Notes and sketches

GILLES COLLETTE

ISBN 978-0-578-02132-4

Publisher's Note 6 7 9 2 7 2 3

AlRaym Publishing

Notes and sketches

Explorations of subject matter and style, Gilles Collette's sketches take us into his creative process. Through these sometimes quickly drawn, sometimes polished images, we follow the artist on his quest to discover new ways of seeing the world. We are allowed a glimpse into his mind and his constant effort to look at everyday things from a fresh perspective. Classically trained, Collette sketches masterly portraits of friends and family, as well as historical and fictional characters. Some of the portraits are academic, realistic, but most are explorations of style and genre. Some are rendered in a single line, some are heavily shaded, others cubist. A deranged man glares from the page wielding a remote control like a weapon. Does he aim to turn the world off?

Landscapes depicting whole worlds, strange interior spaces, portraits, geometric shapes, cubist nudes, mythical creatures rendered in a baroque style, or a more modern, streamlined style. A variation of the familiar pear-shaped nude, local architecture and everyday objects: an ornate fork, a knife, bending in a surreal wind. And throughout words, poetry. This is a documentation of one artist's quest to challenge accepted views of the world, and to question his own.

Anne Collette

Notes and

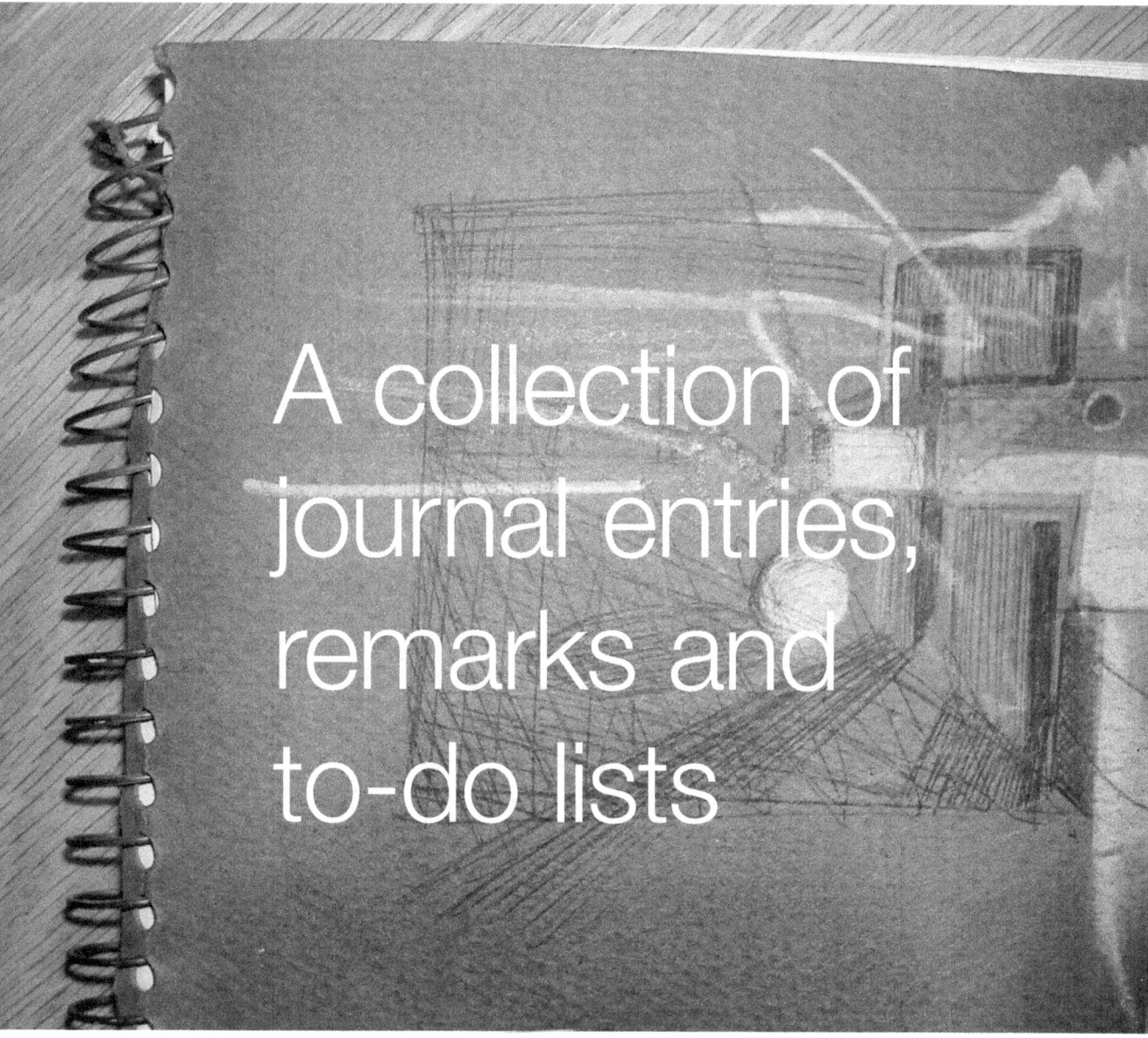

A collection of
journal entries,
remarks and
to-do lists

sketches

Gilles COLLETTE

Notes and sketches

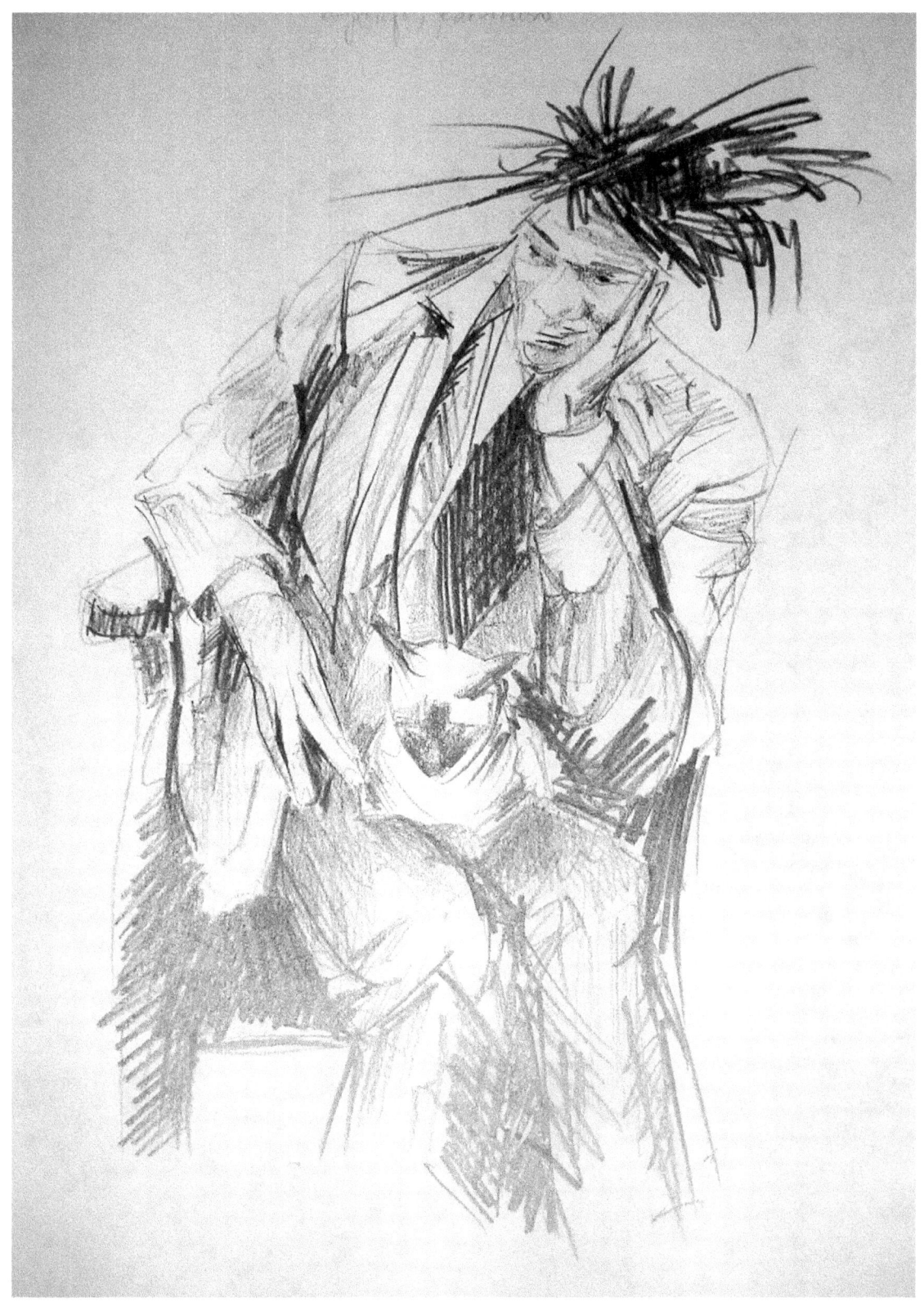

Gilles COLLETTE

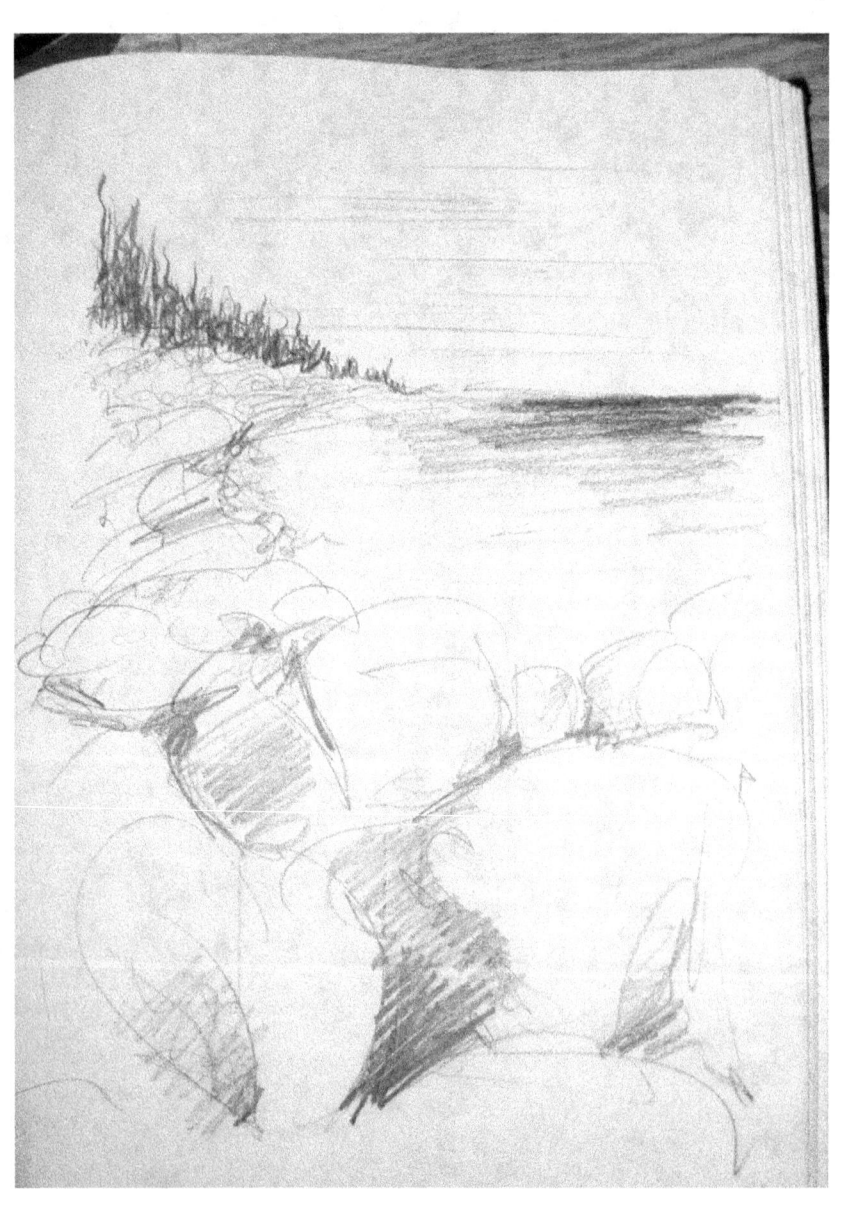

Notes and sketches

Gilles COLLETTE

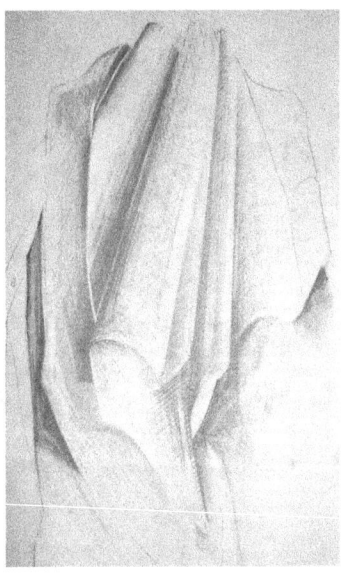

Notes and sketches

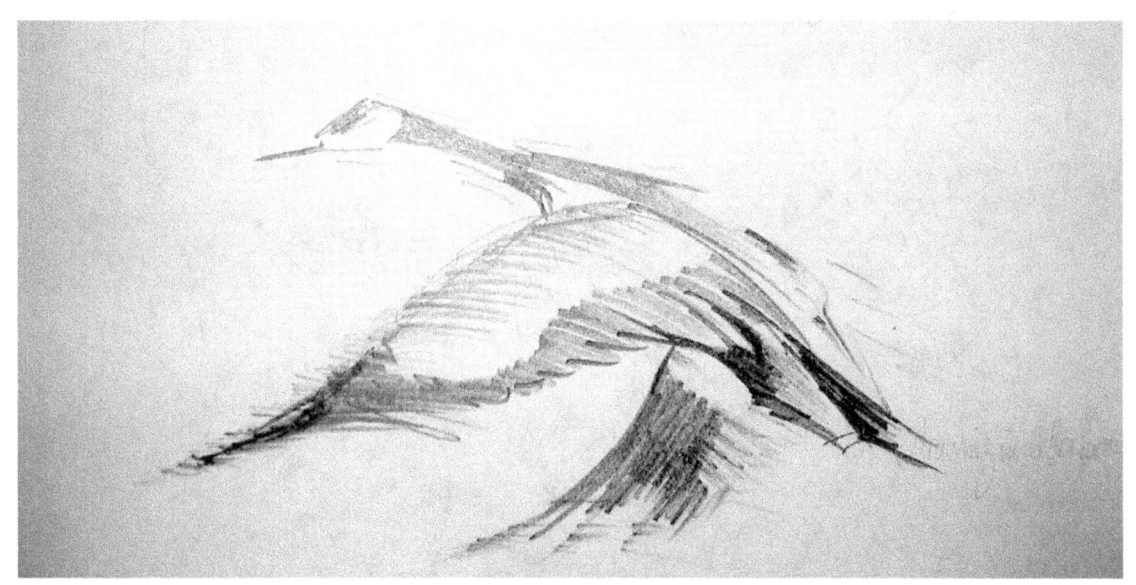

Gilles COLLETTE

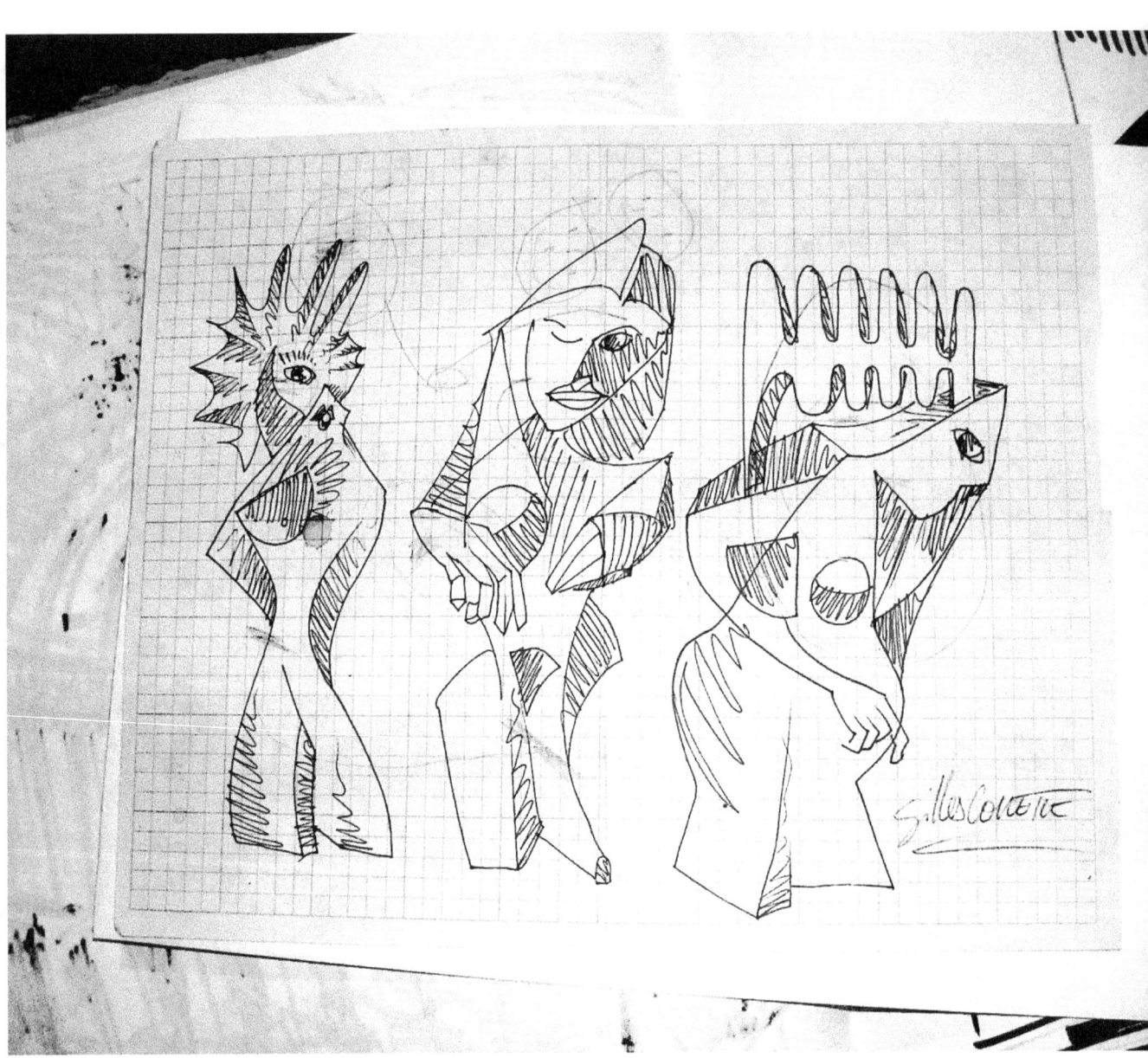

Notes and sketches

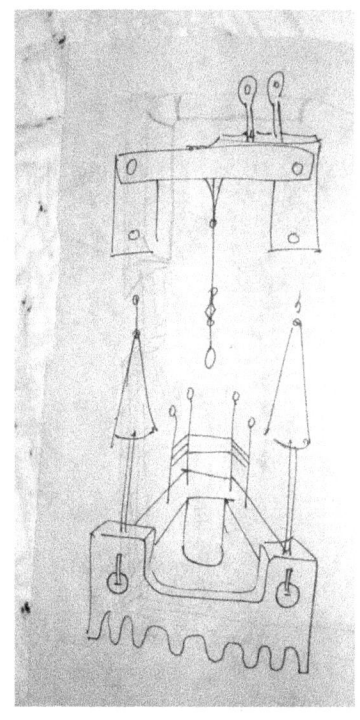 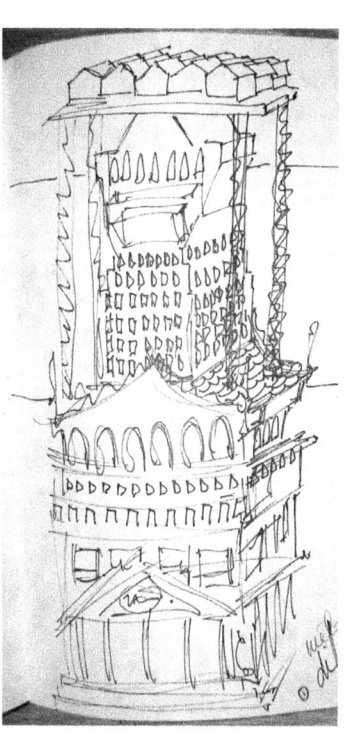

Gilles COLLETTE

9

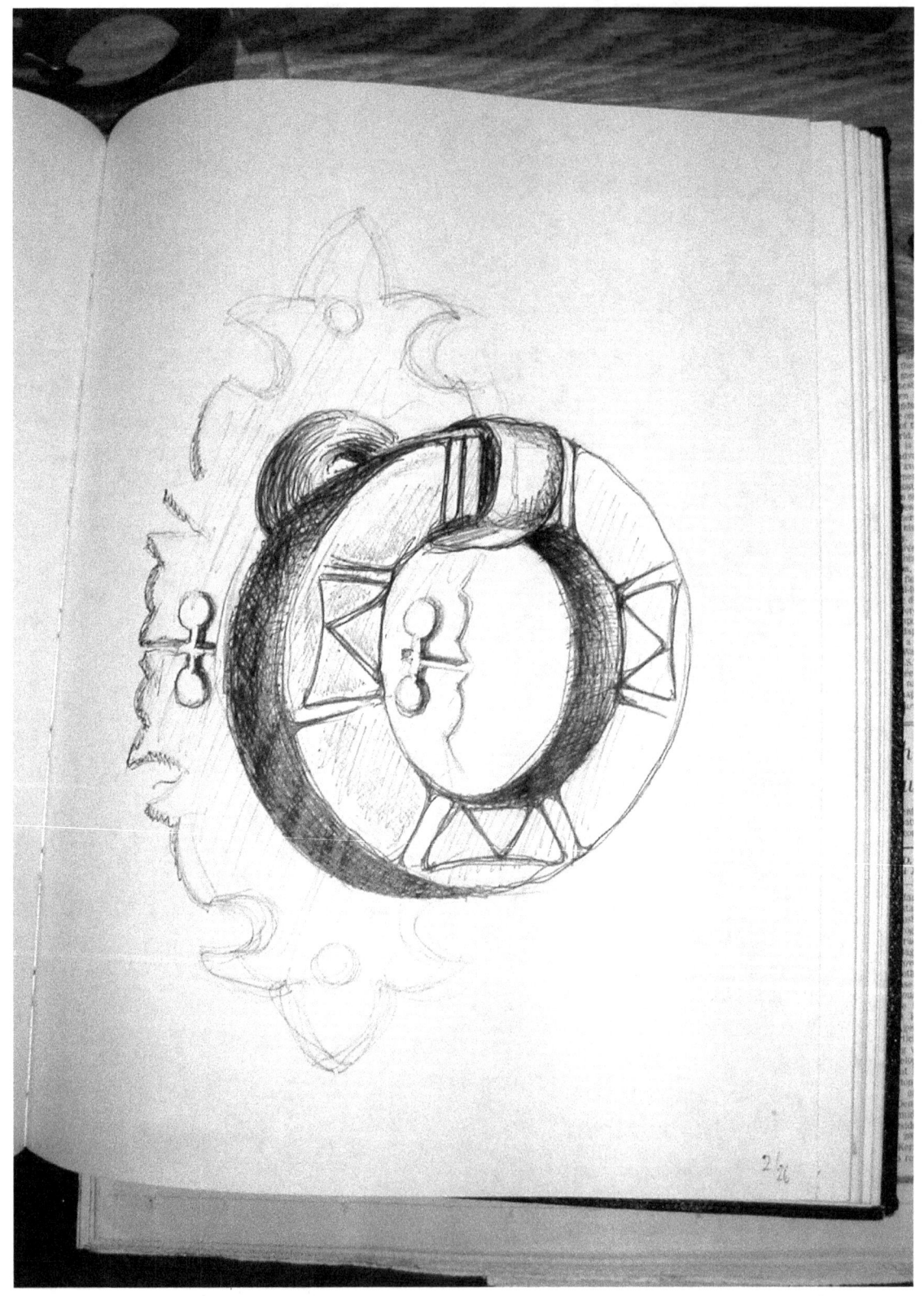

Notes and sketches

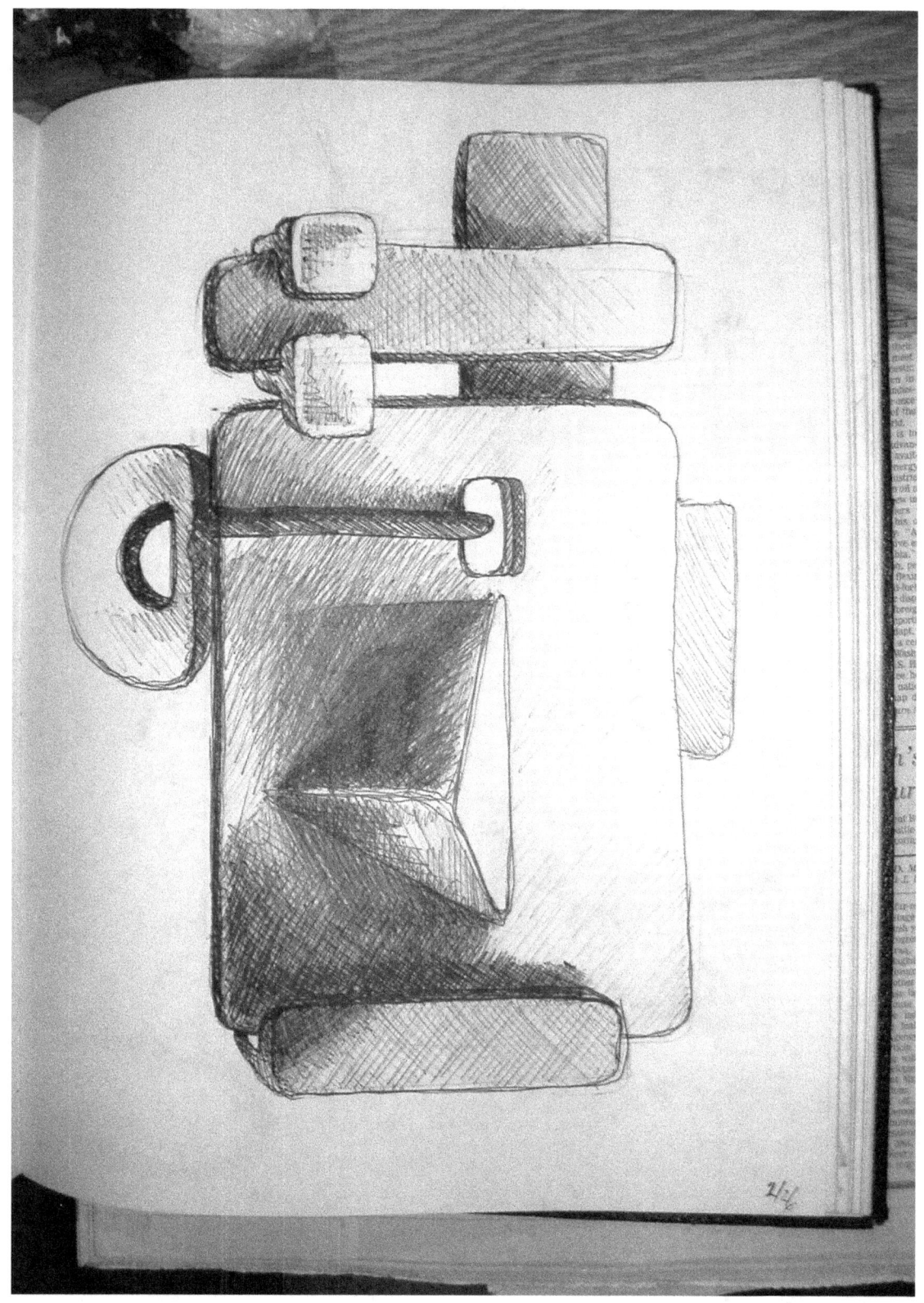

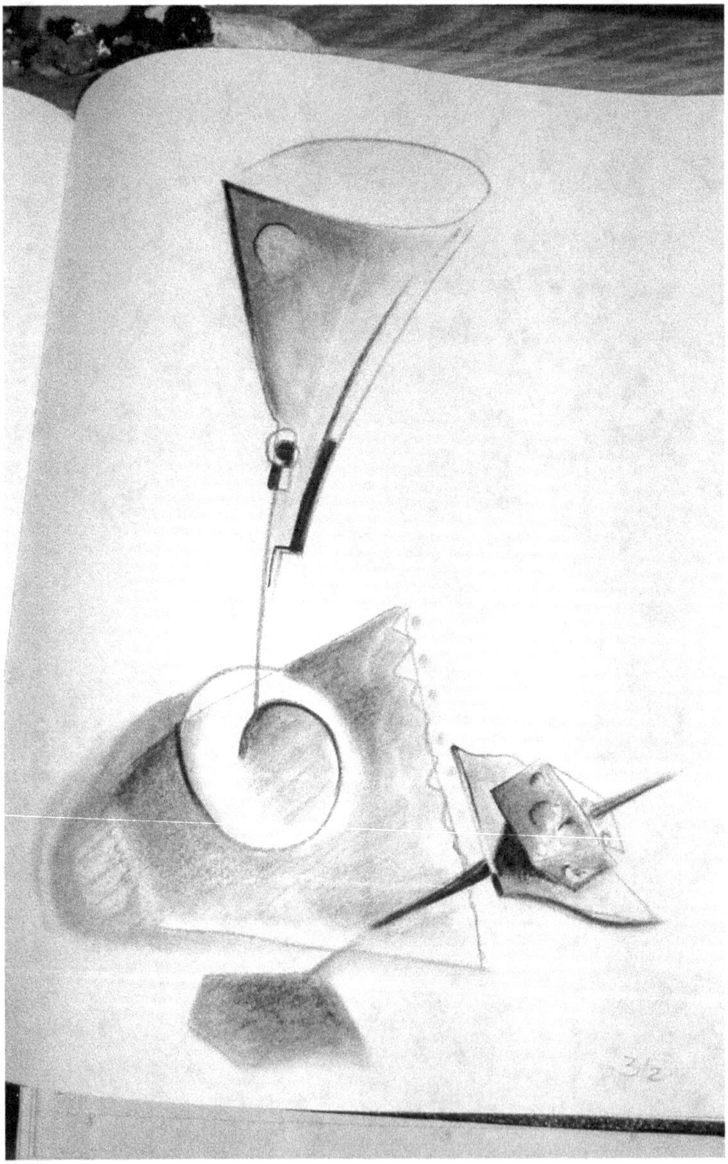

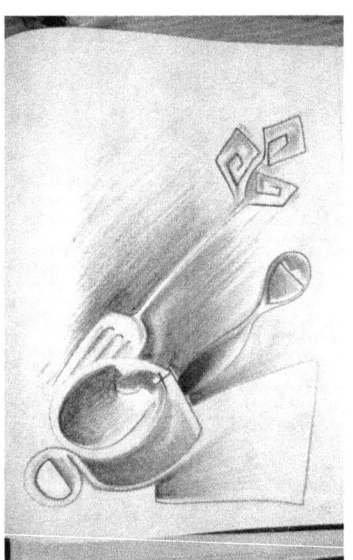

Notes and sketches

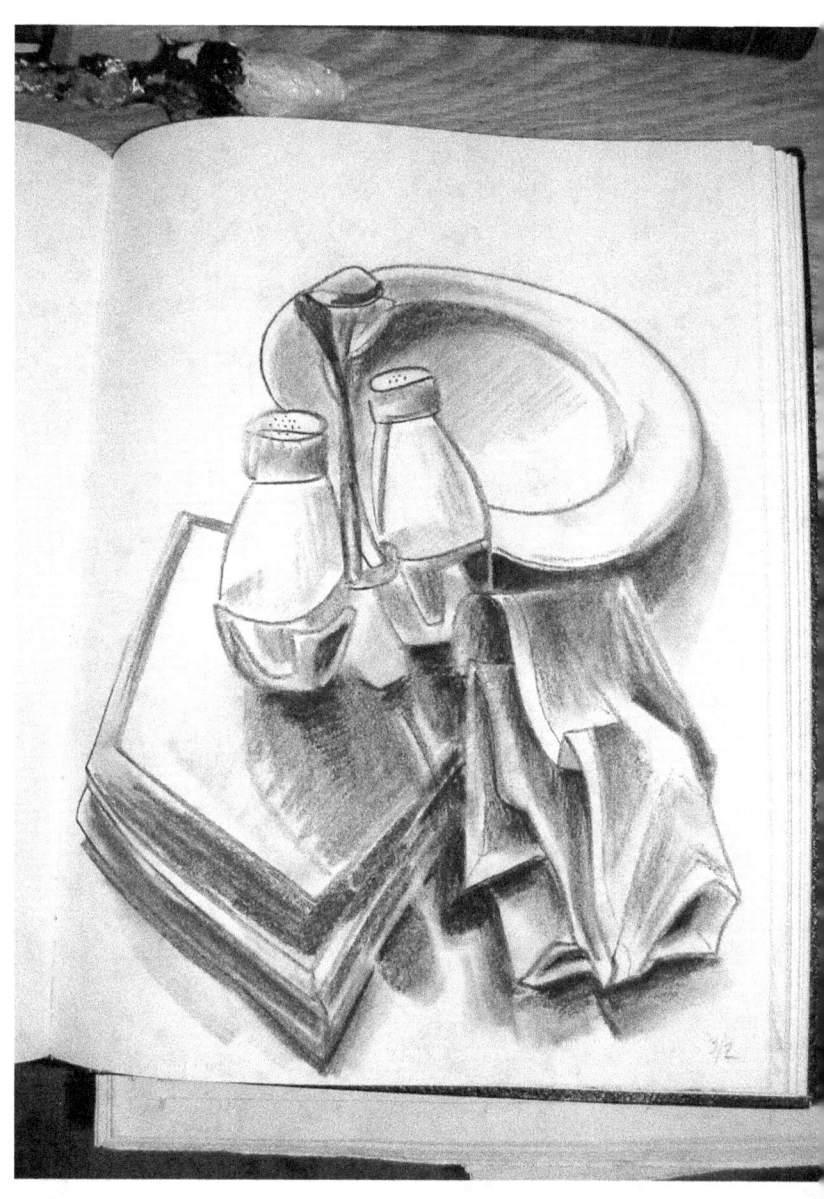

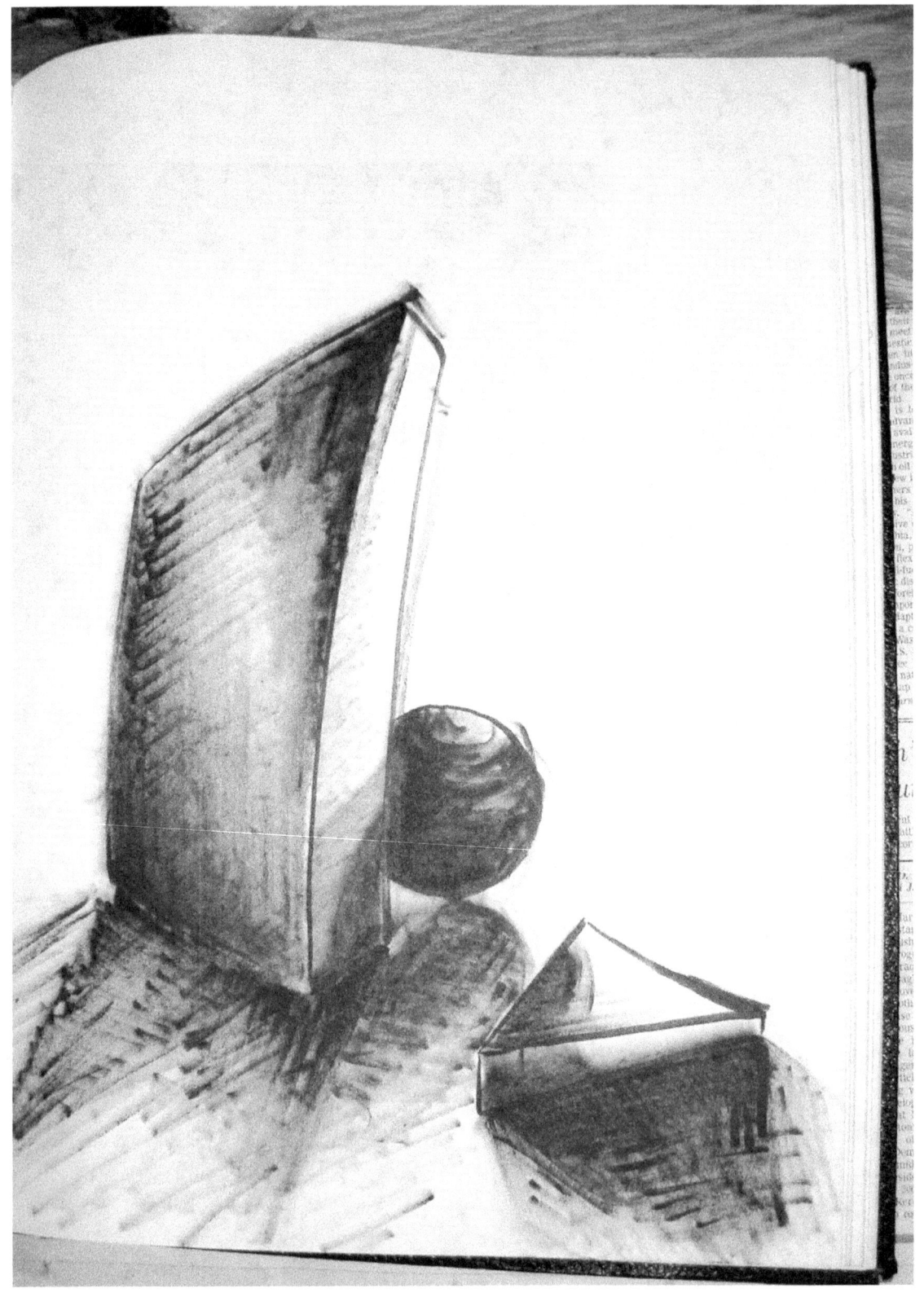

Notes and sketches

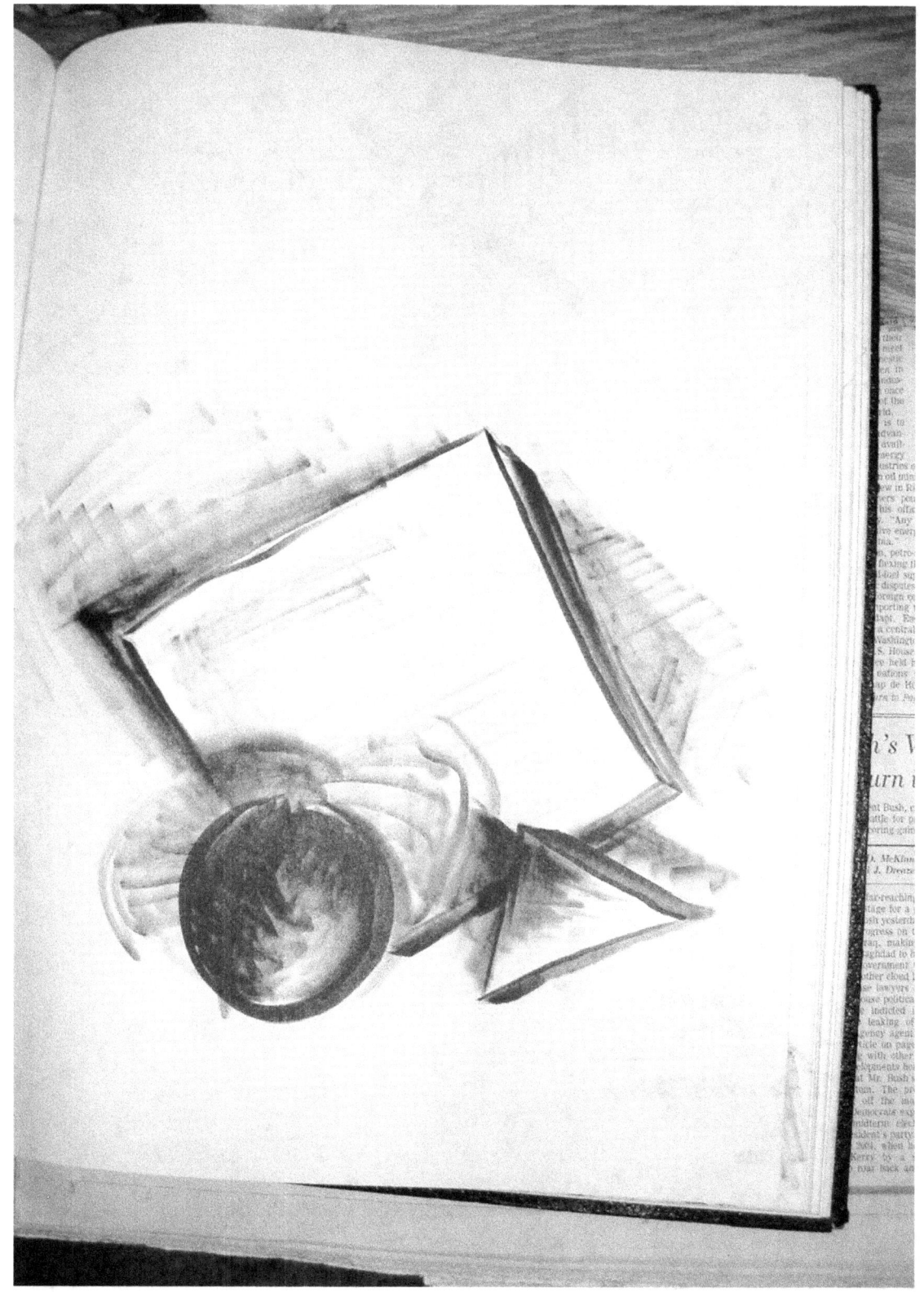

Gilles COLLETTE

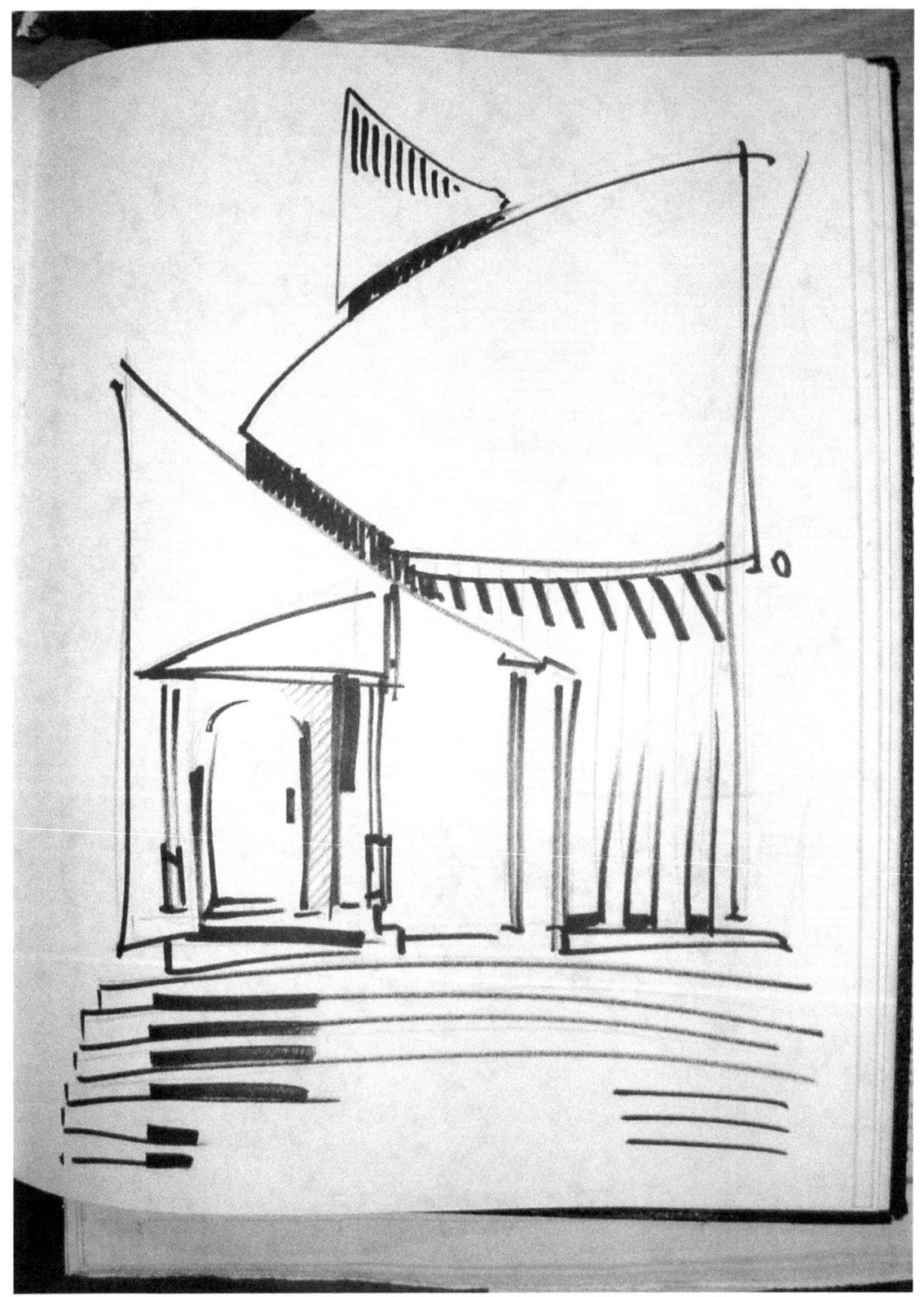

Notes and sketches

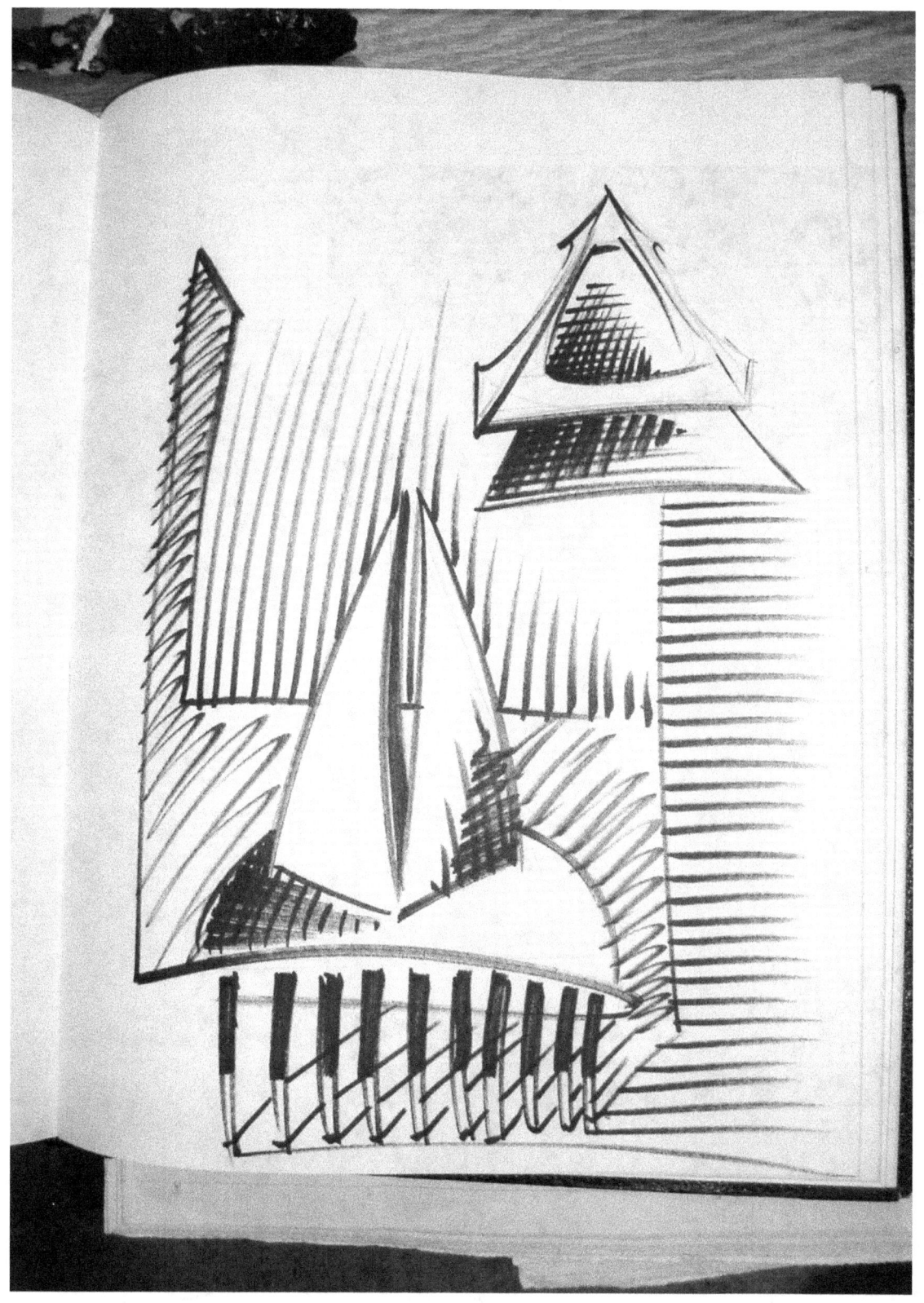

Gilles COLLETTE

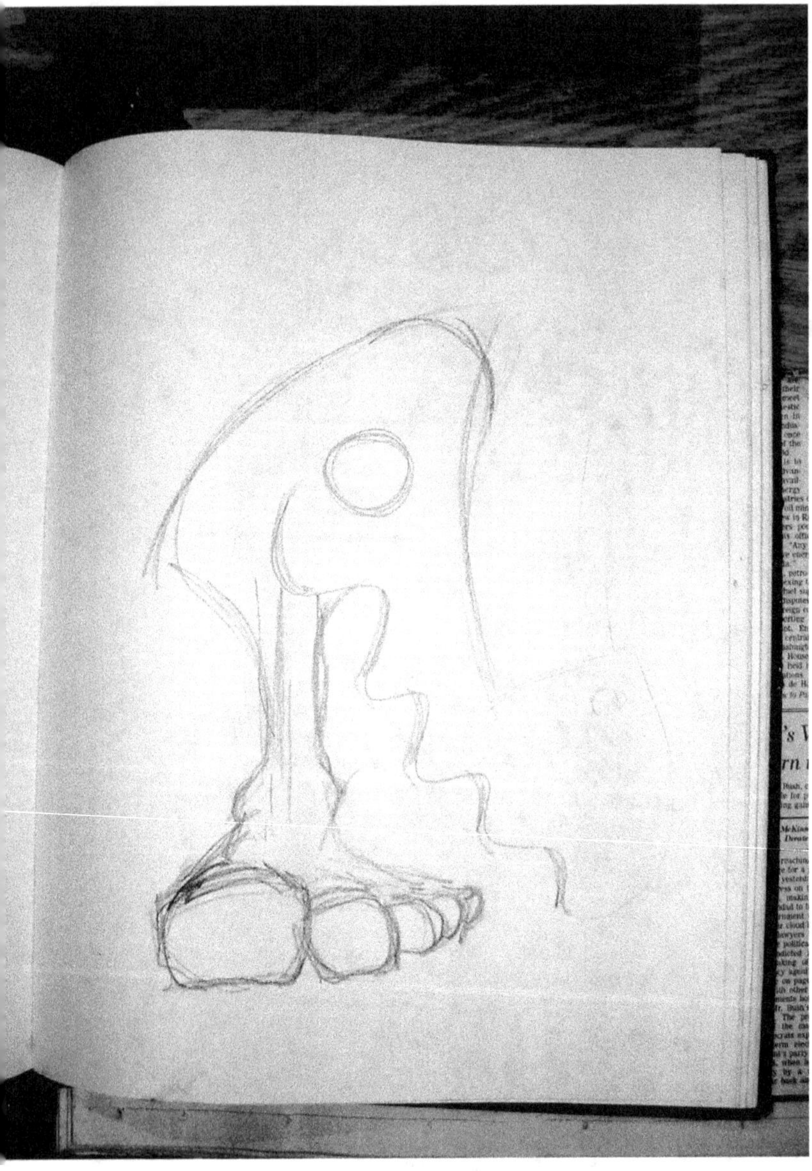

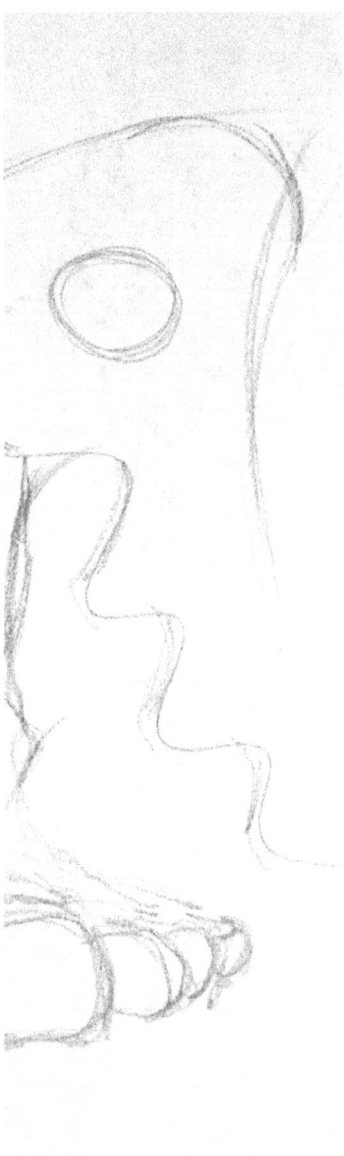

Notes and sketches

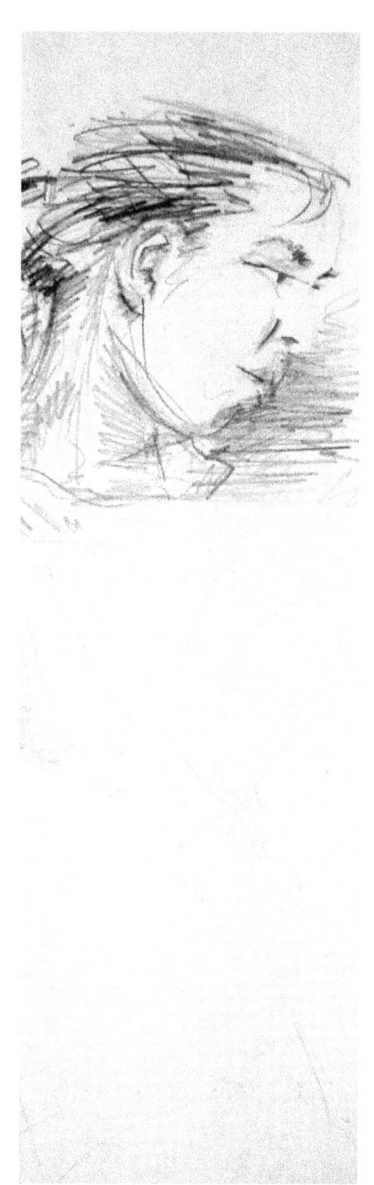

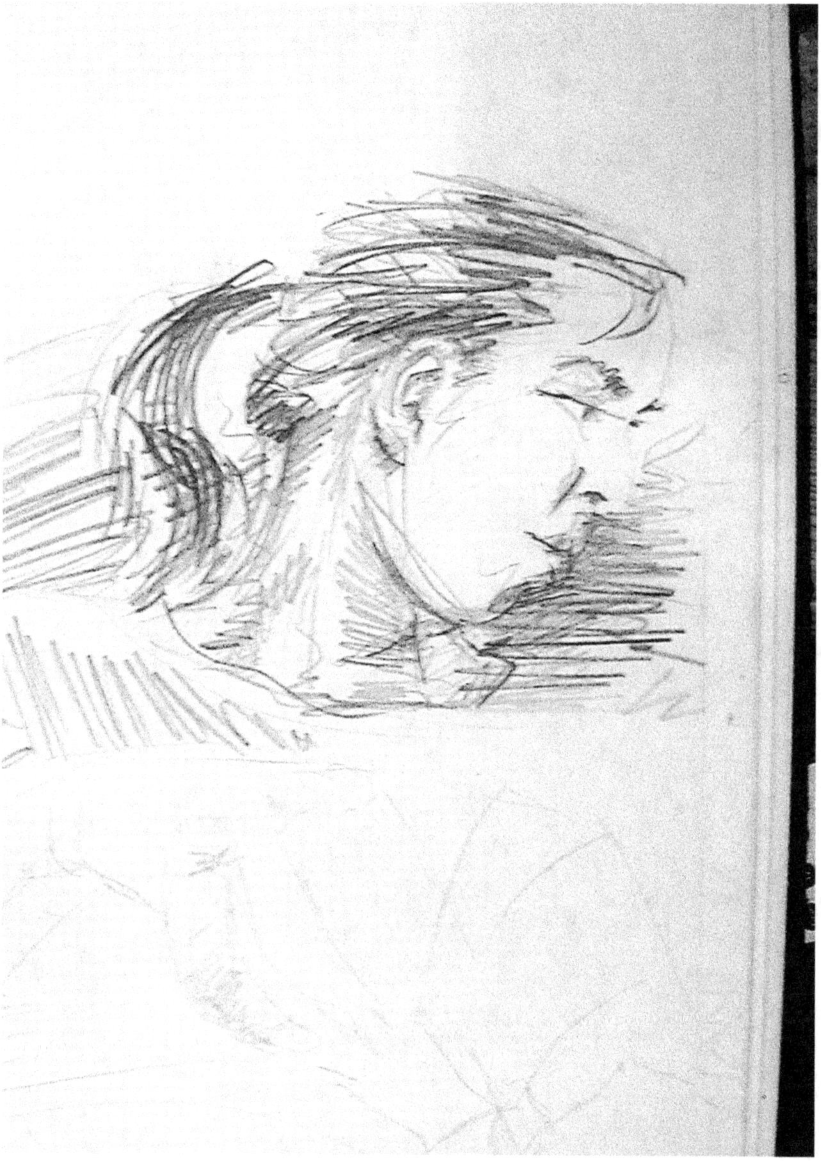

Gilles COLLETTE

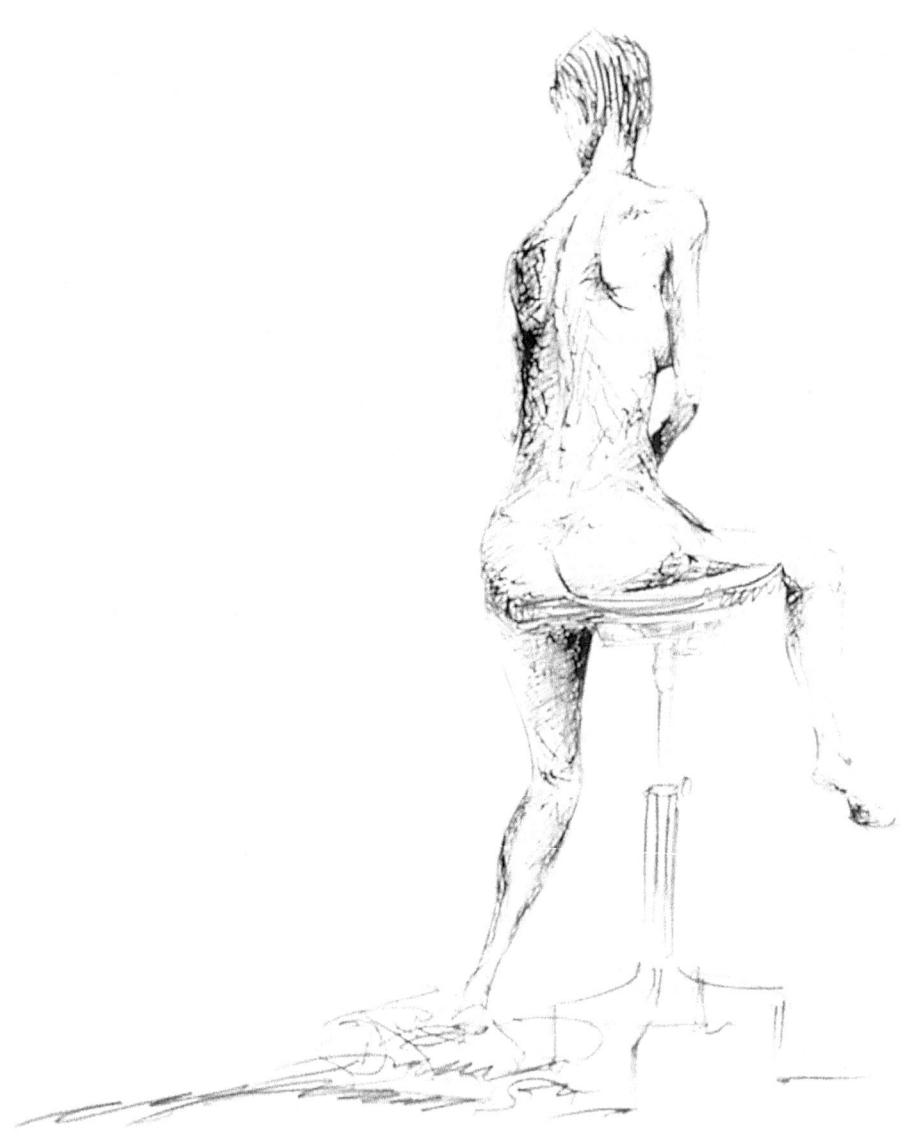

Notes and sketches

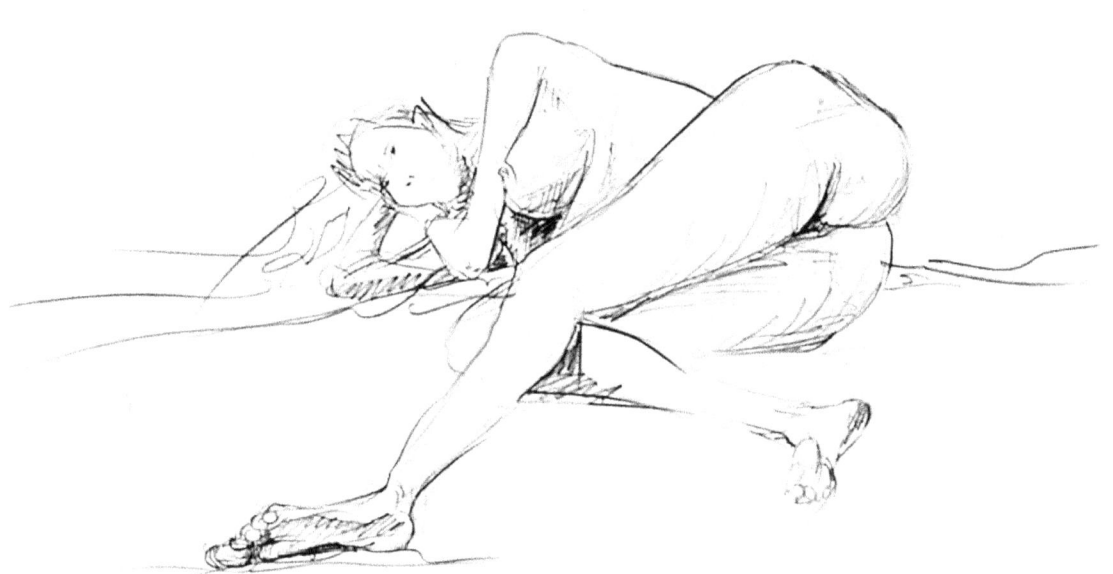

Gilles COLLETTE

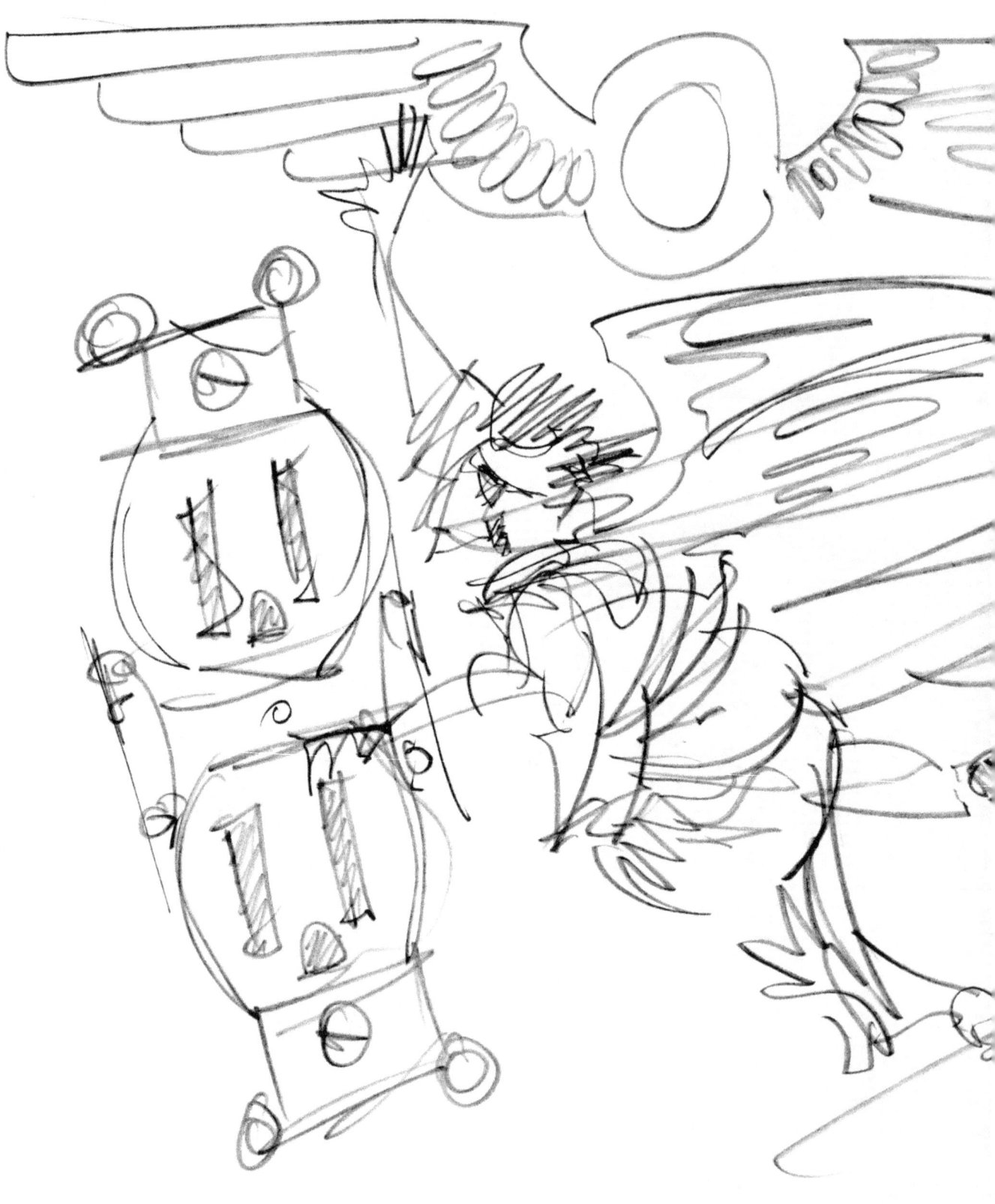

Notes and sketches

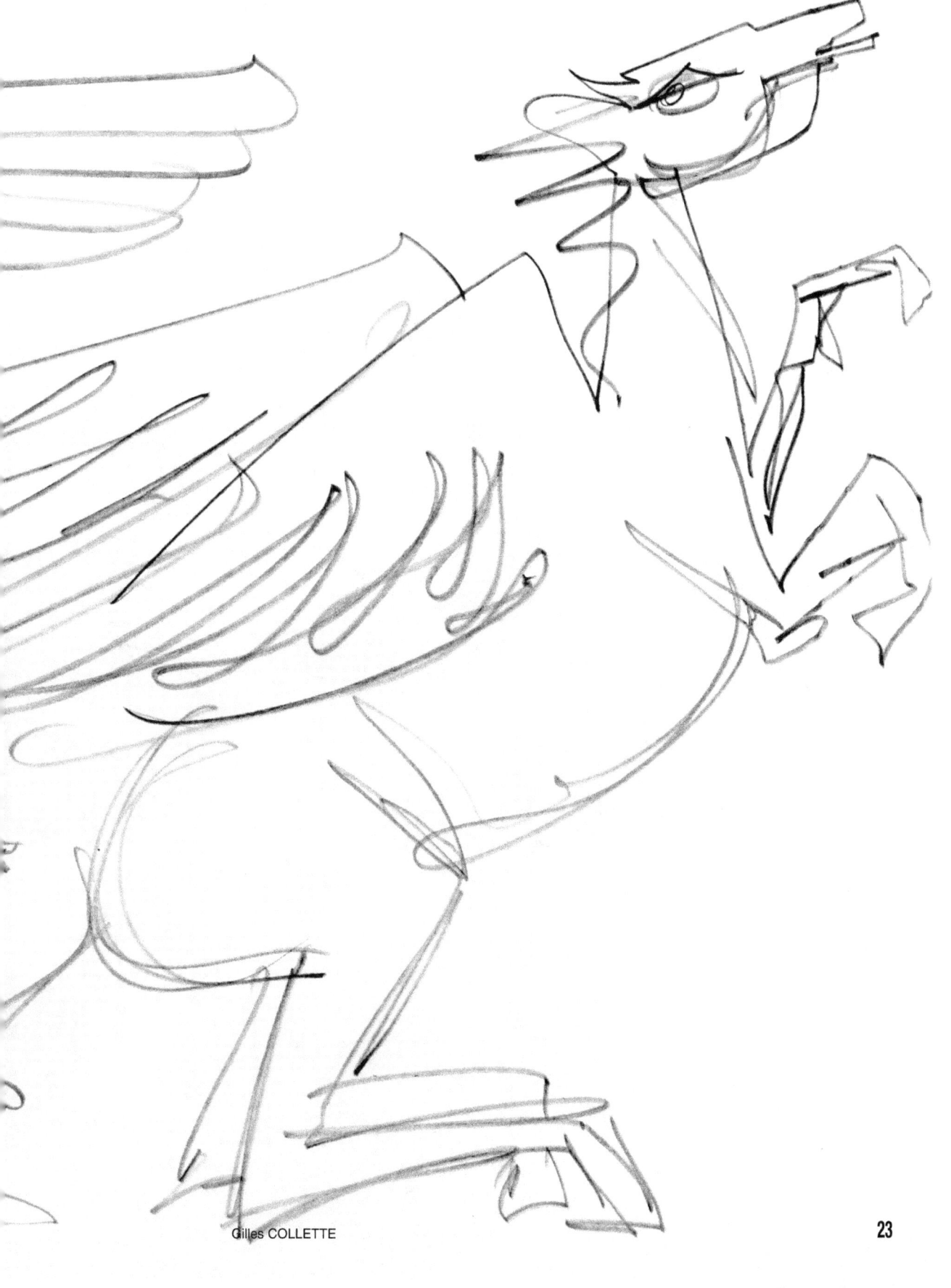

Gilles COLLETTE

23

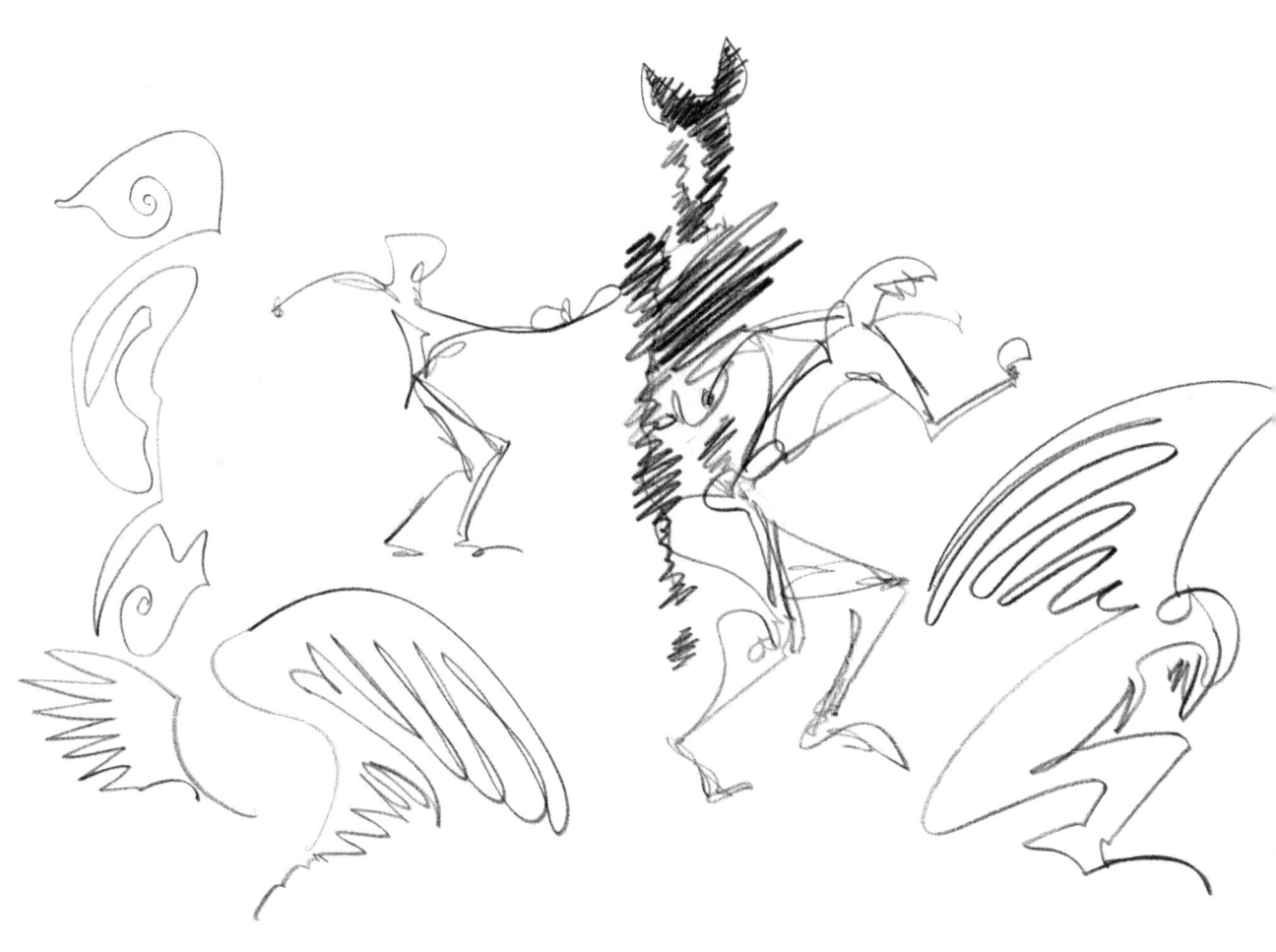

Notes and sketches

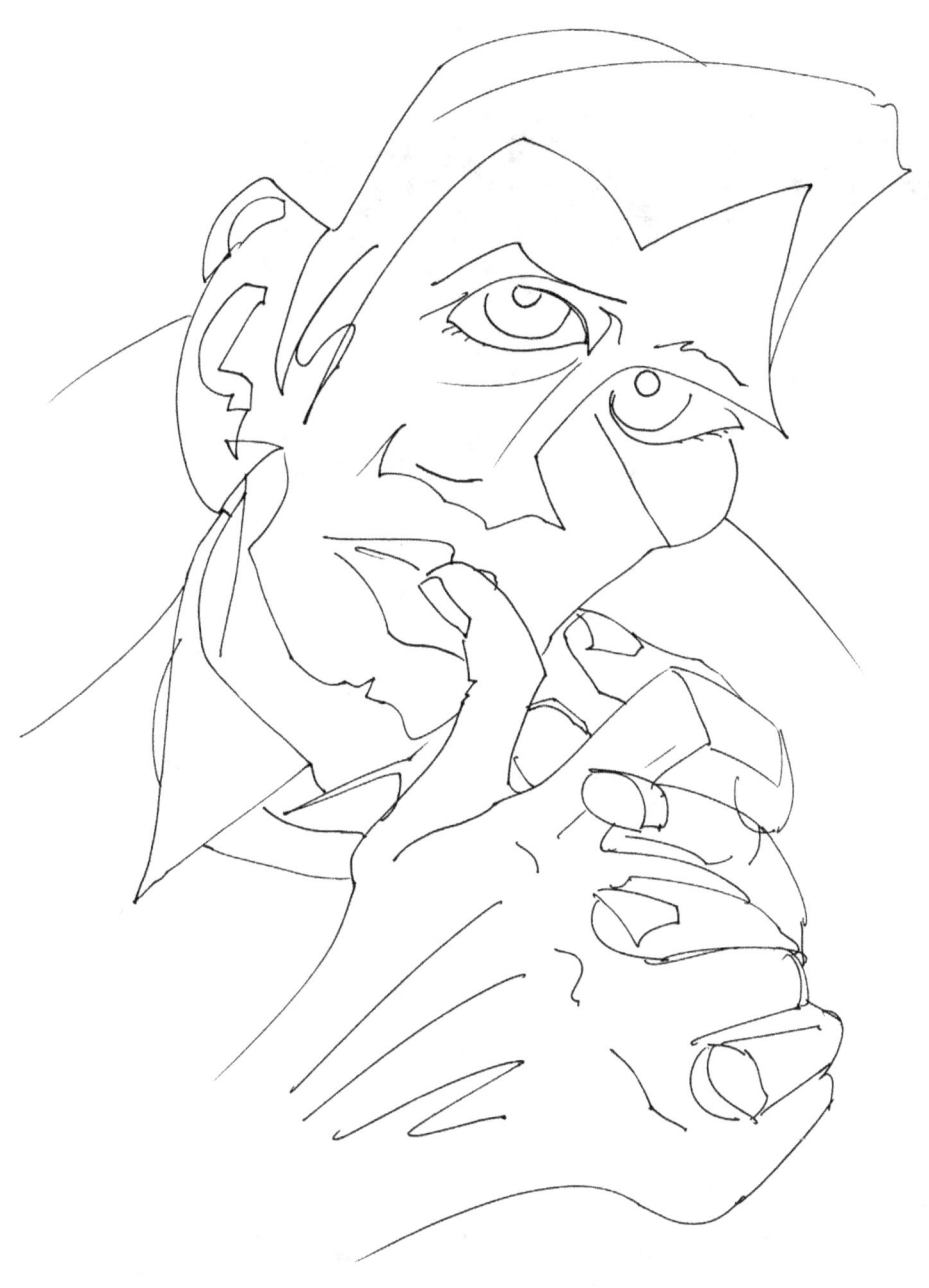

Gilles COLLETTE

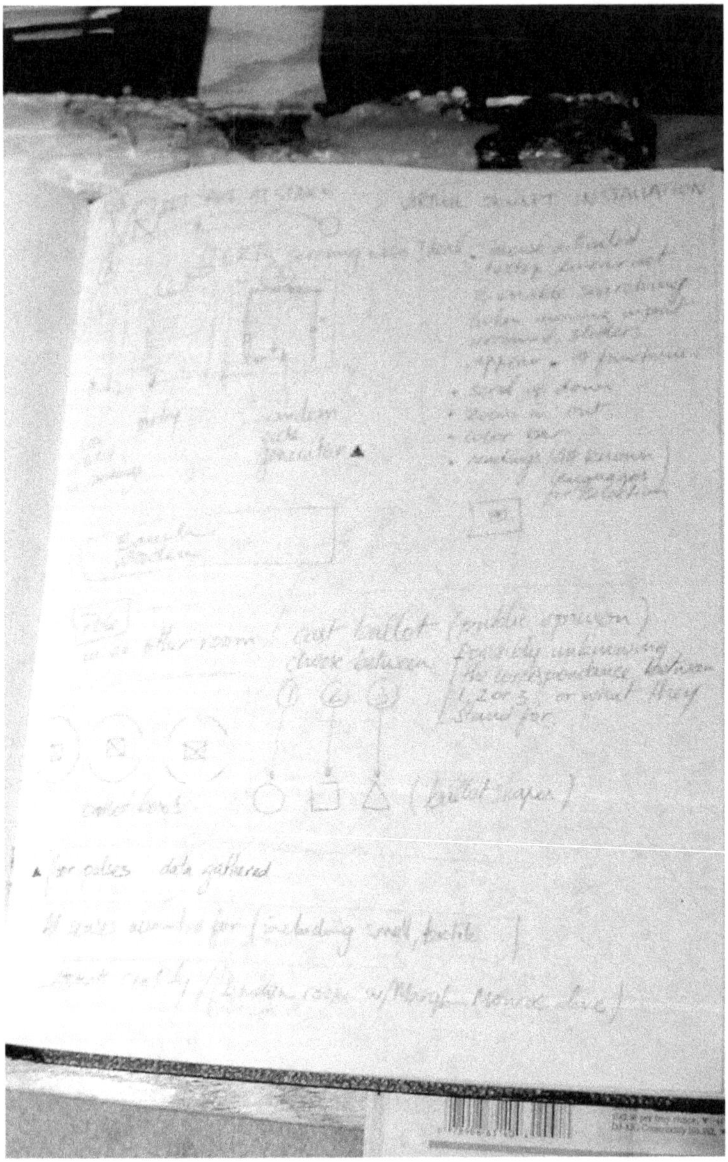

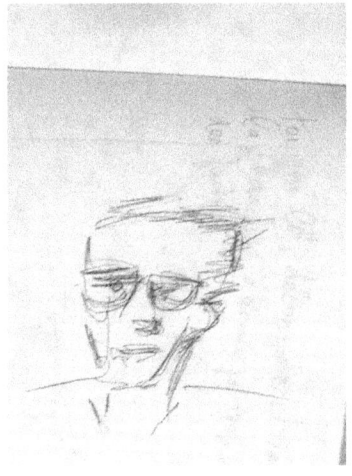

Notes and sketches

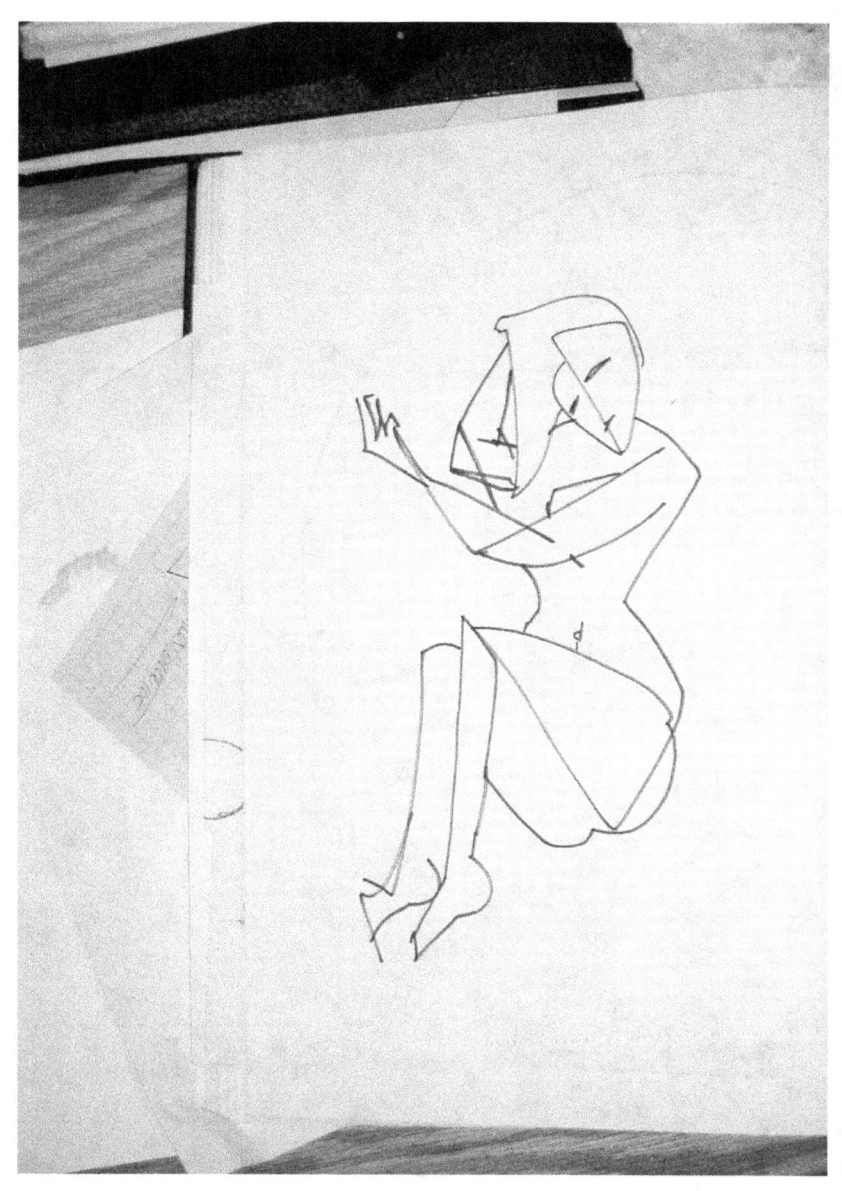

Gilles COLLETTE

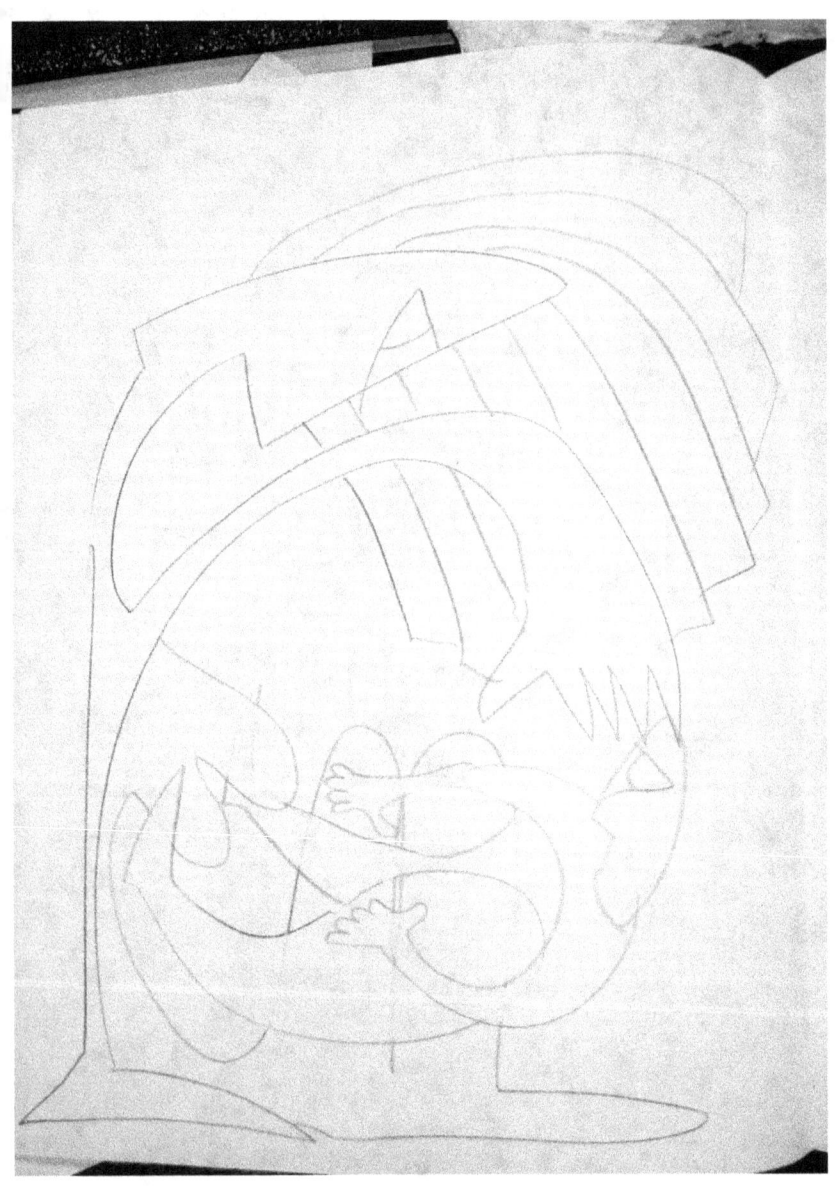

Notes and sketches

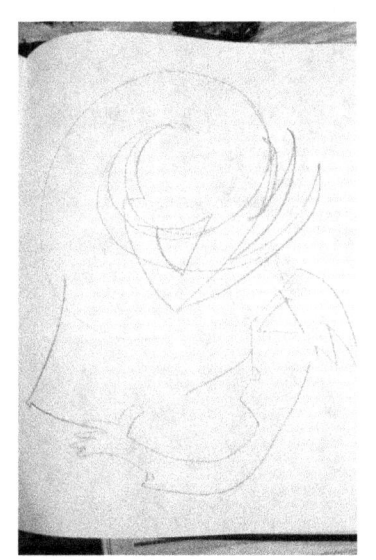

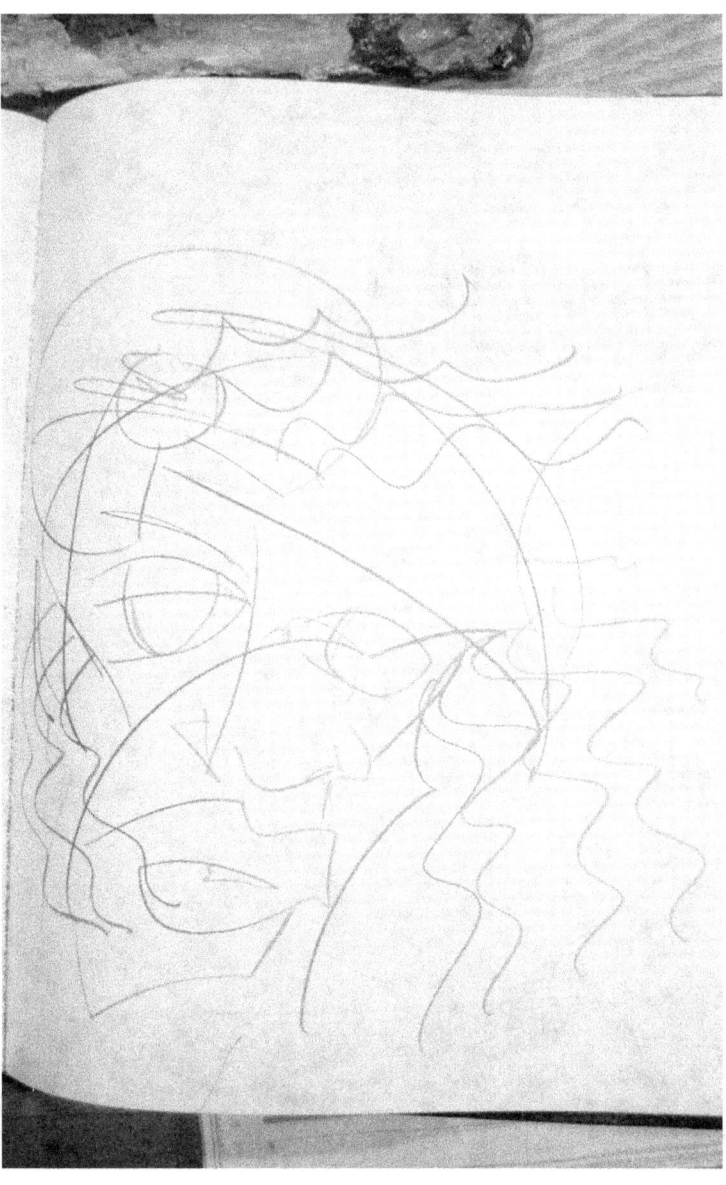

Gilles COLLETTE

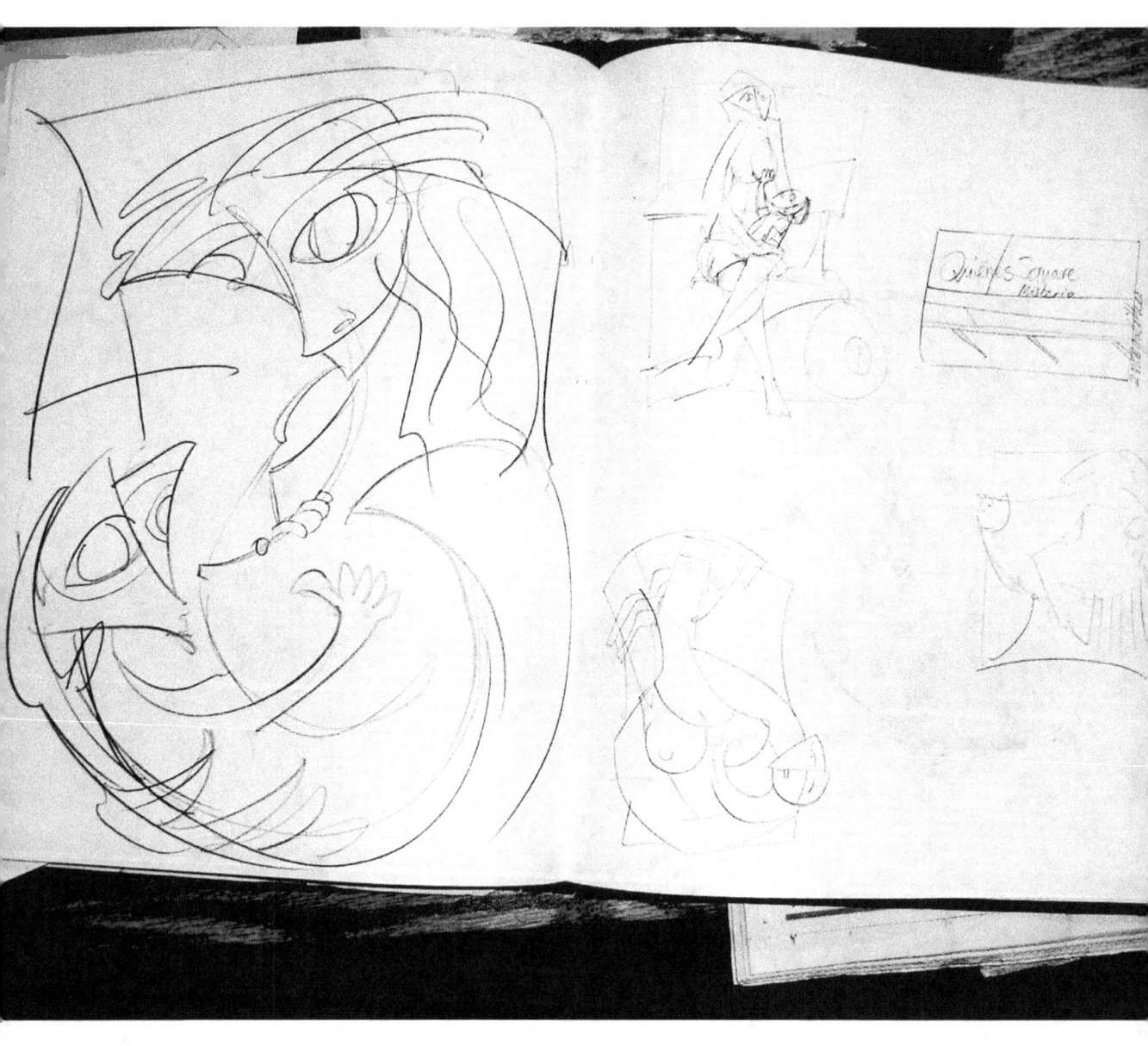

30   Notes and sketches

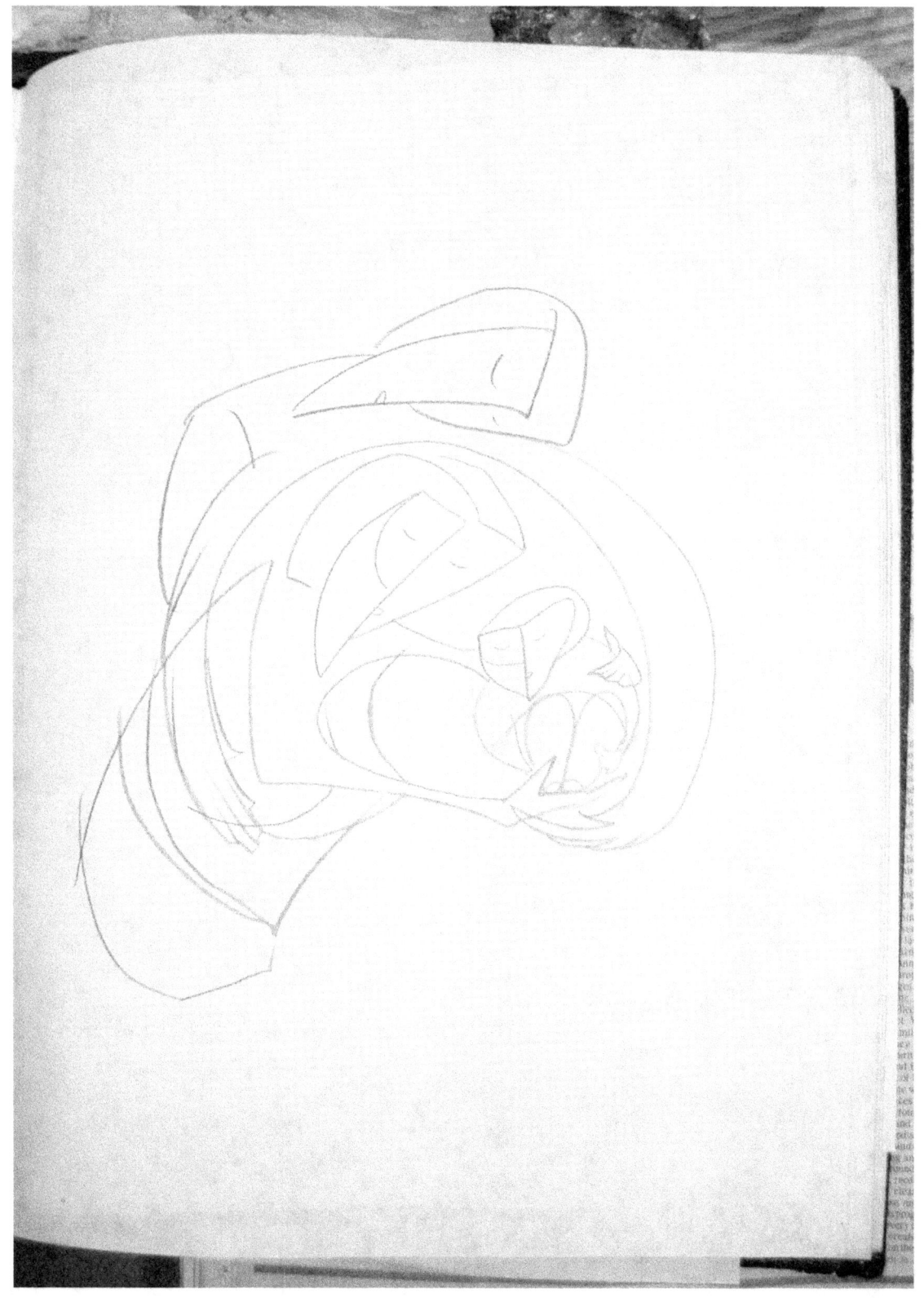

Gilles COLLETTE

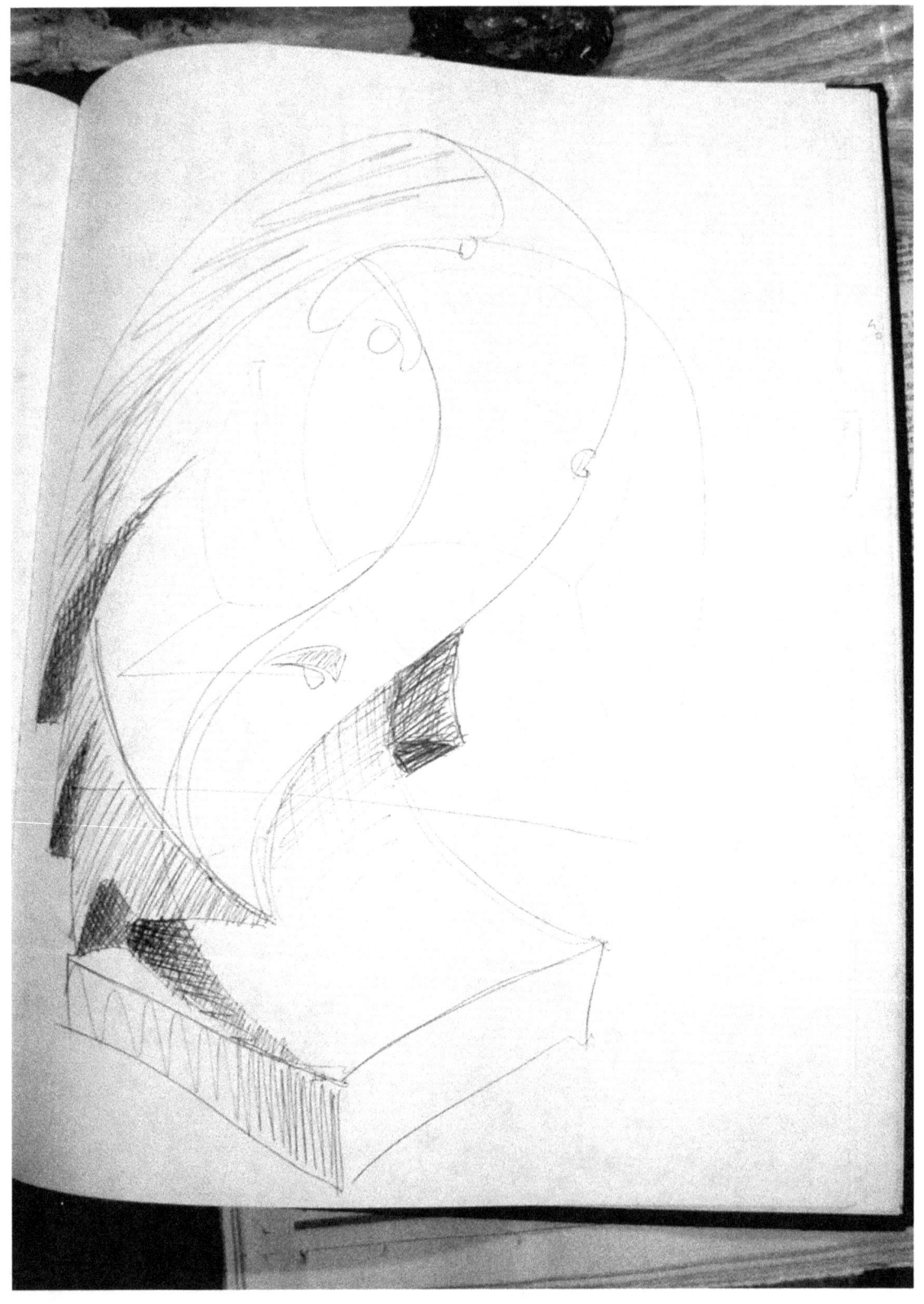

Notes and sketches

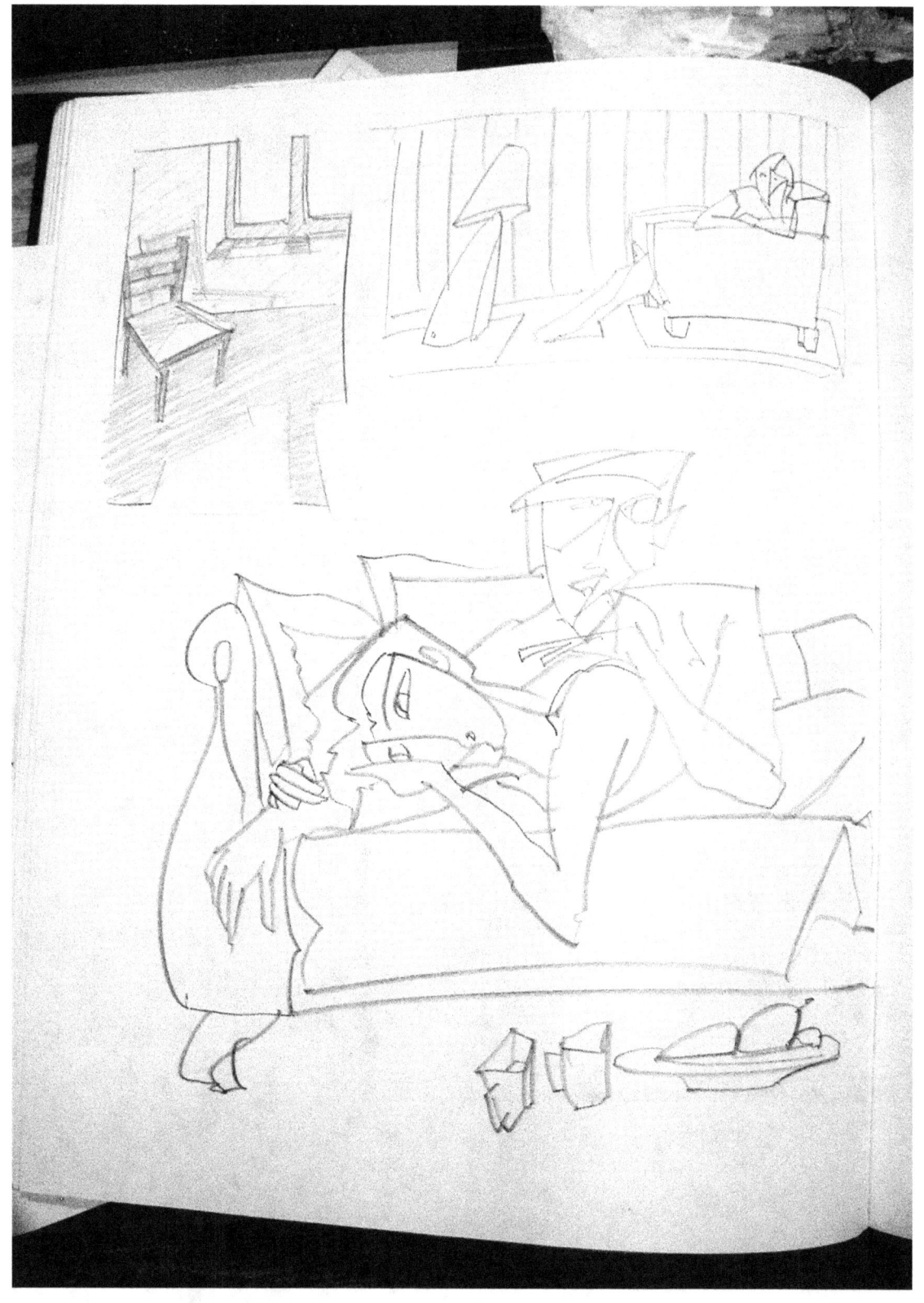

Gilles COLLETTE

33

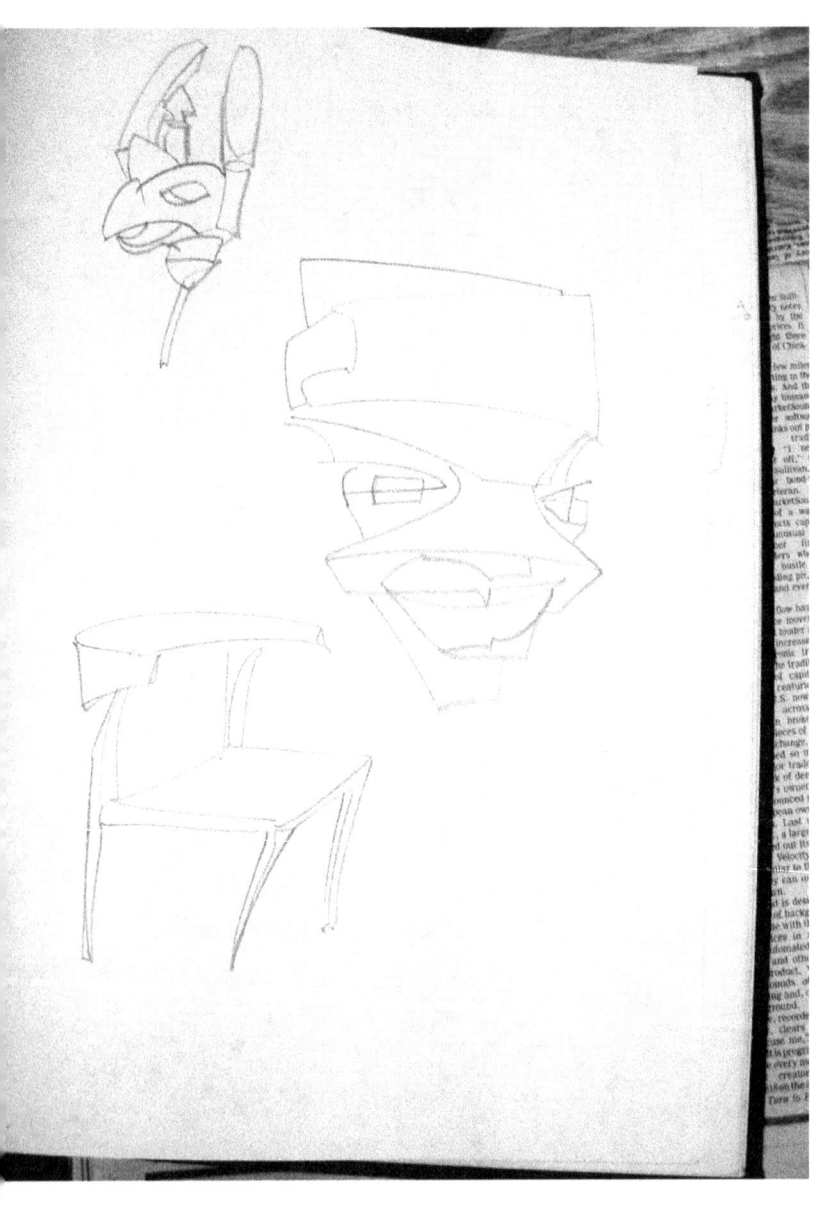

Notes and sketches

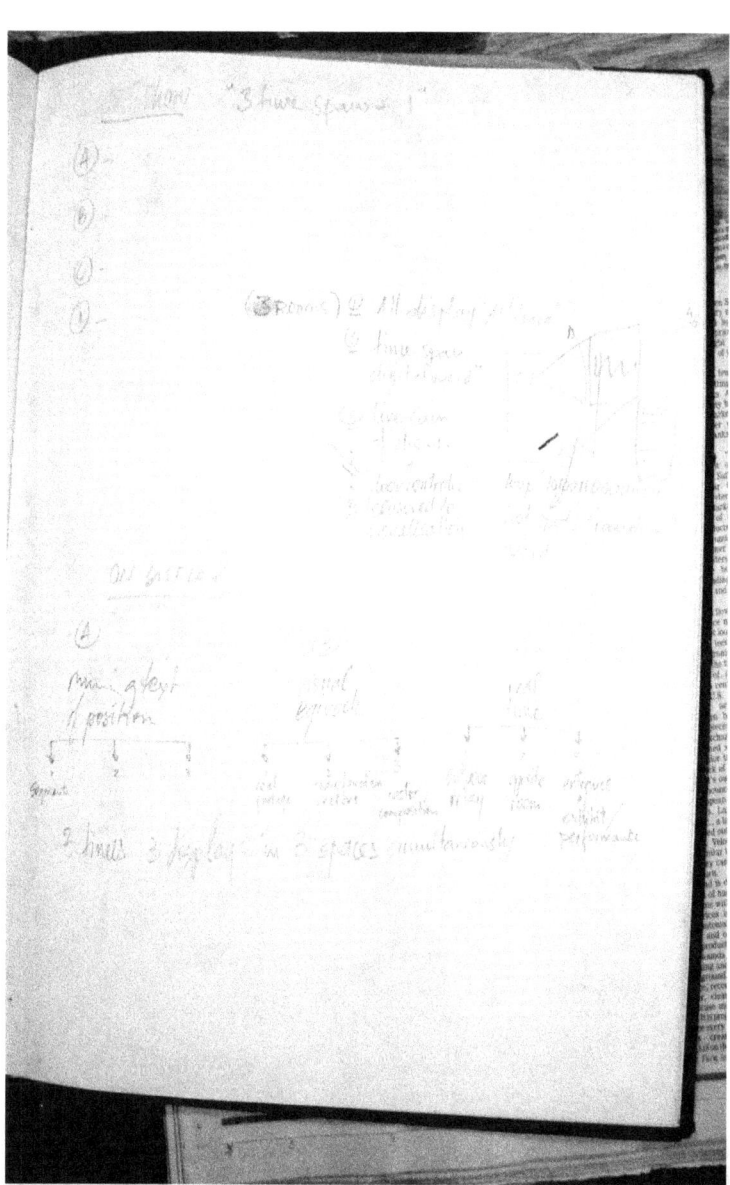

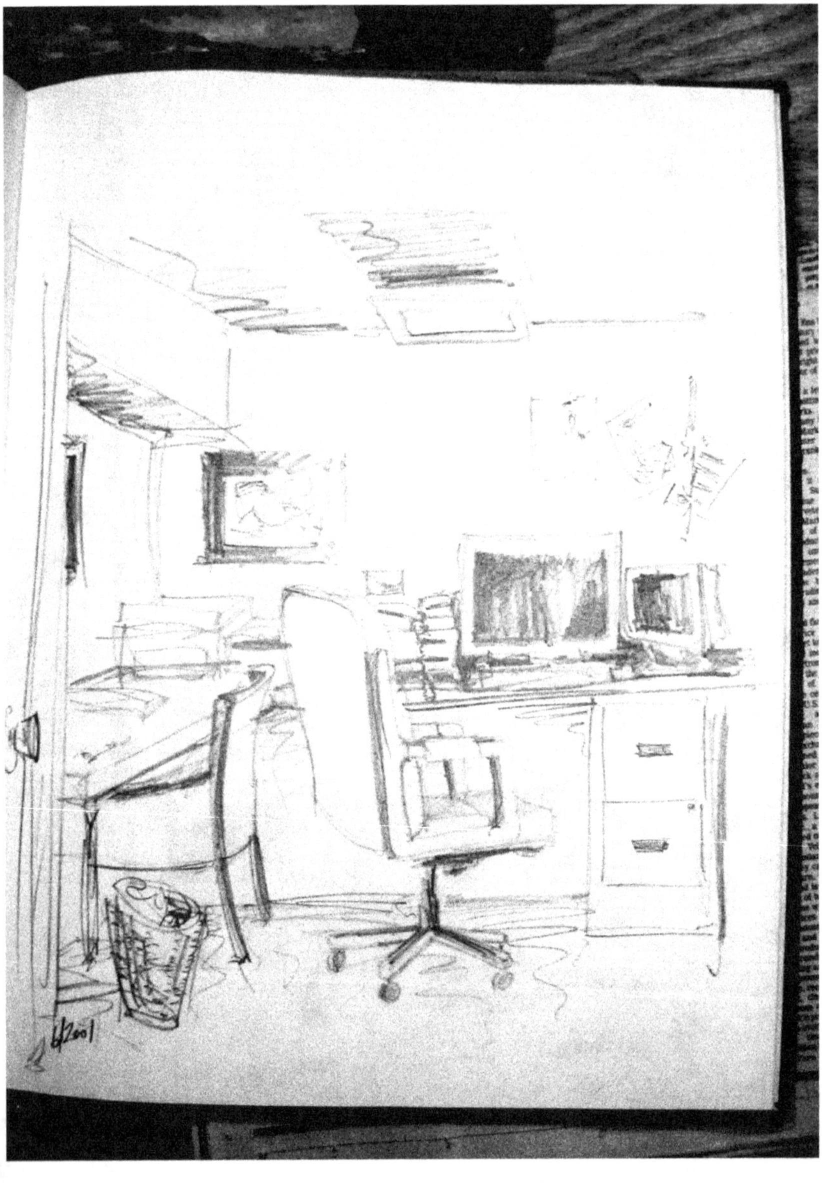

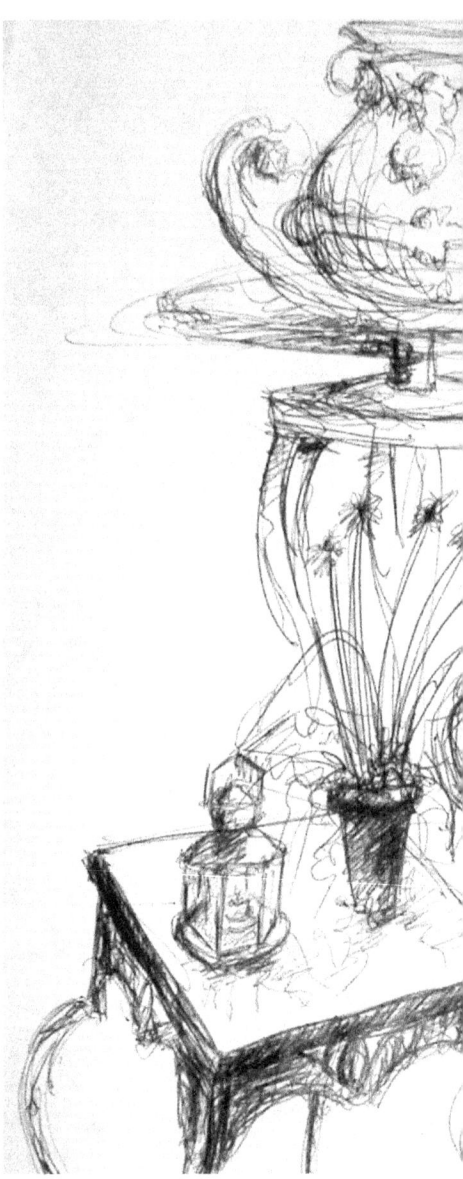

Notes and sketches

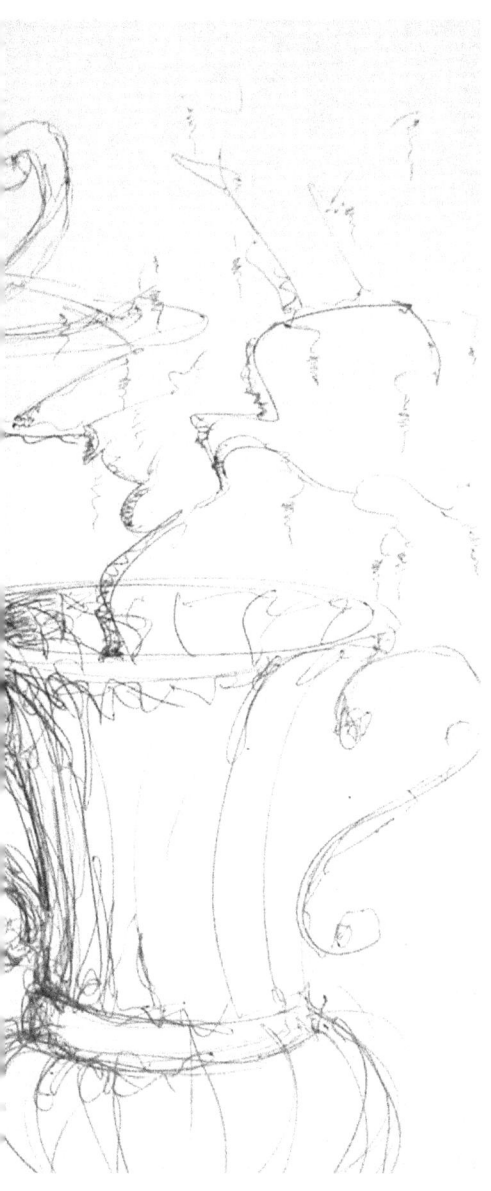

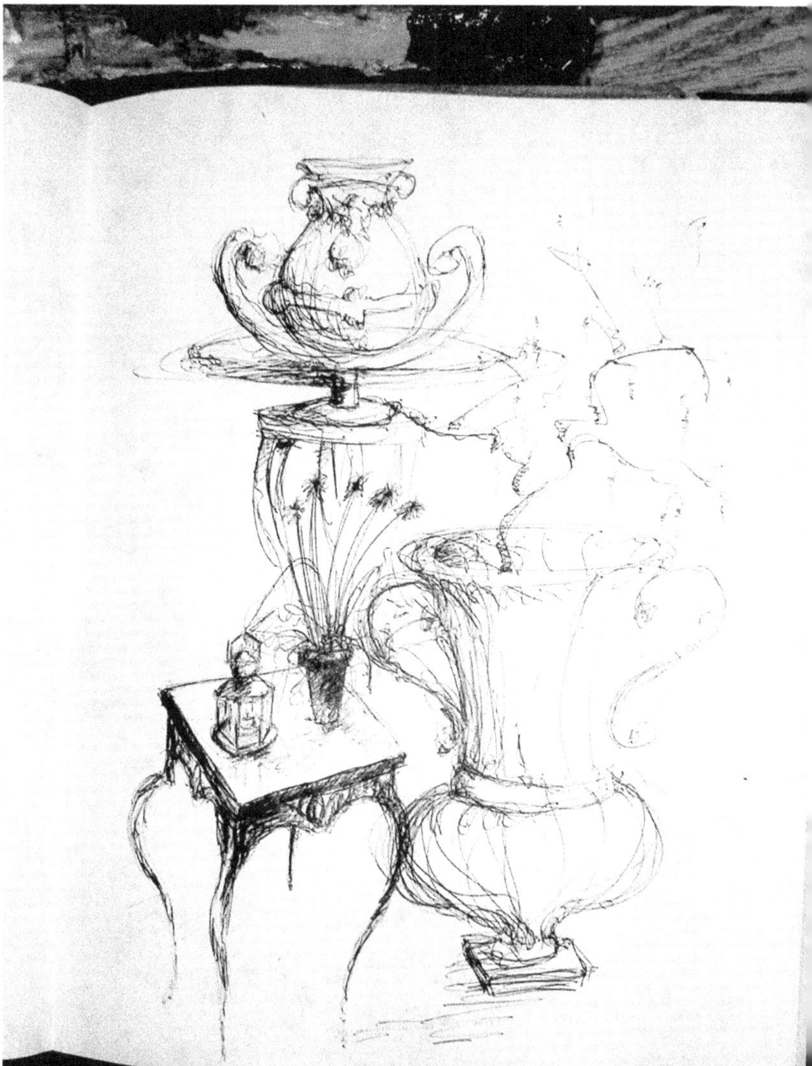

Gilles COLLETTE

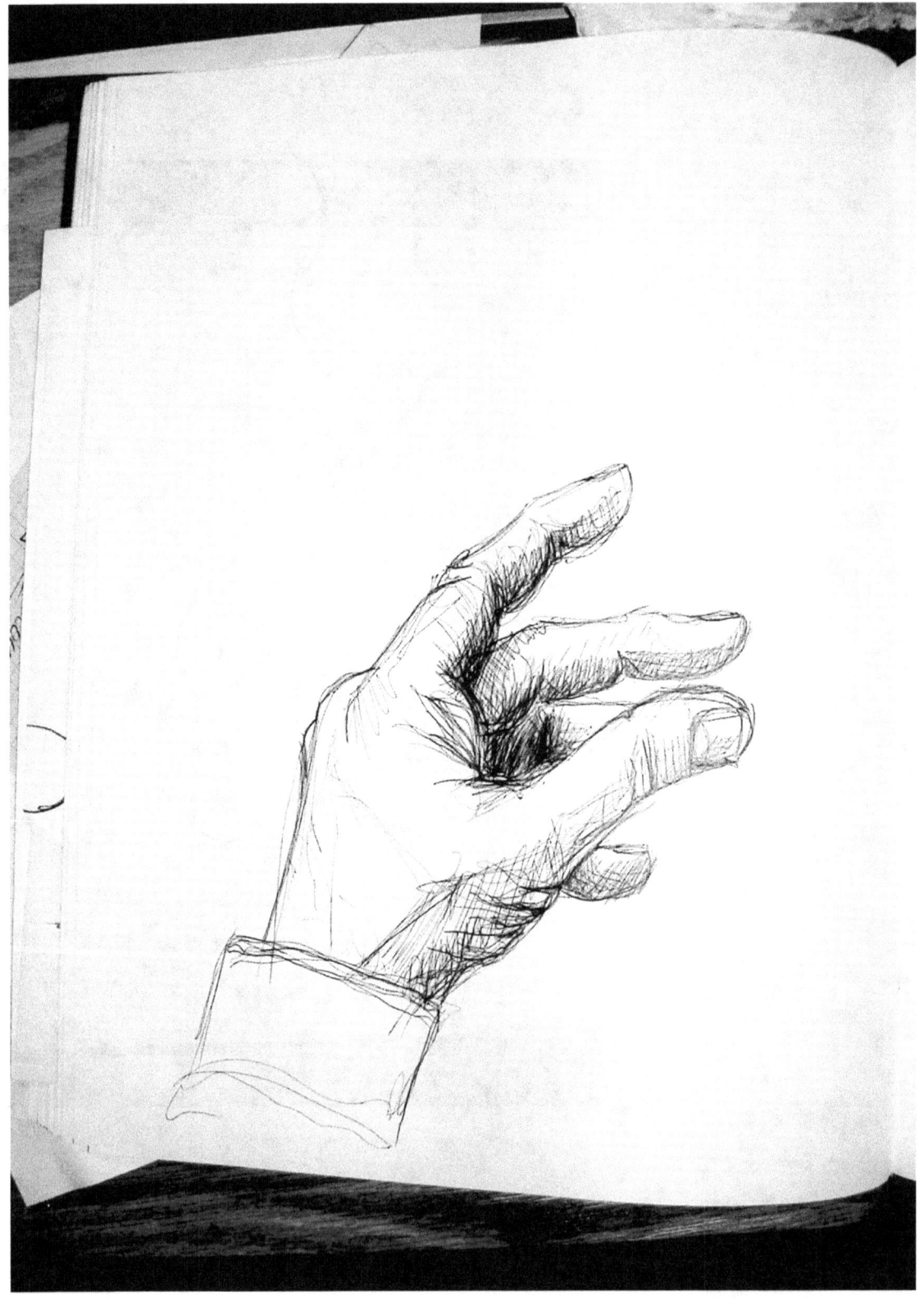

Notes and sketches

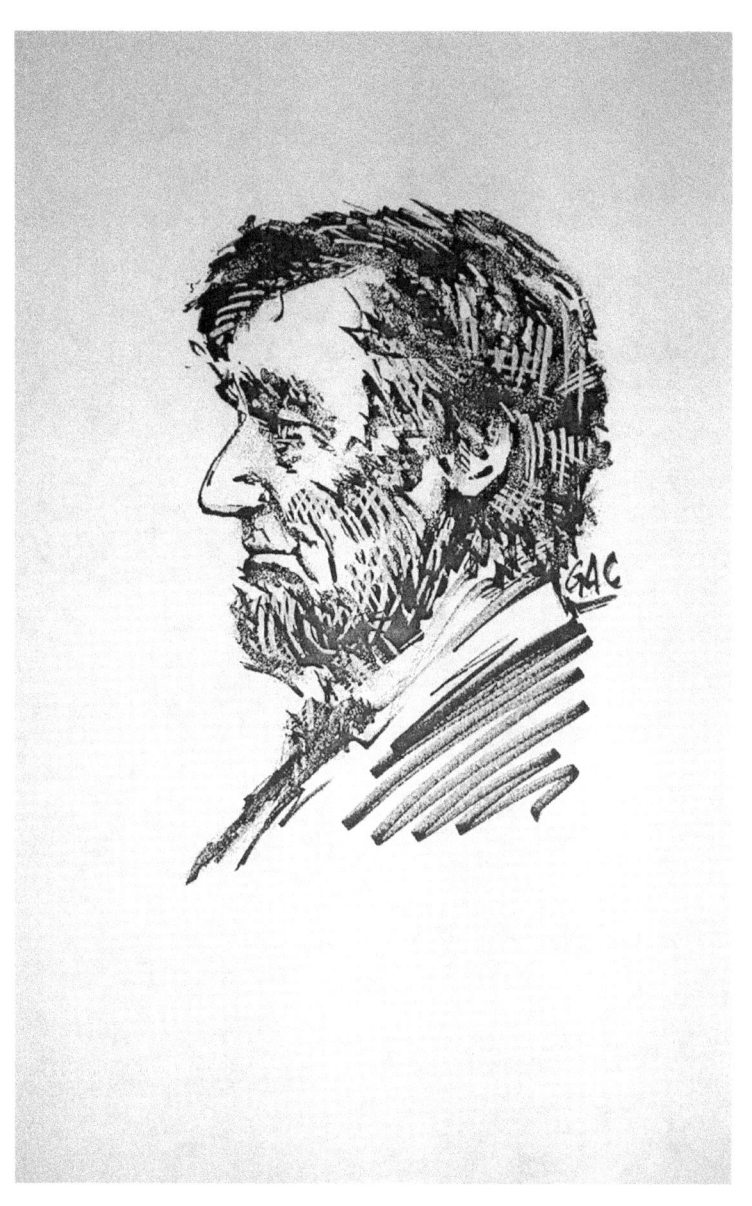

Gilles COLLETTE

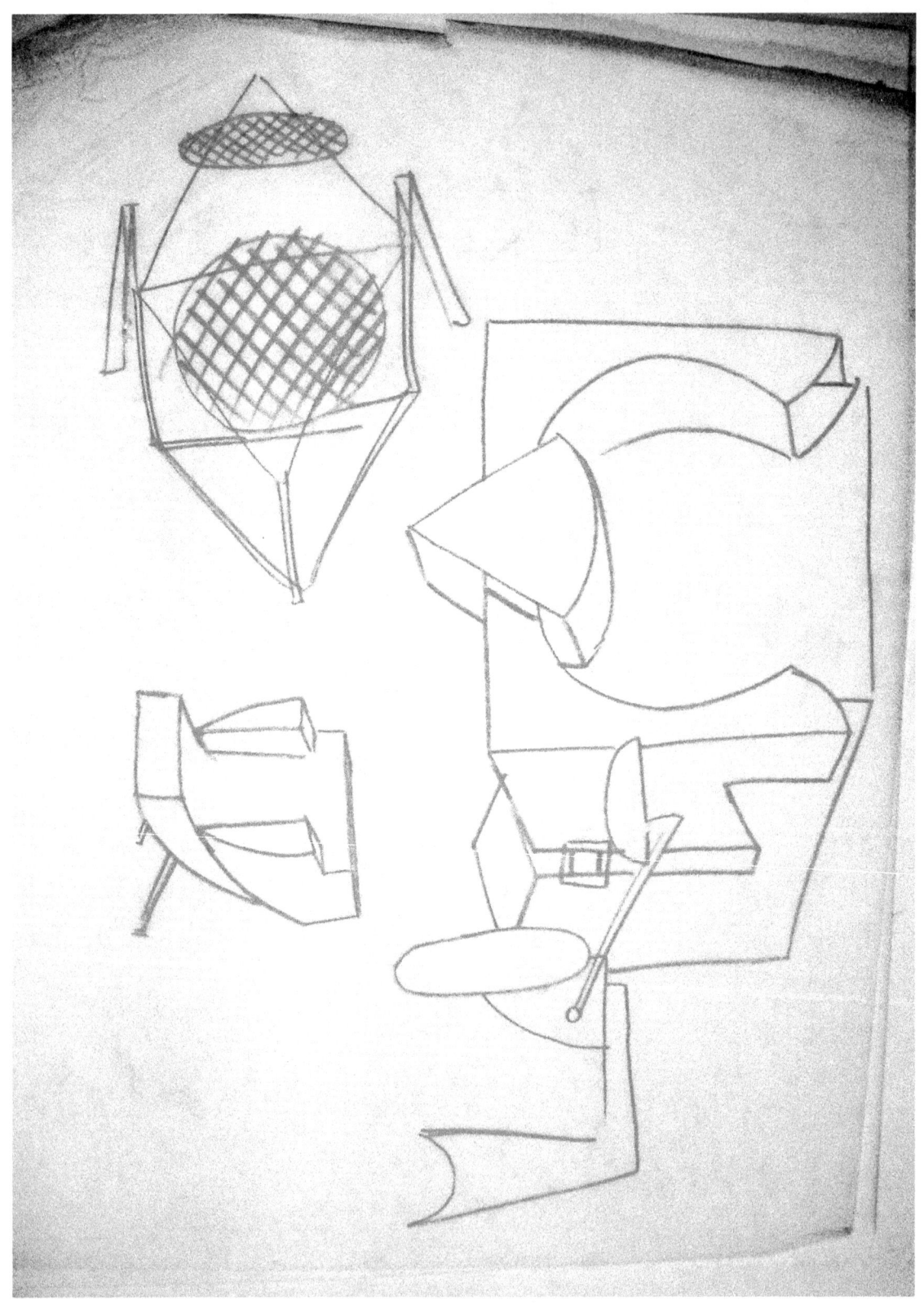

Notes and sketches

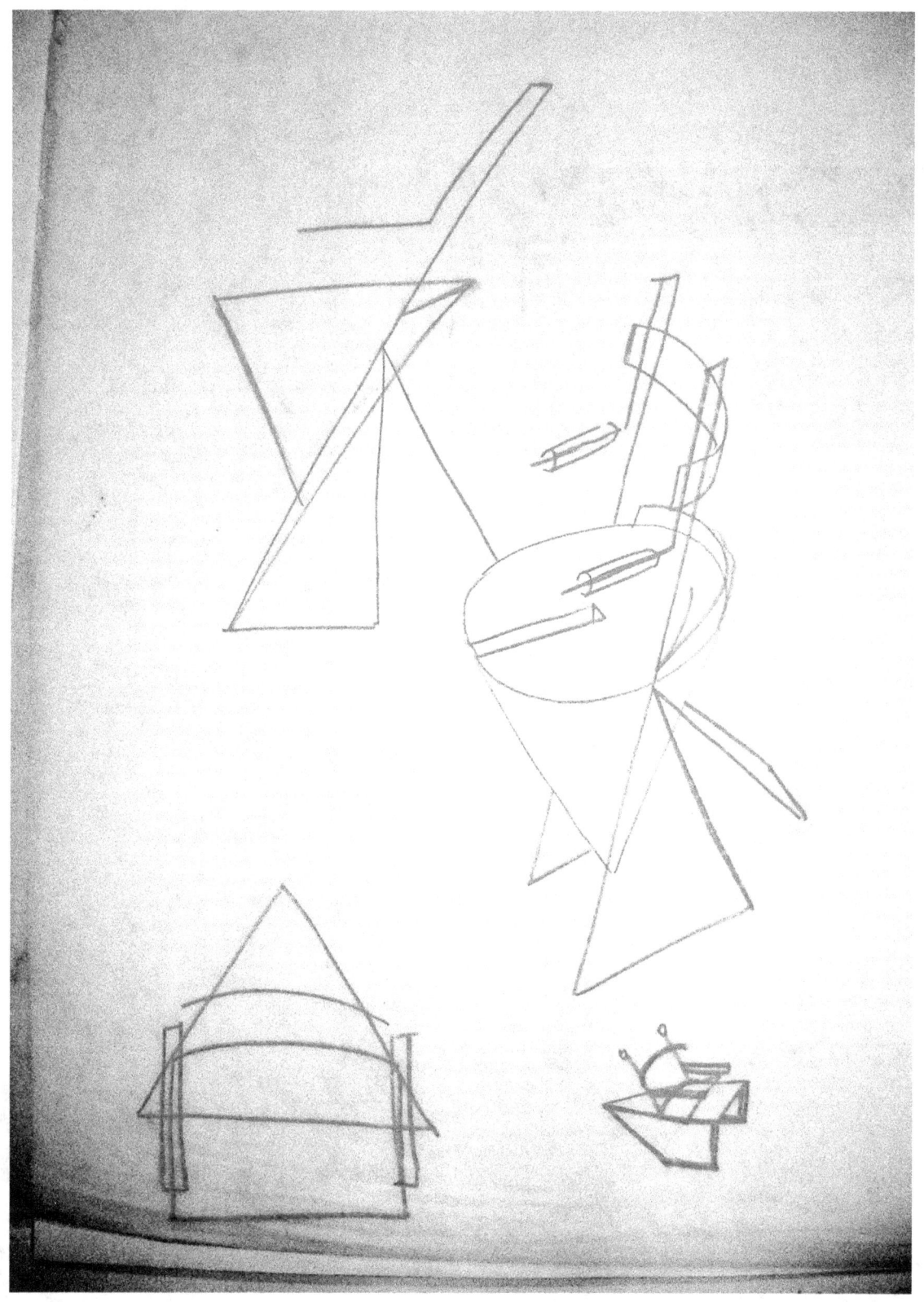

Gilles COLLETTE

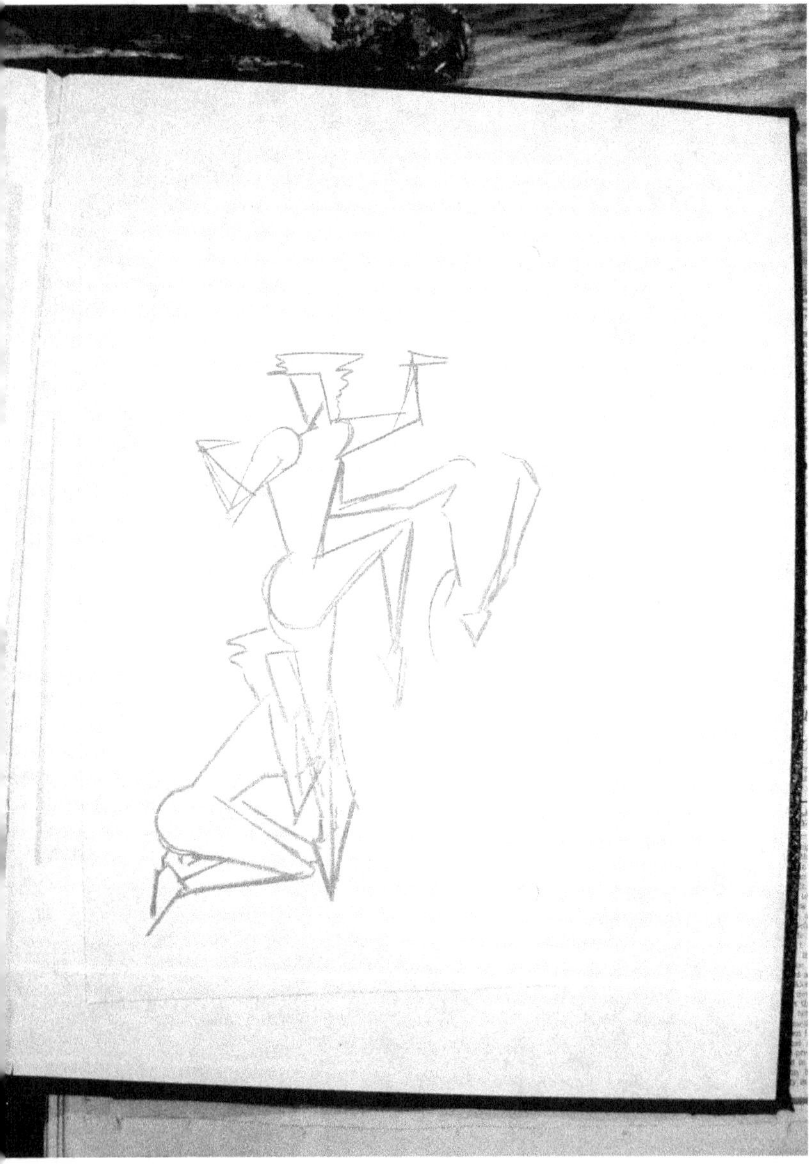

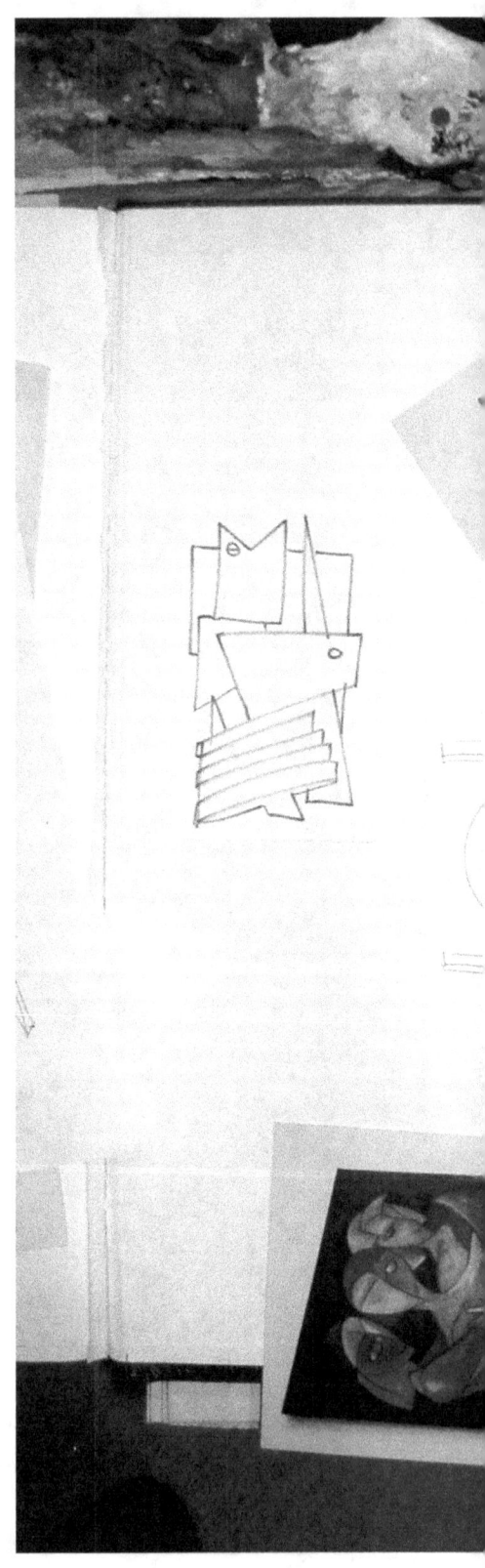

Notes and sketches

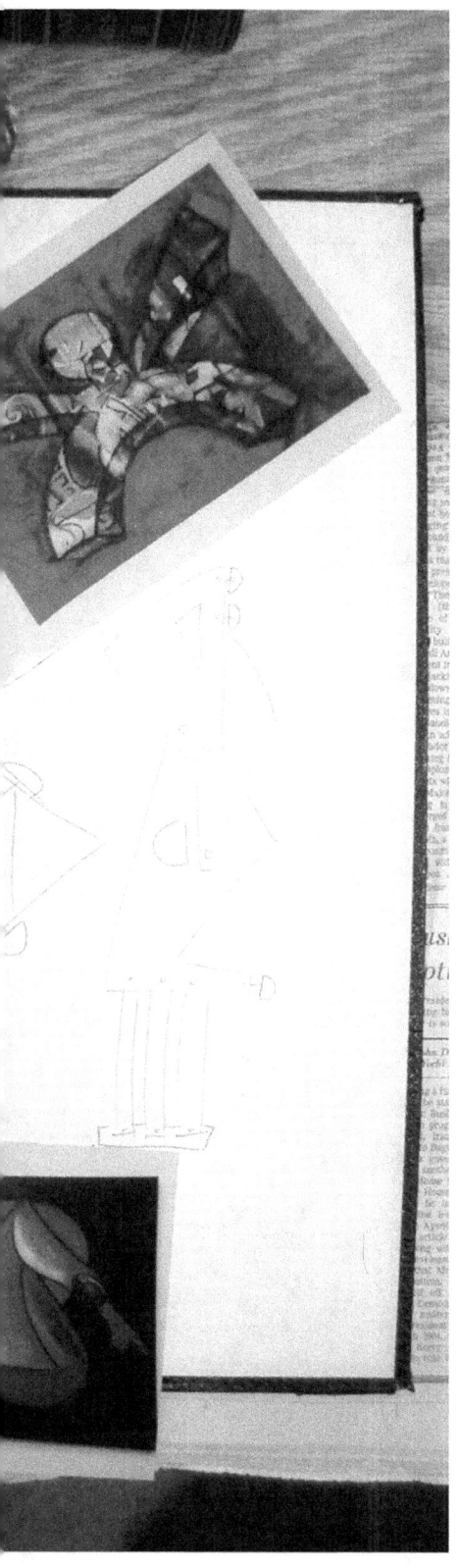

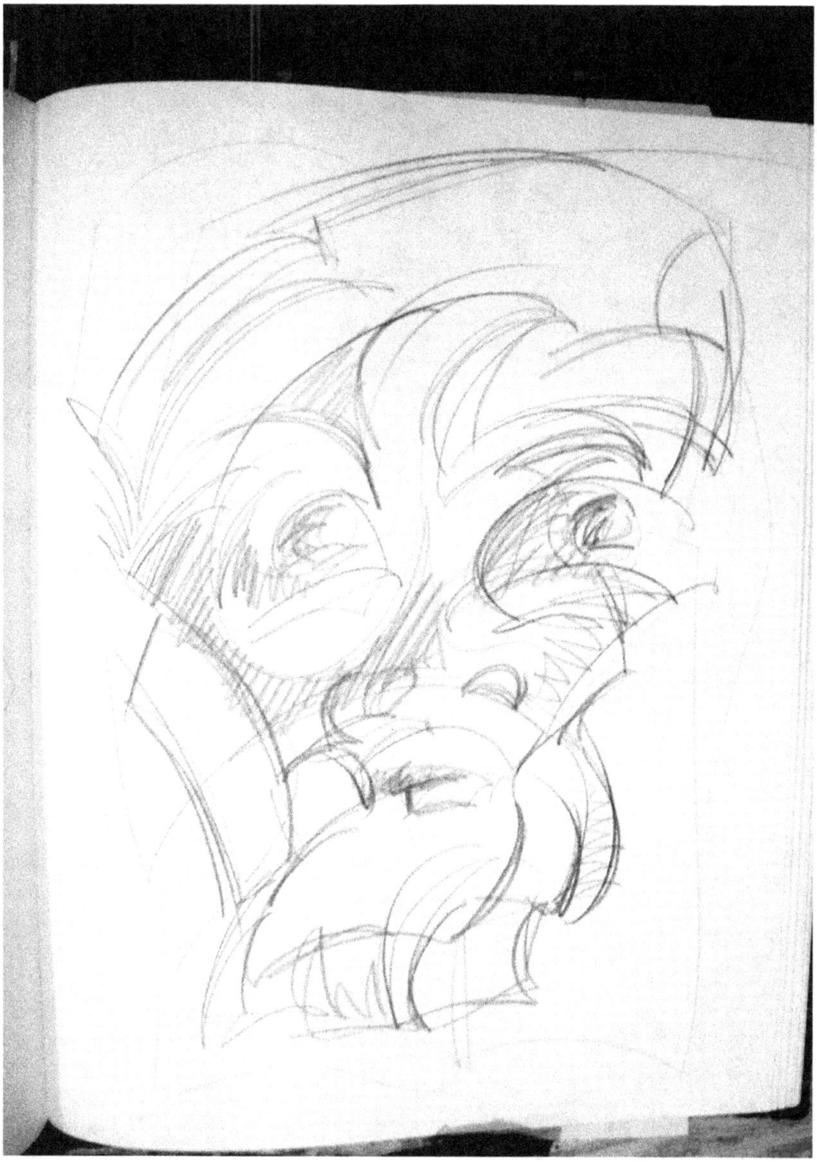

Gilles COLLETTE

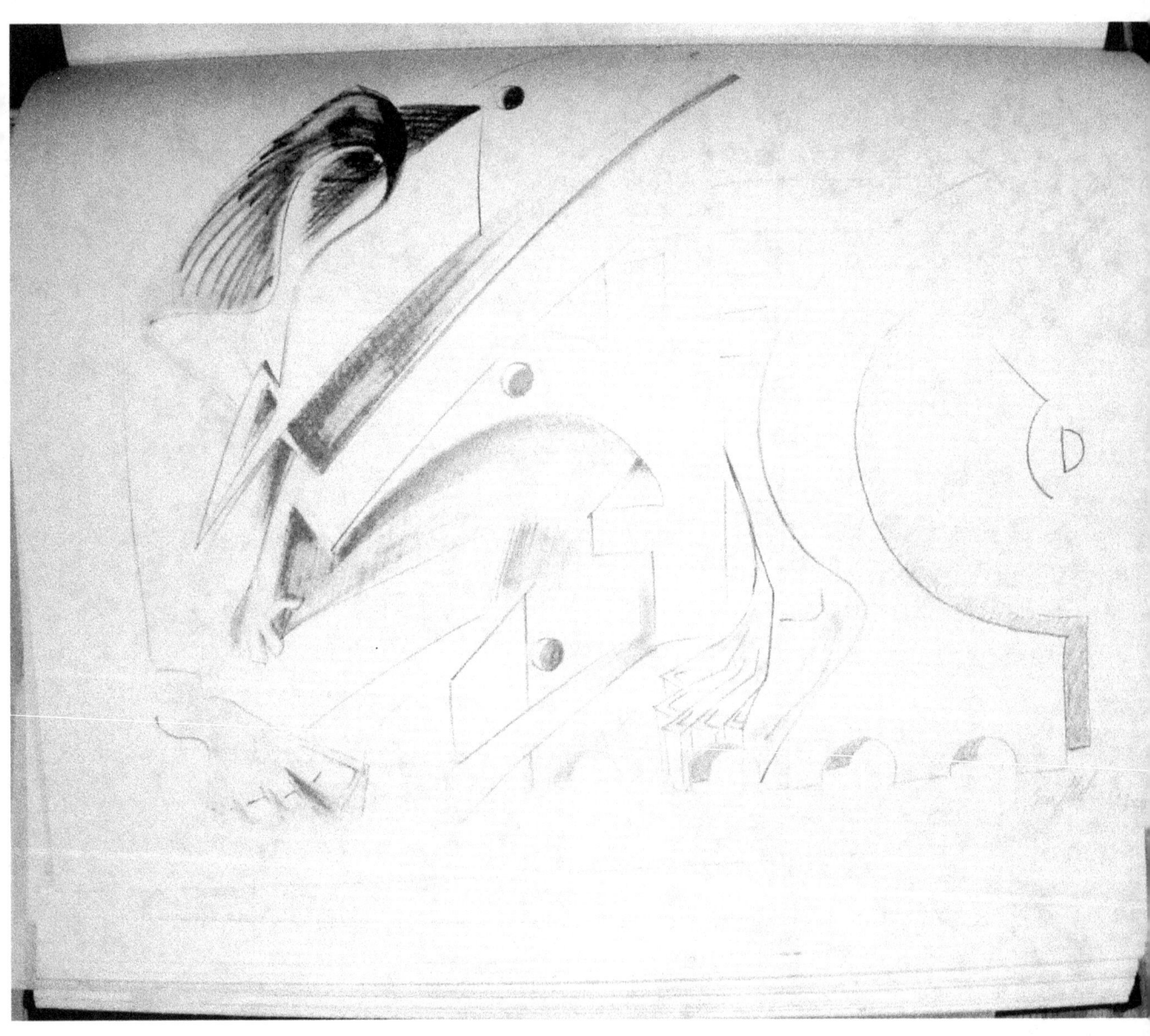

Notes and sketches

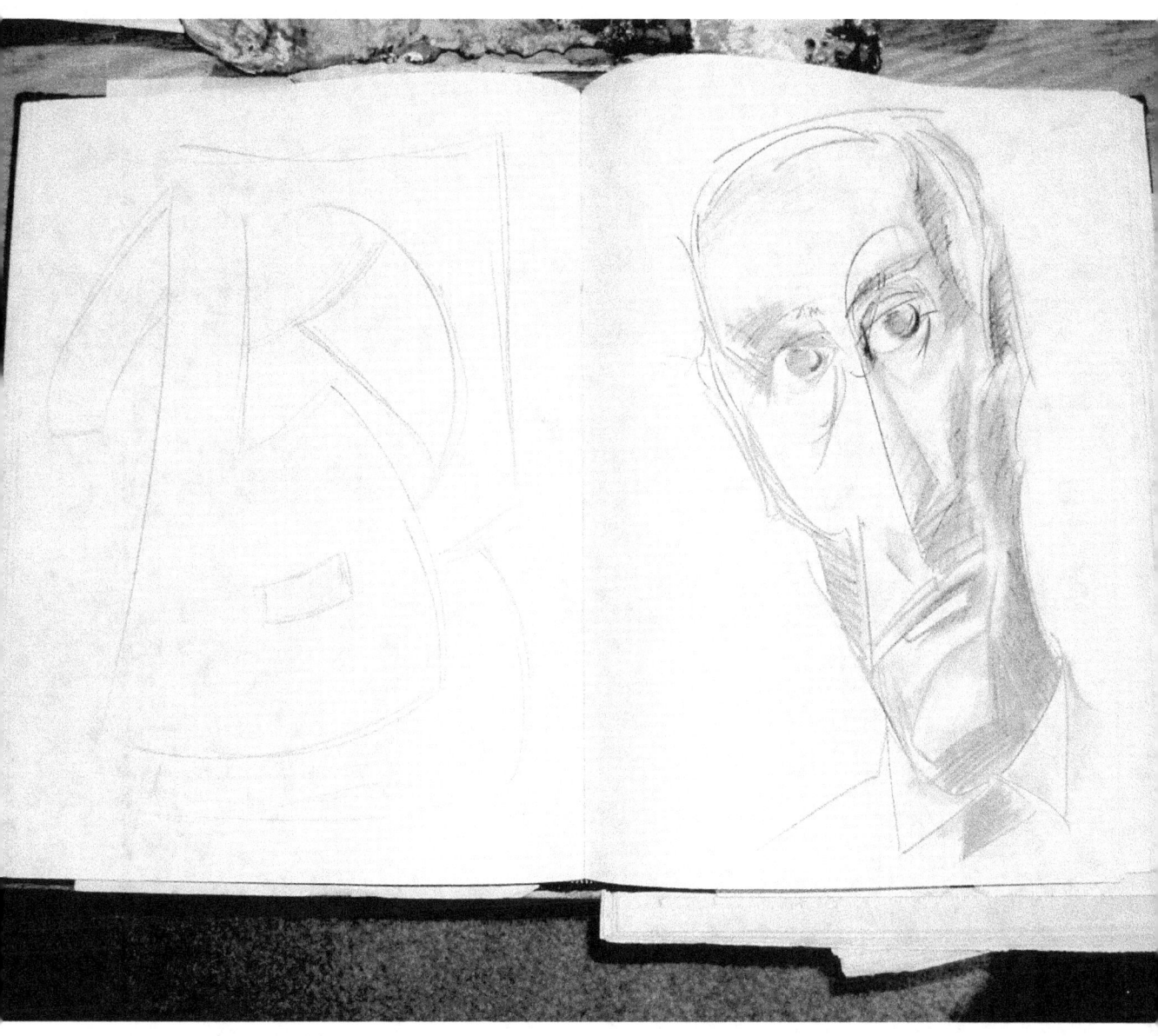

Gilles COLLETTE

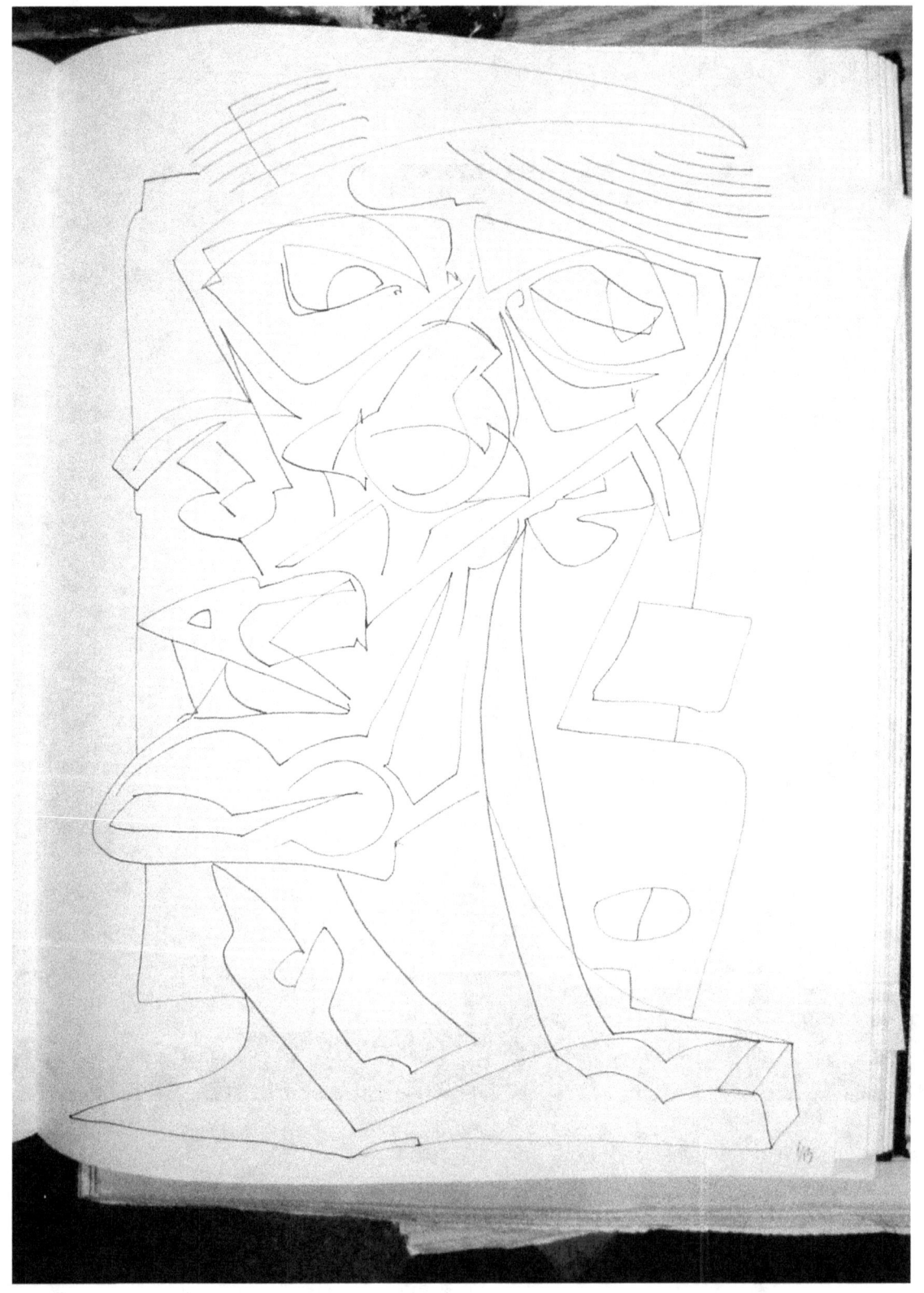

Notes and sketches

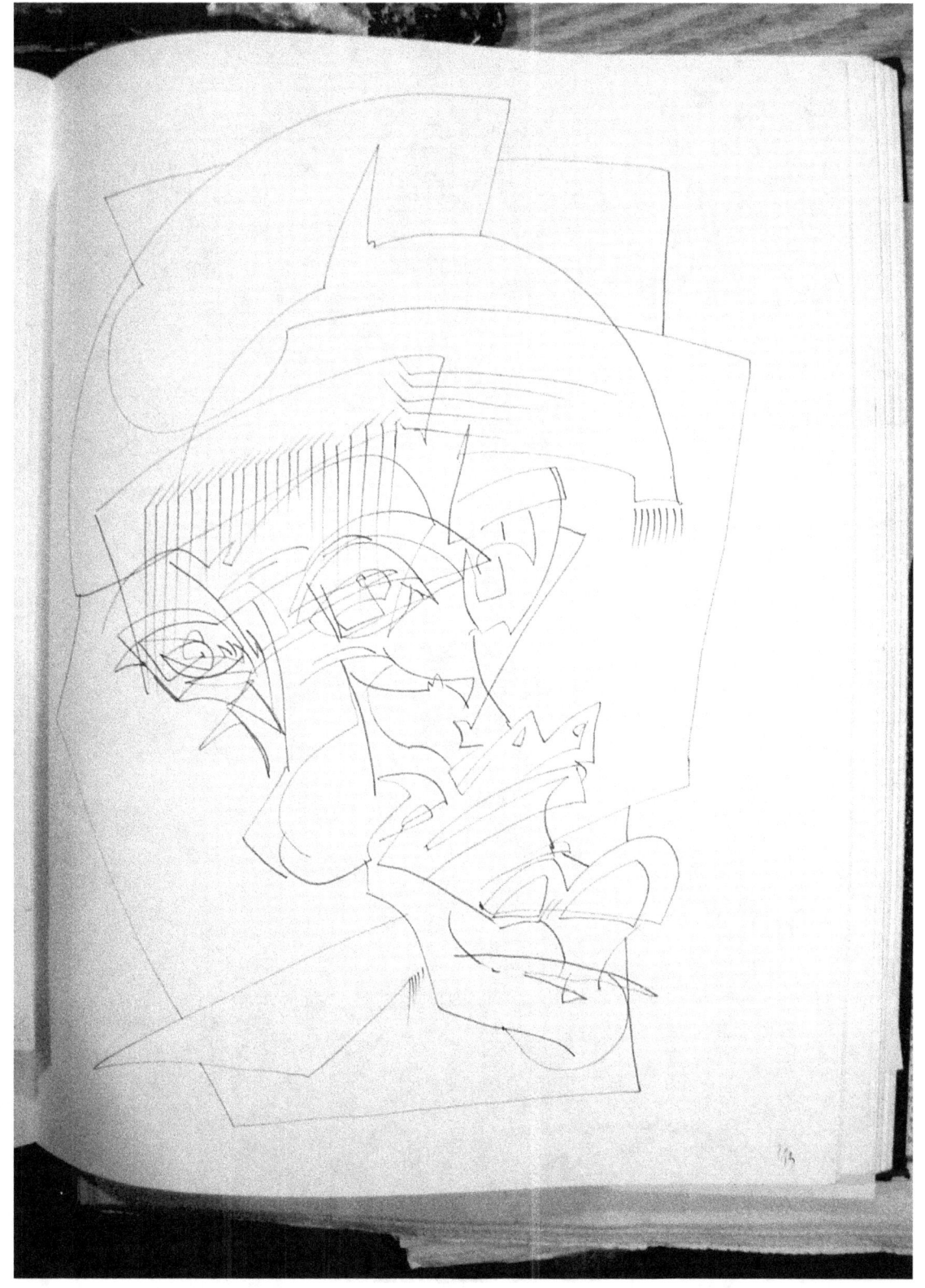

Gilles COLLETTE

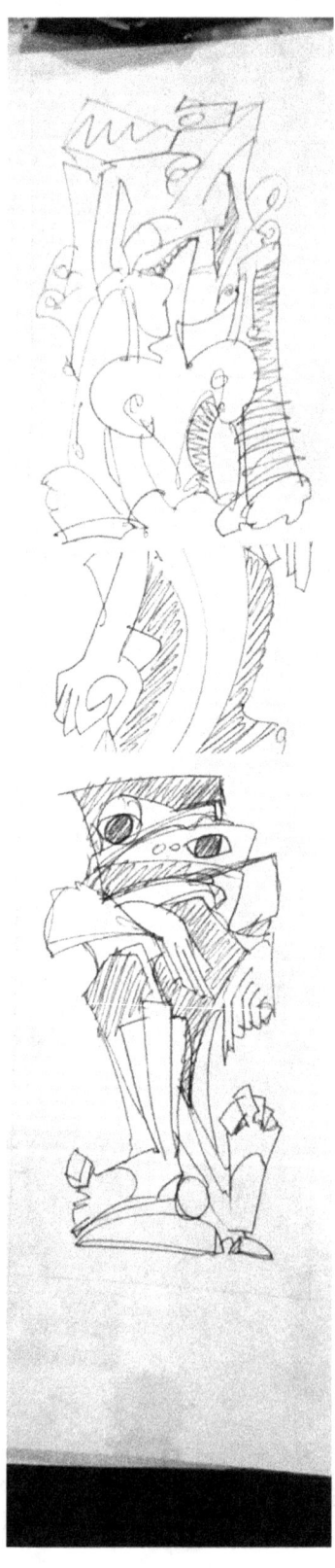

Notes and sketches

équilibrium :

A Au départ il y a le cercle (Terre, soleil, lune...)

A' Du cercle est sorti le parrallélépipède (demeure ; délimita-
tion des champs / grilles ..)

A².en compressant le p. ou en extrayant une moitié, nous
arrivons au triangle (pédiment pyramide) que je
qualifierais comme point d'entente entre le cercle et le carré
ou synthèse pour cette démonstration

B ce symbole universel assimilé avec l'humanité, la
nature

B' parral... ou plus simplement le geste carré représente

la singularité d'une des races qui peuplent l'humanité.
ou plus globalement toutes avec leur différence

B² le triangle serait donc rennessent de l'entente _
les principes commun seraient sous jacent

Gilles COLLETTE

49

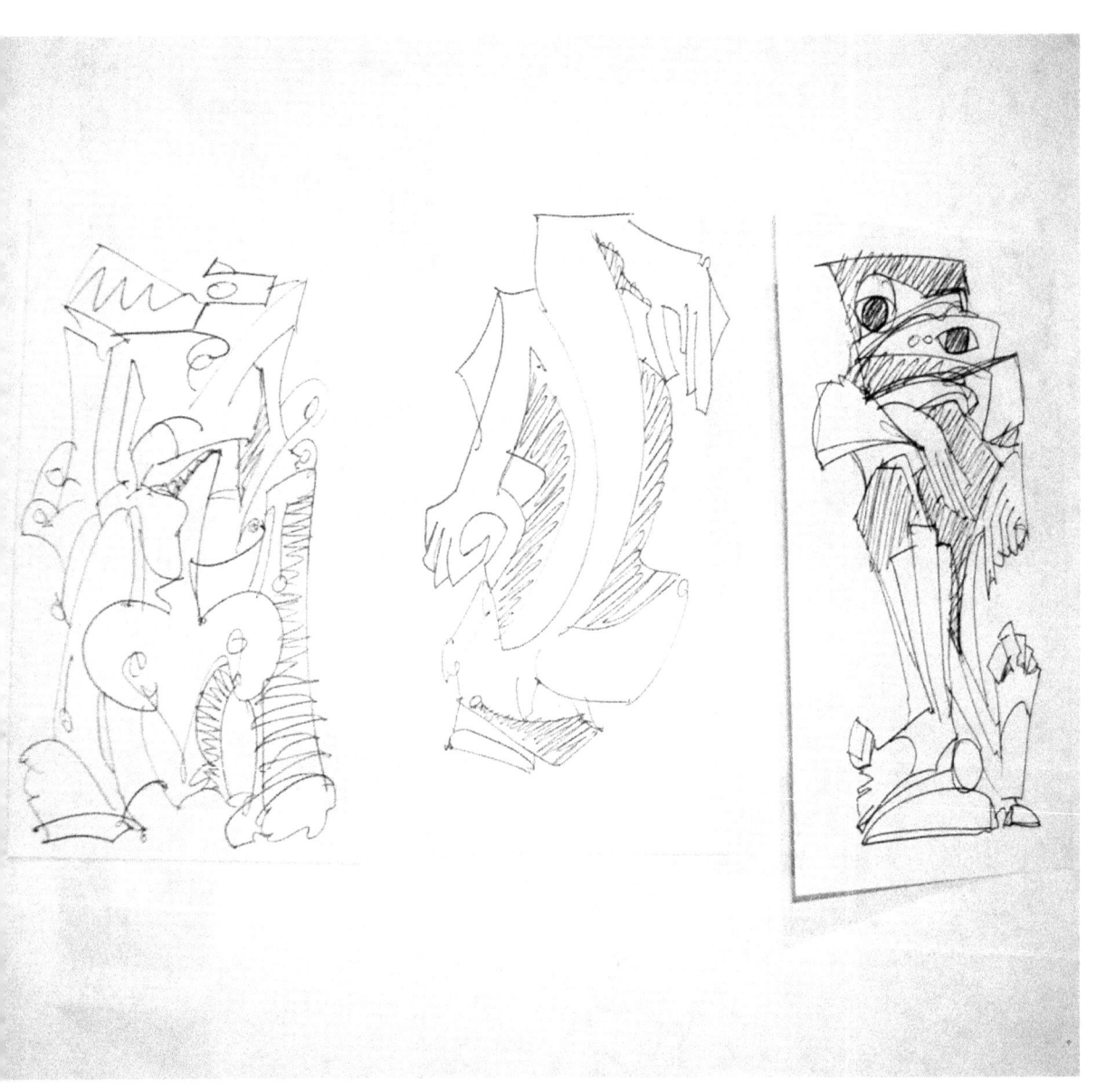

Notes and sketches

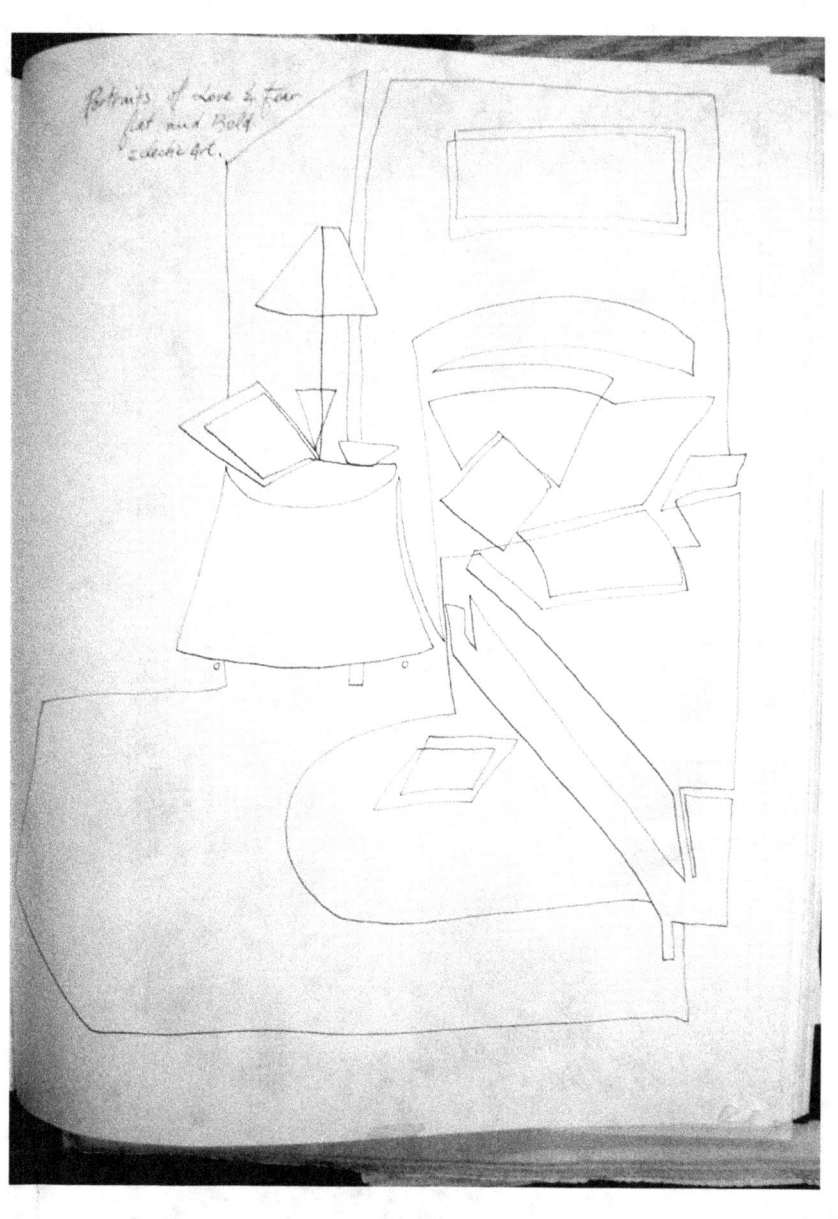

Gilles COLLETTE

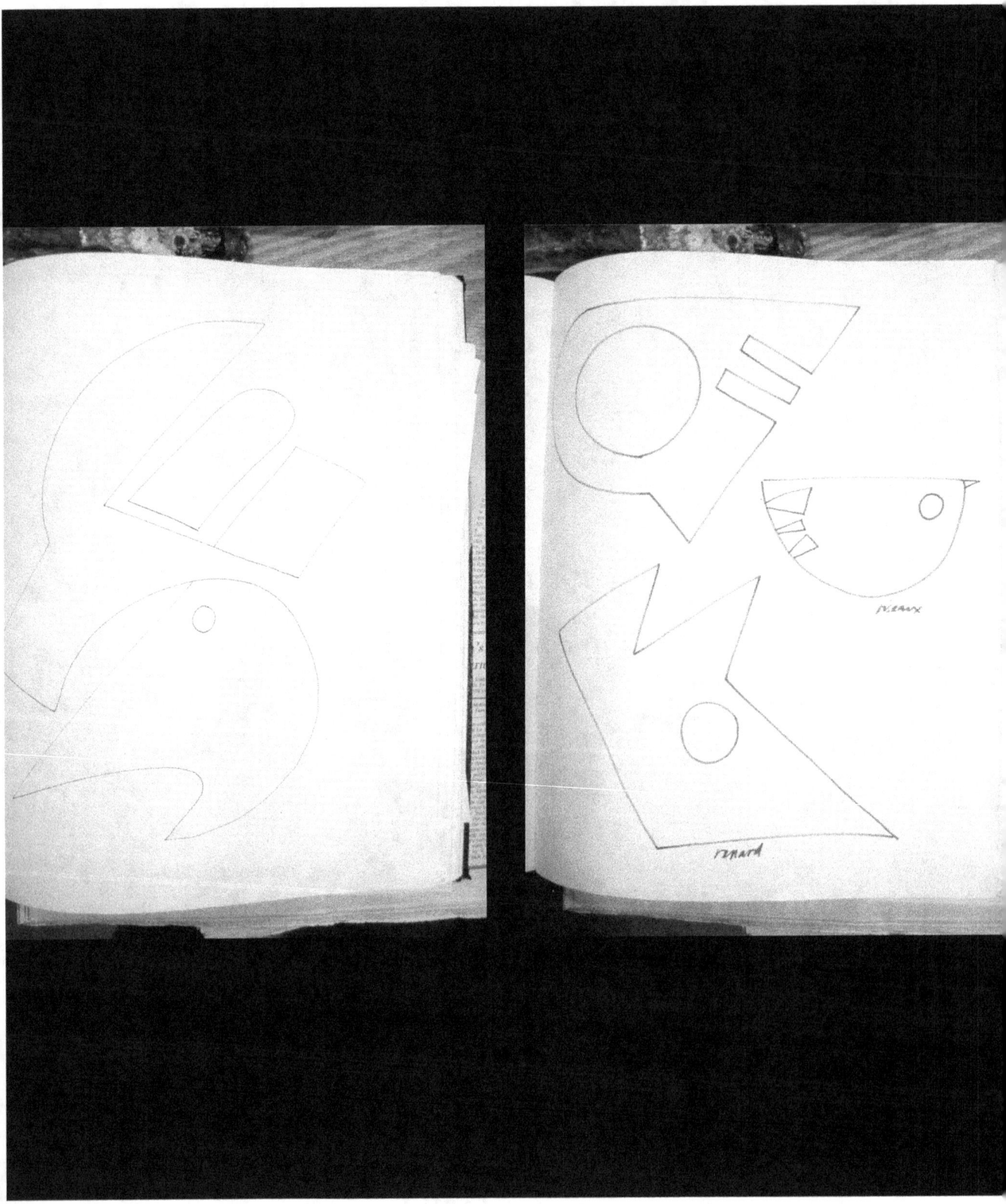

Notes and sketches

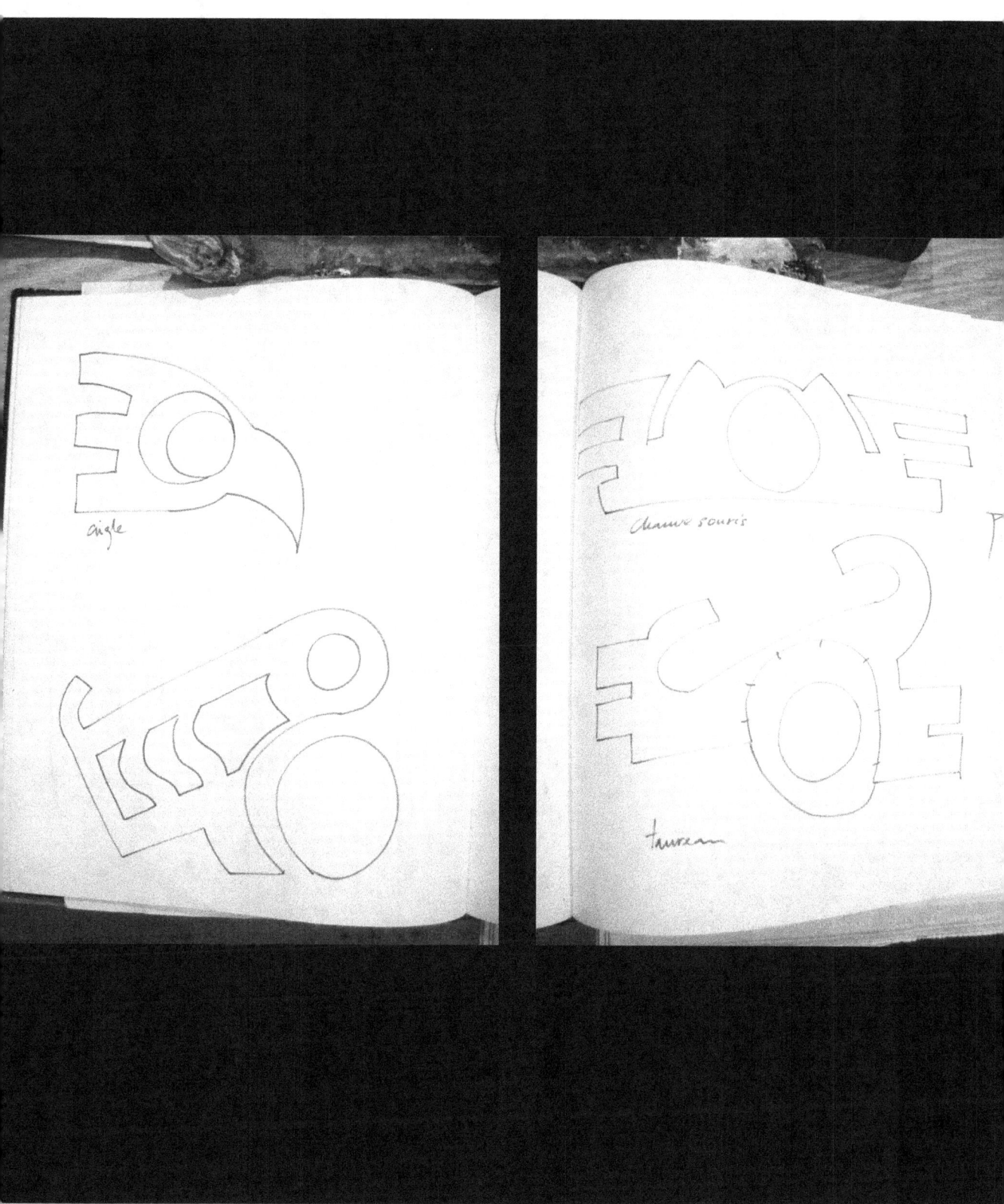

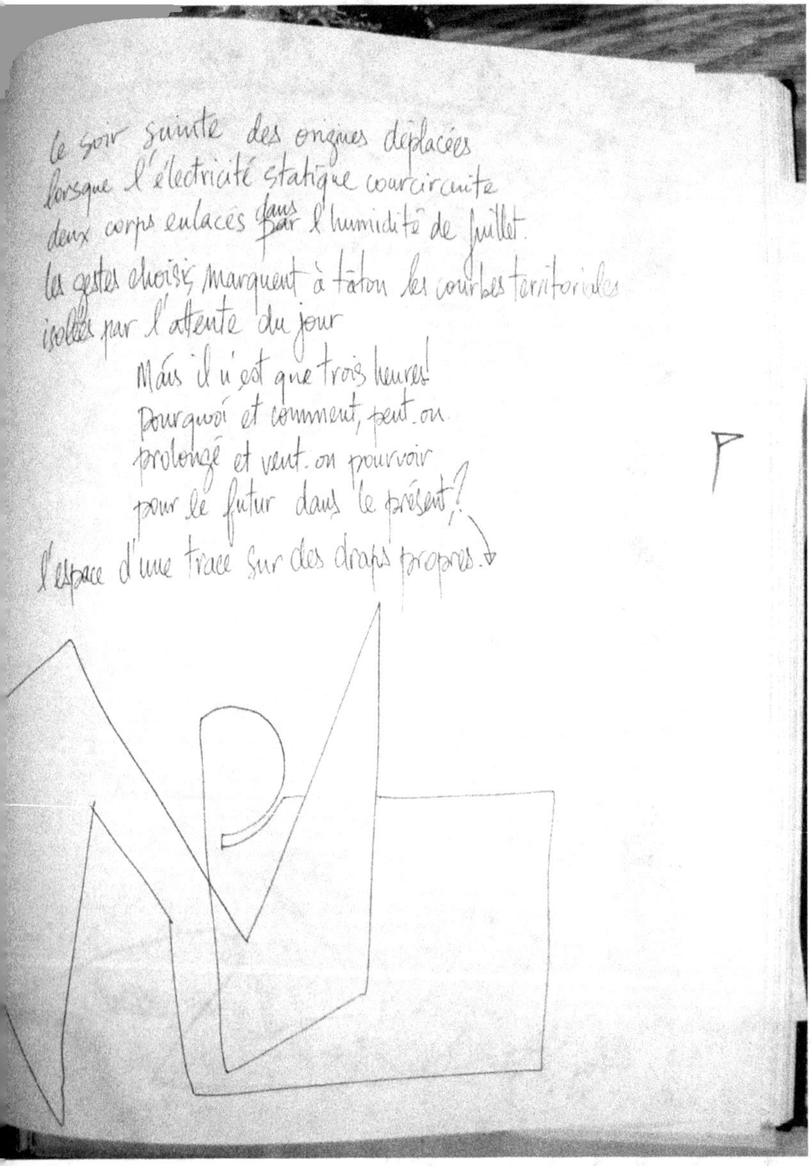

Le soir suinte des ongines déplacées
lorsque l'électricité statique courcircuite
deux corps enlacés par l'humidité de Juillet.

Les gestes choisis marquent à tâton les courbes territoriales
isolées par l'attente du jour

      Mais il n'est que trois heures!
      Pourquoi et comment, peut-on
      prolonger et veut-on pourvoir
      pour le futur dans le présent?

l'espace d'une trace sur des draps propres.

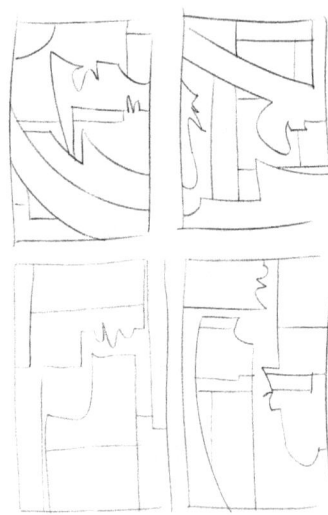

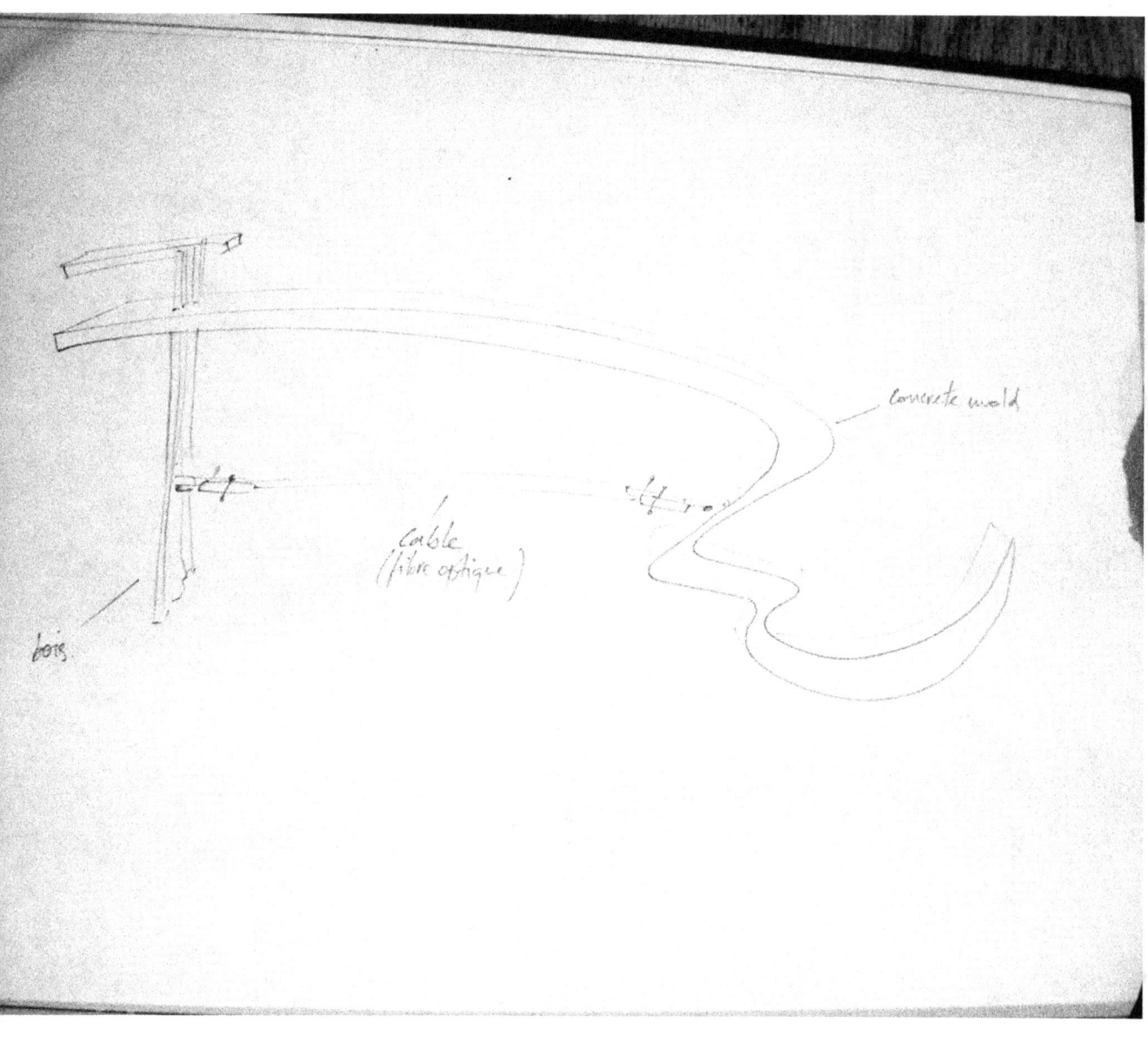

bois

câble
(fibre optique)

concrete mould

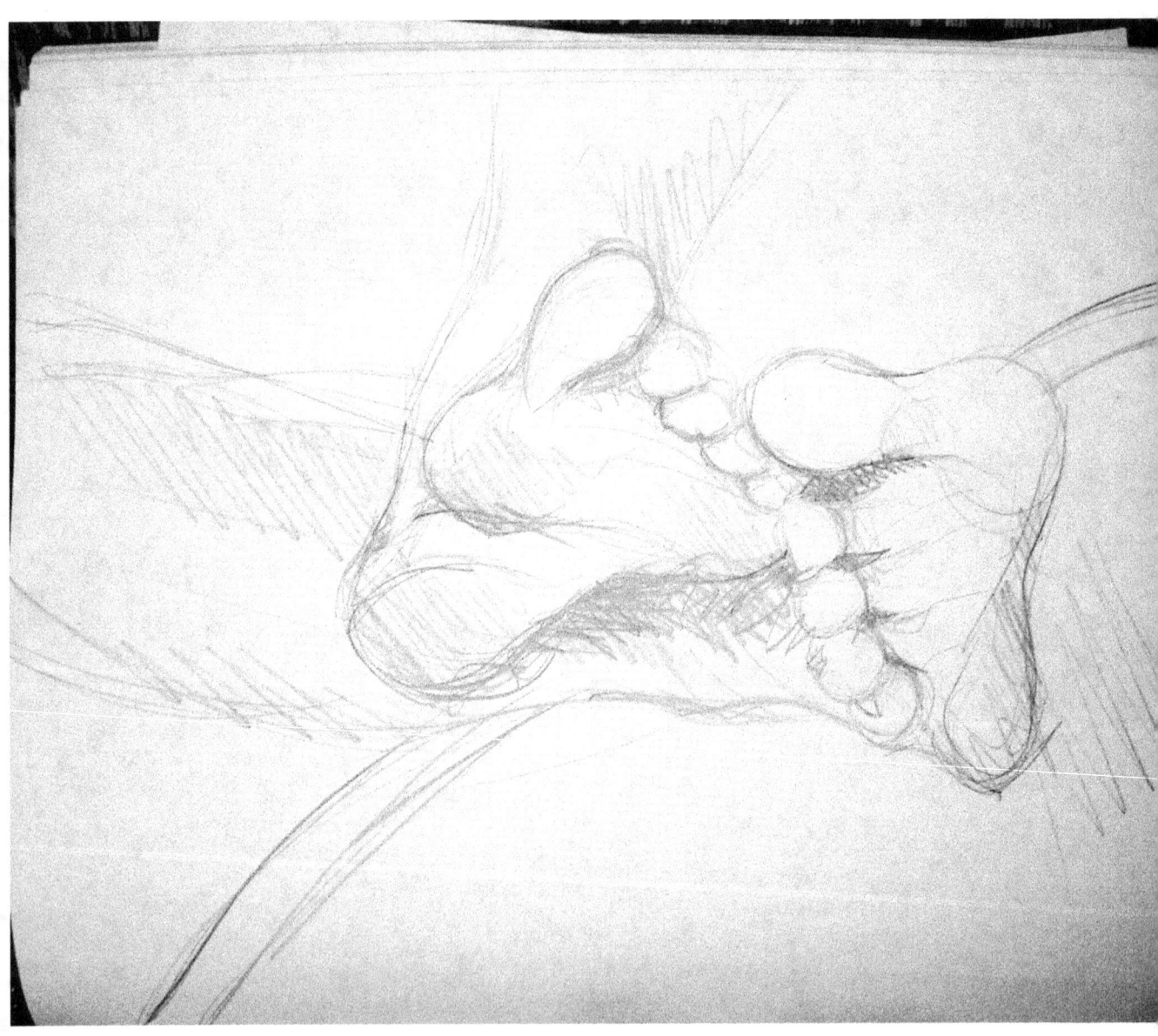

Notes and sketches

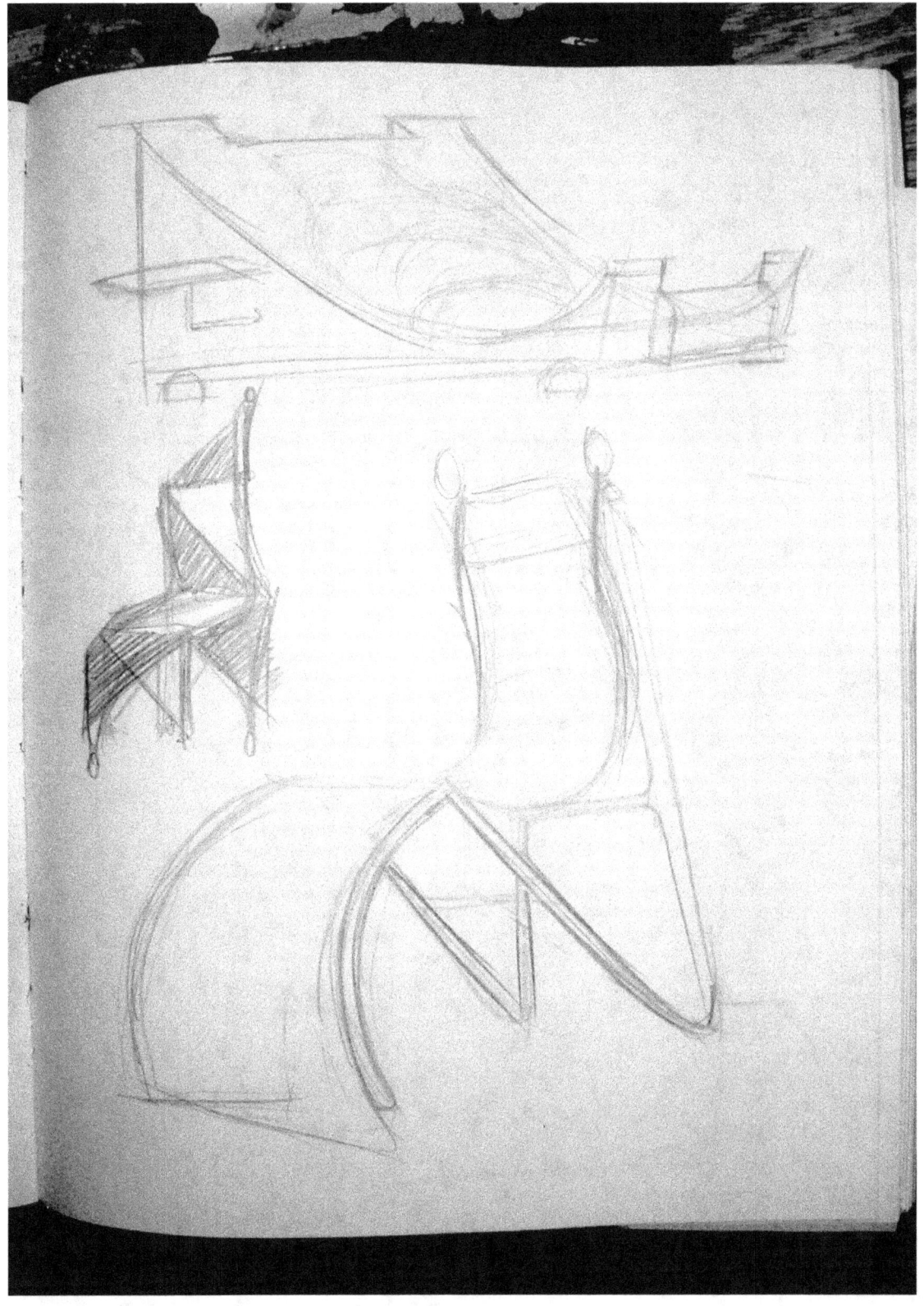

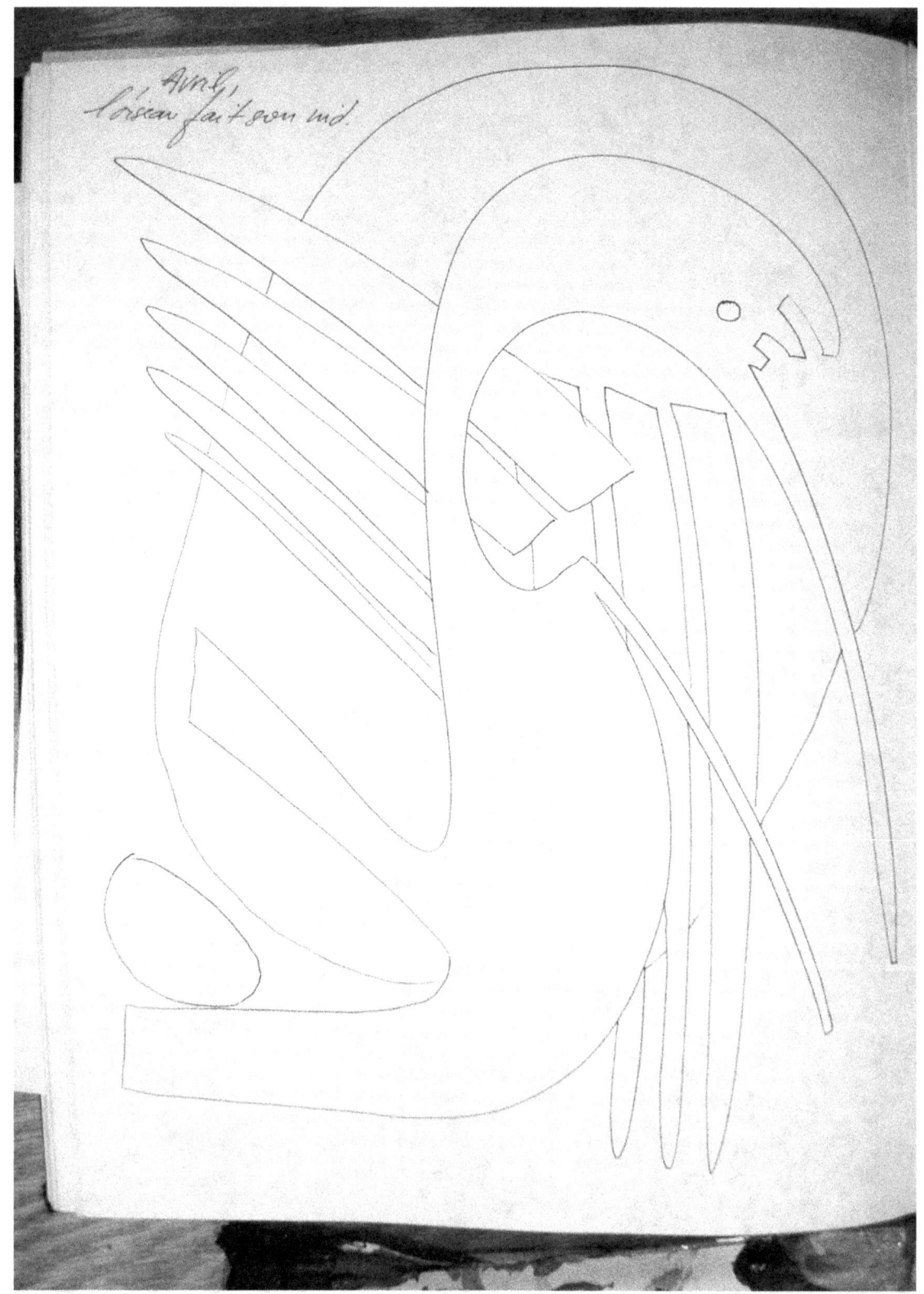

Avril,
l'oiseau fait son nid.

Notes and sketches

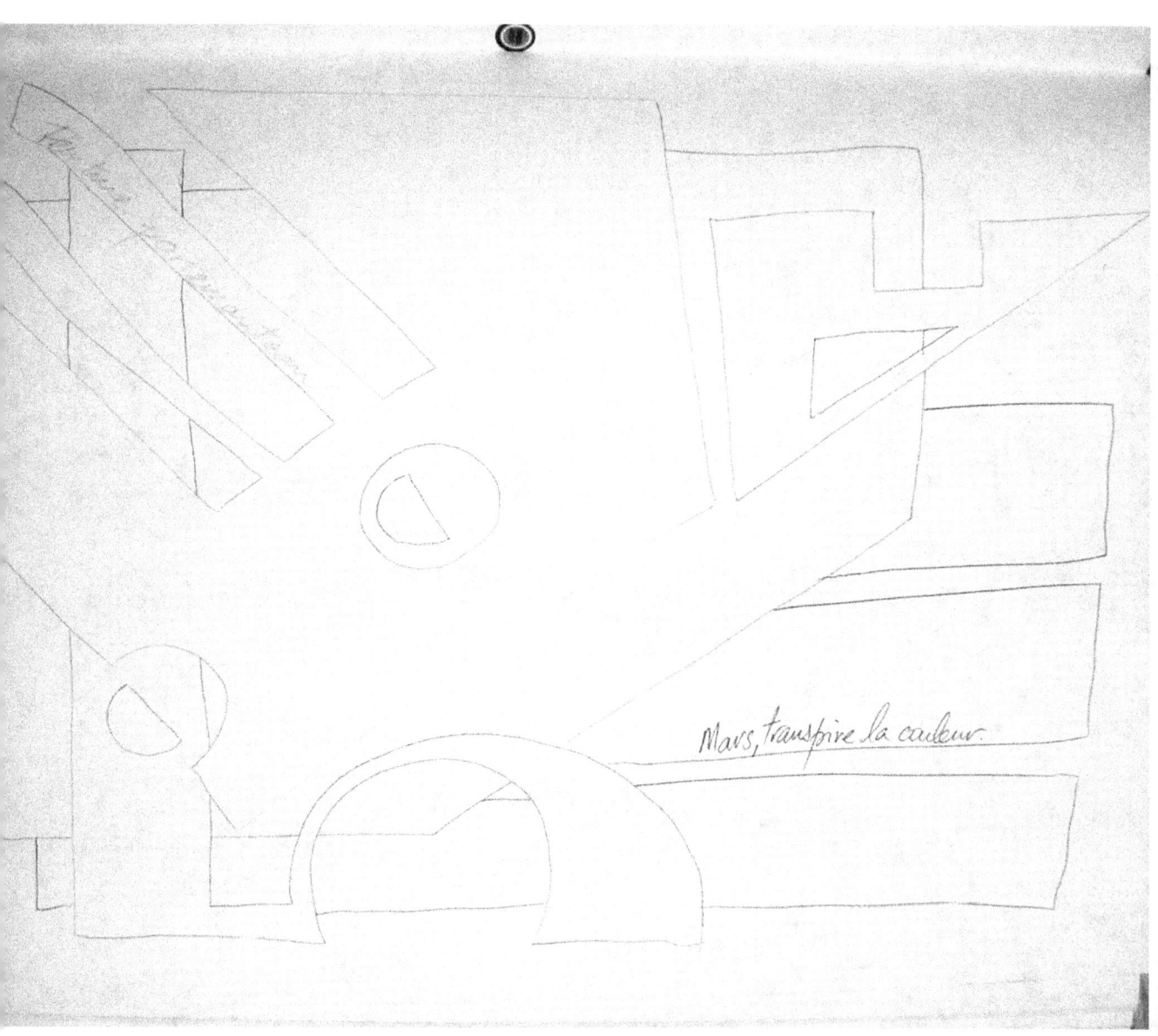

Mars, transpire la couleur.

Gilles COLLETTE

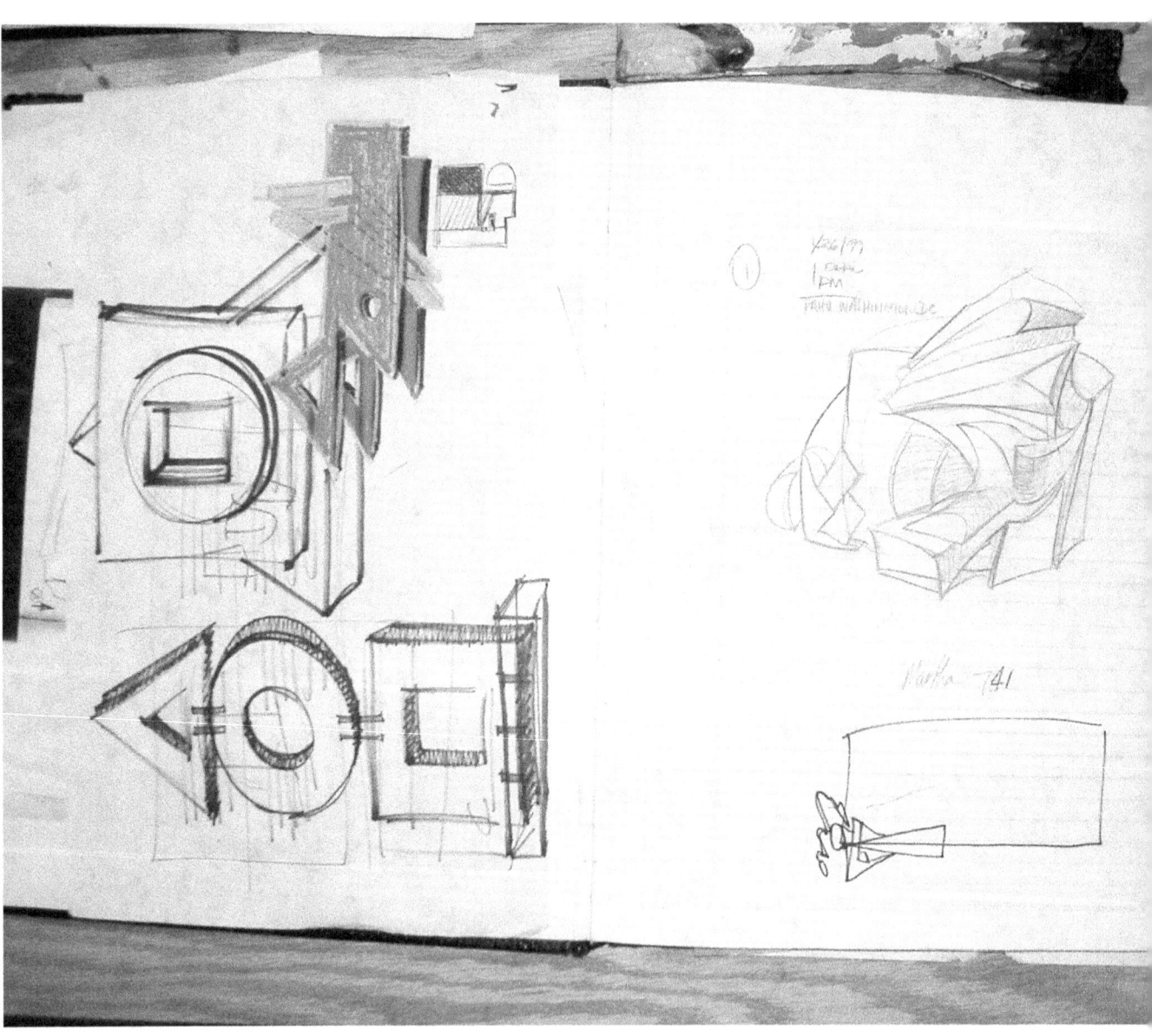

Notes and sketches

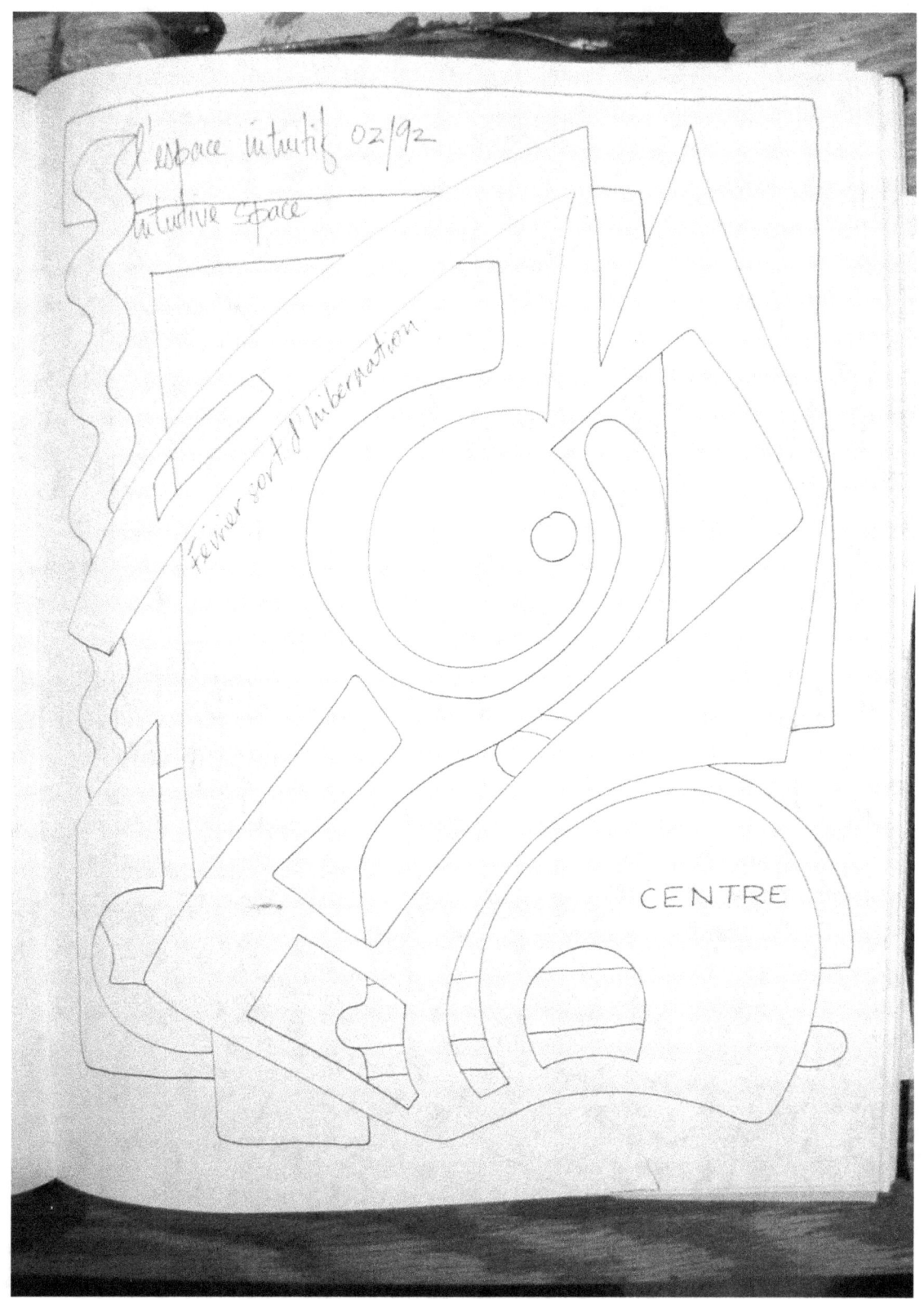

l'espace intuitif 02/92

Intuitive Space

Février sort d'hibernation

CENTRE

Gilles COLLETTE

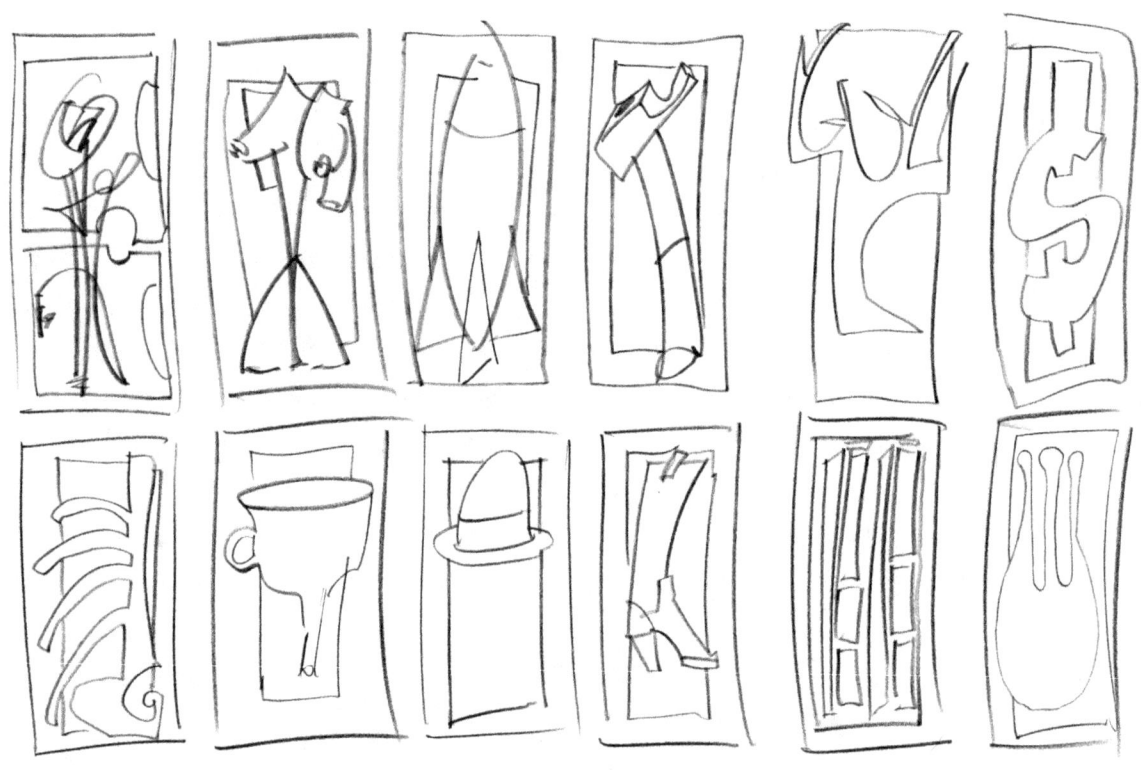

Notes and sketches

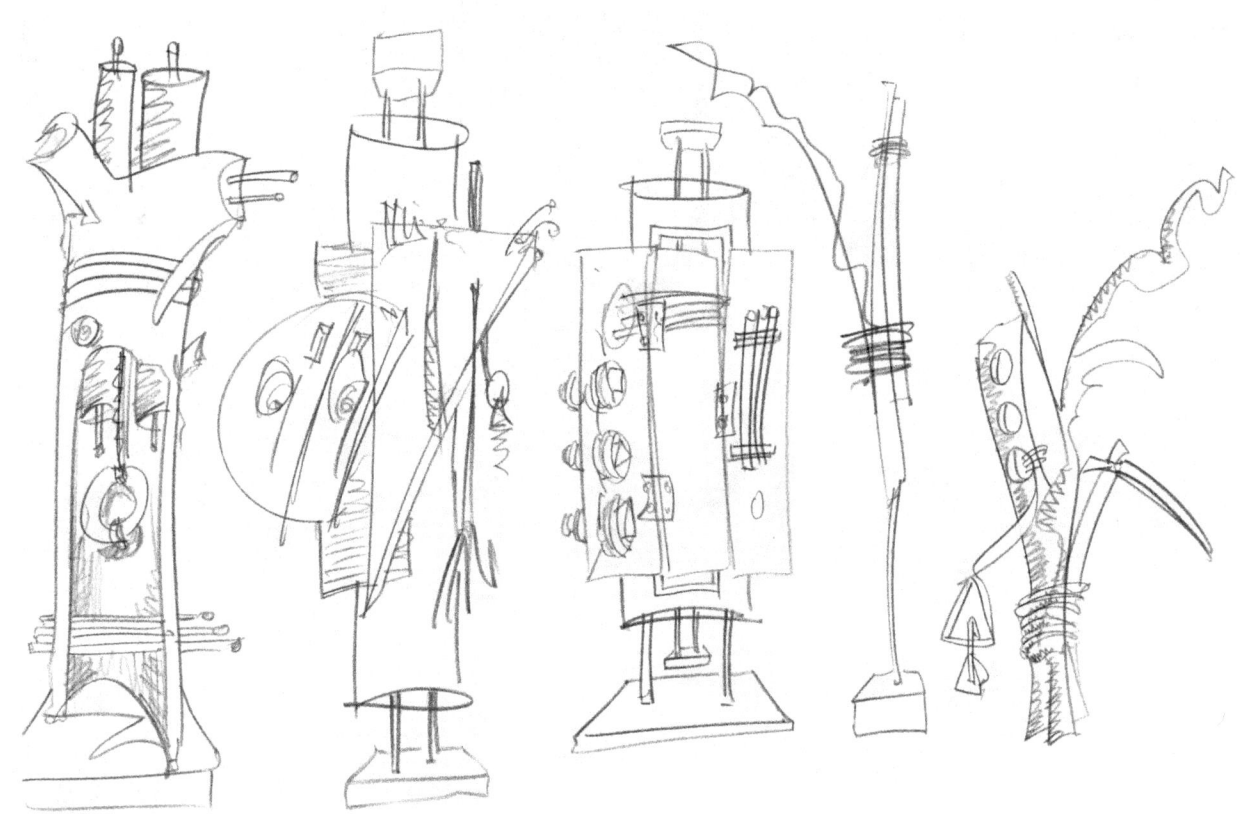

Gilles COLLETTE

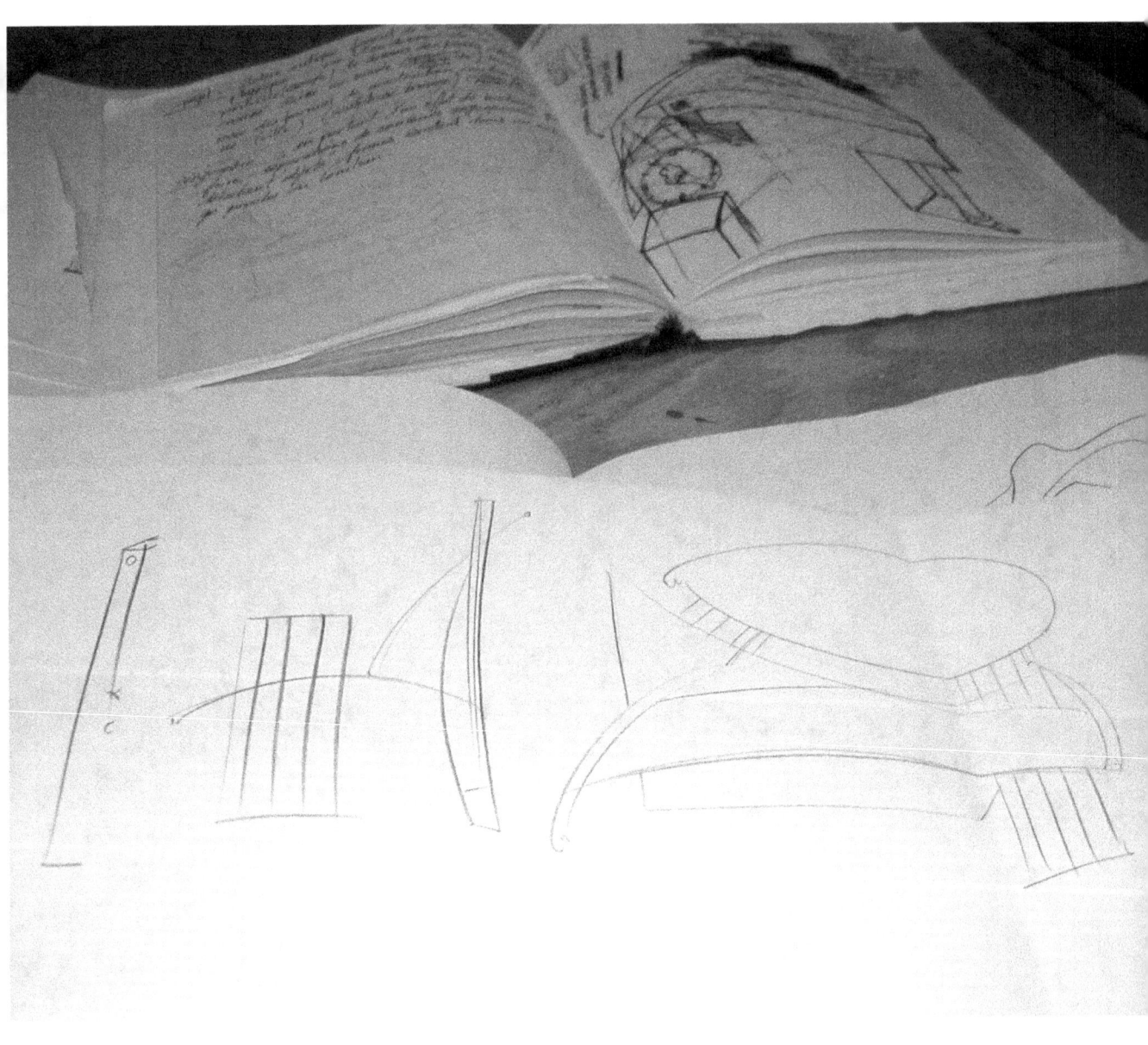

Notes and sketches

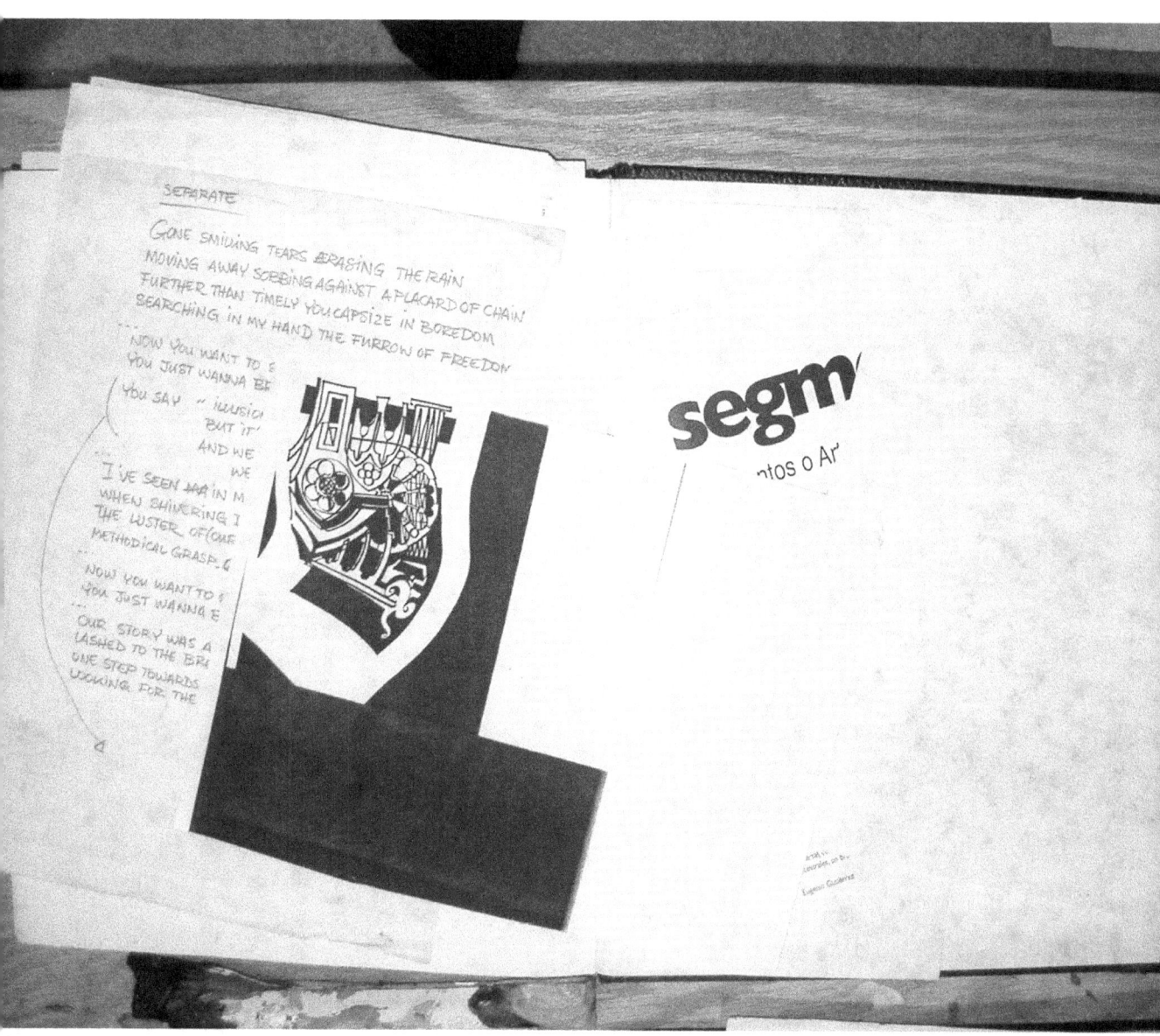

Series
Femmes au natural
drawings for paintings and
sculptures (dimensional size)

Each woman will pick-up the name of
a flower which colors and forms shall
serve as basis for selection of tonalities—

Notes and sketches

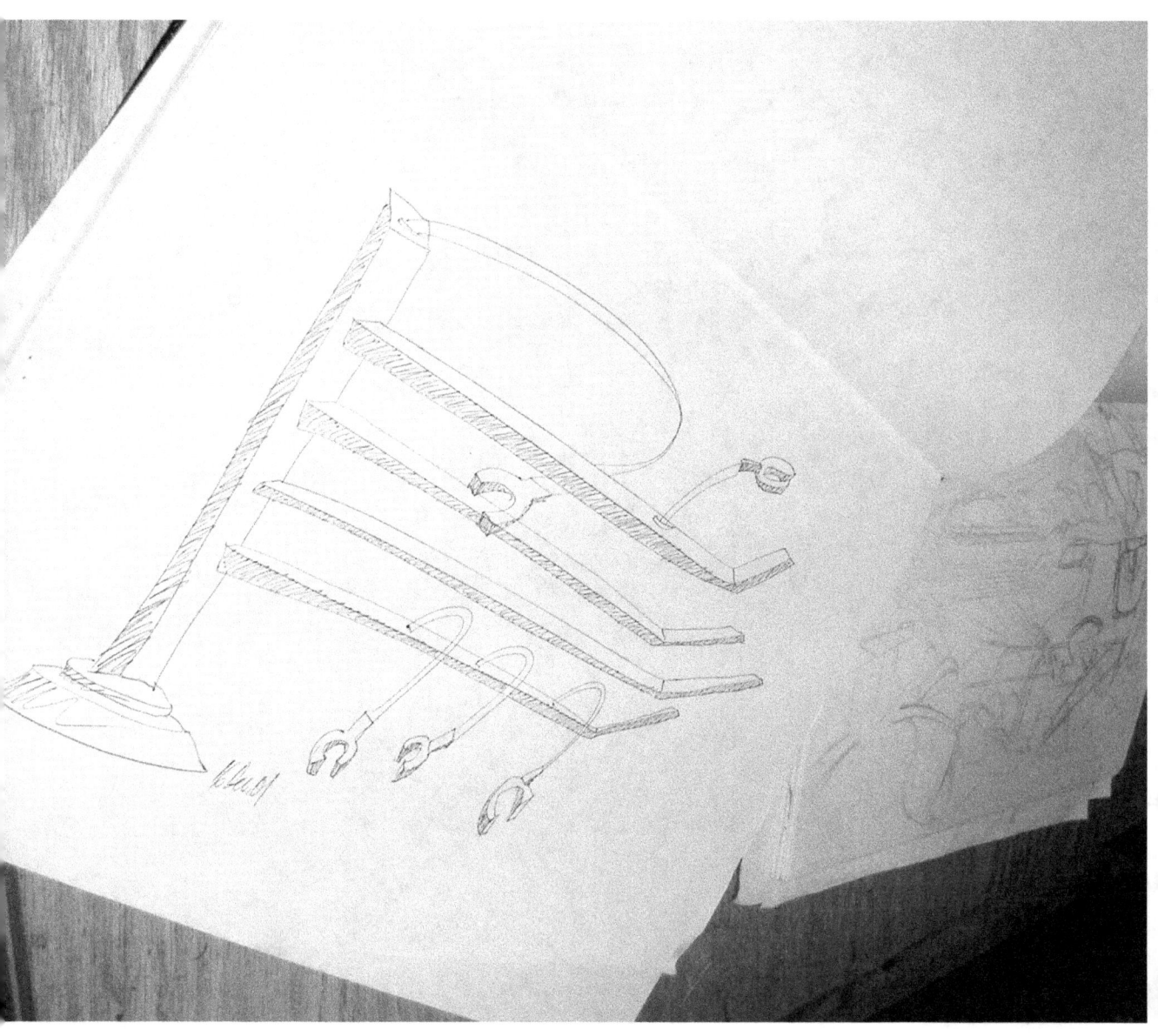

Gilles COLLETTE

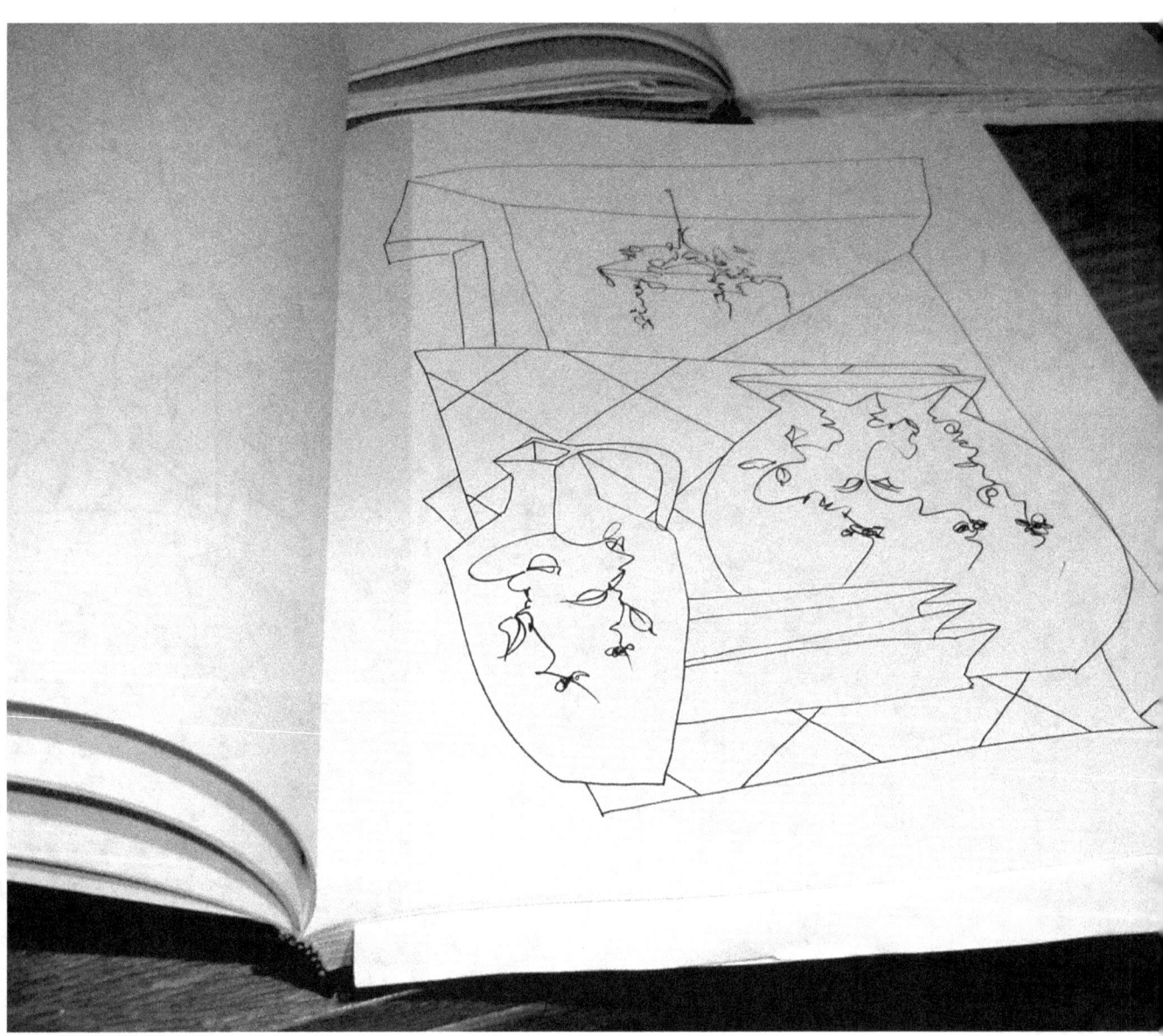

Notes and sketches

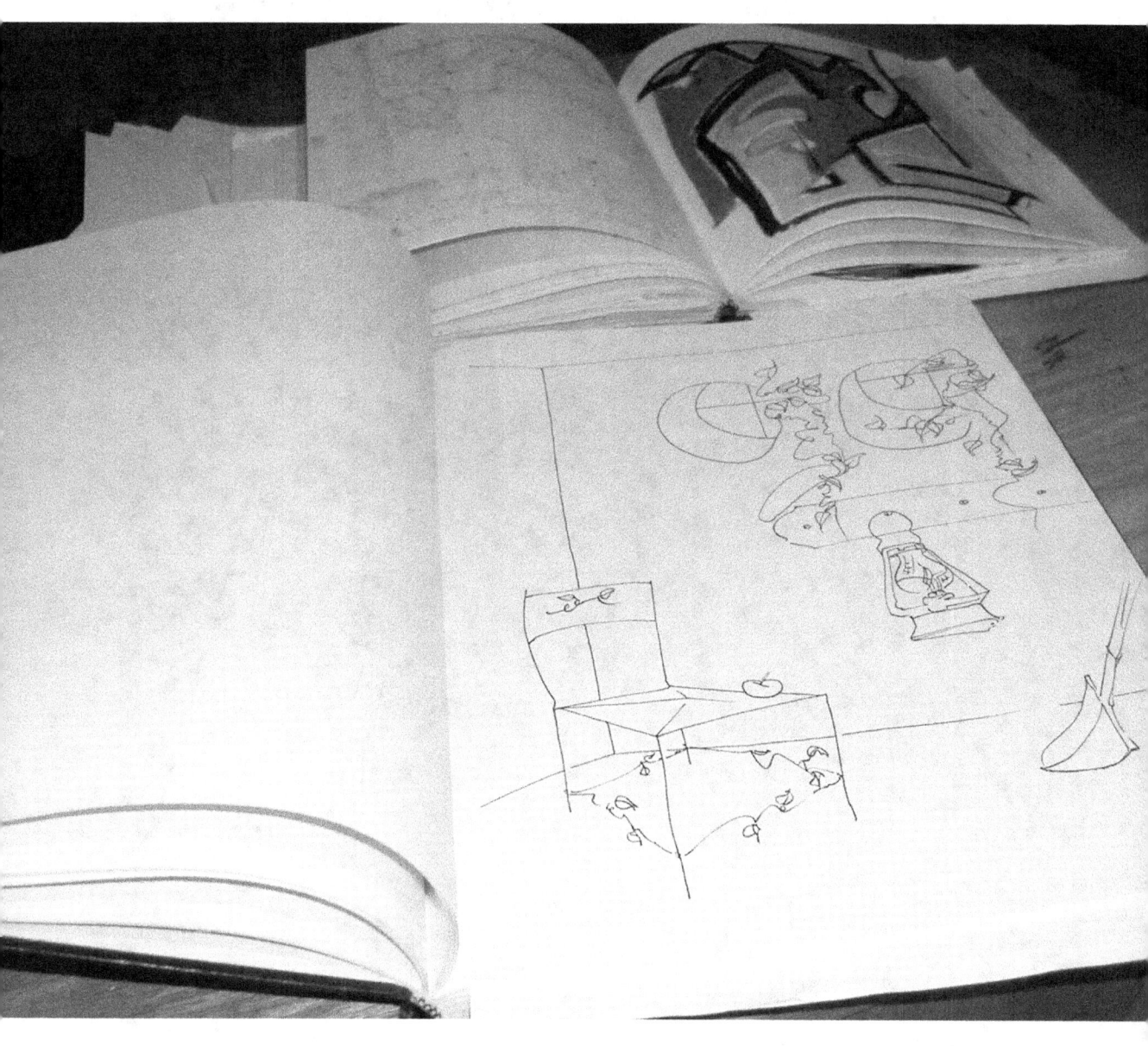

Gilles COLLETTE

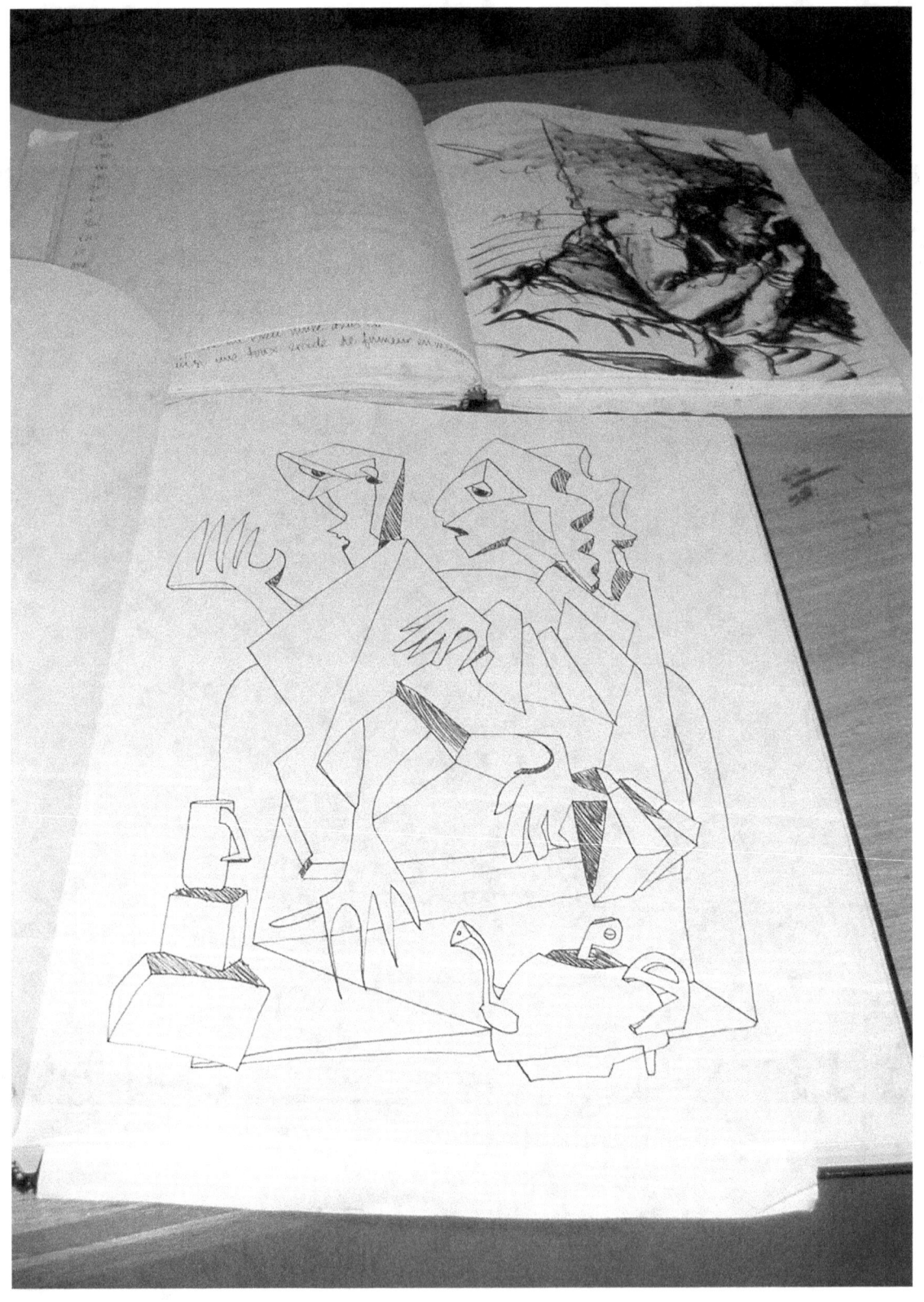

Notes and sketches

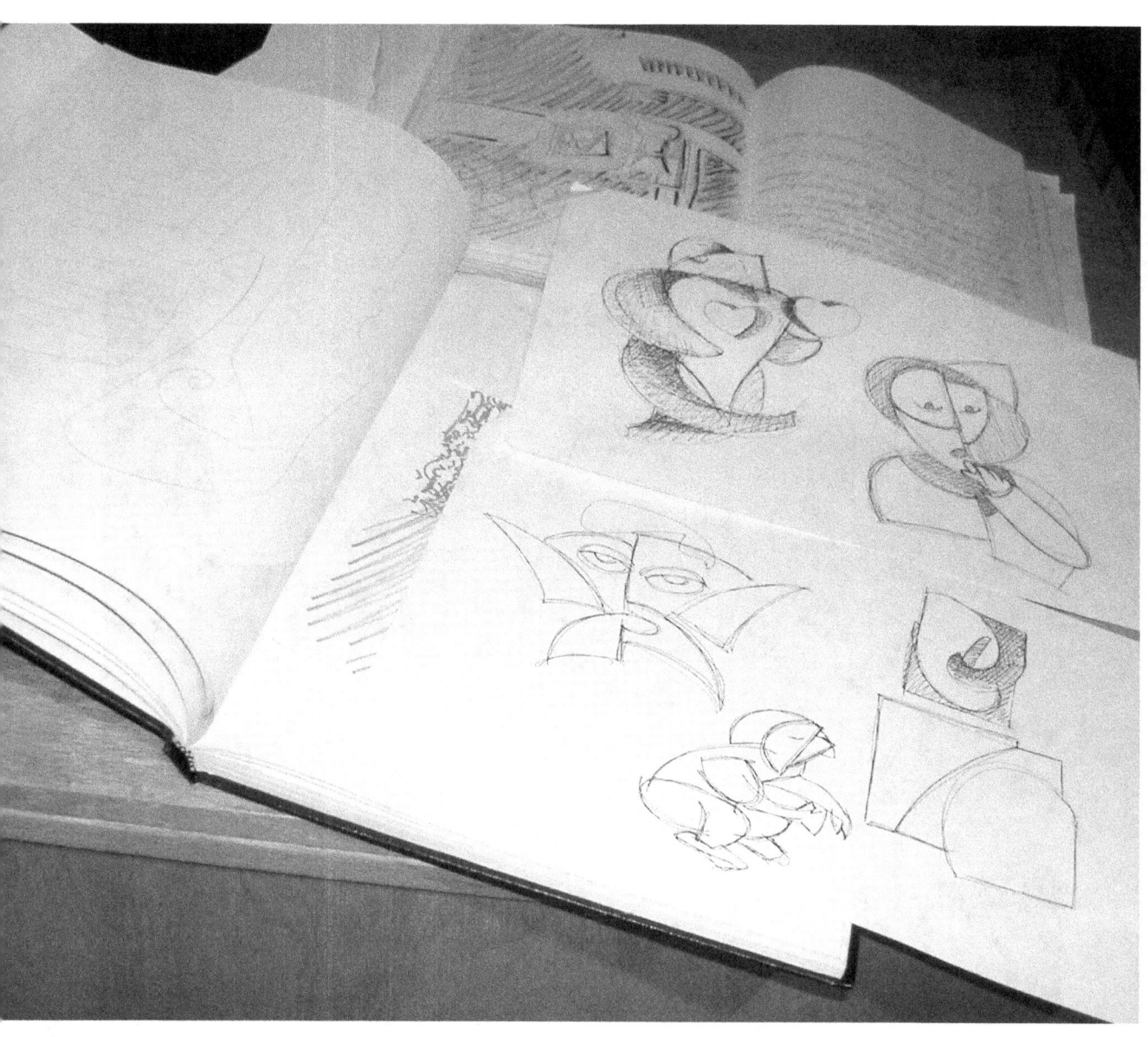

Gilles COLLETTE

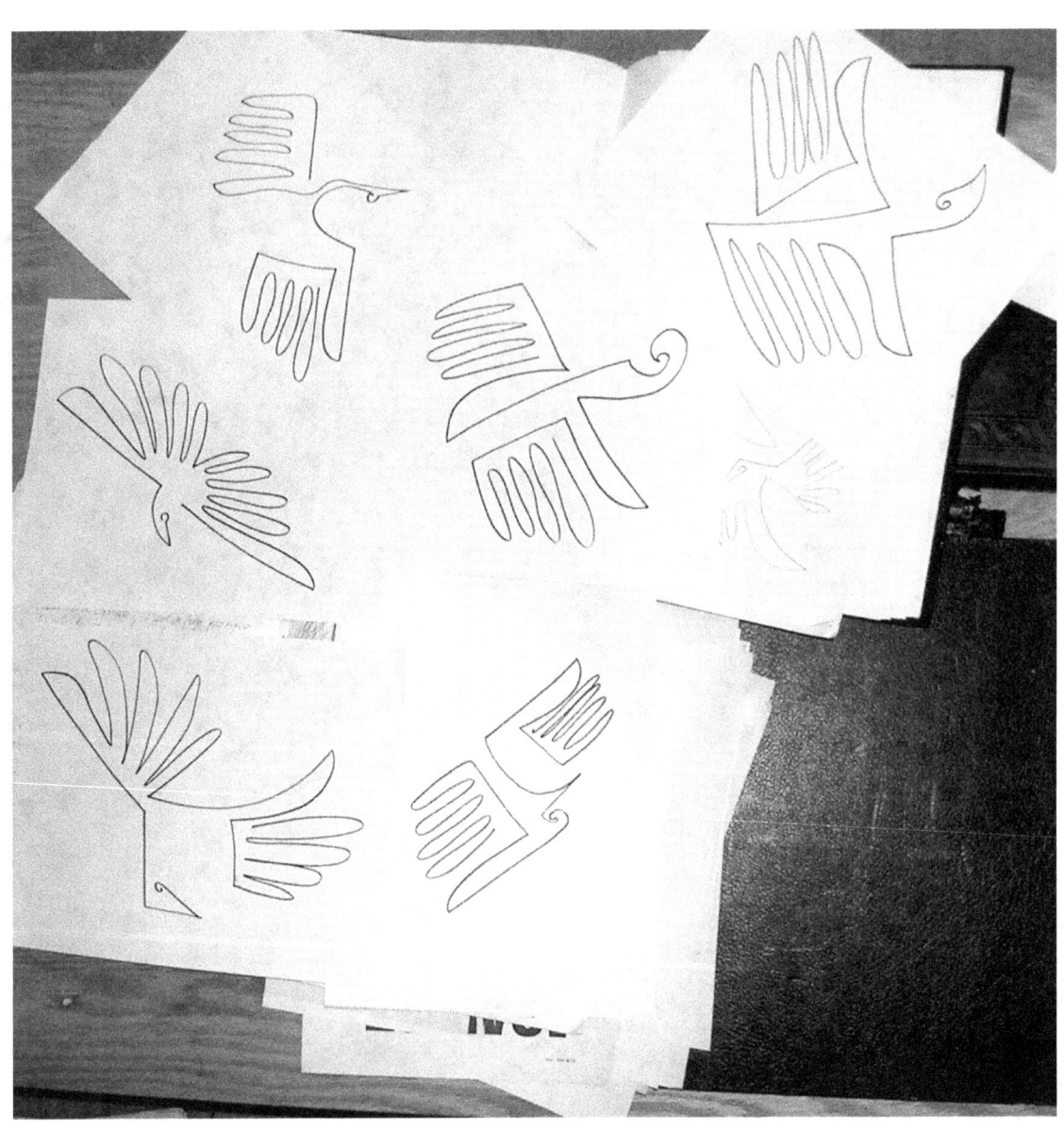

Notes and sketches

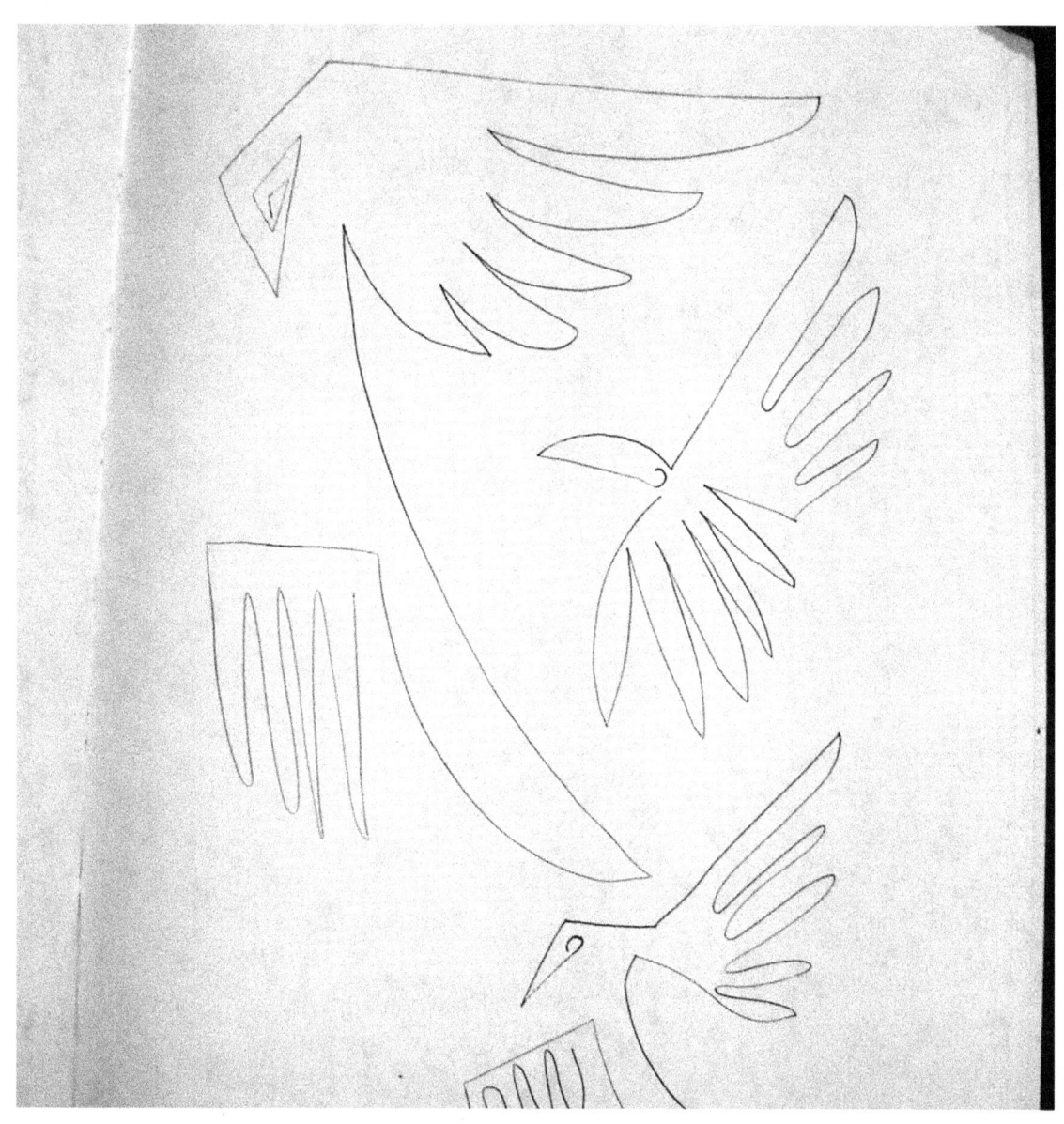

Gilles COLLETTE

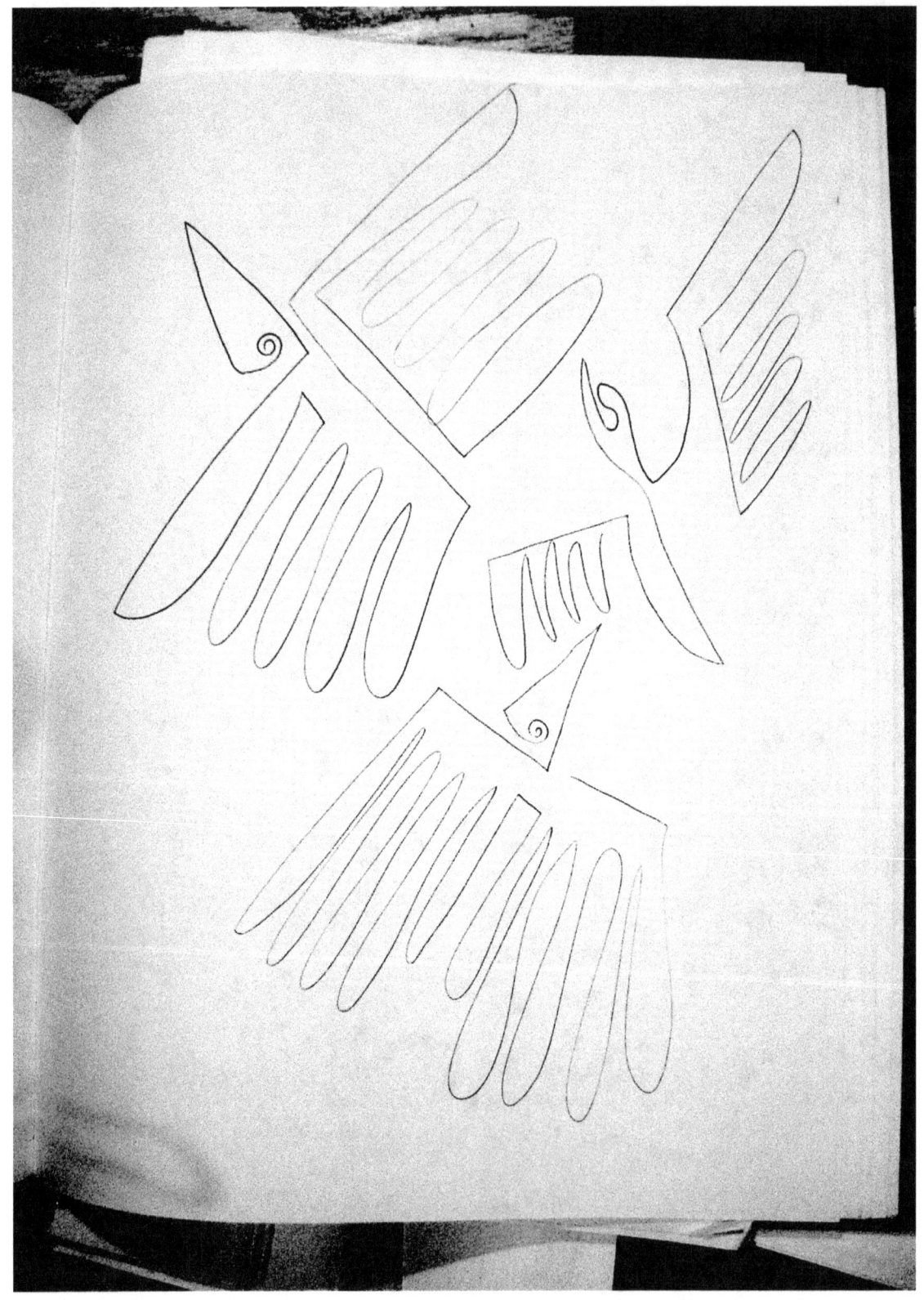

Notes and sketches

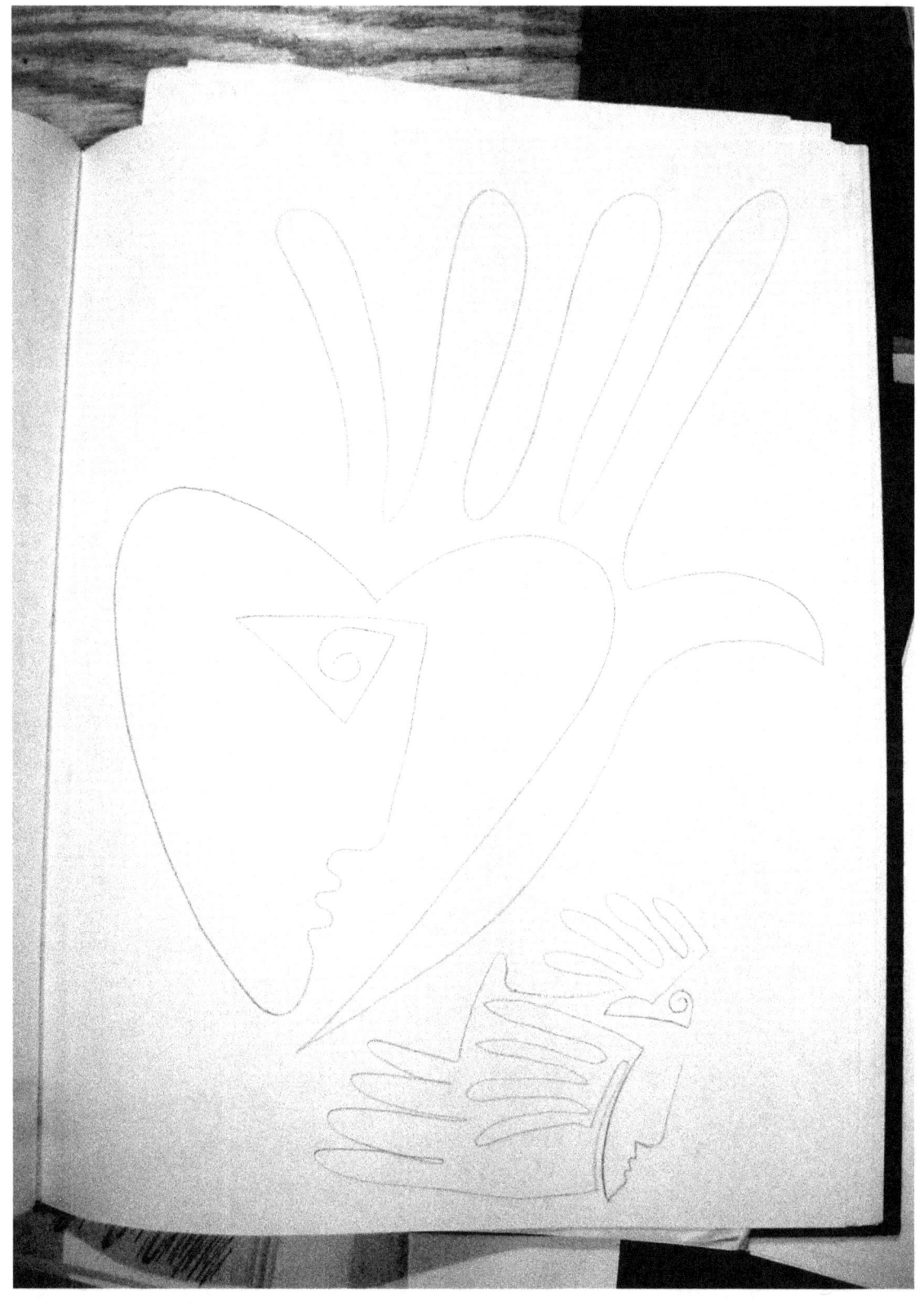

Gilles COLLETTE

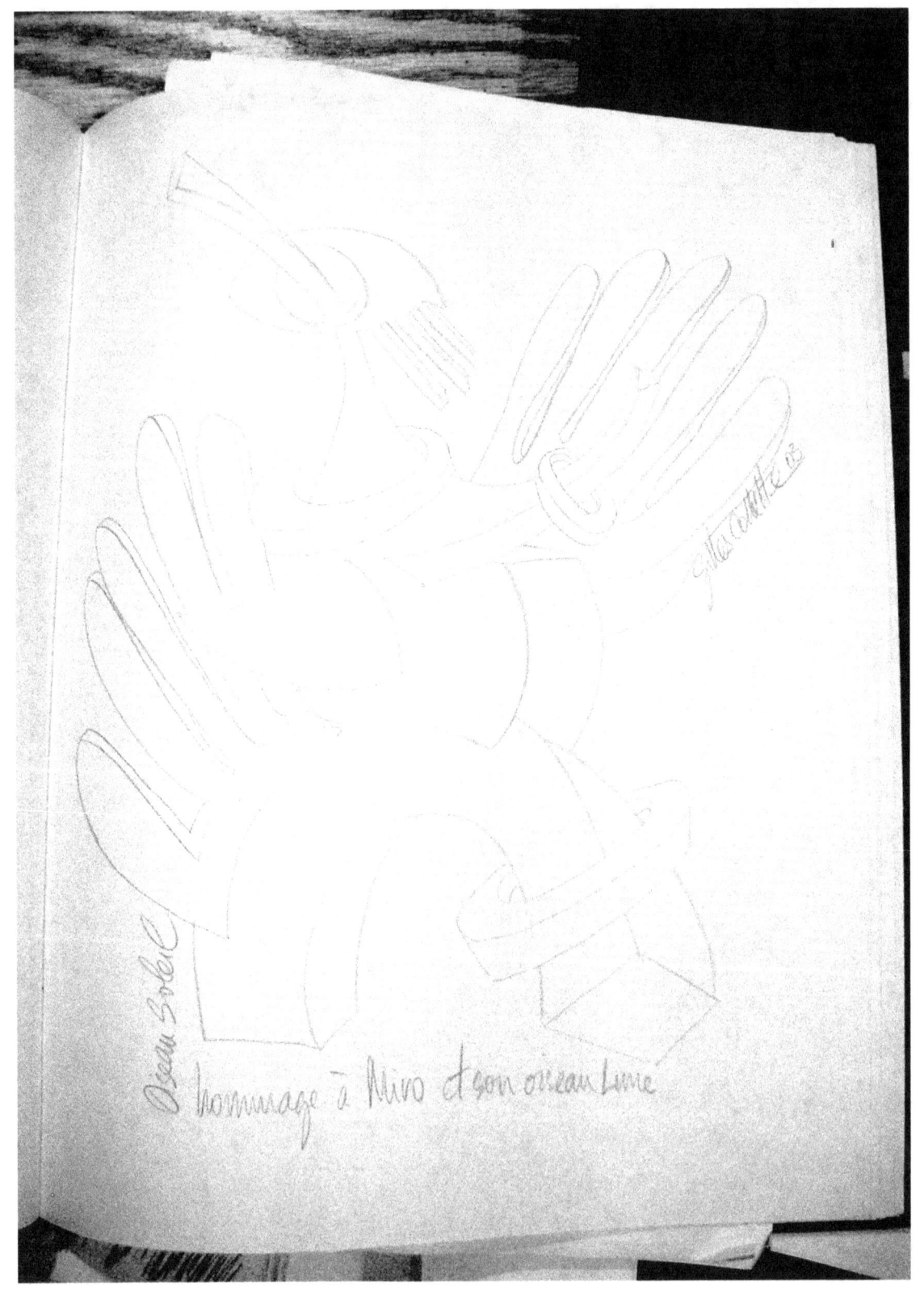

Oiseau Soleil

hommage à Miro et son oiseau lune

Notes and sketches

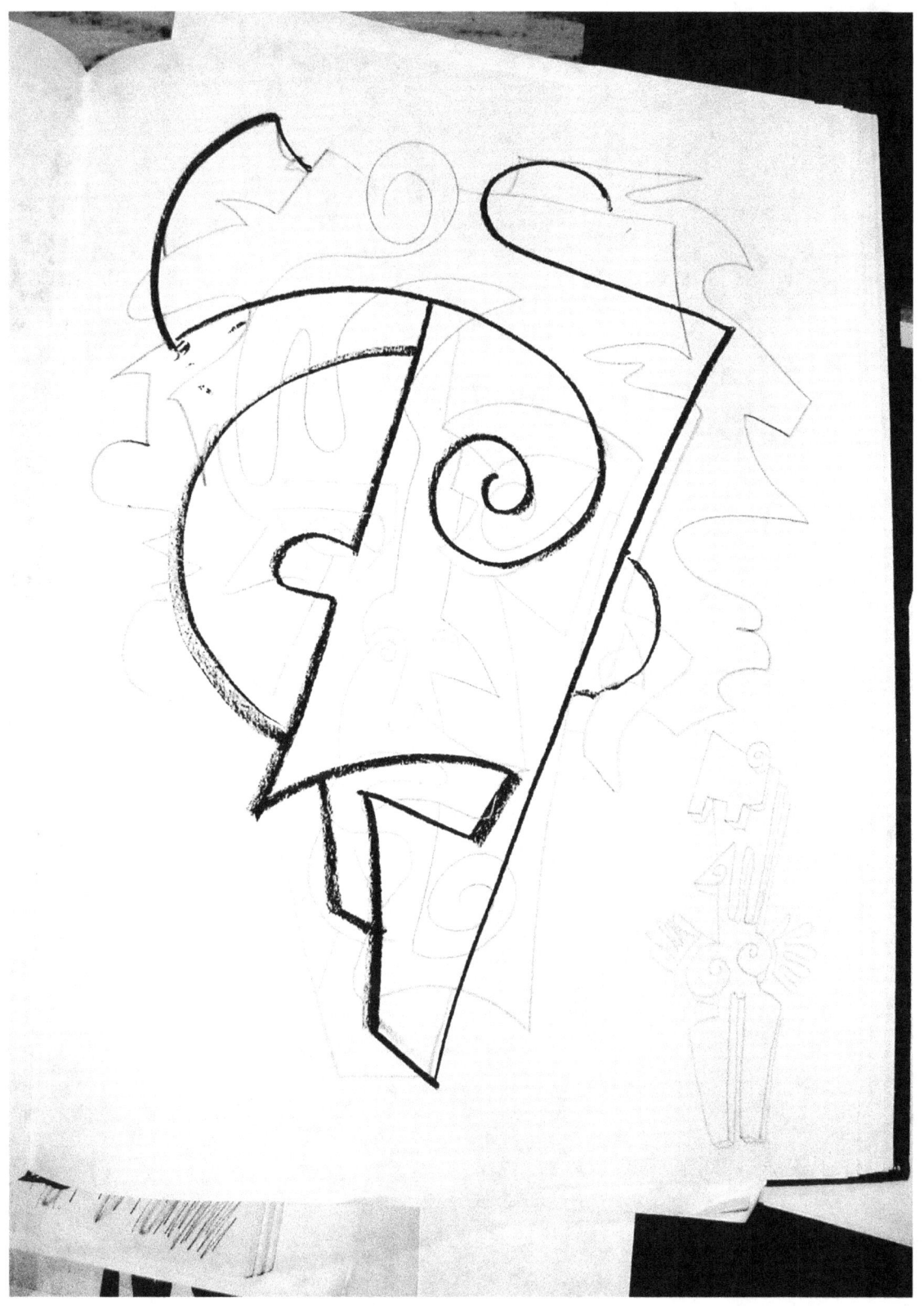

Gilles COLLETTE

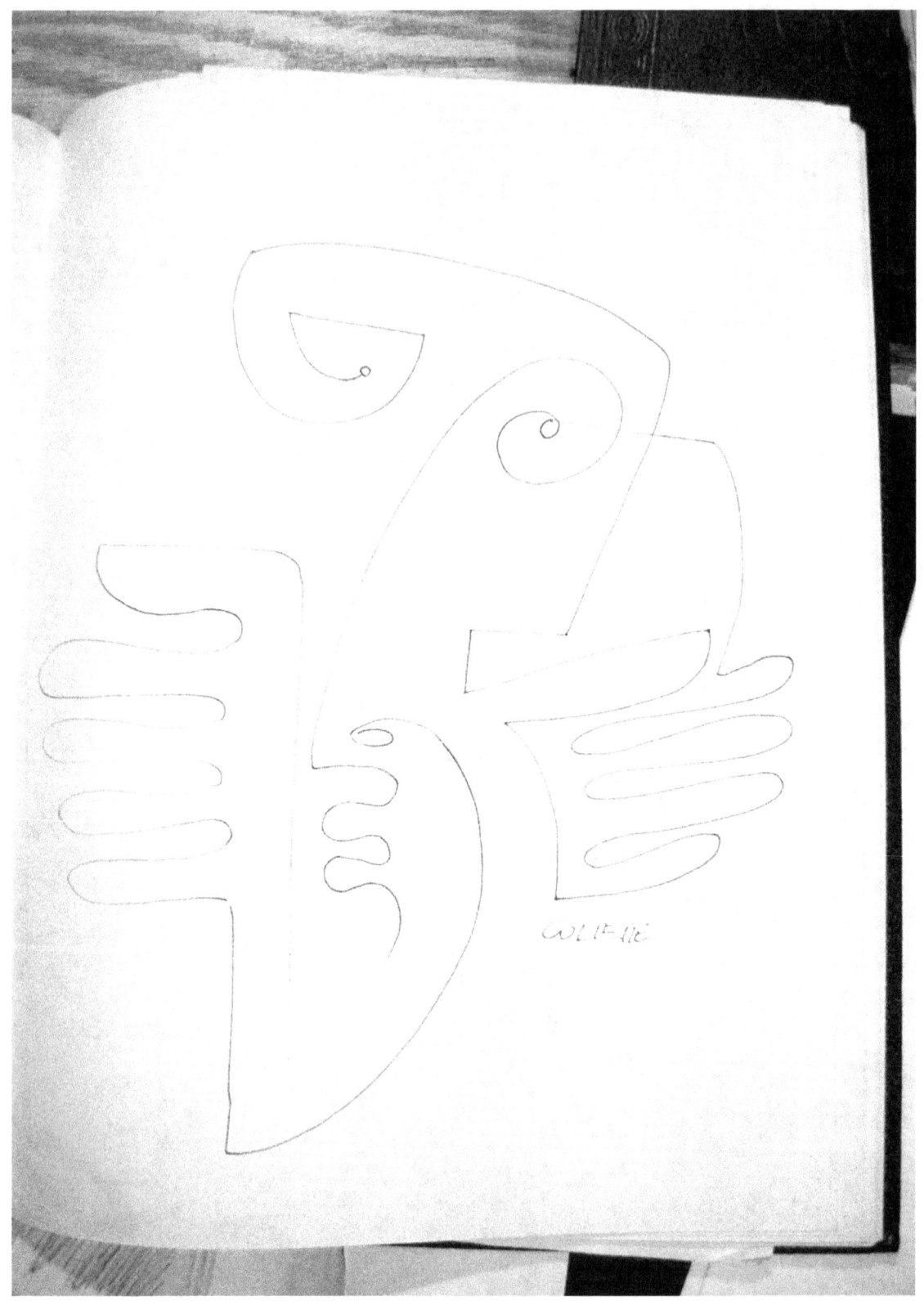

Notes and sketches

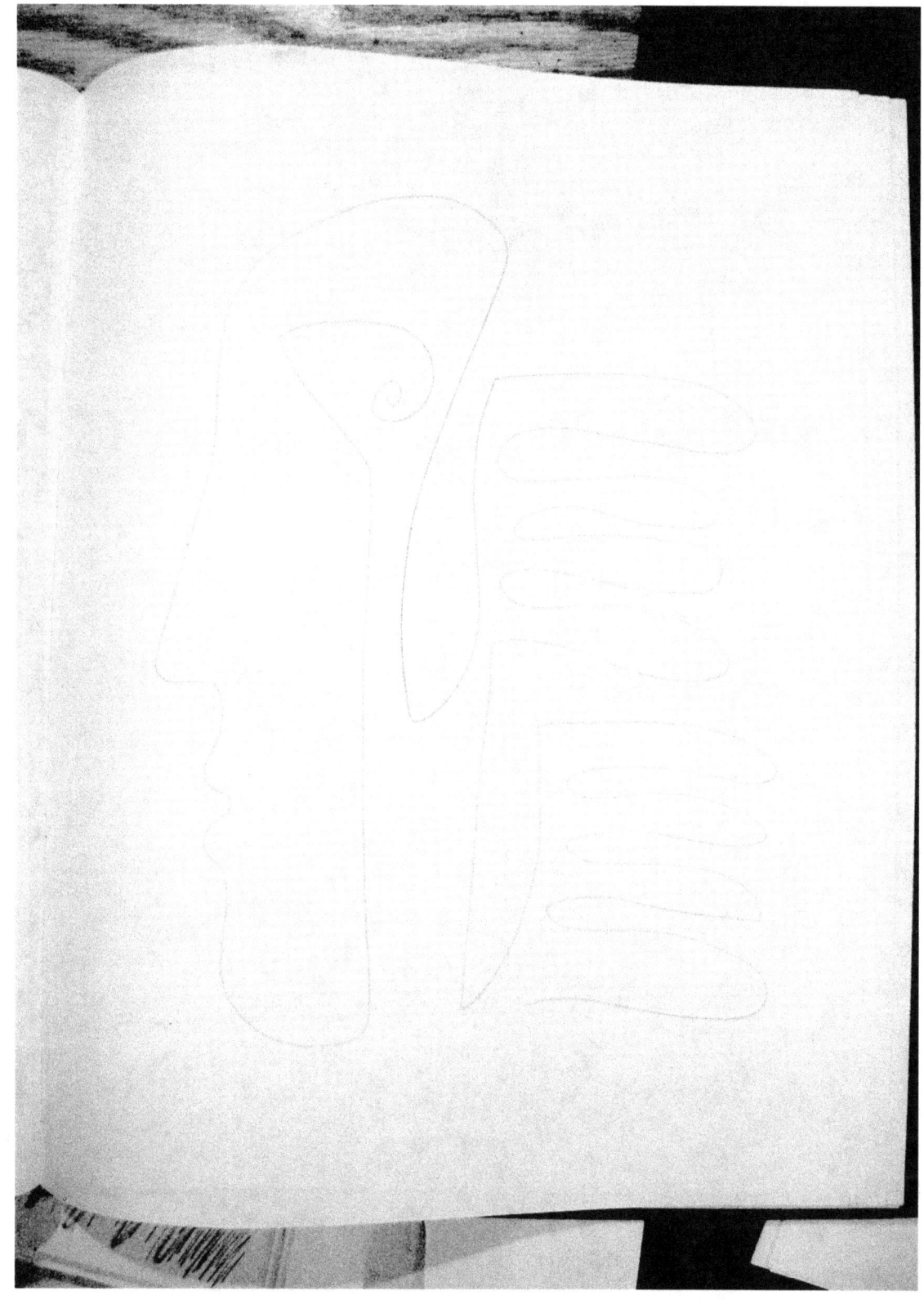

Gilles COLLETTE

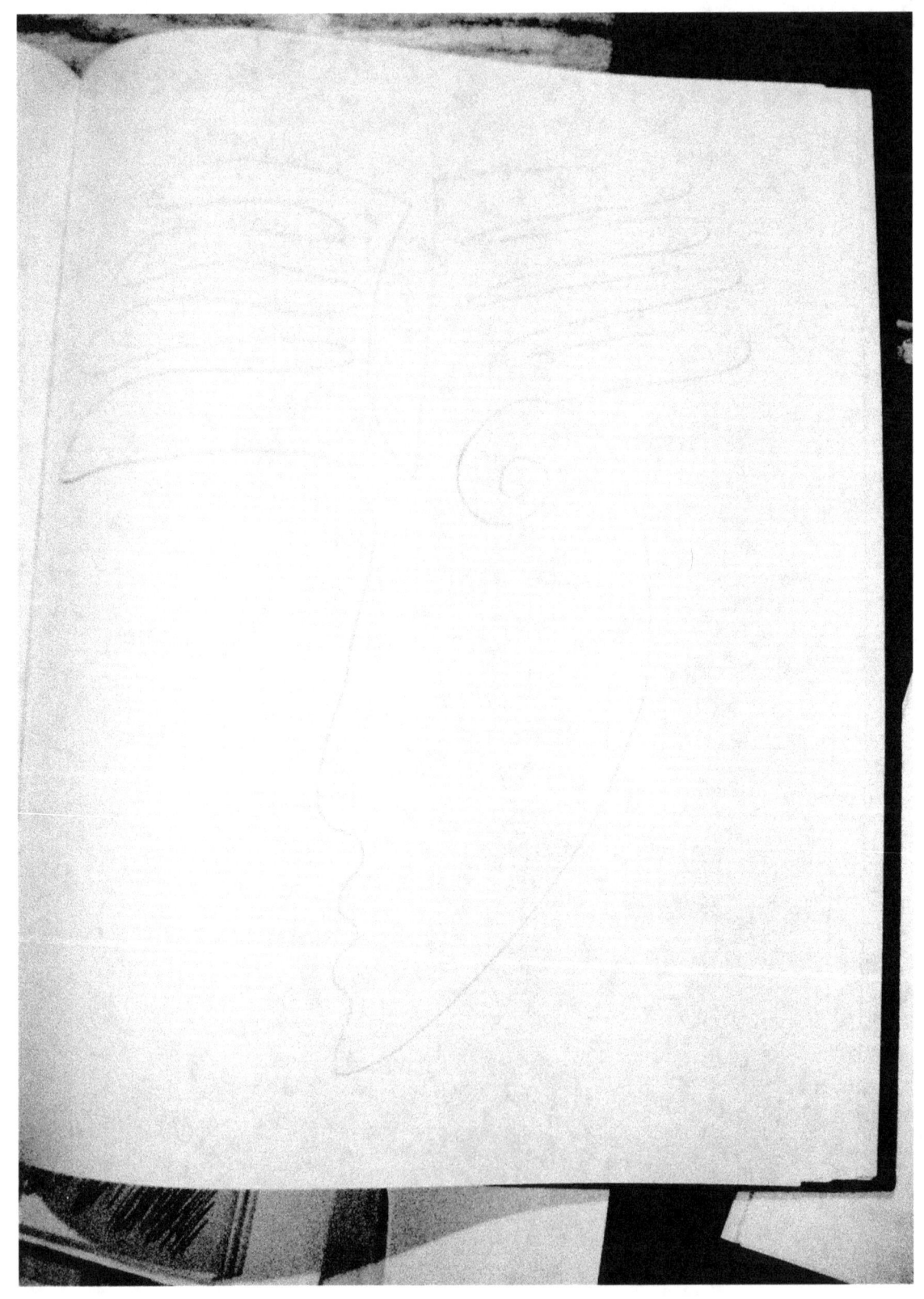

Notes and sketches

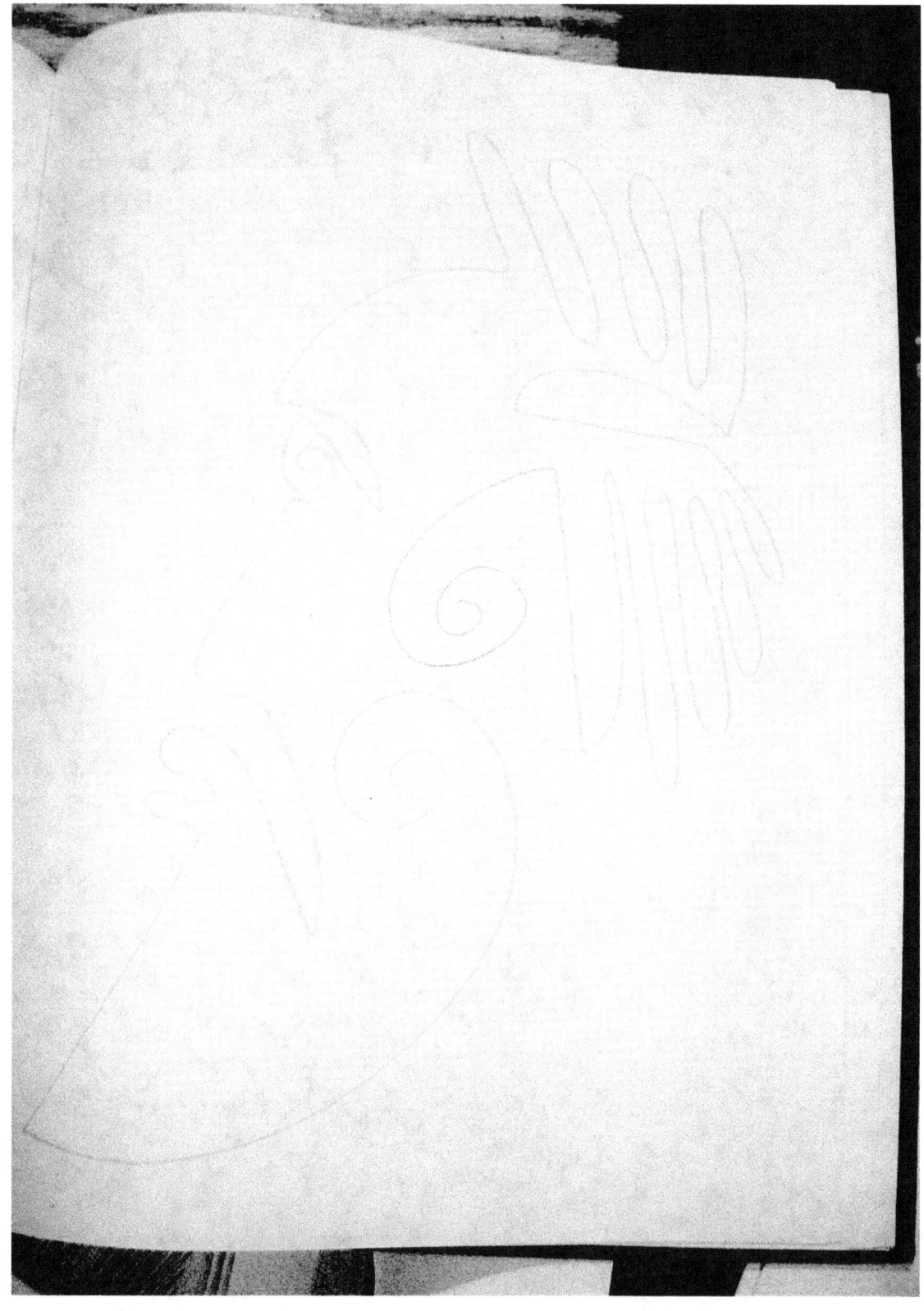

Gilles COLLETTE

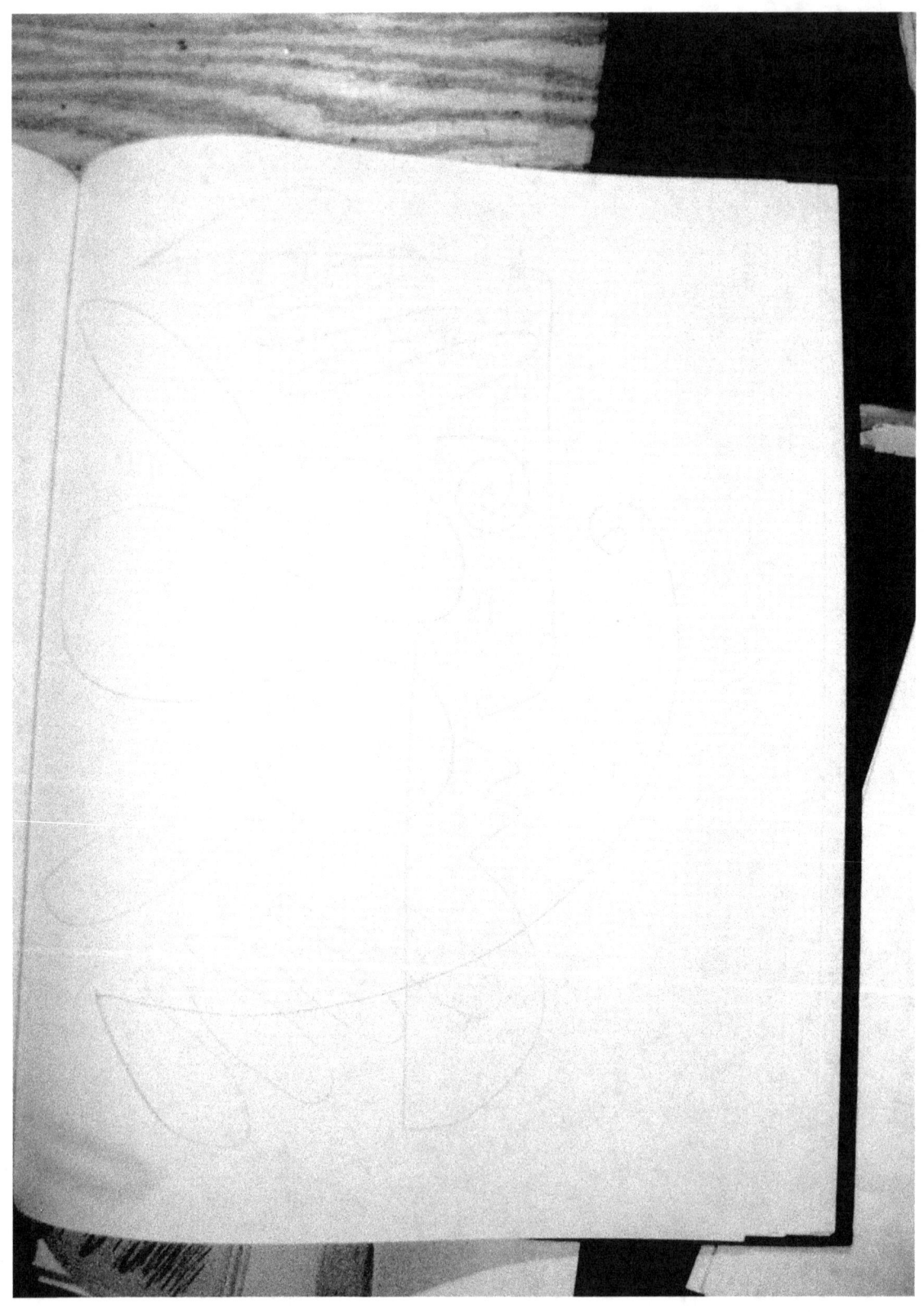

Notes and sketches

Gilles COLLETTE

Notes and sketches

Gilles COLLETTE

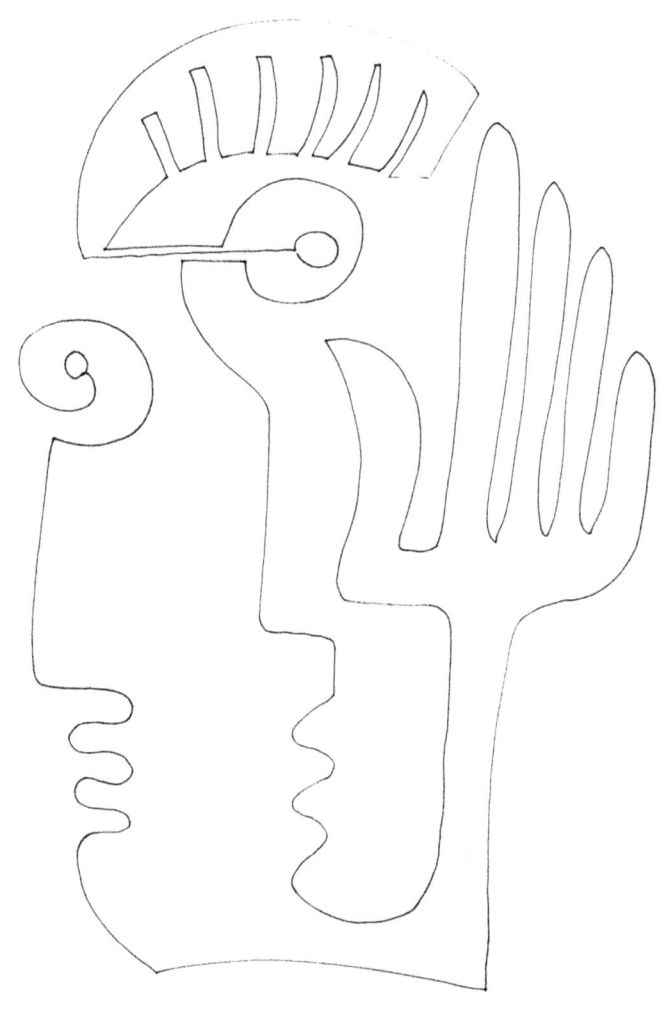

Notes and sketches

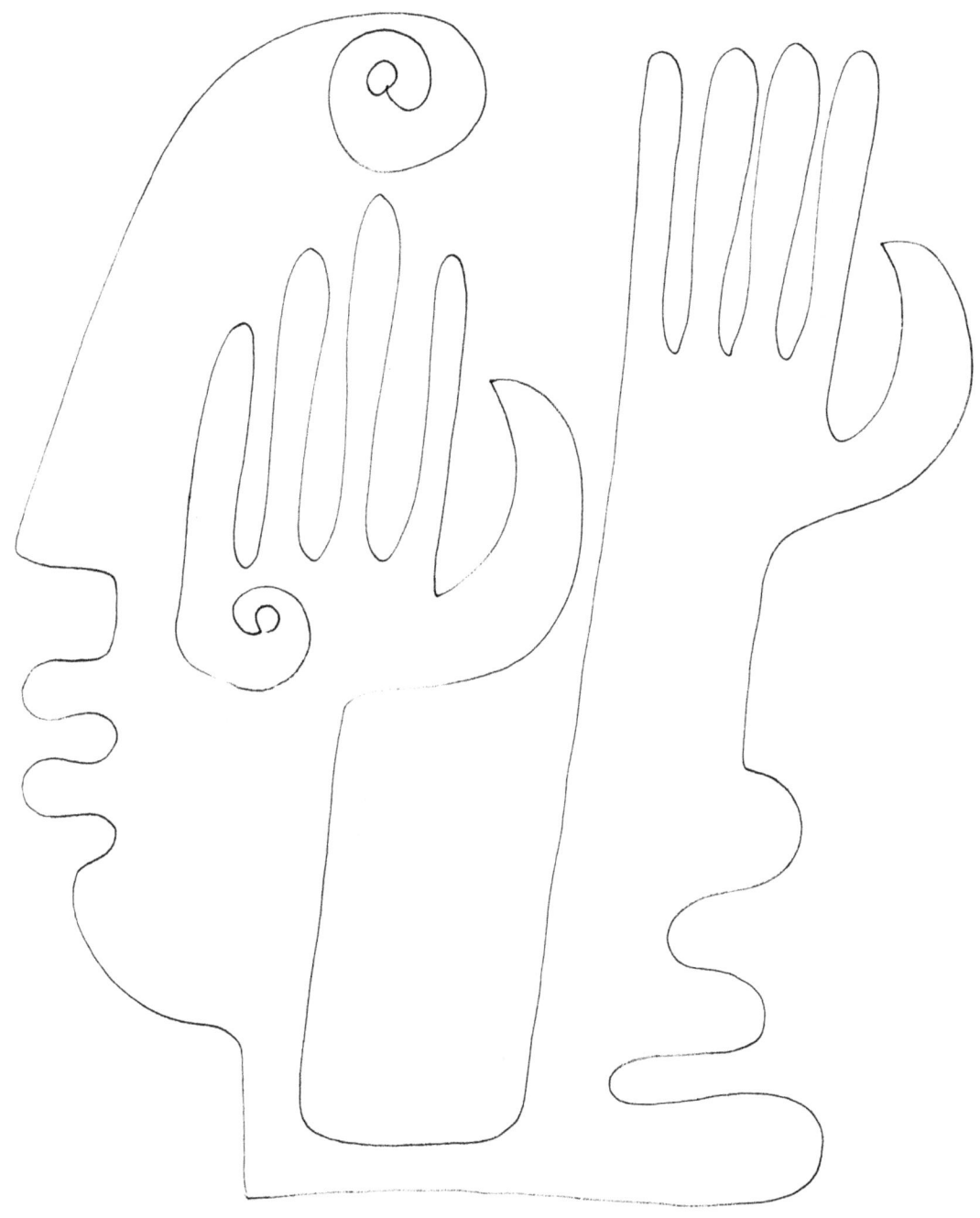

Gilles COLLETTE

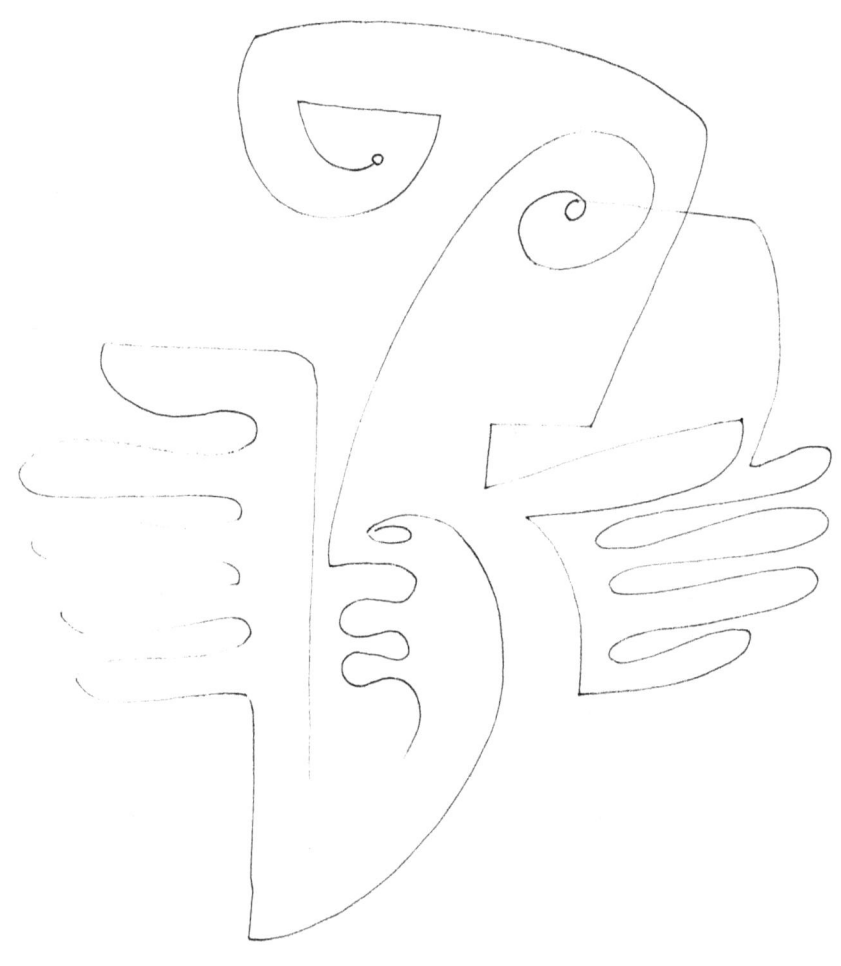

Notes and sketches

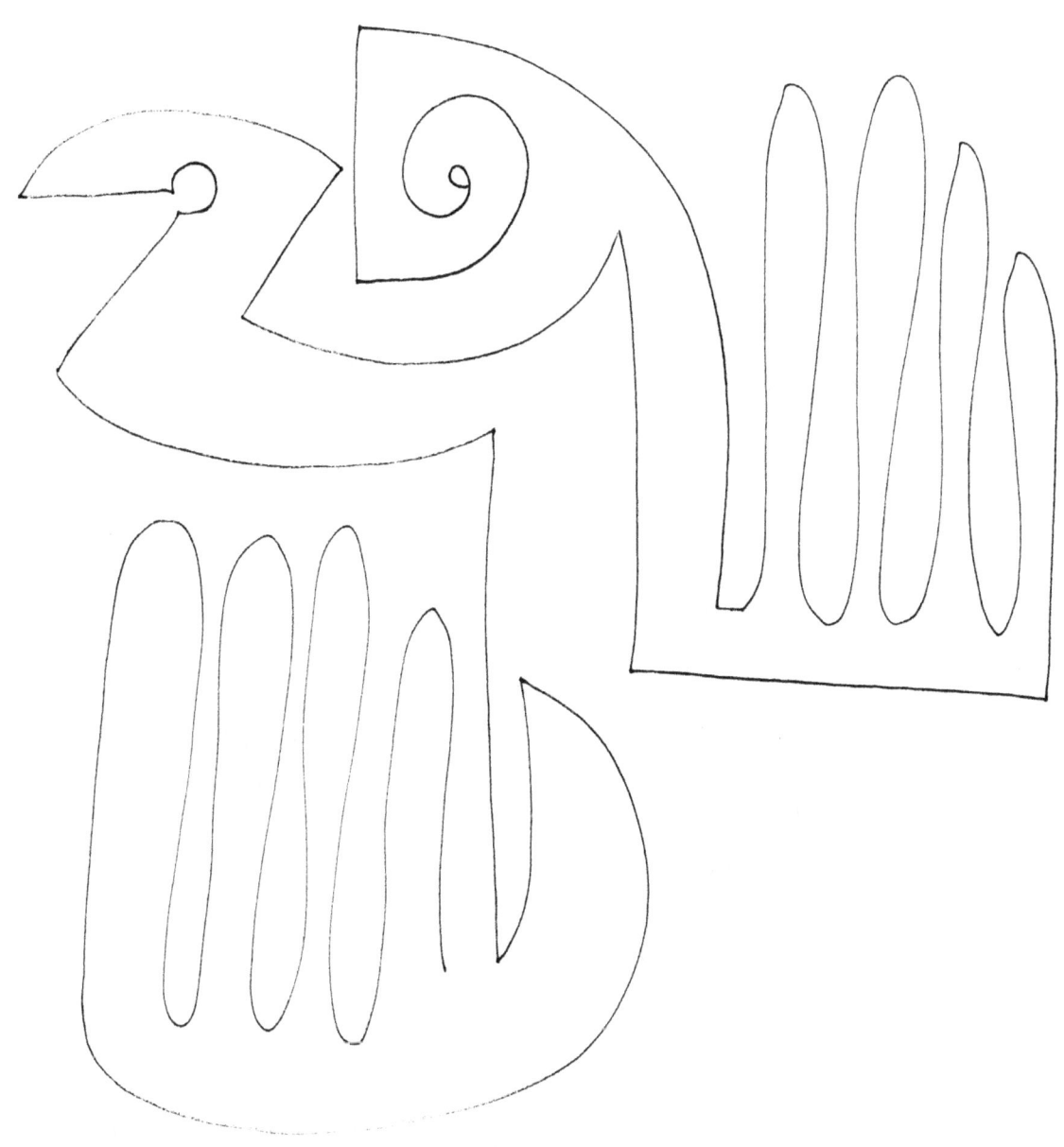

Gilles COLLETTE

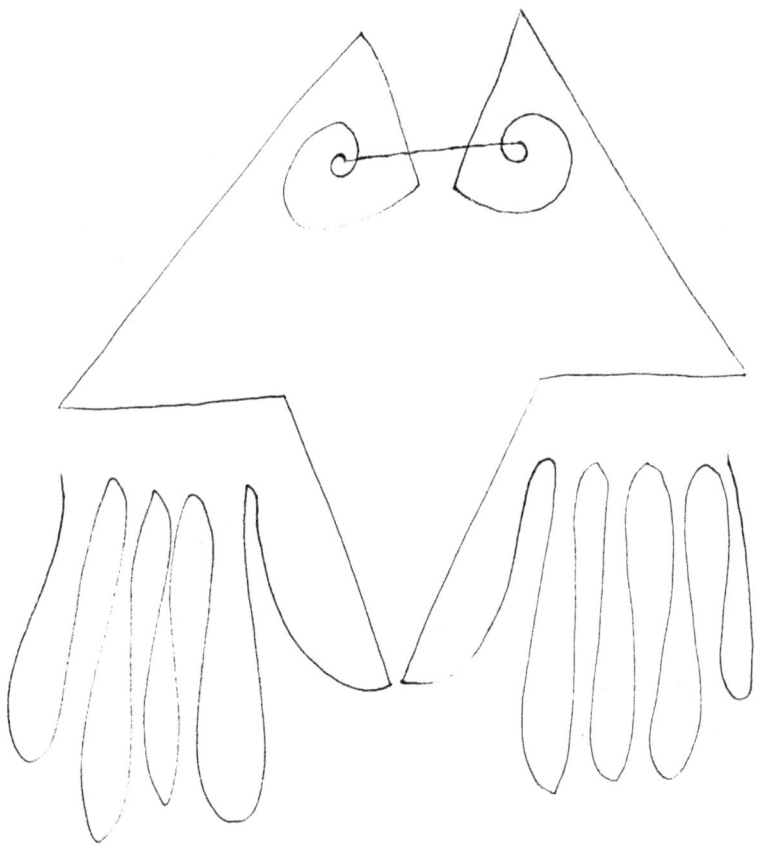

Notes and sketches

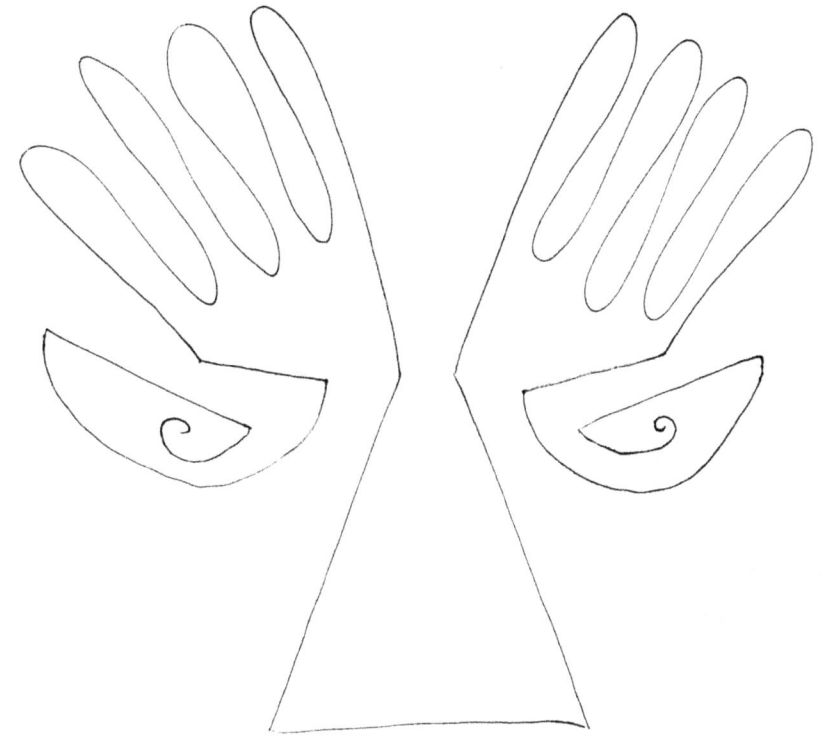

Gilles COLLETTE

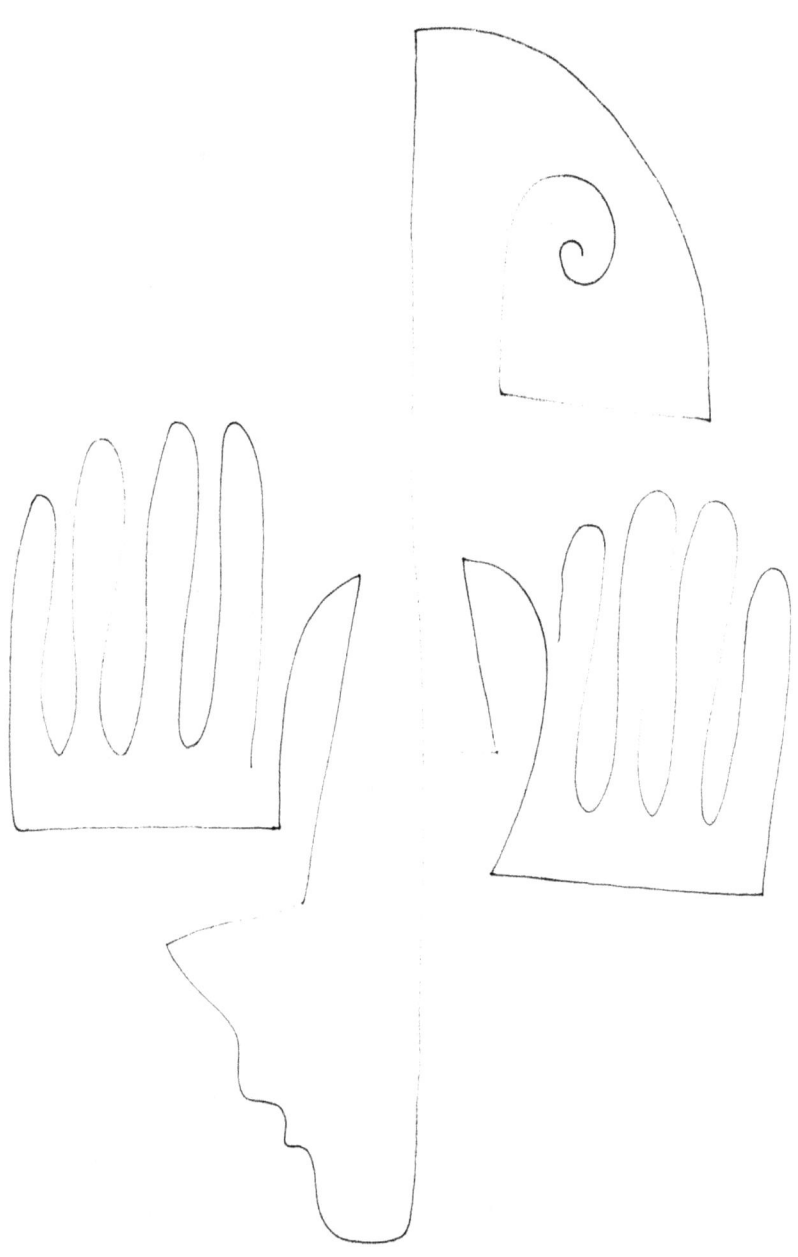

Notes and sketches

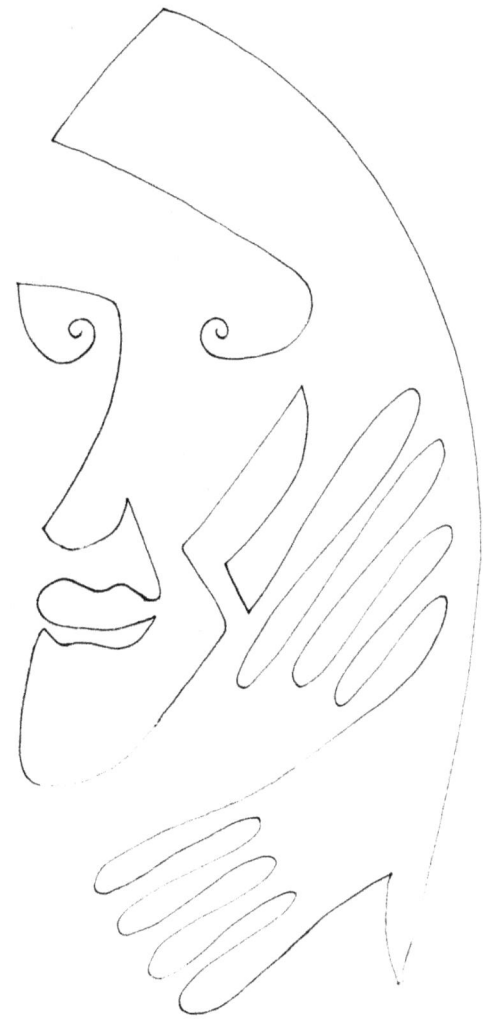

Gilles COLLETTE

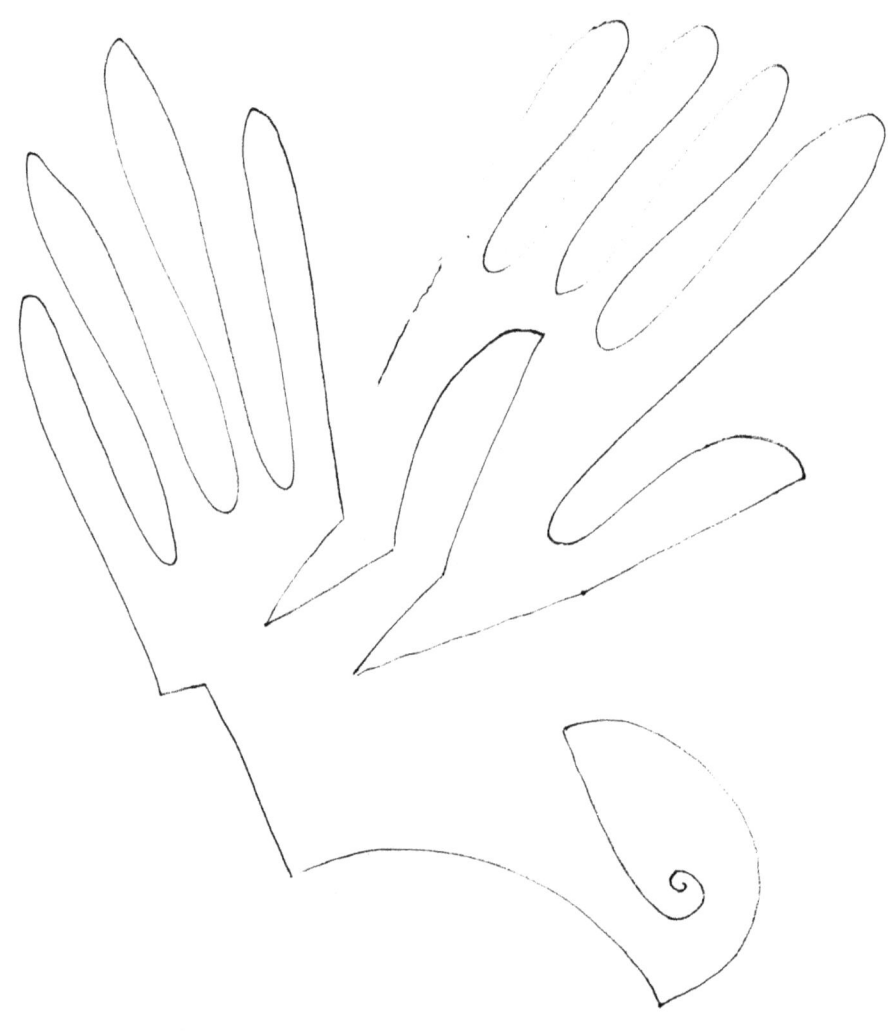

Notes and sketches

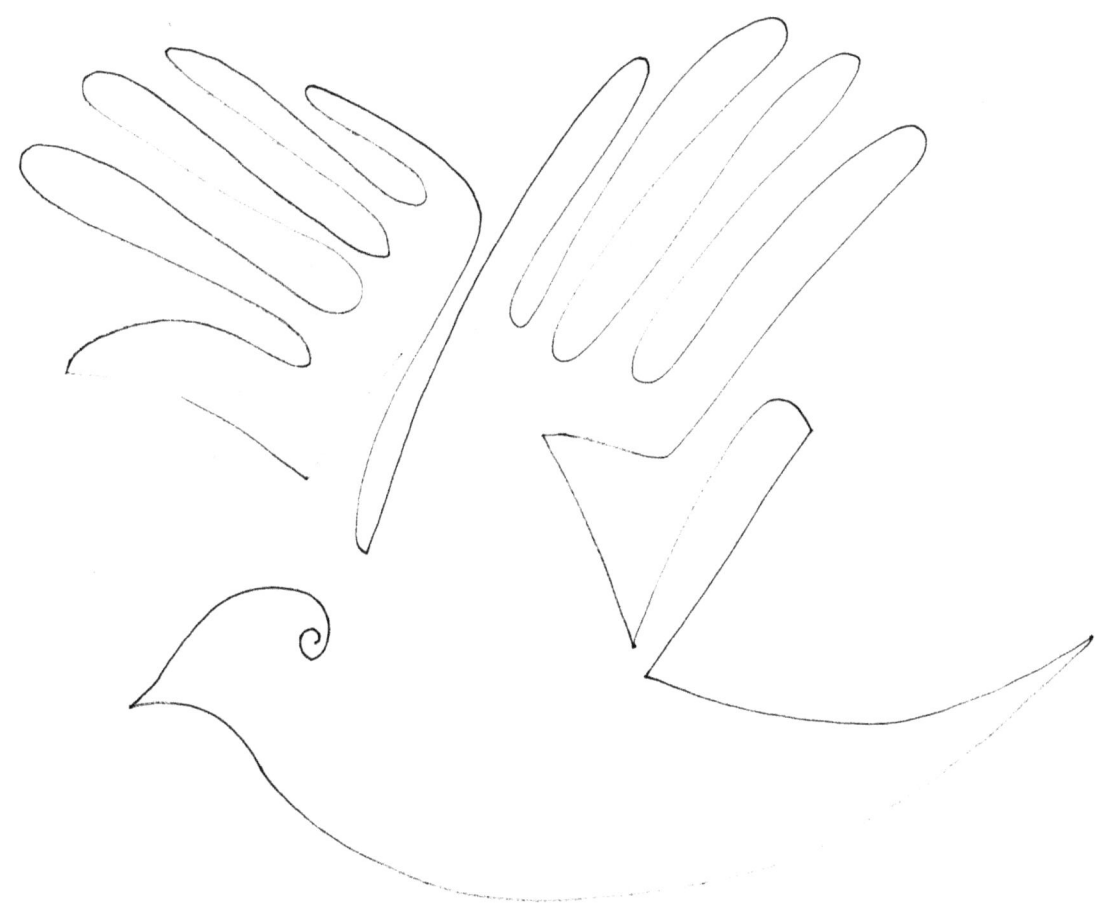

Gilles COLLETTE

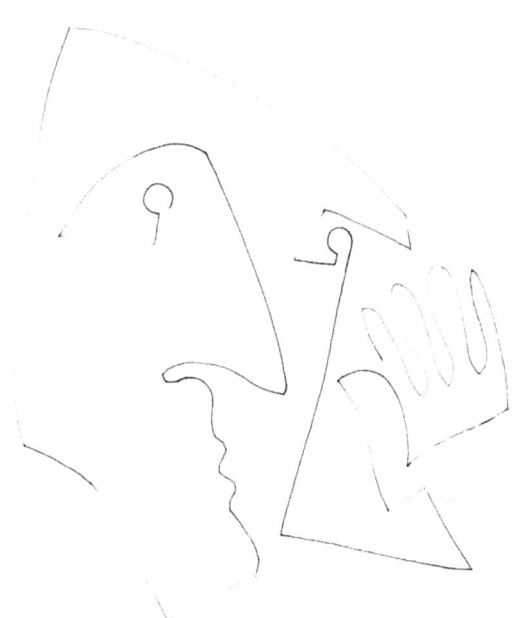

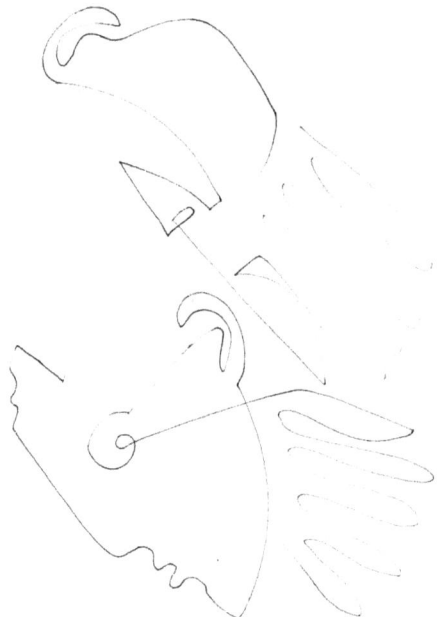

Notes and sketches

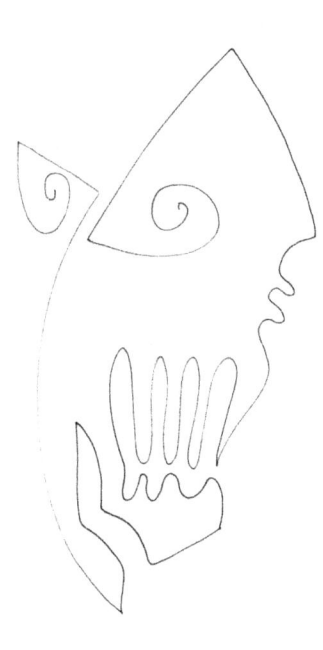
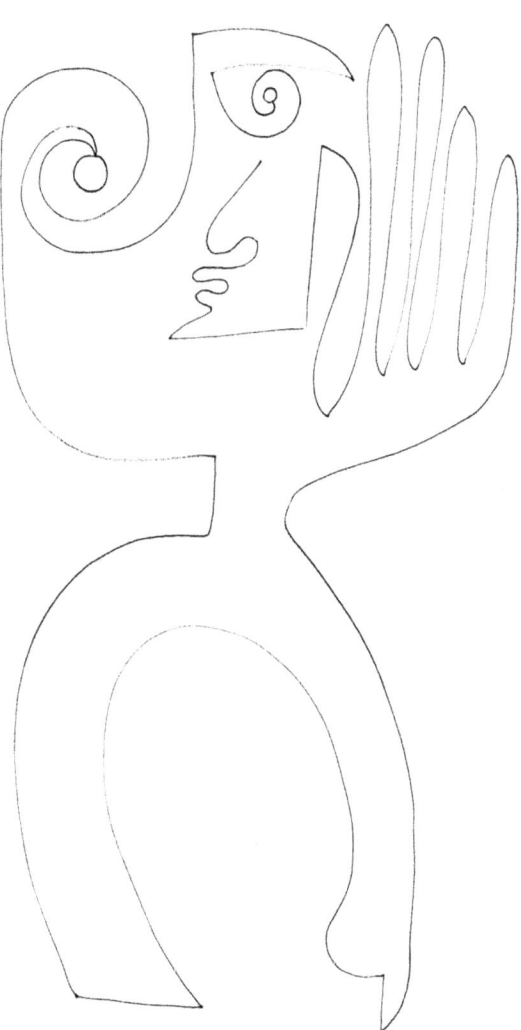

Gilles COLLETTE

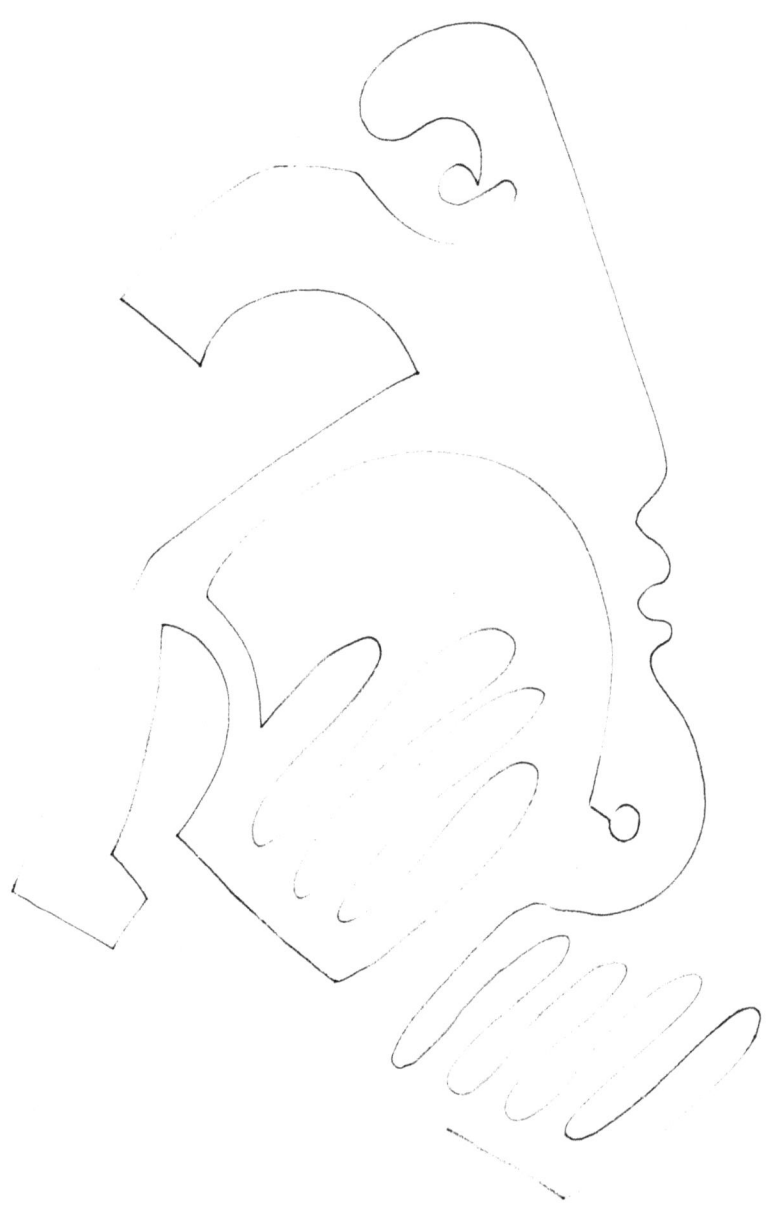

Notes and sketches

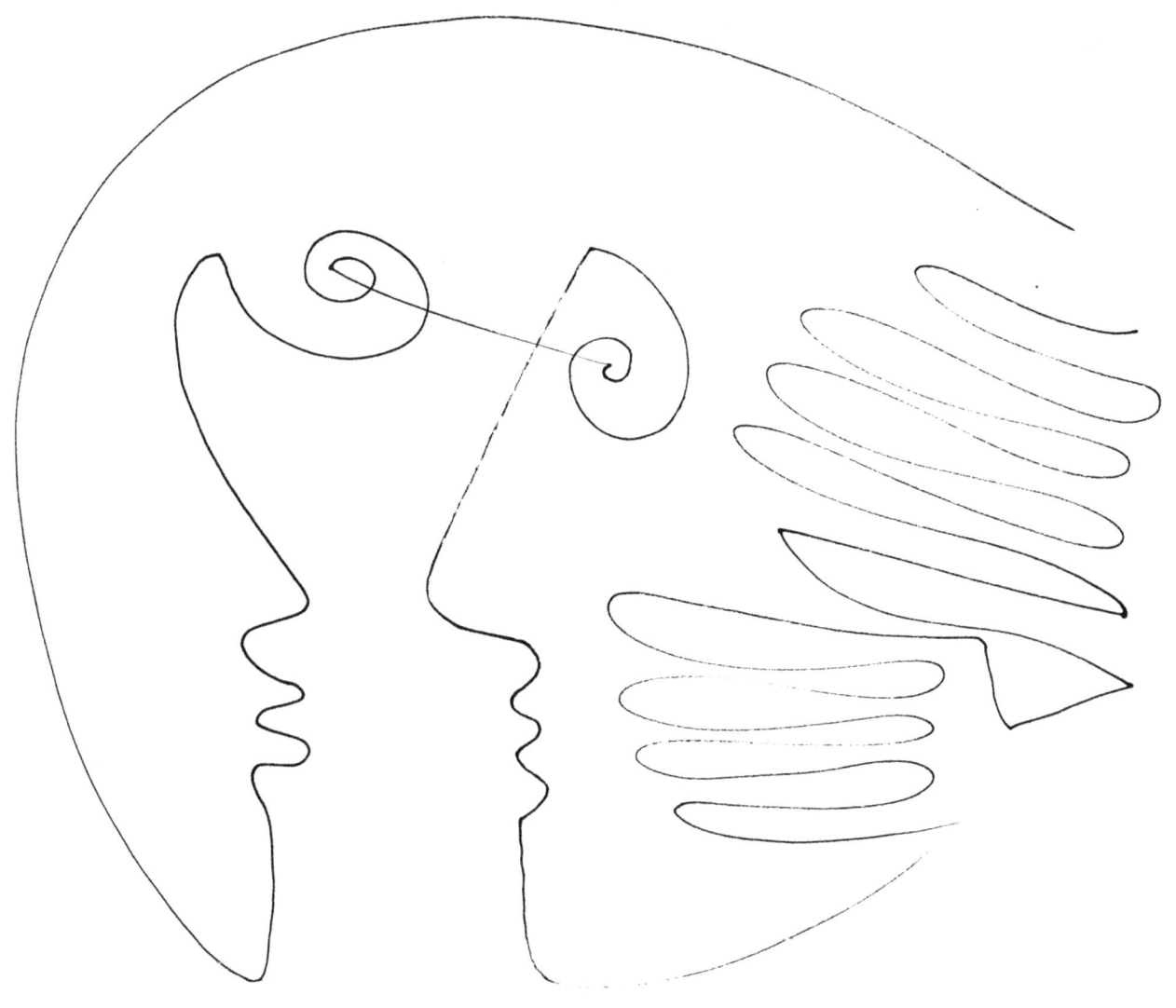

Gilles COLLETTE

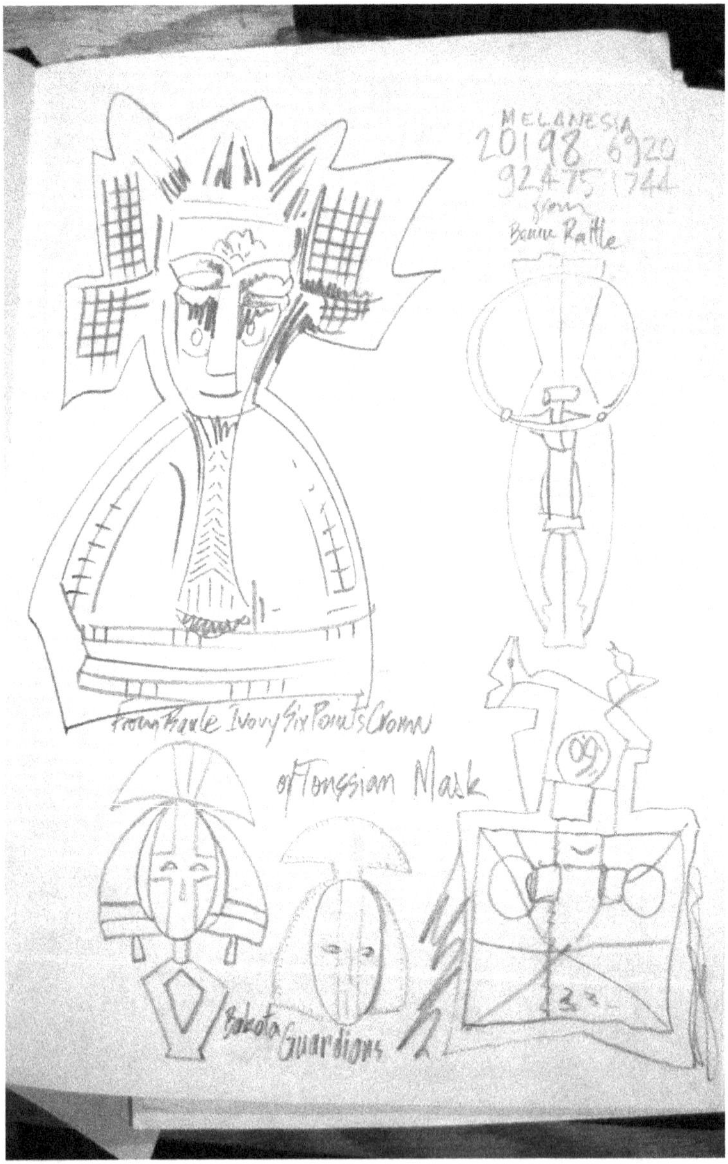

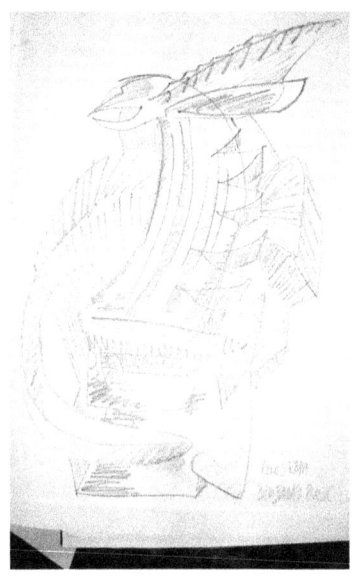

MELANESIA
20198 6920
92475 1744
from
Benin Rattle

From Baule Ivory Six Point's Crown

of Tongsian Mask

Bakota Guardians

Notes and sketches

Gilles COLLETTE

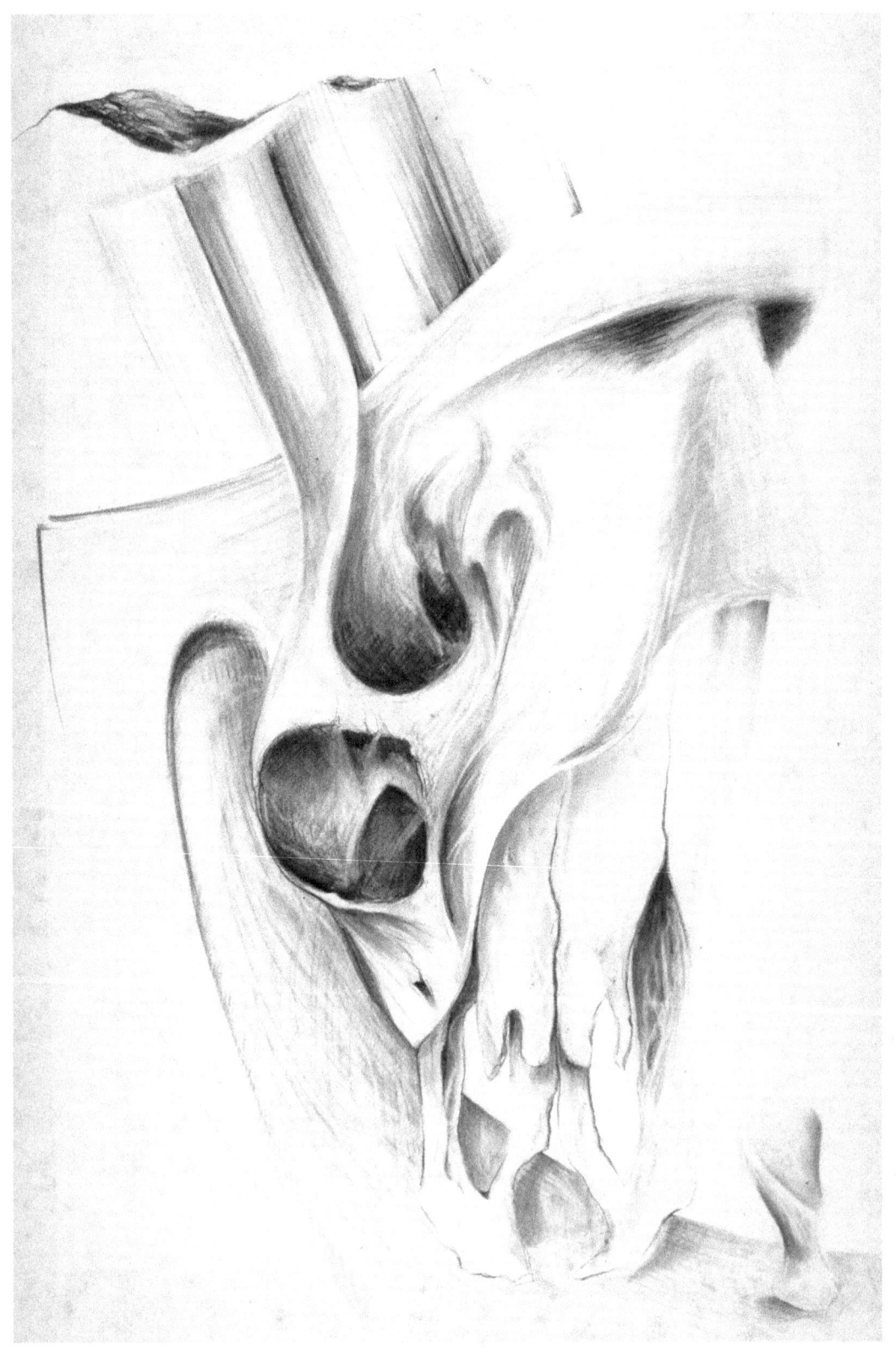

Notes and sketches

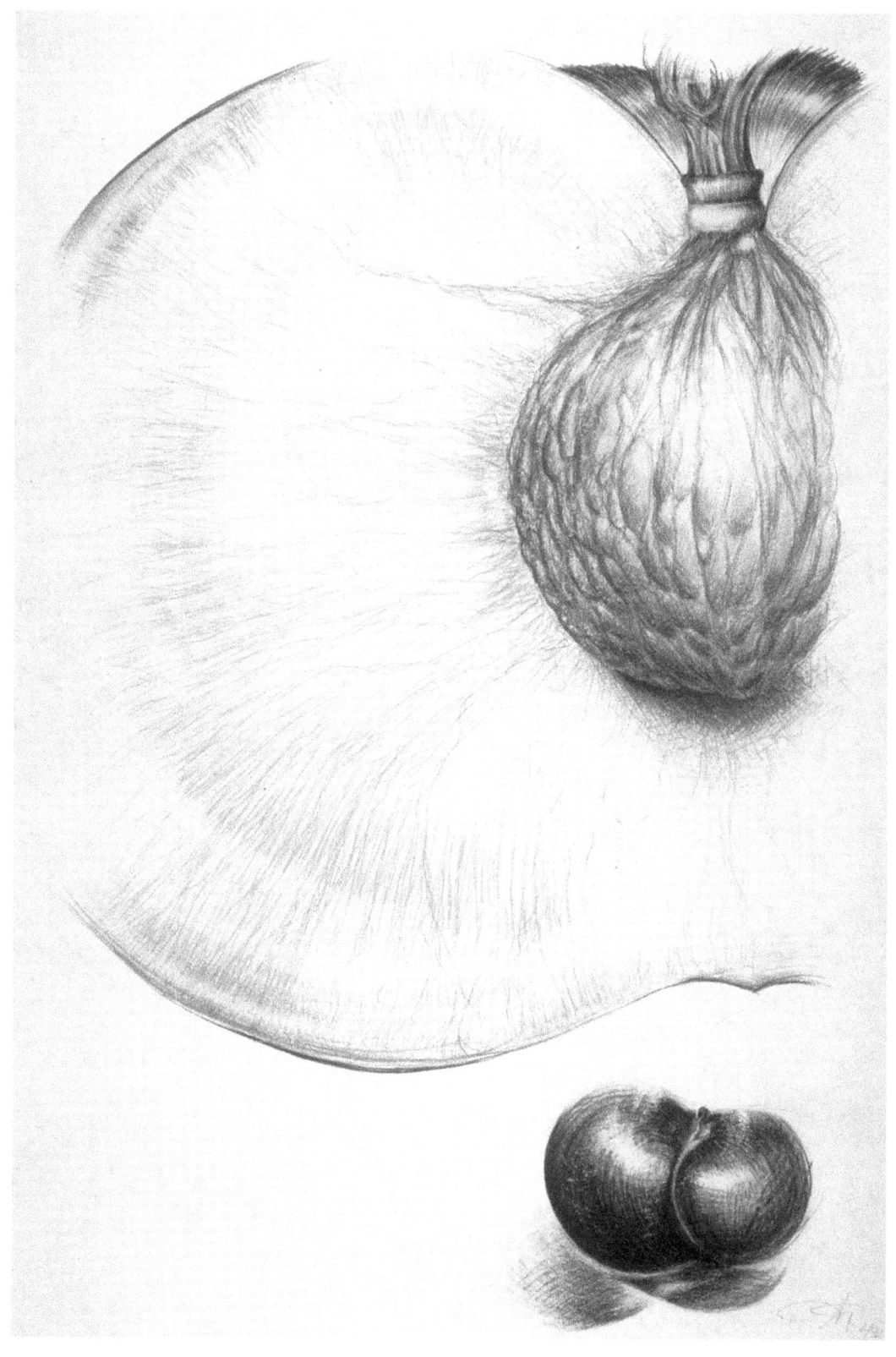

Gilles COLLETTE

104

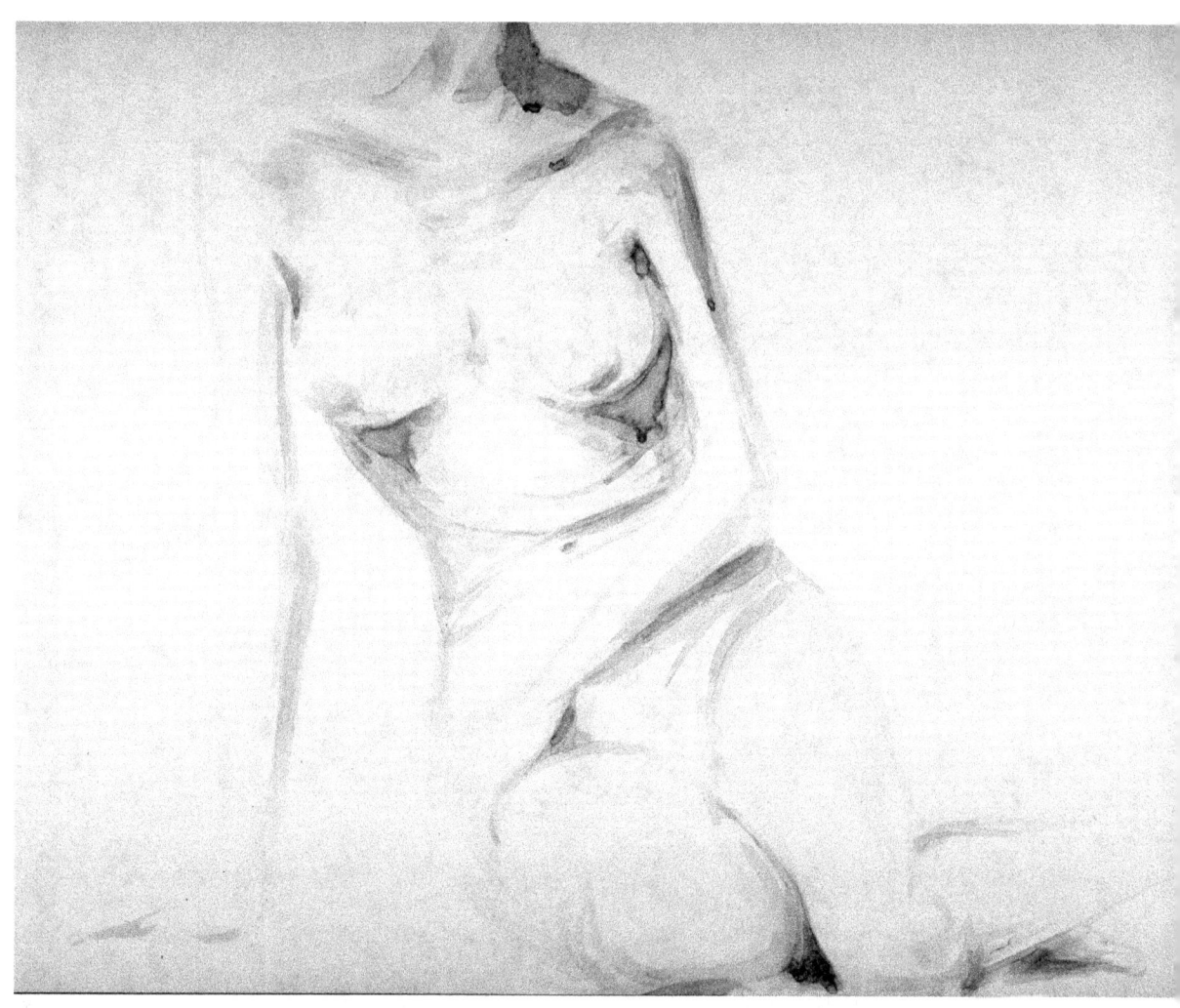

Gilles COLLETTE

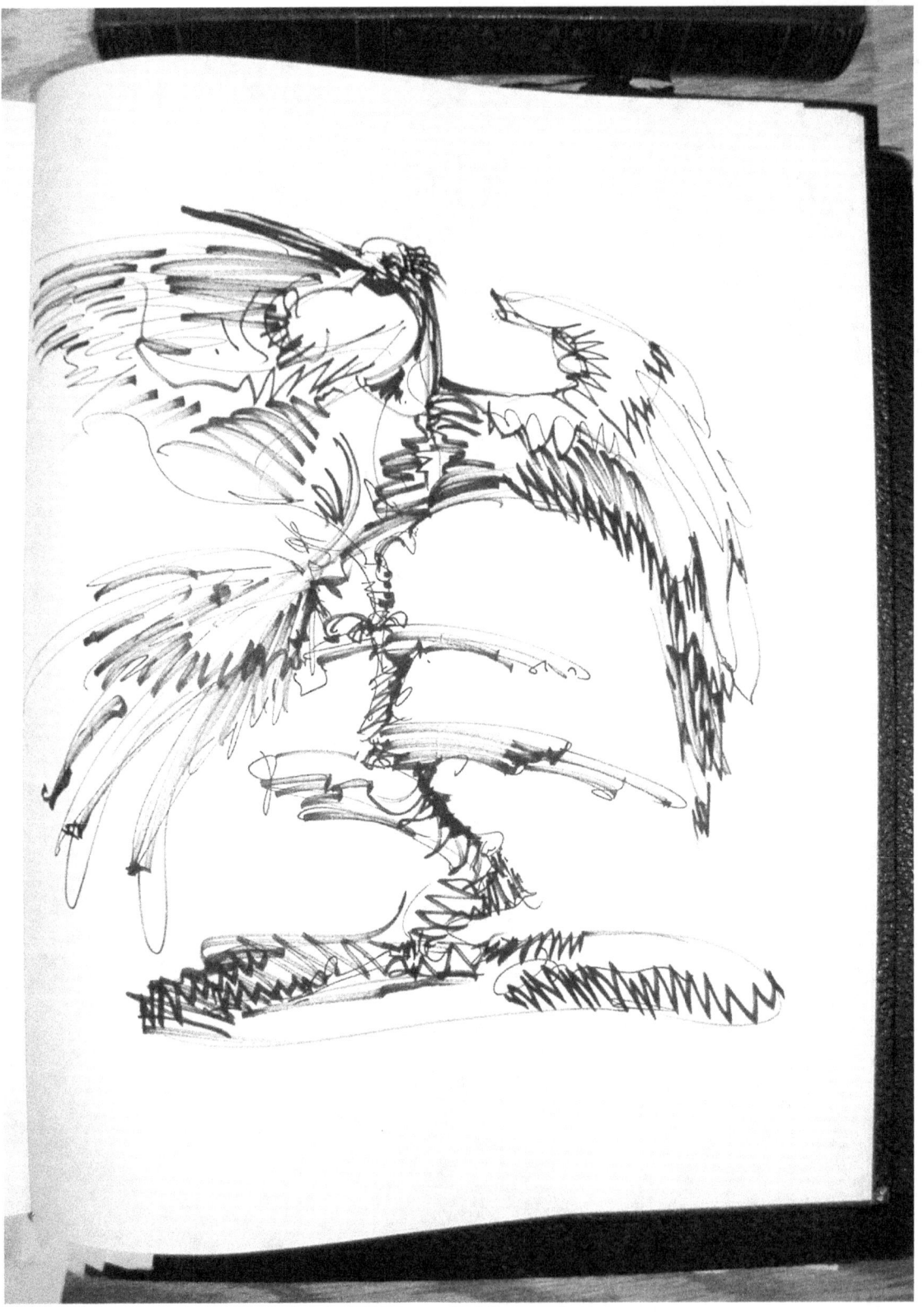

Notes and sketches

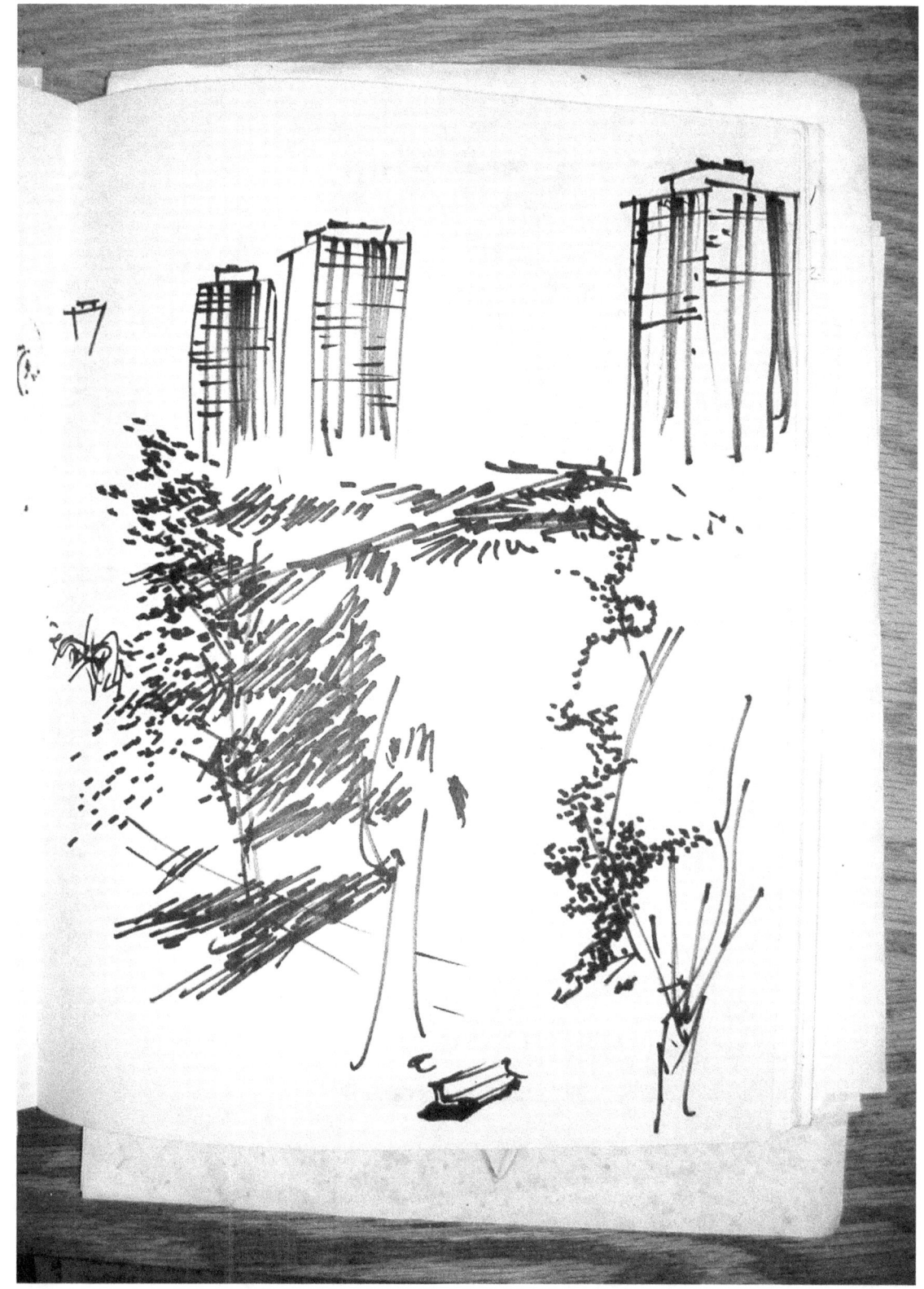

Gilles COLLETTE

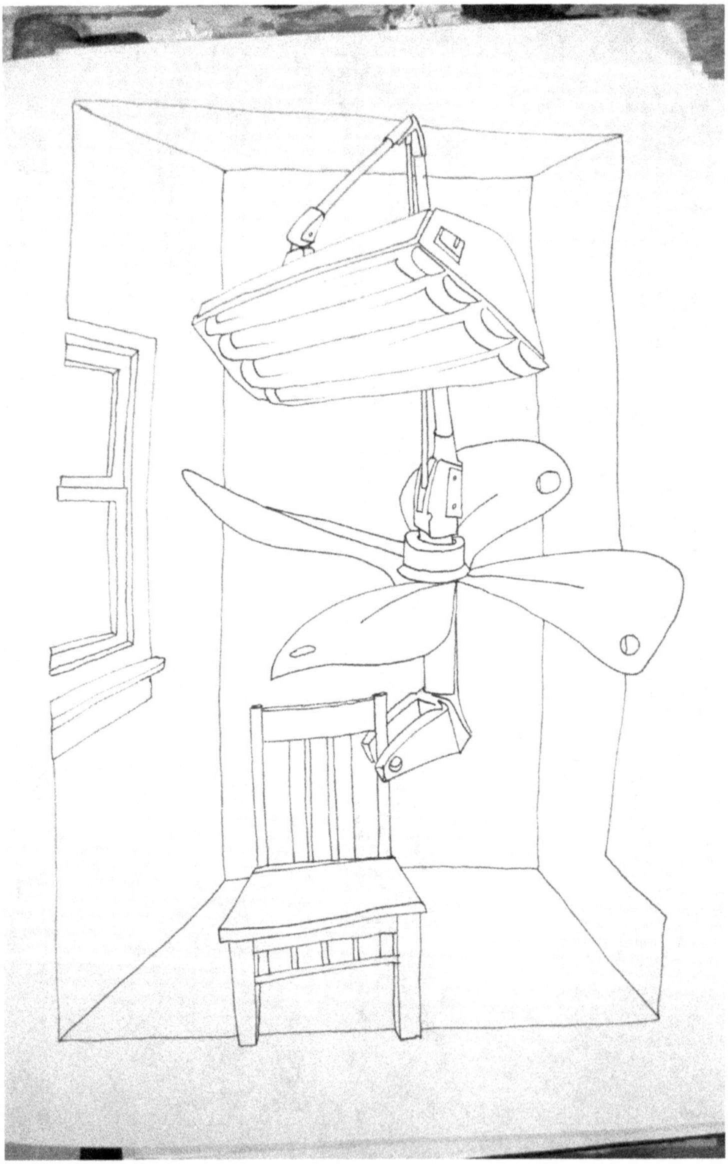

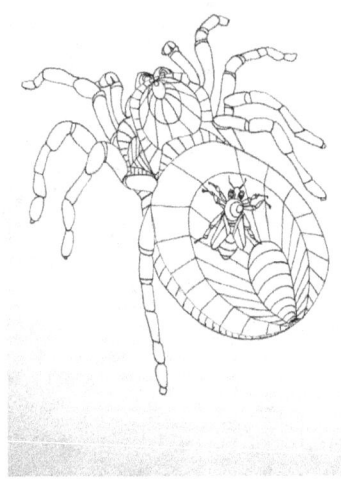

Notes and sketches

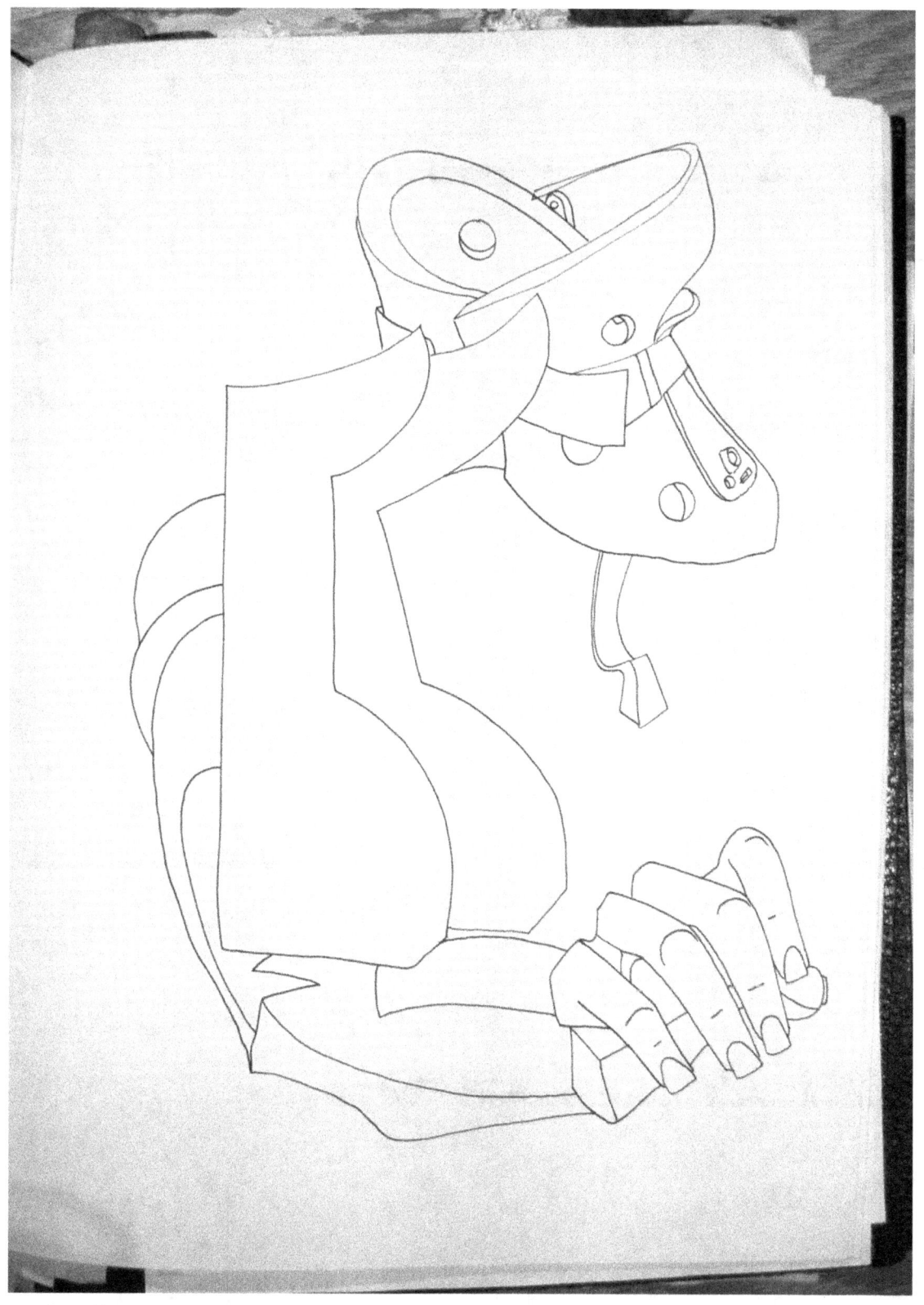

Gilles COLLETTE

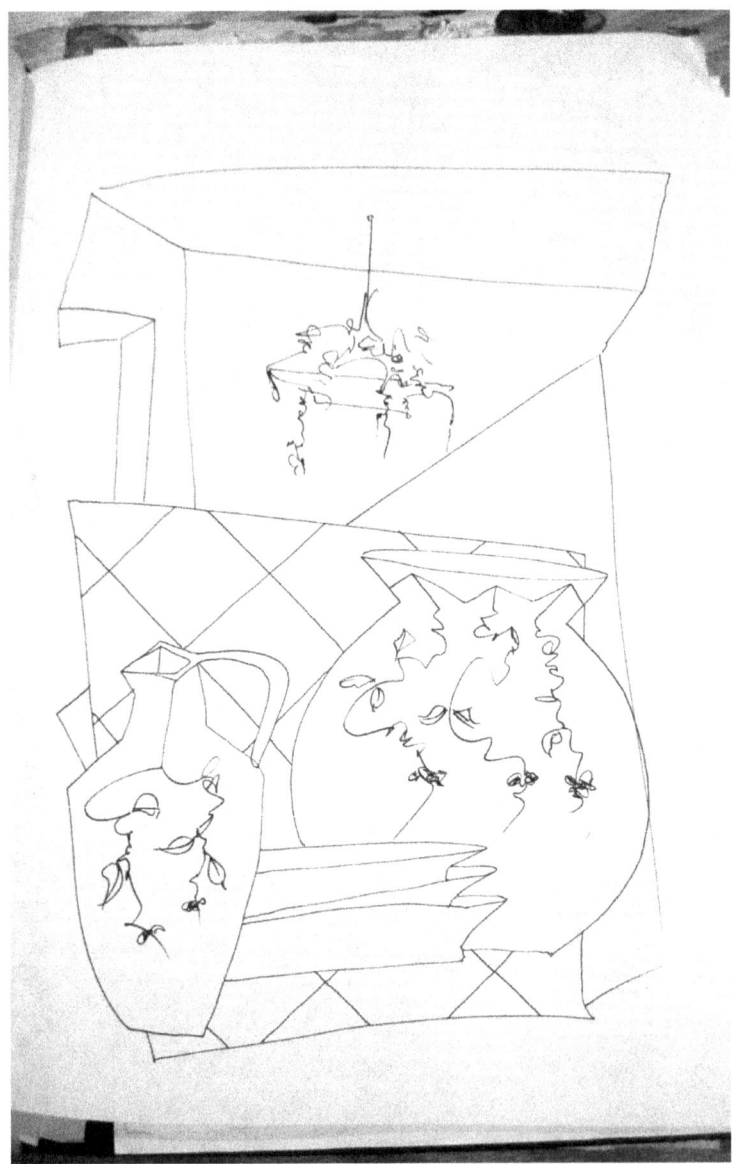

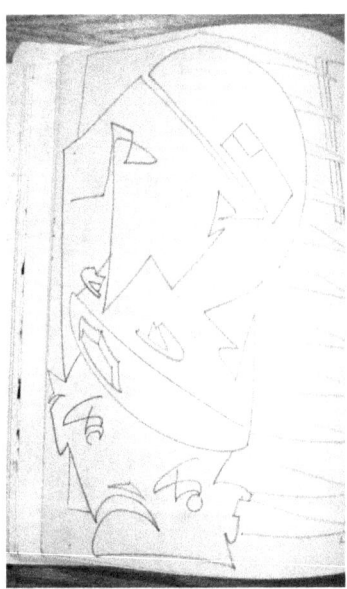

Notes and sketches

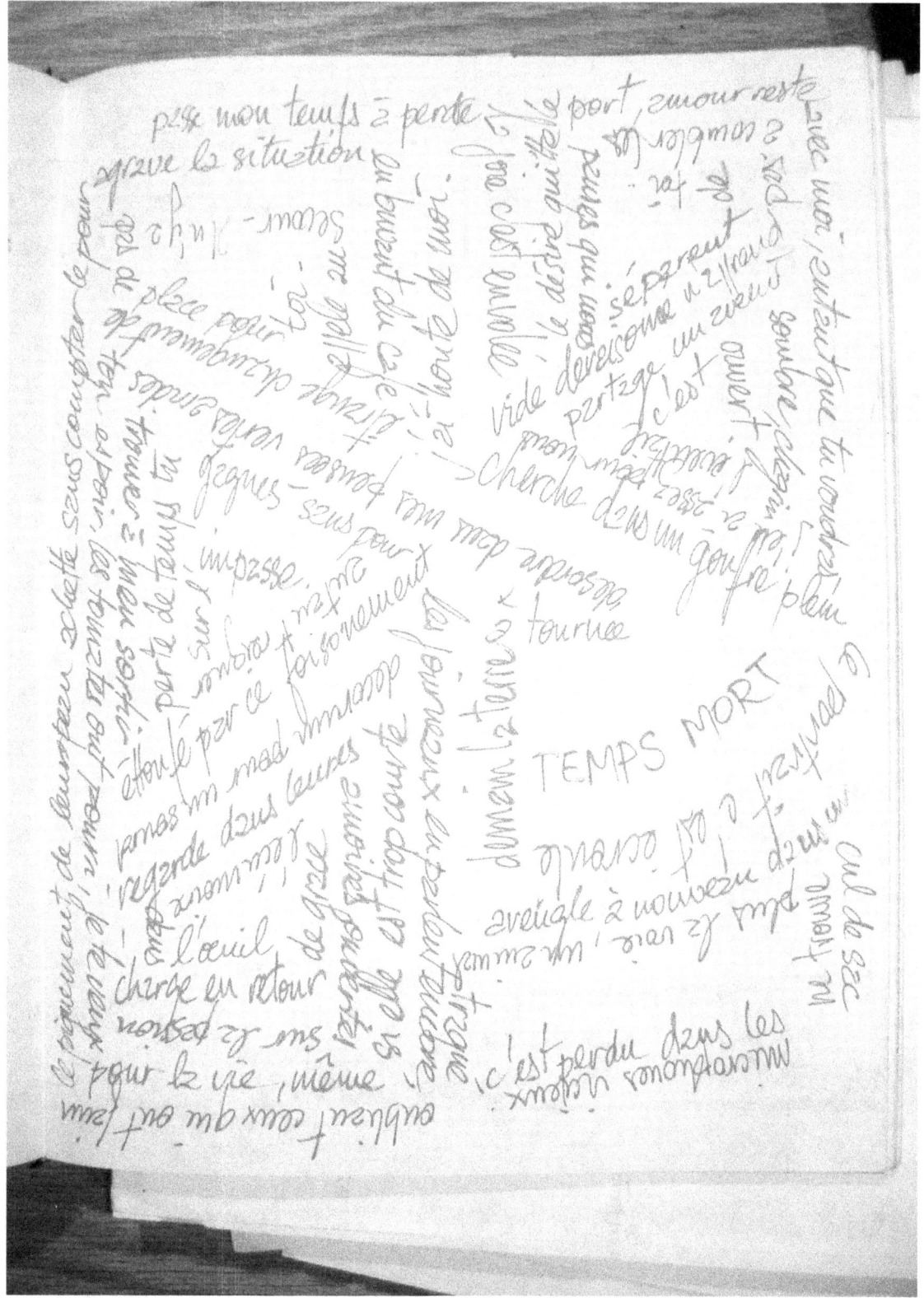

TEMPS MORT

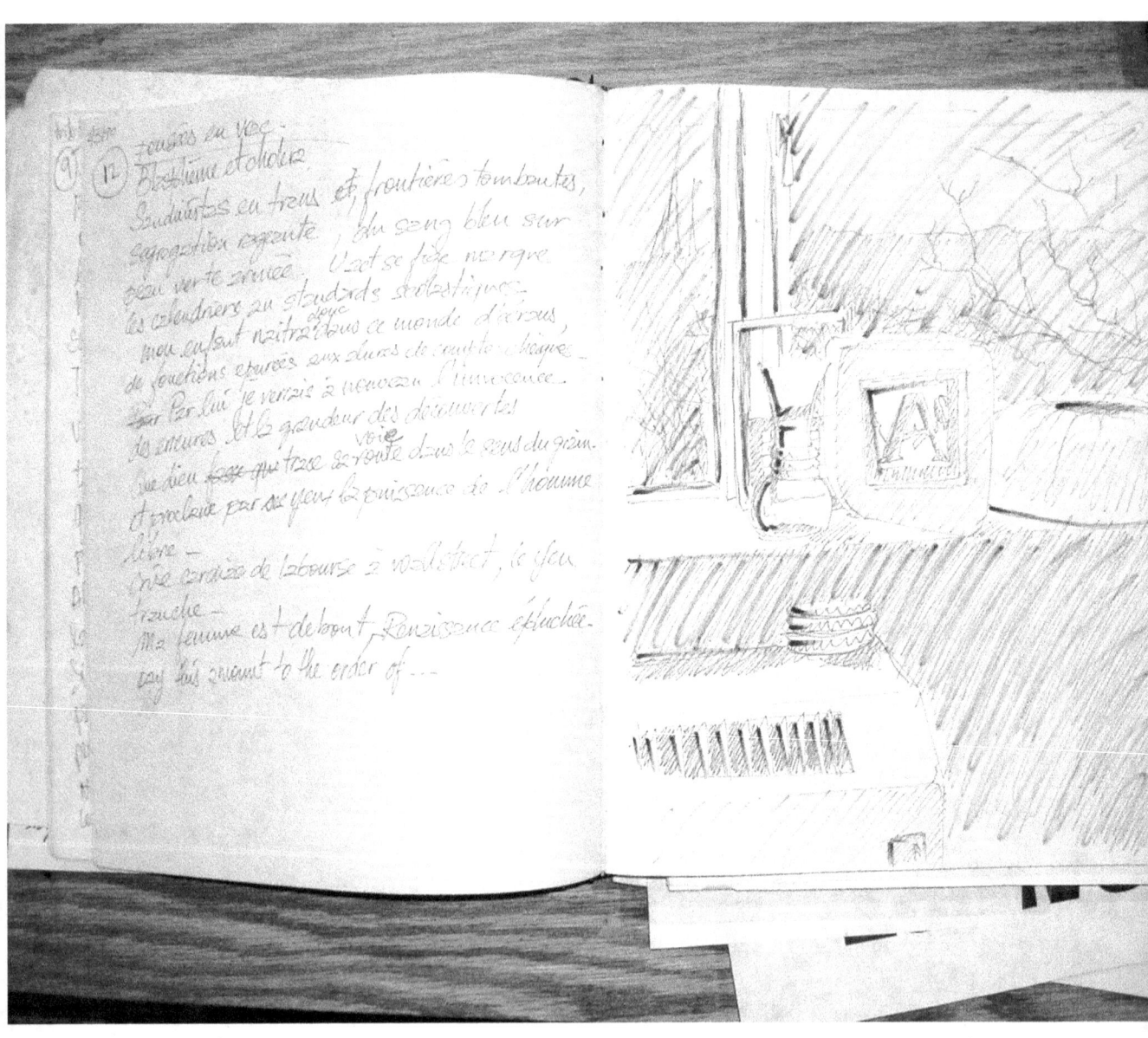

Notes and sketches

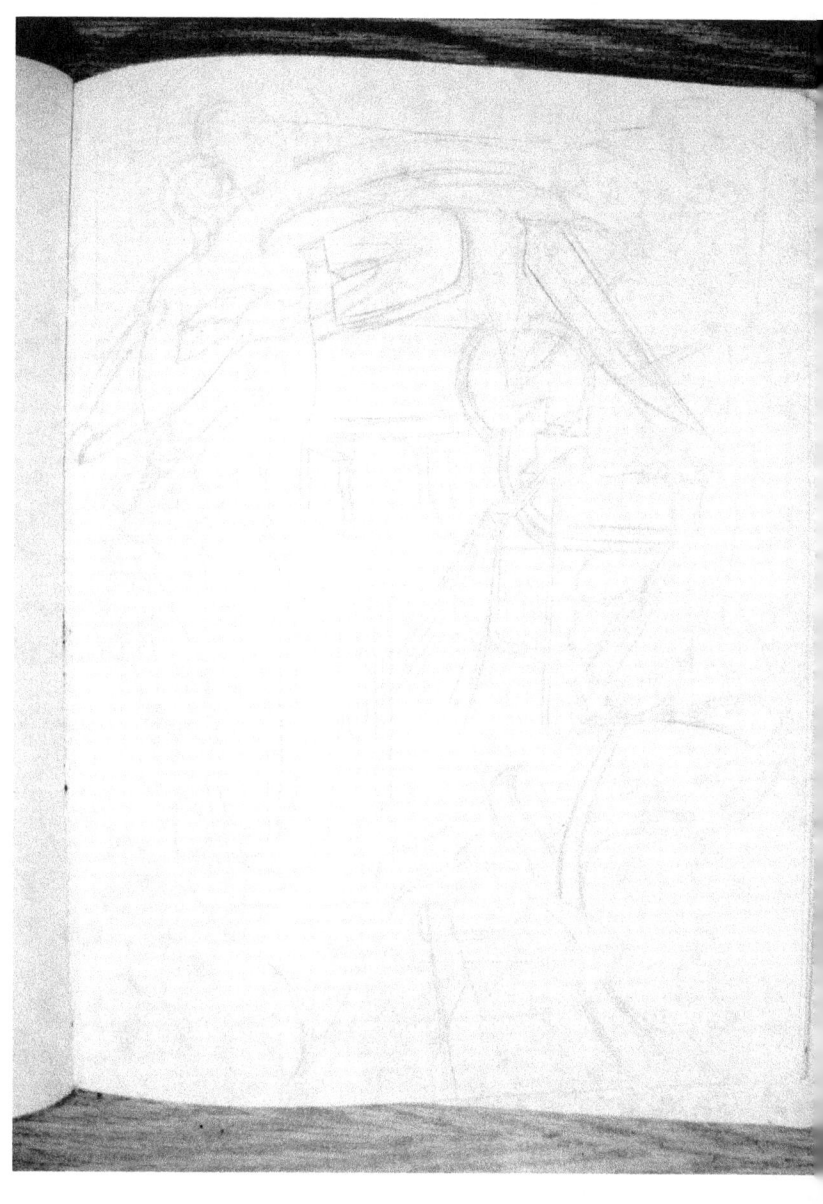

Gilles COLLETTE

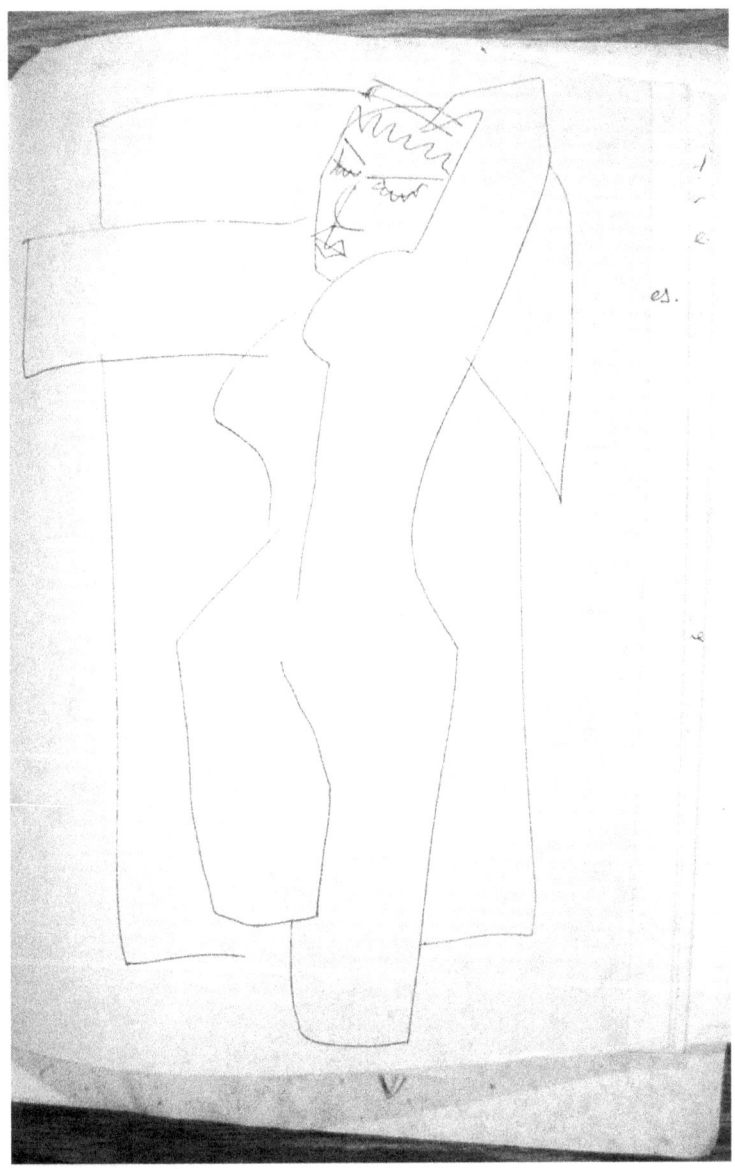

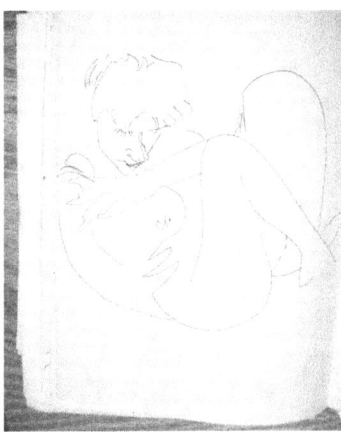

Notes and sketches

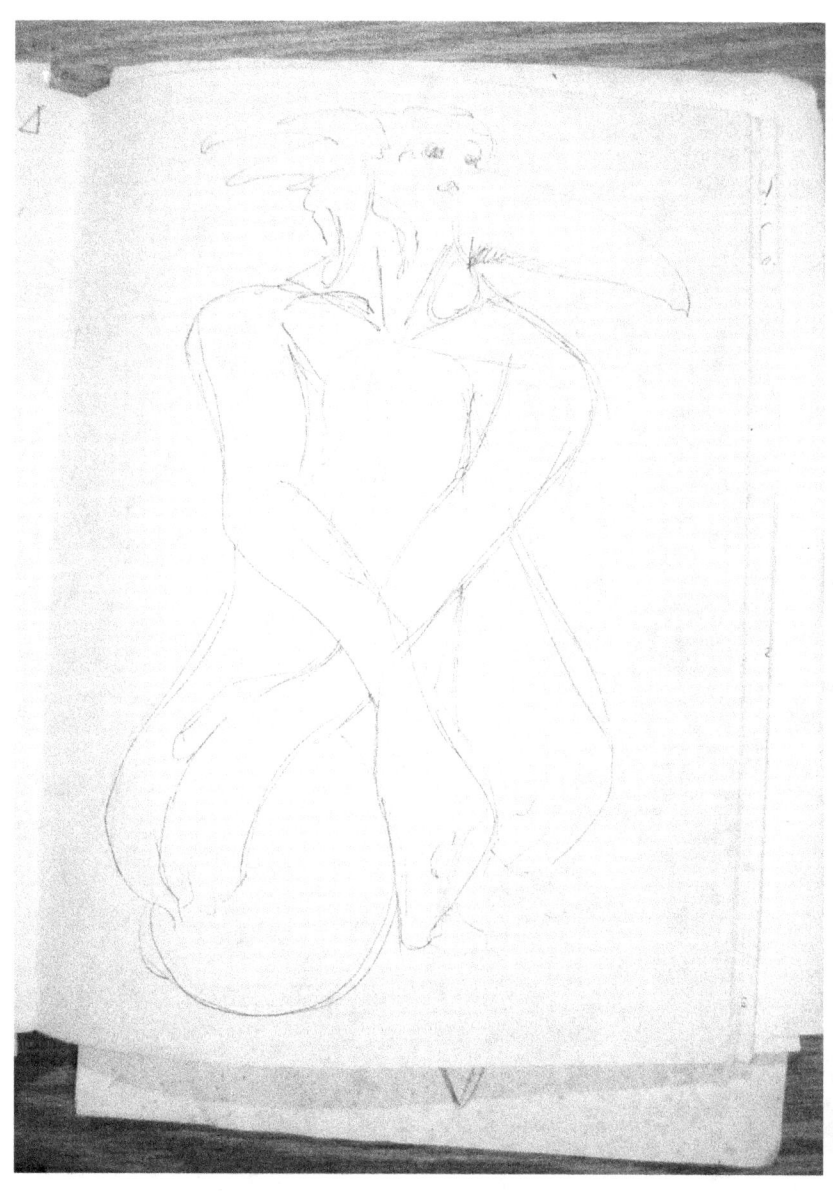

Gilles COLLETTE

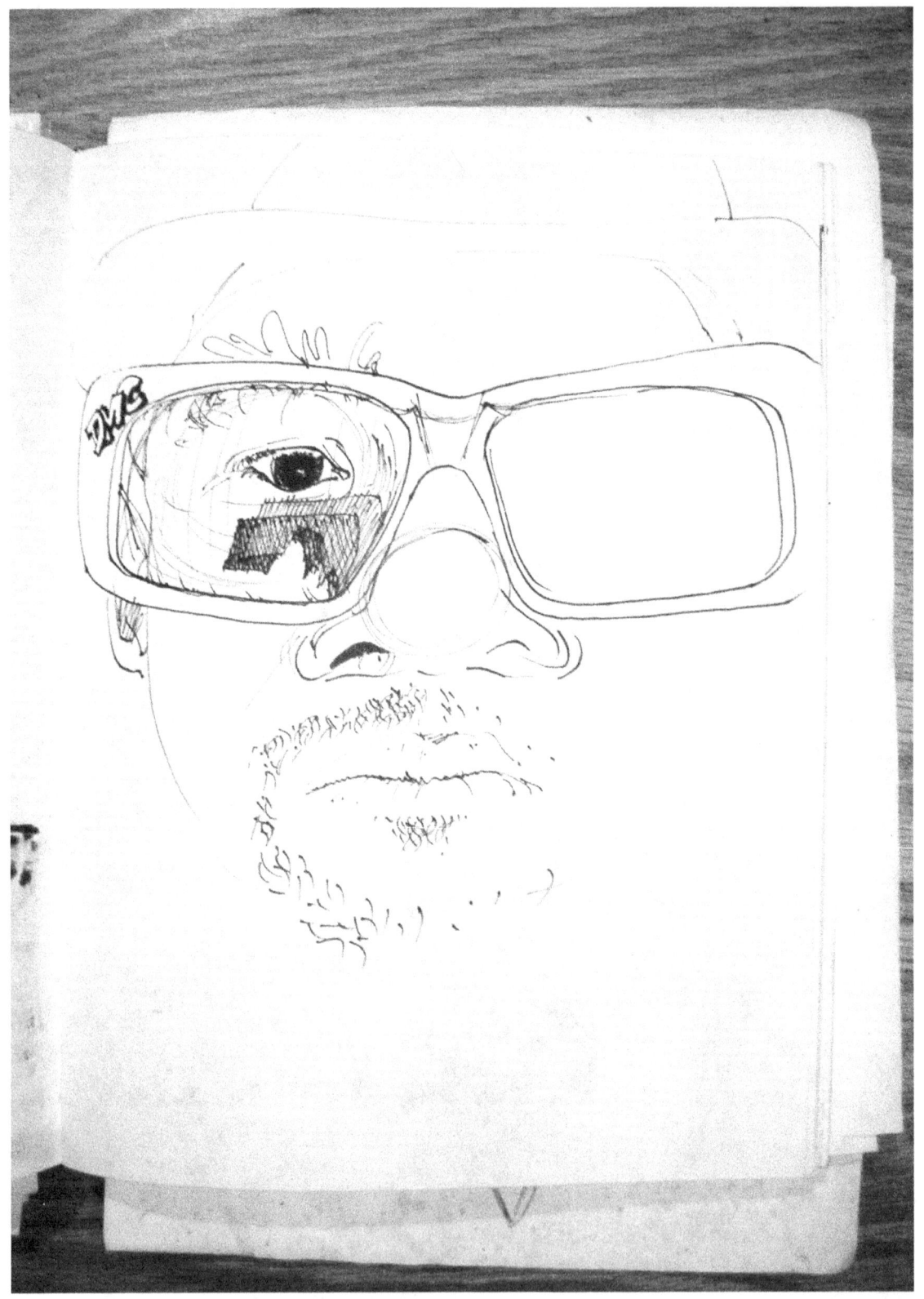

Notes and sketches

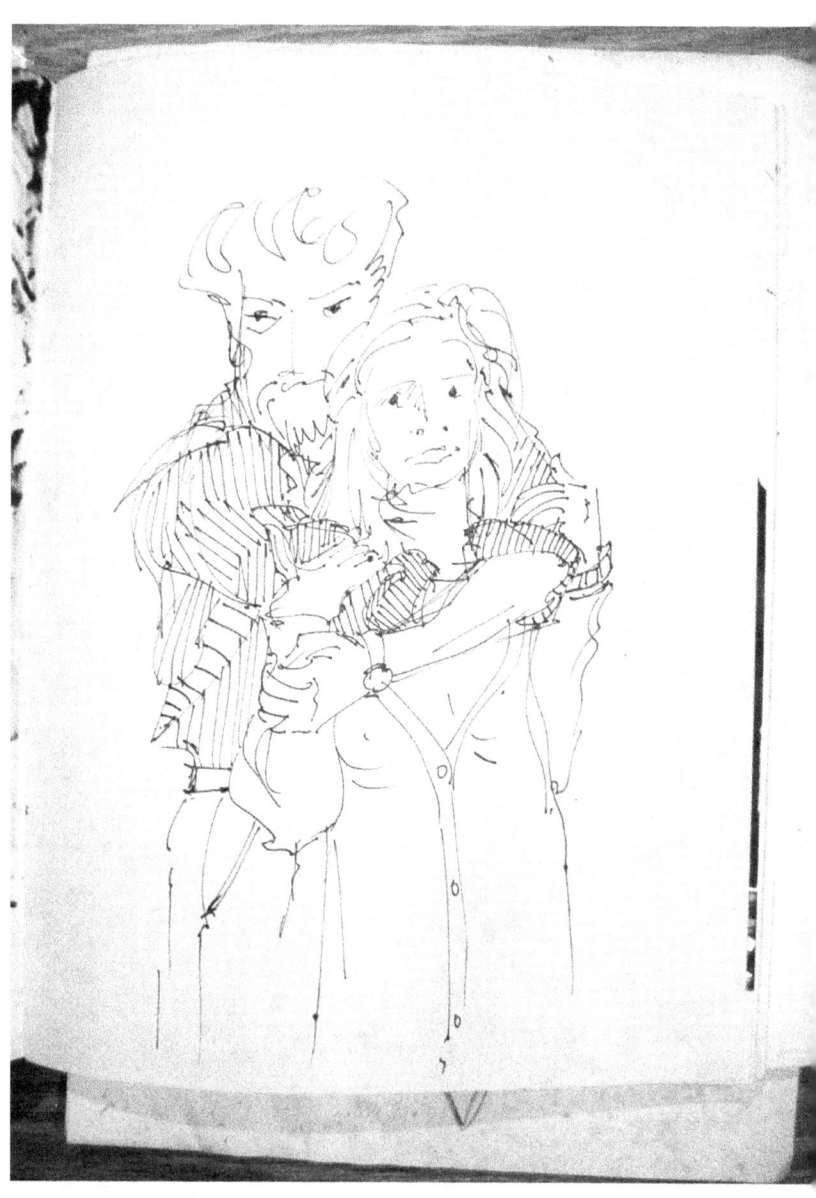

Gilles COLLETTE

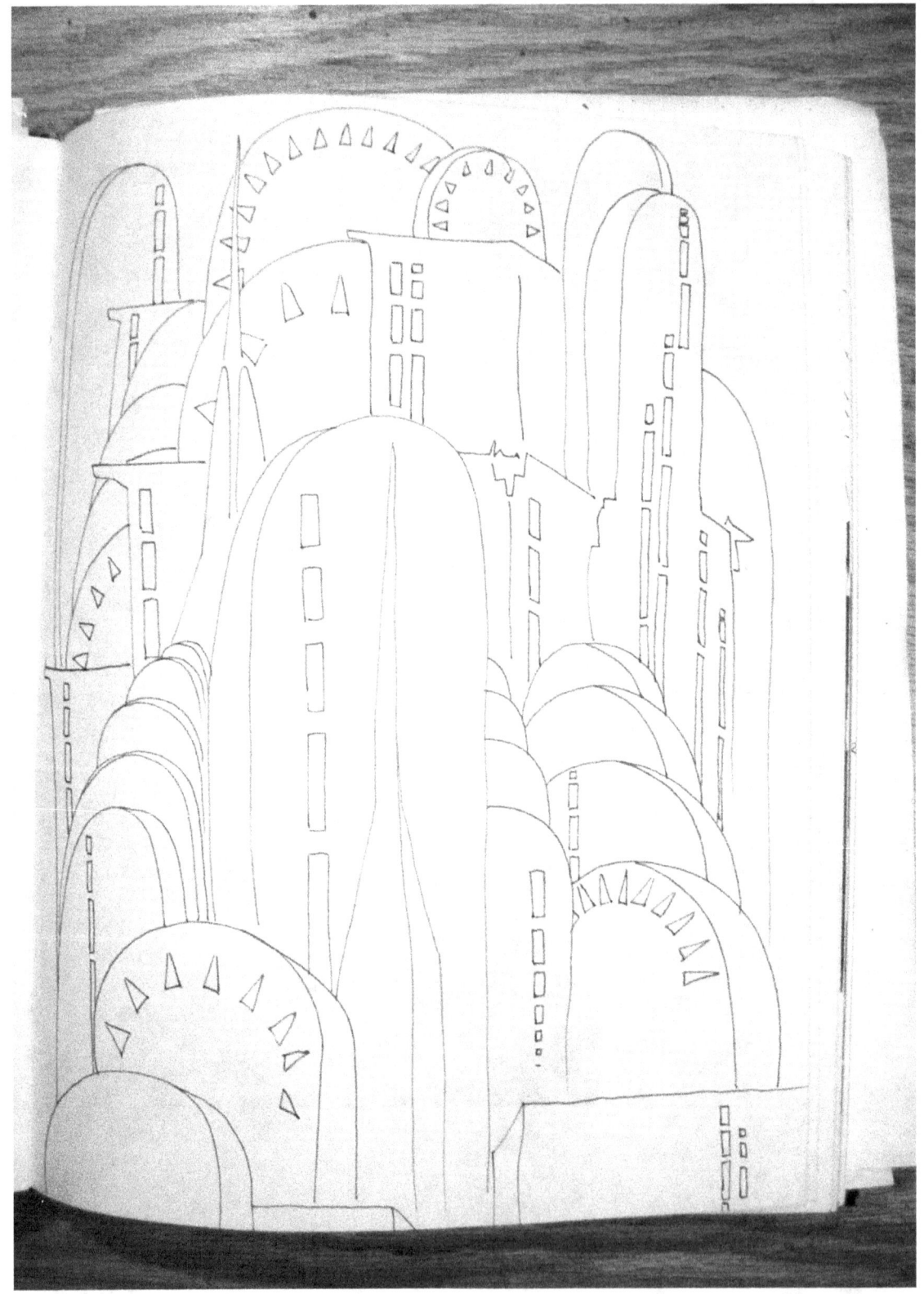

Notes and sketches

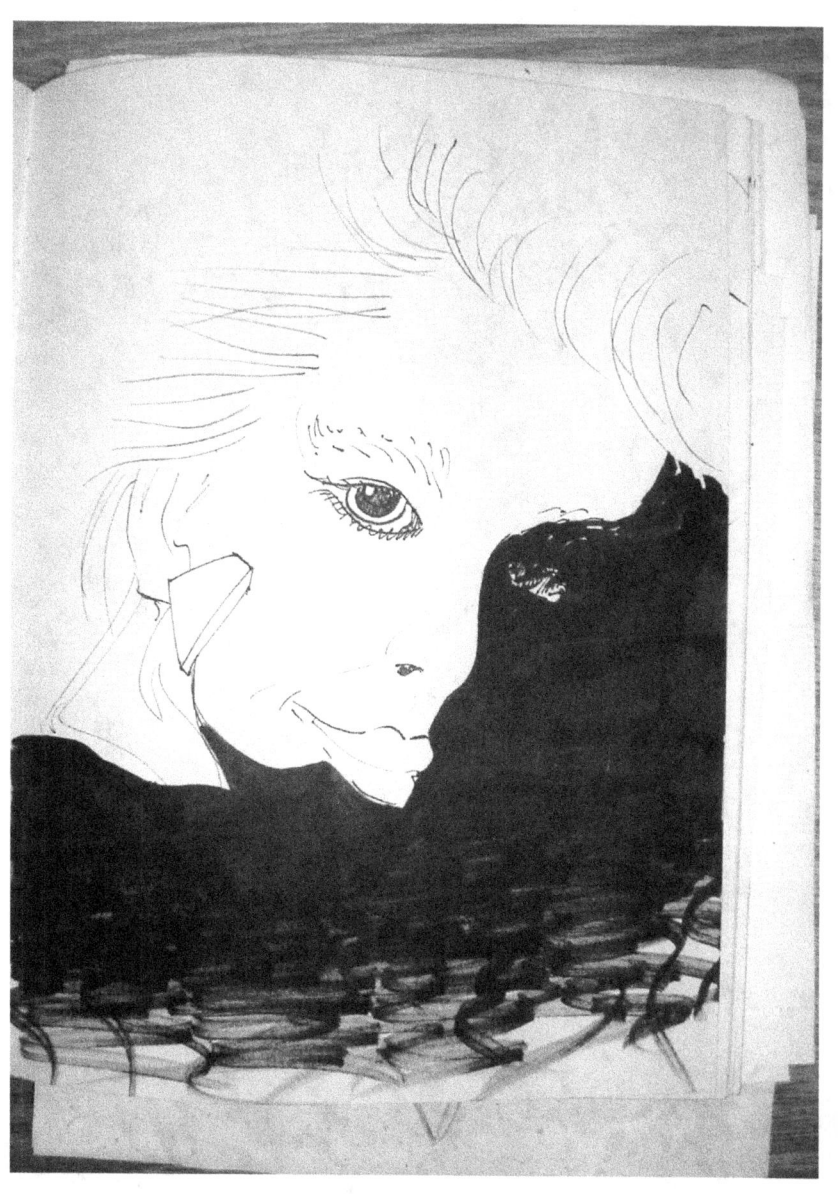

Gilles COLLETTE

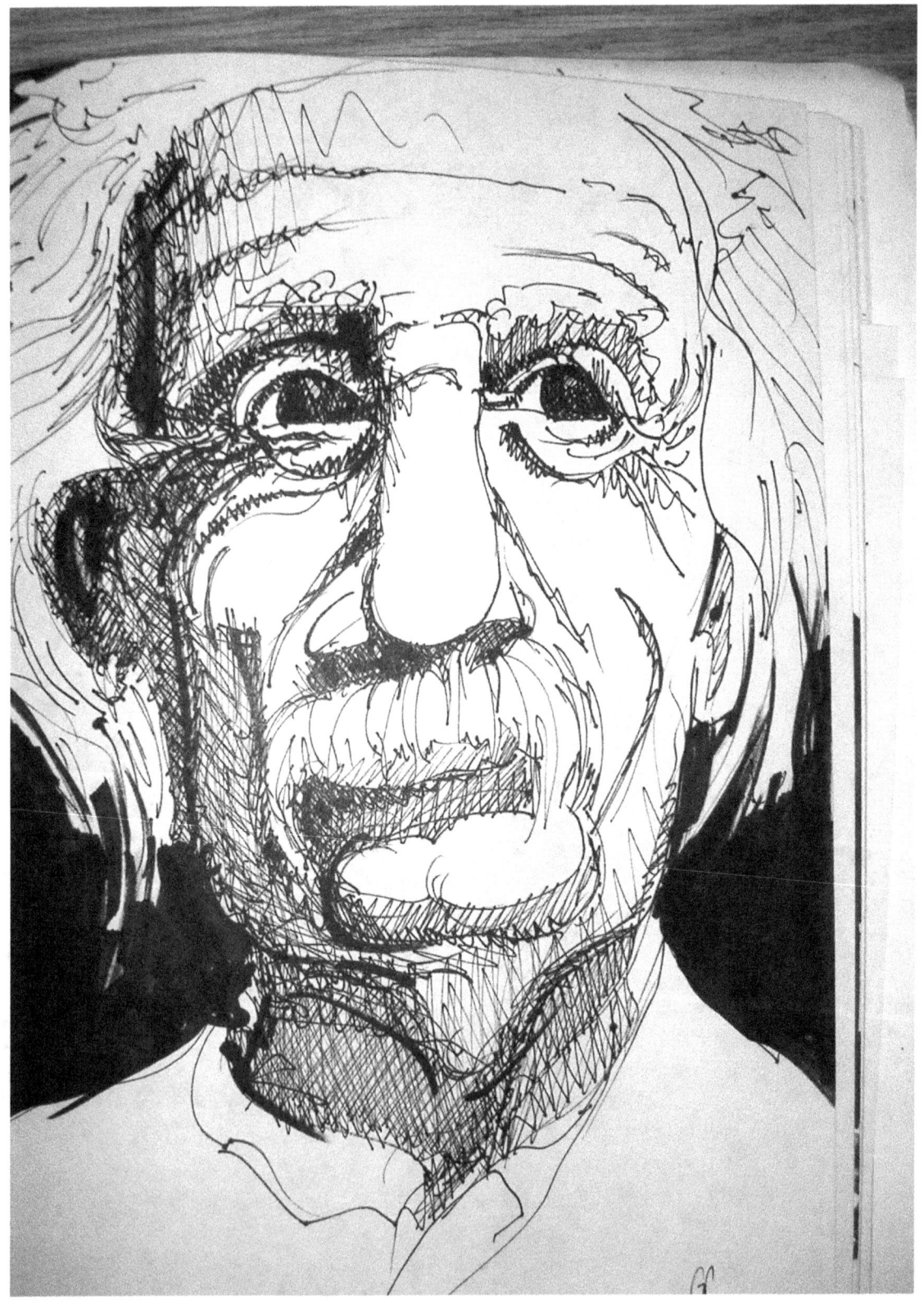

Notes and sketches

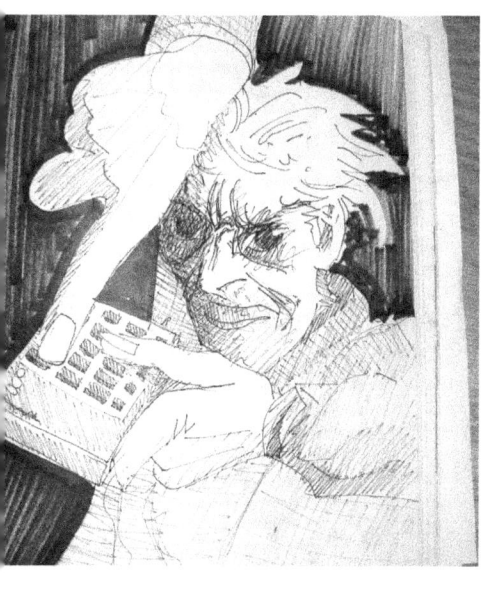
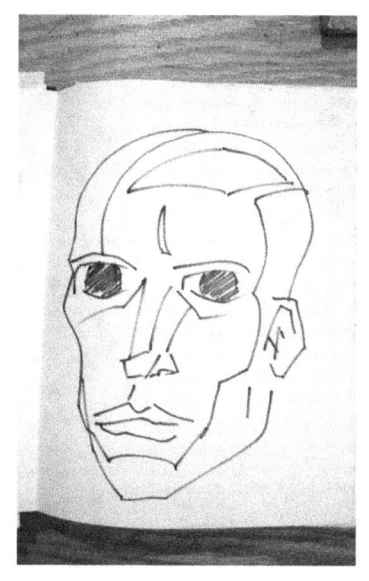
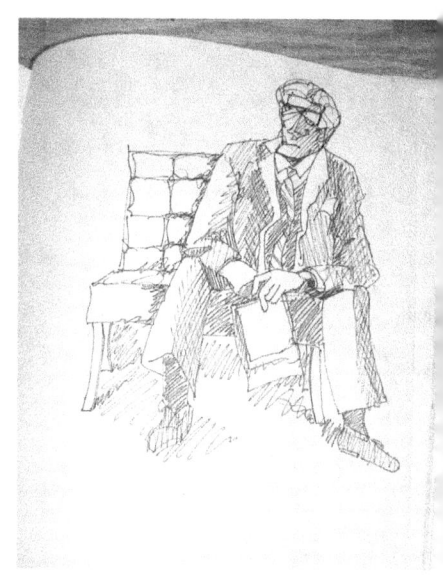
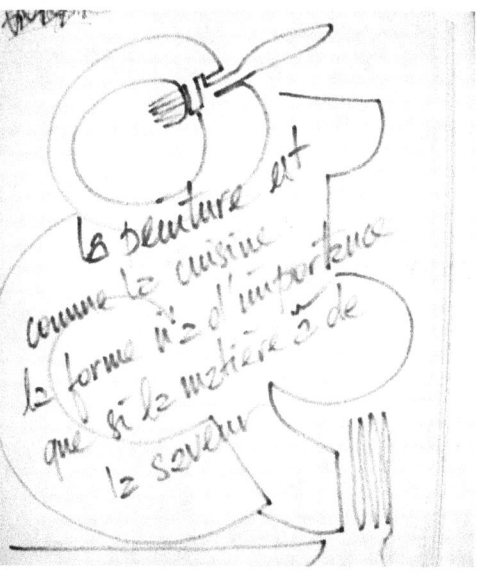
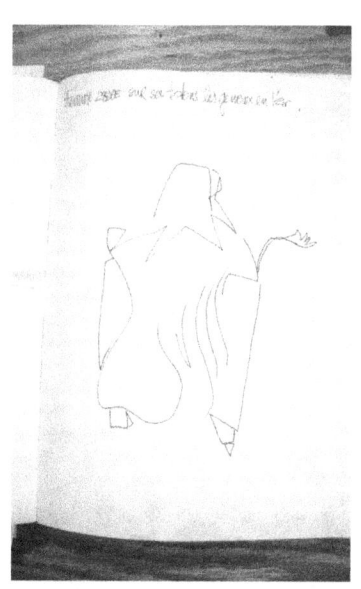
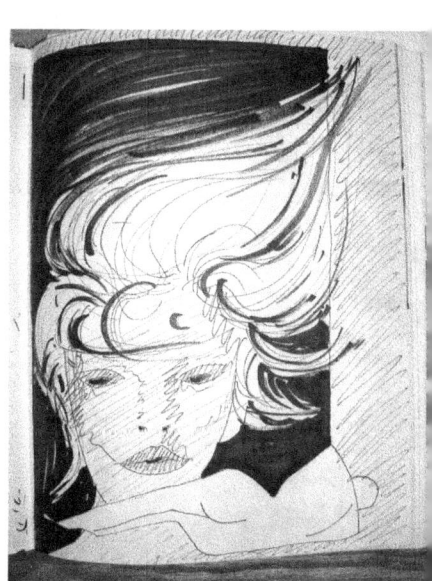

Gilles COLLETTE

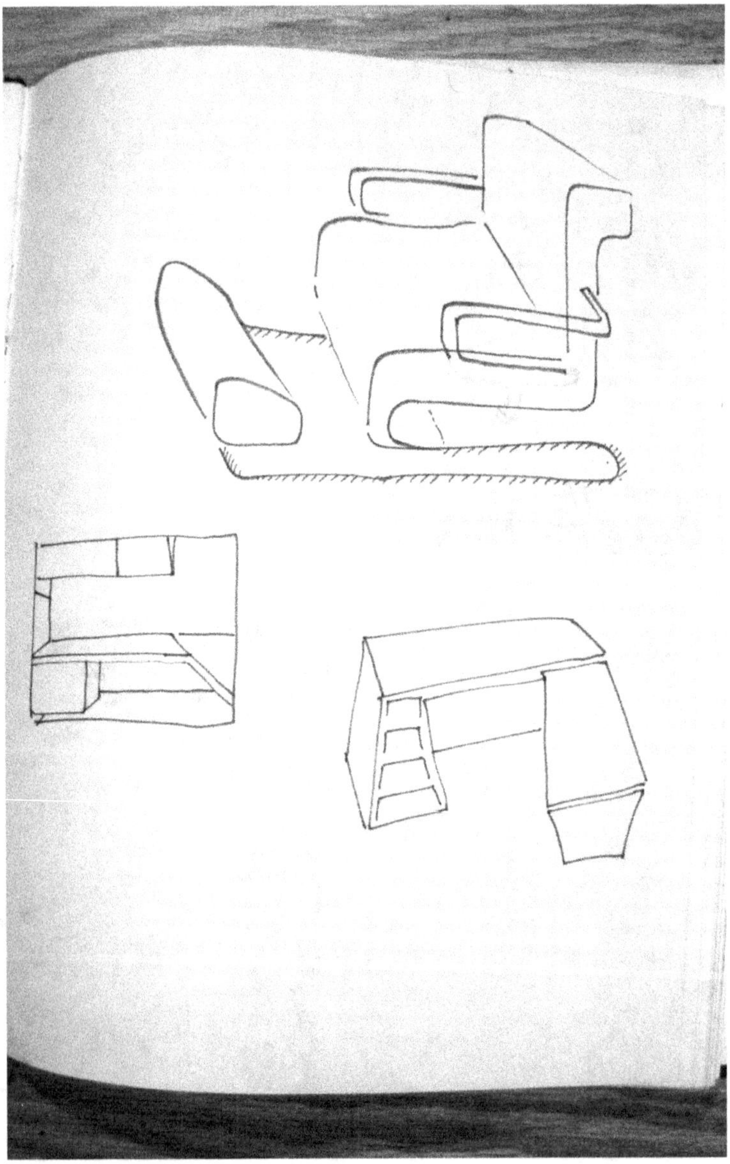

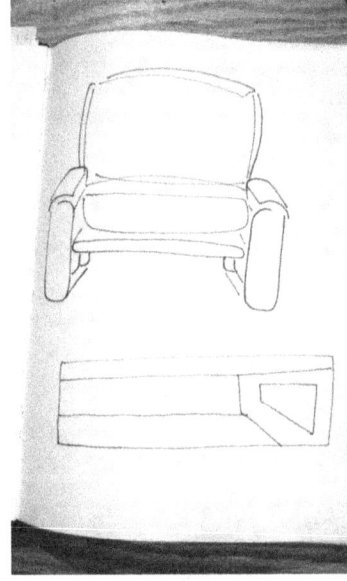

Notes and sketches

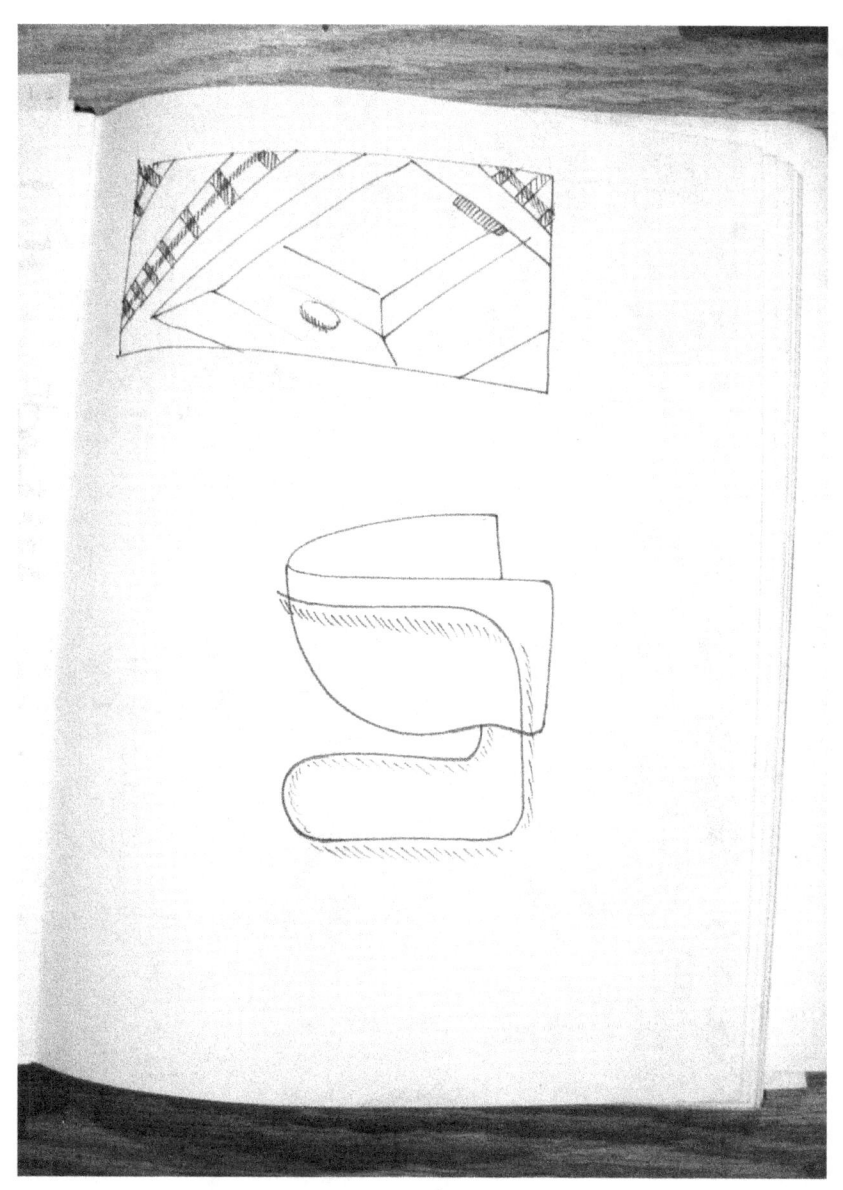

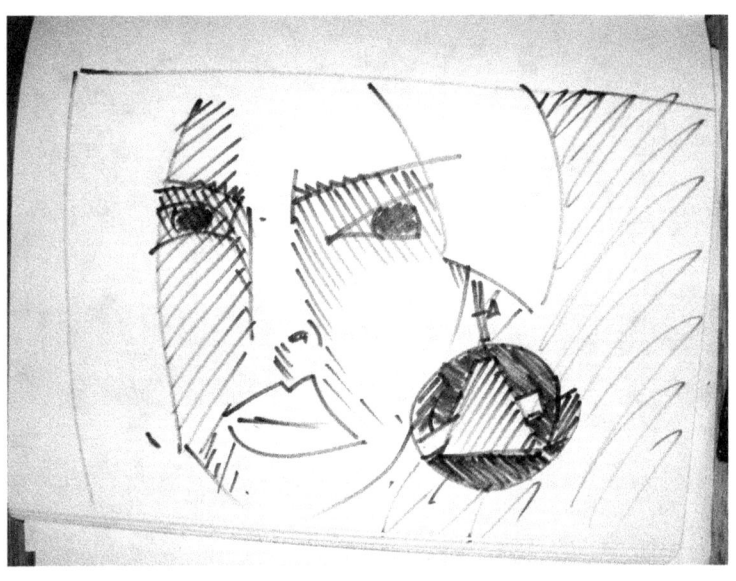

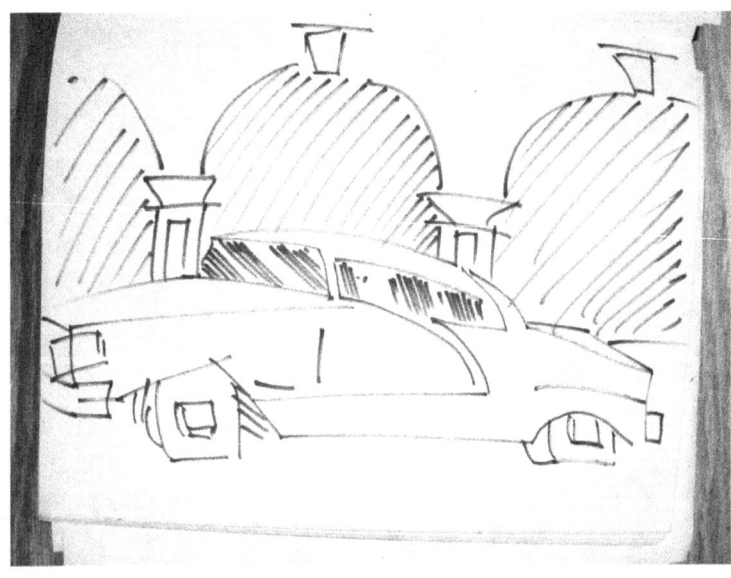

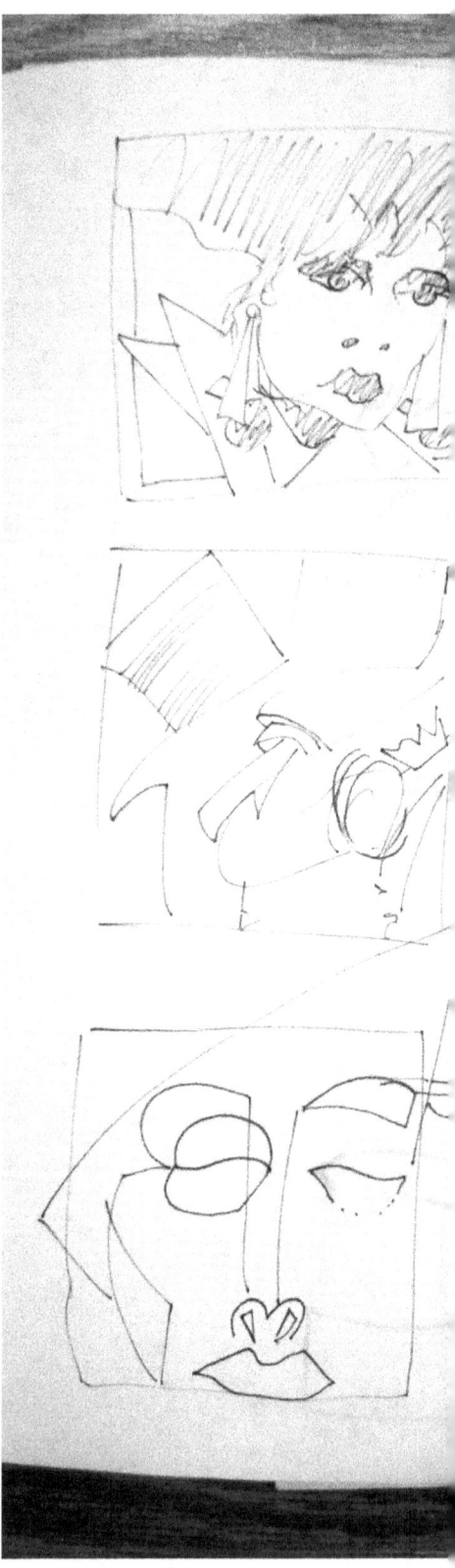

124 Notes and sketches

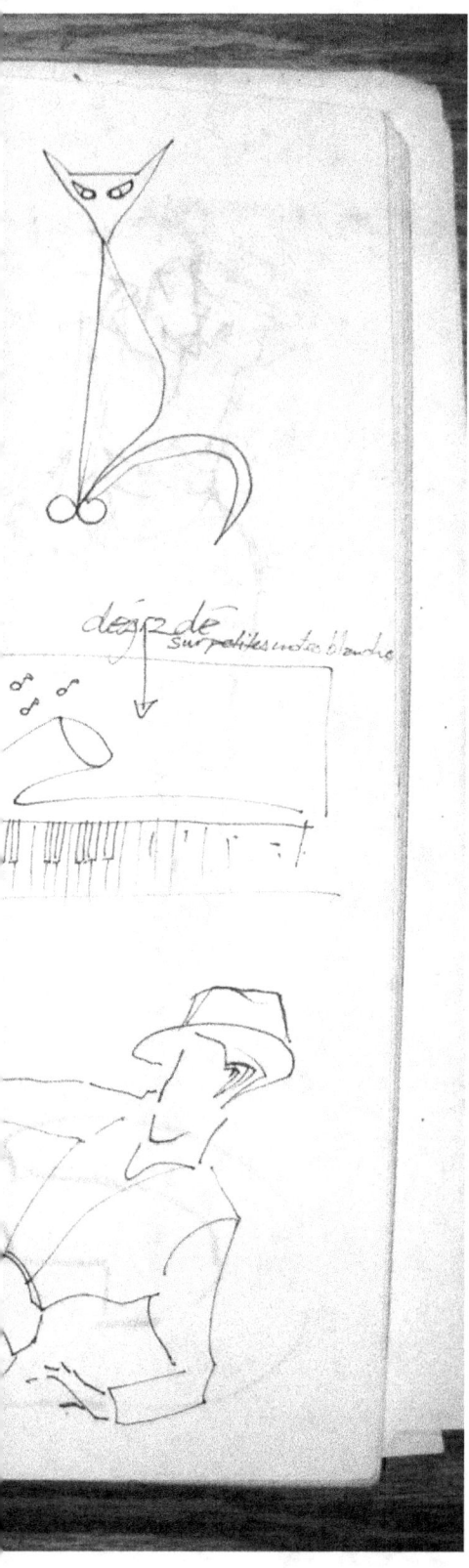

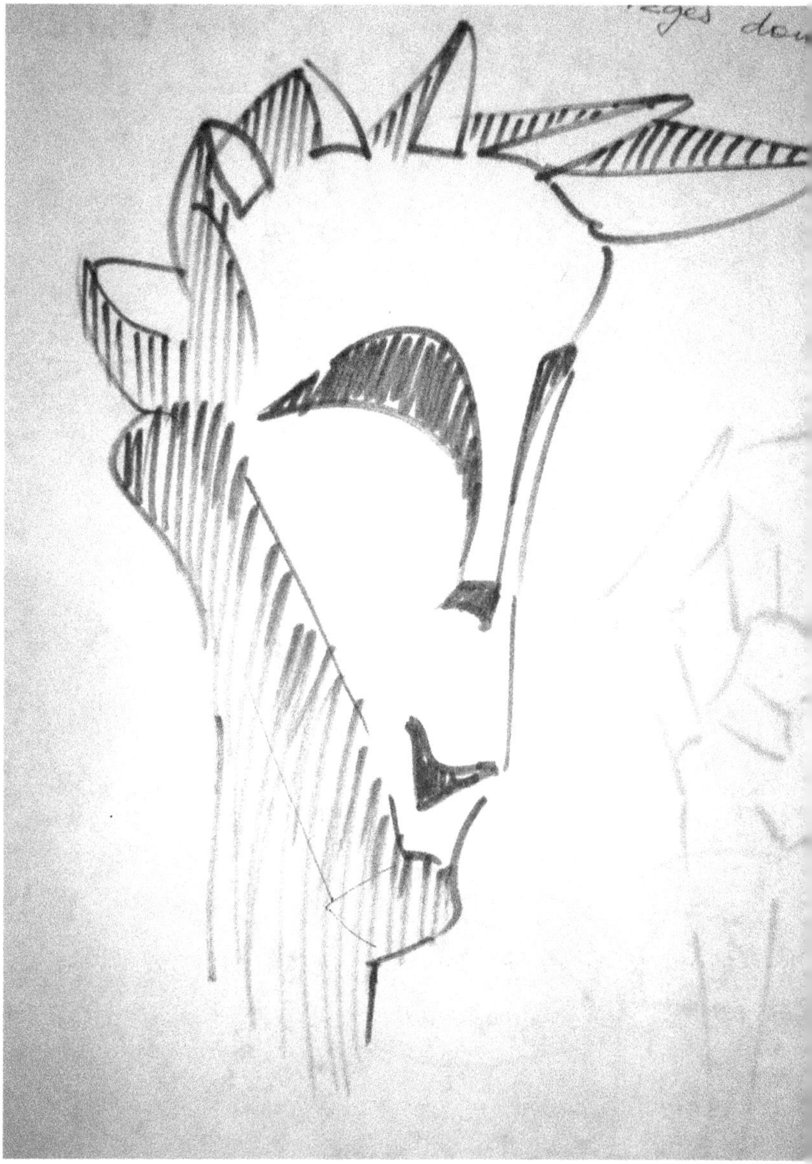

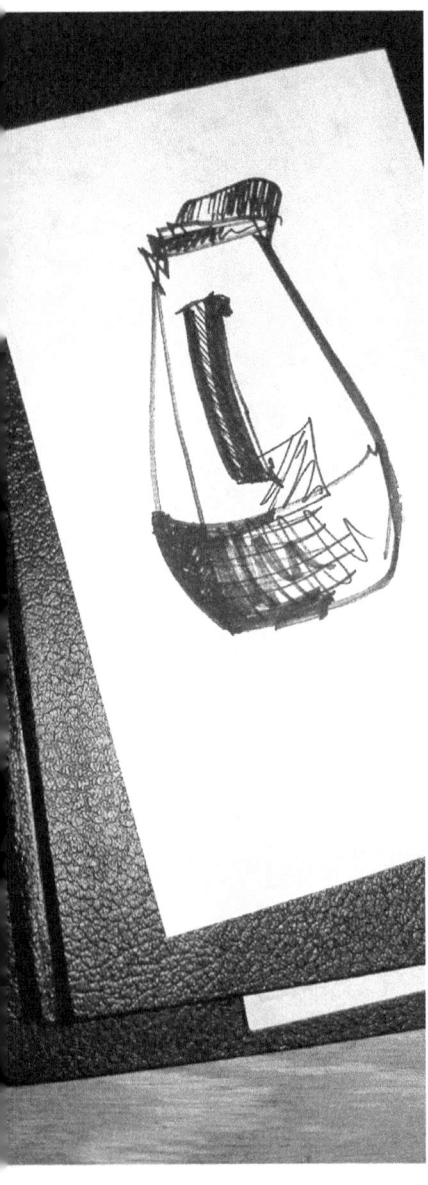

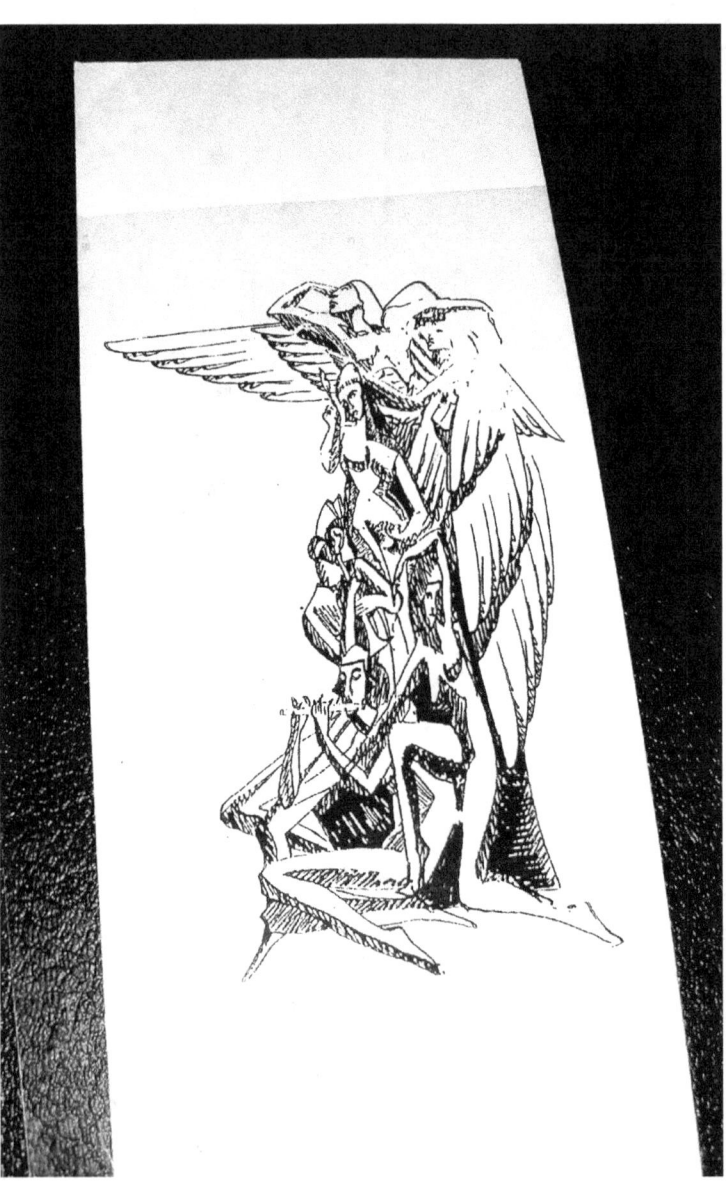

Notes and sketches

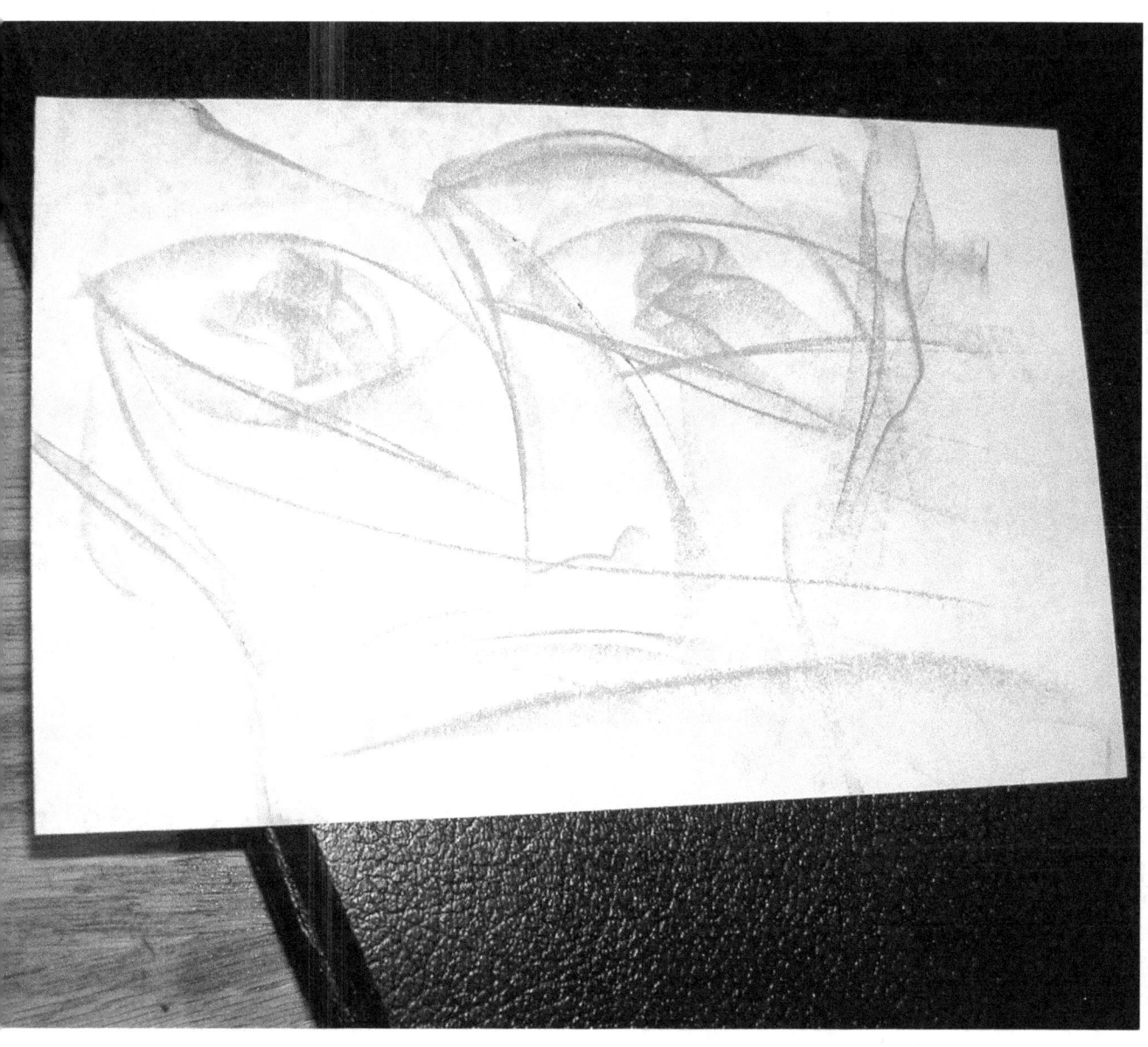

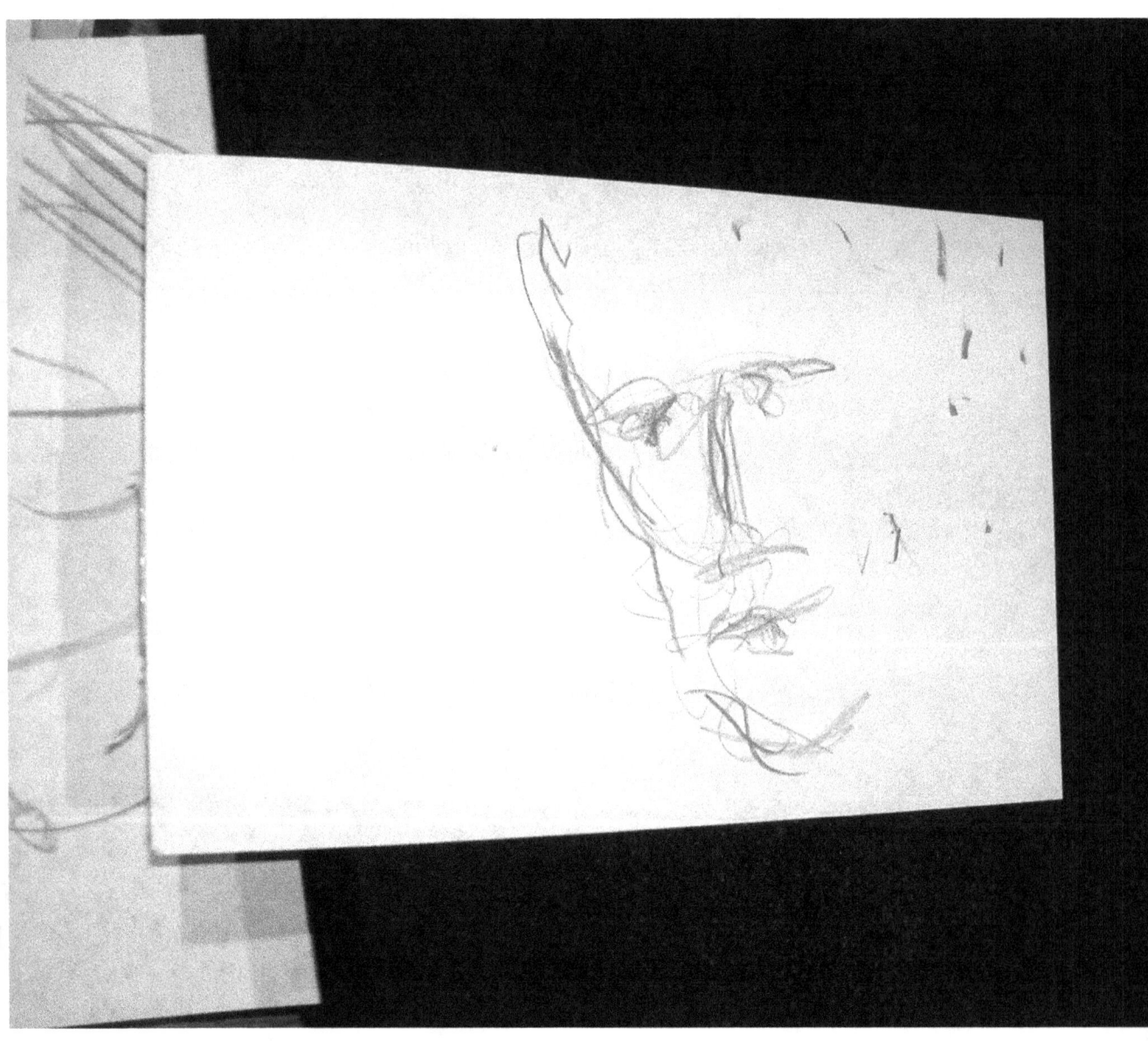

Notes and sketches

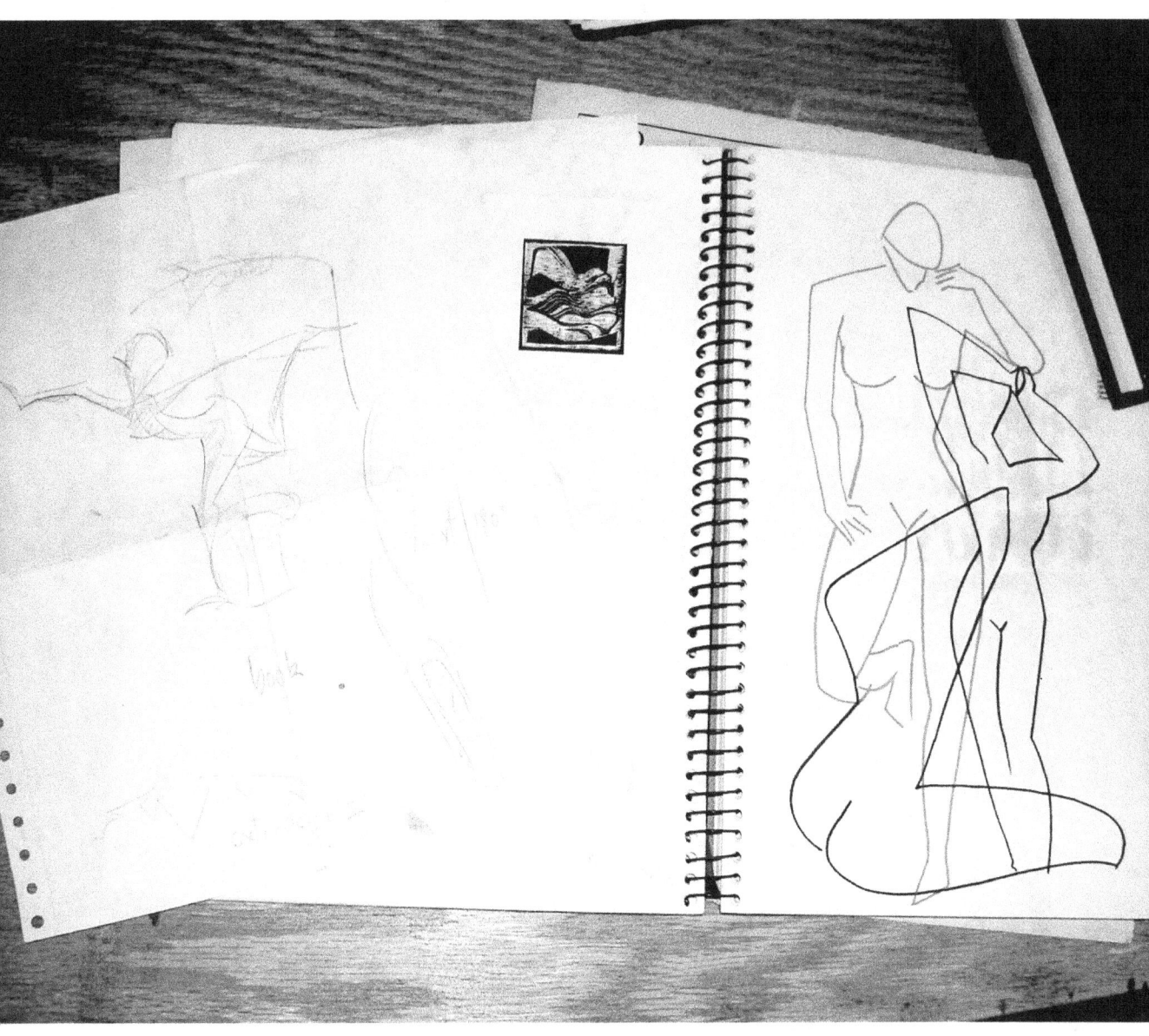

Gilles COLLETTE

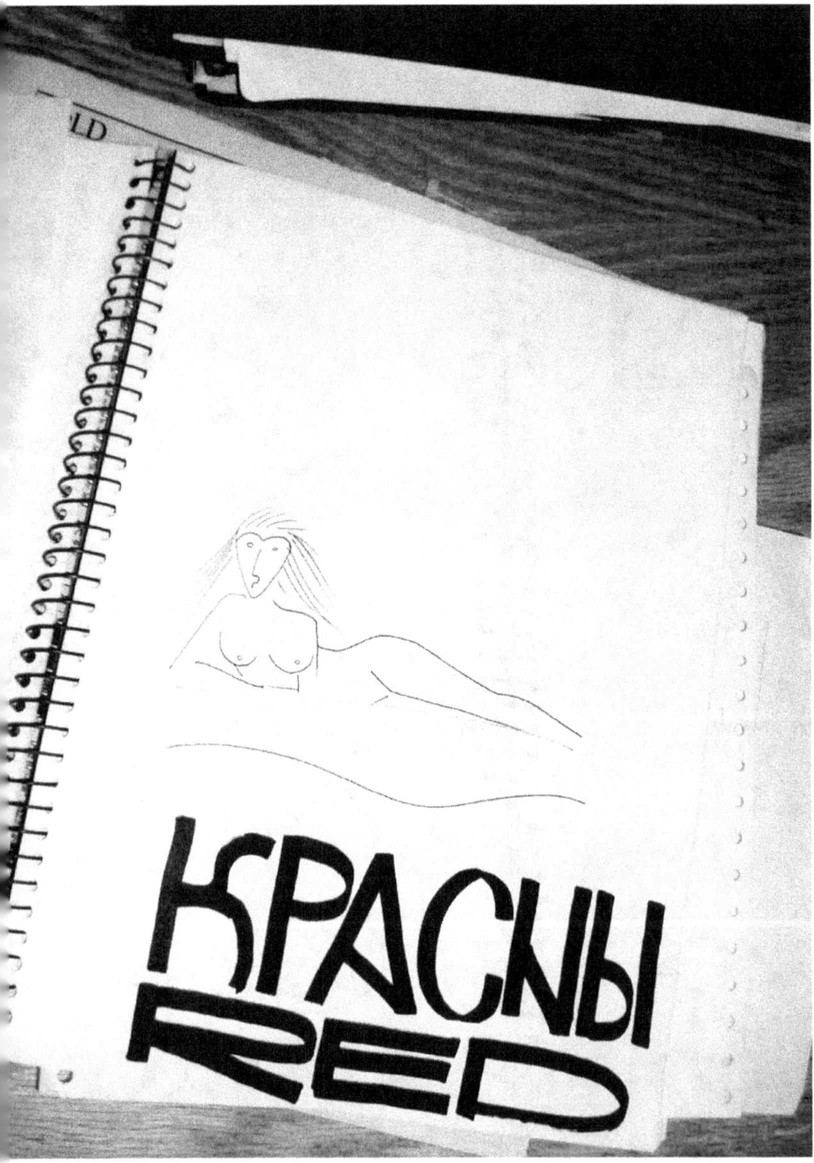

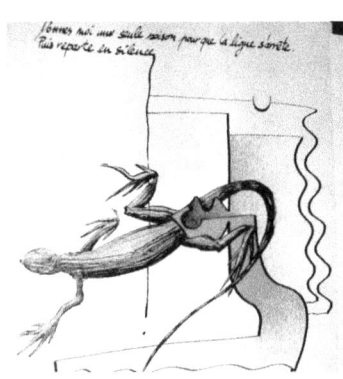

Notes and sketches

...itions et a rempli mon cœur d'un
... vermillon.

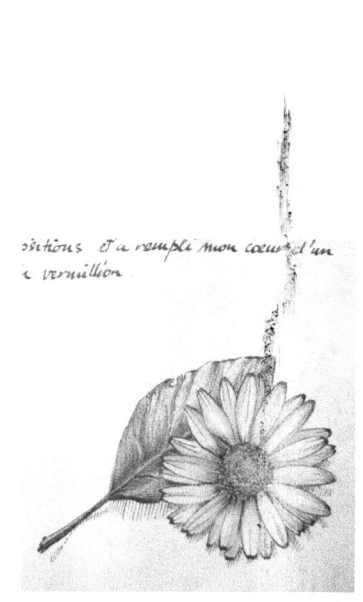

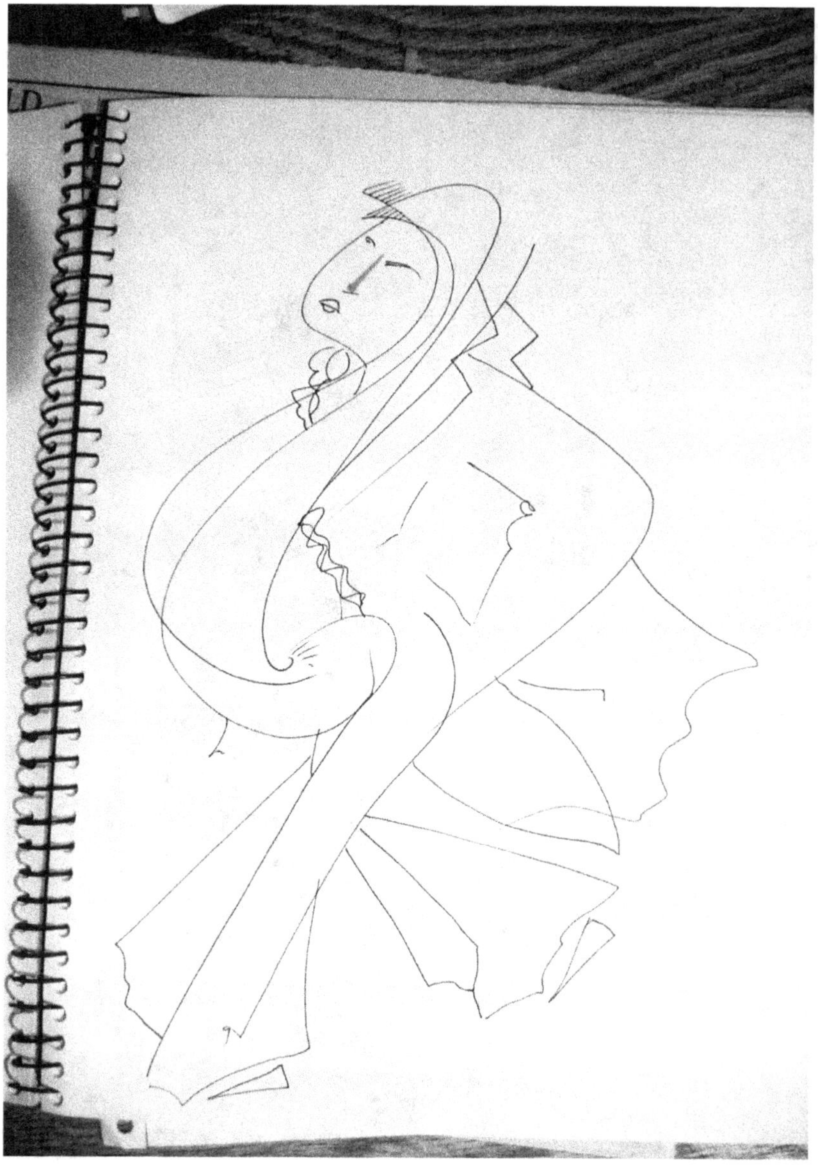

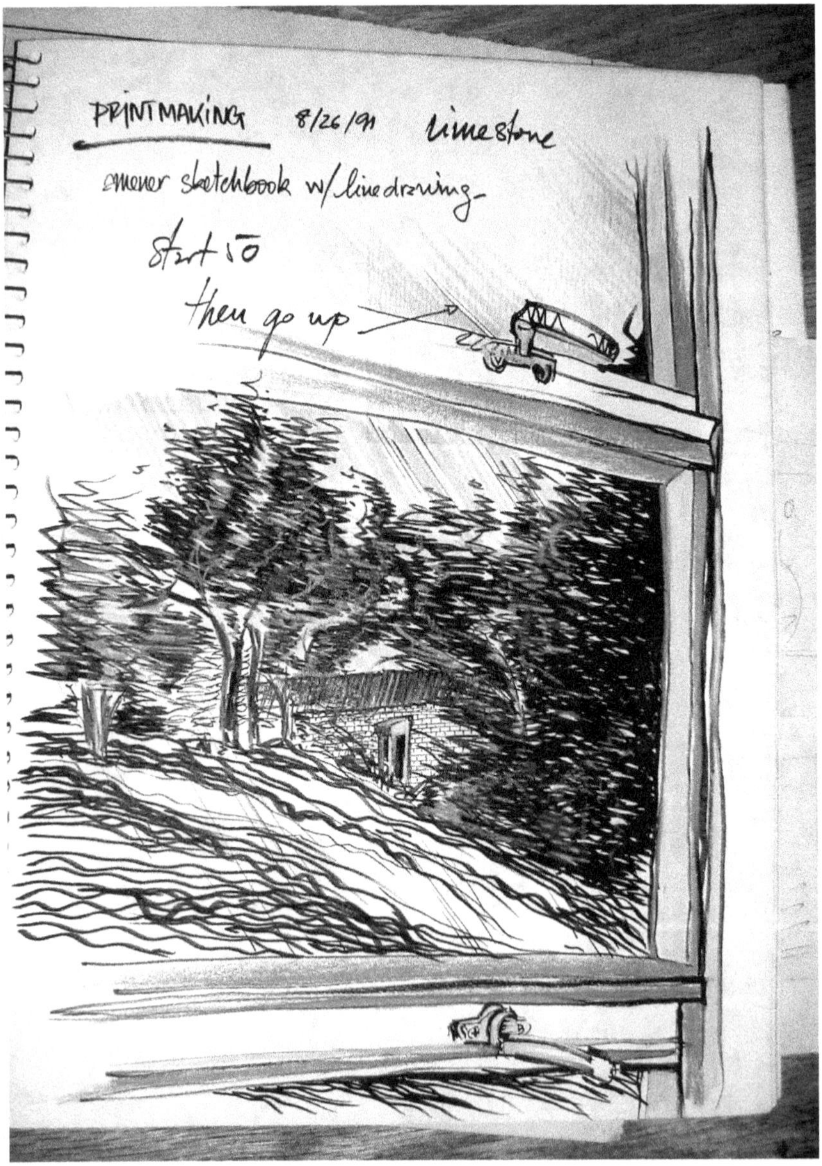

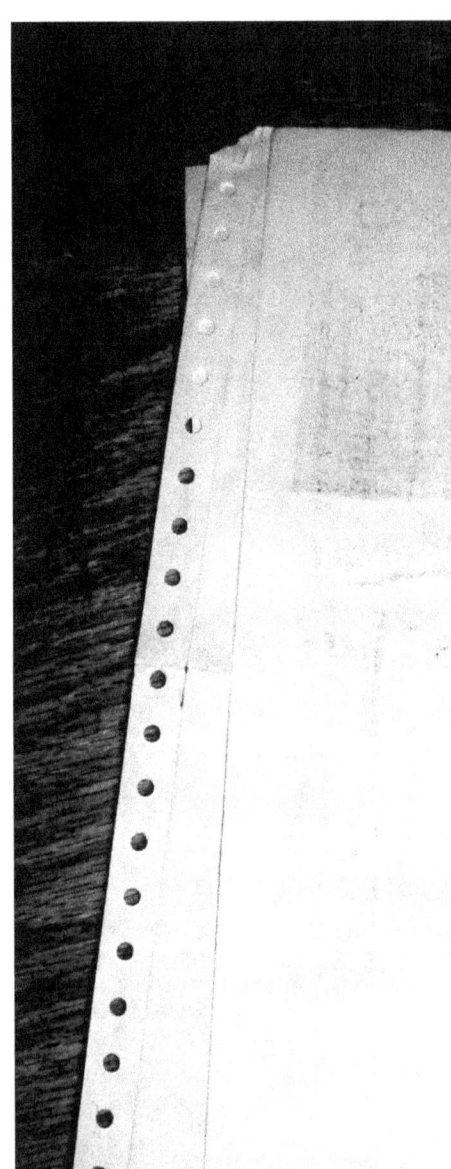

PRINTMAKING 8/26/91 limestone

smaller sketchbook w/ line drawing

start 50

then go up →

Notes and sketches

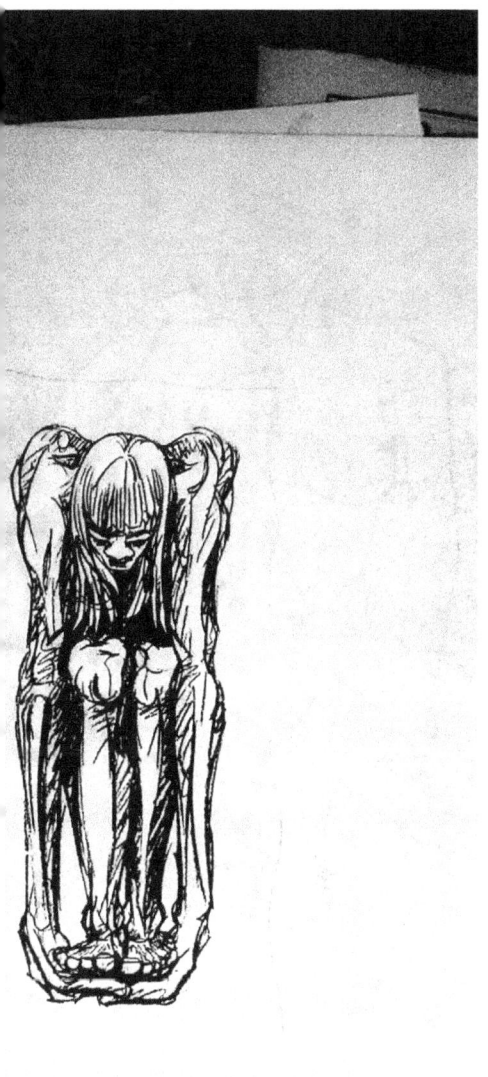

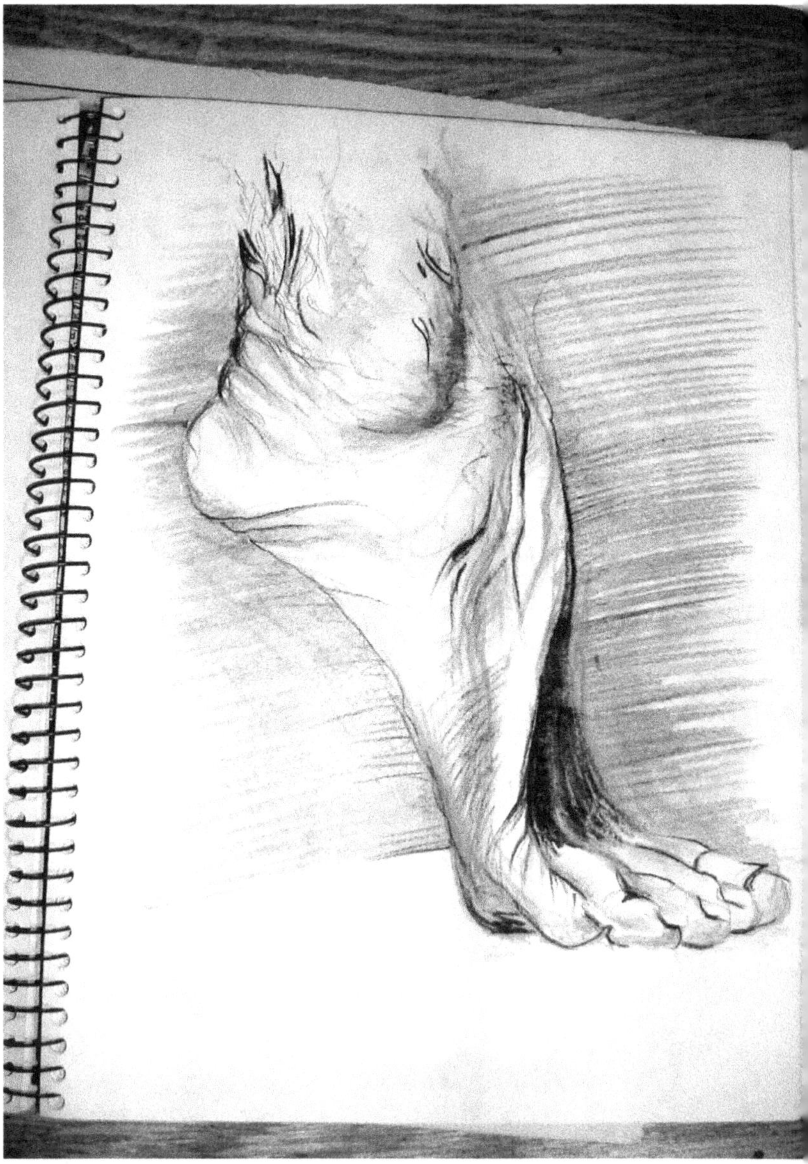

Gilles COLLETTE

133

134

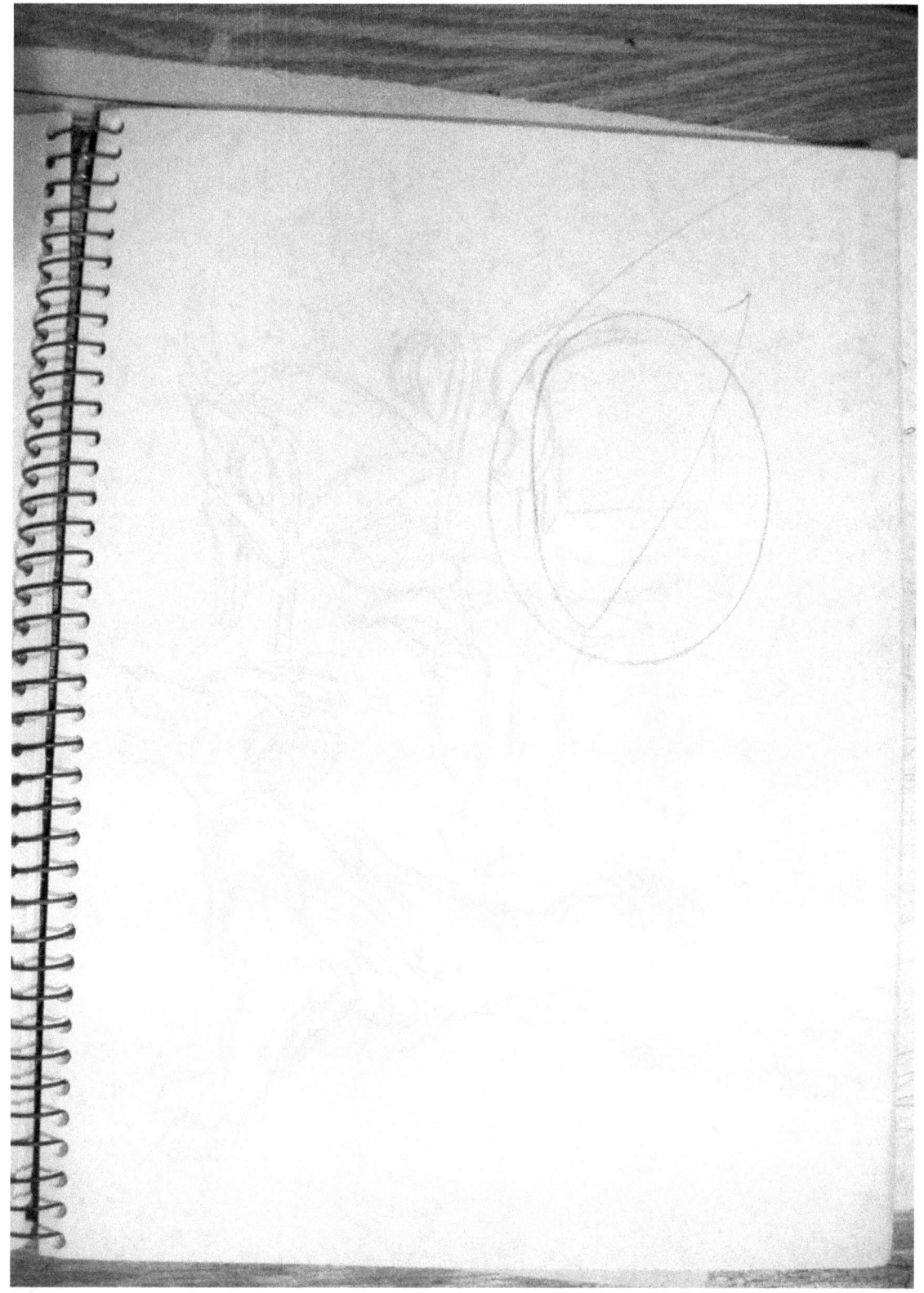

Gilles COLLETTE

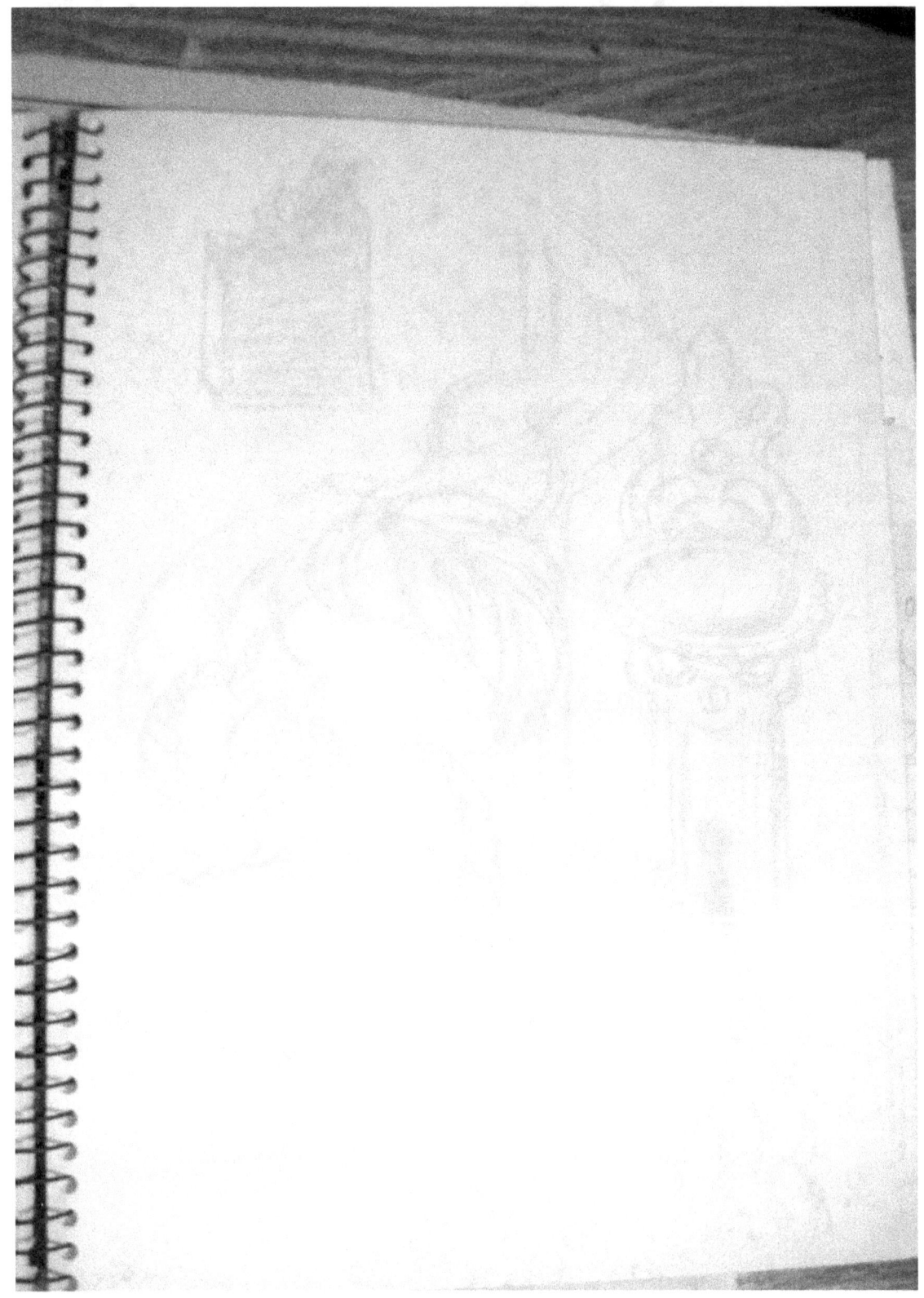

136

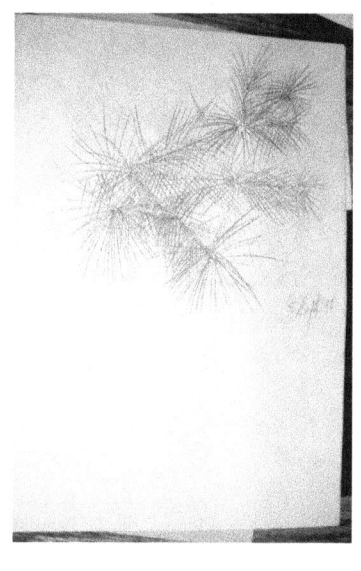
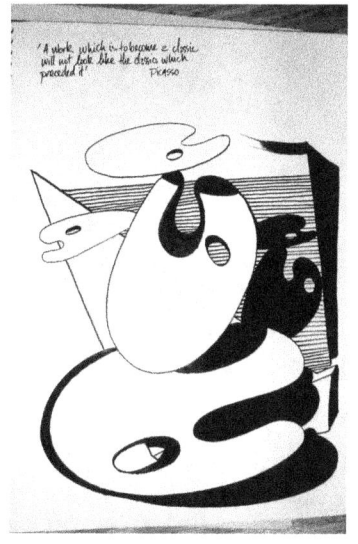
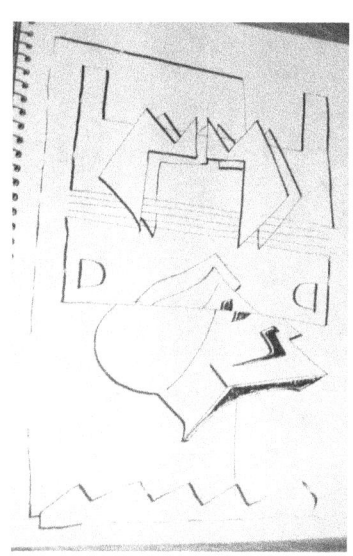
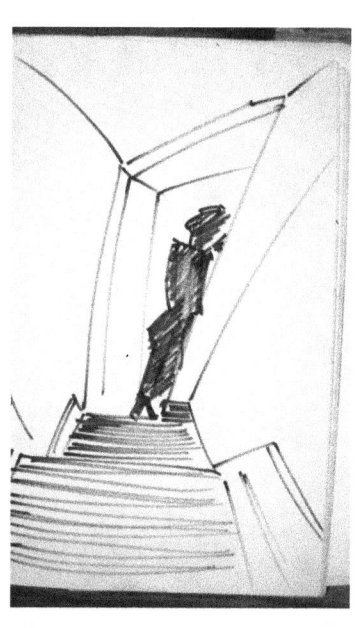
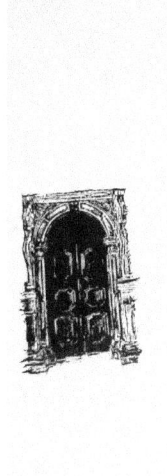
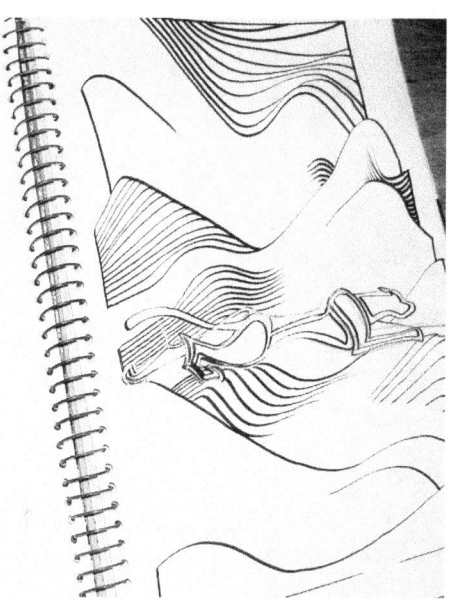

Gilles COLLETTE

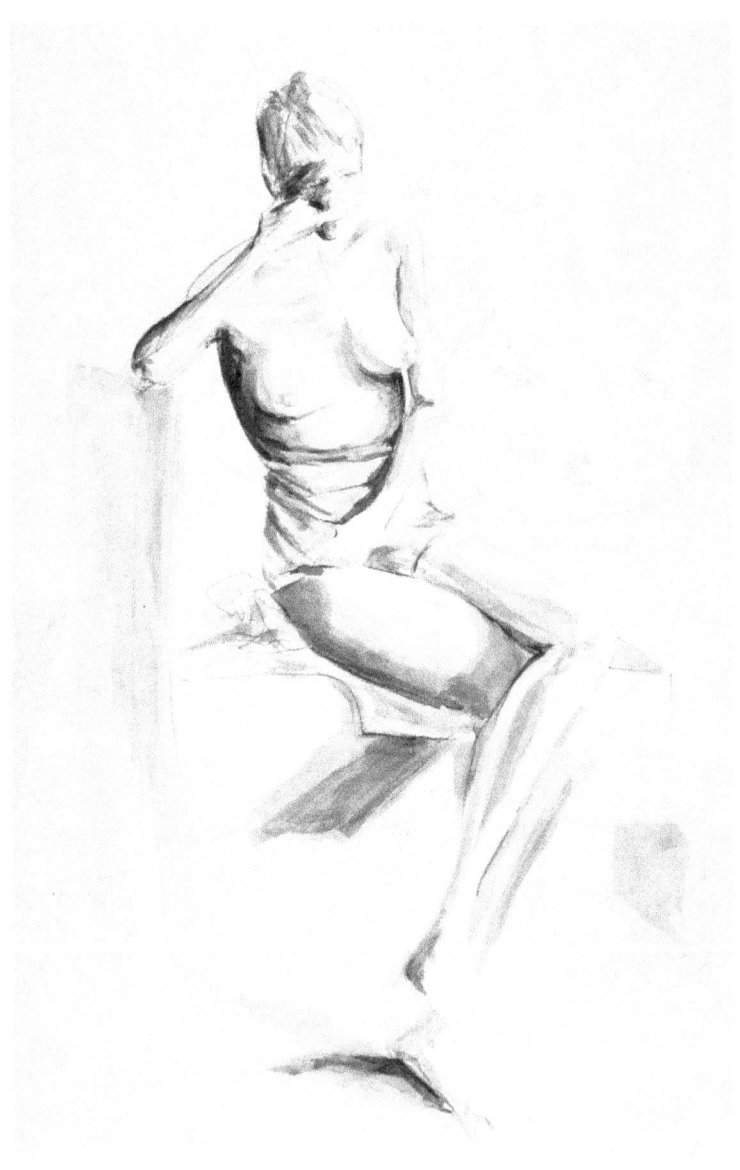

Notes and sketches

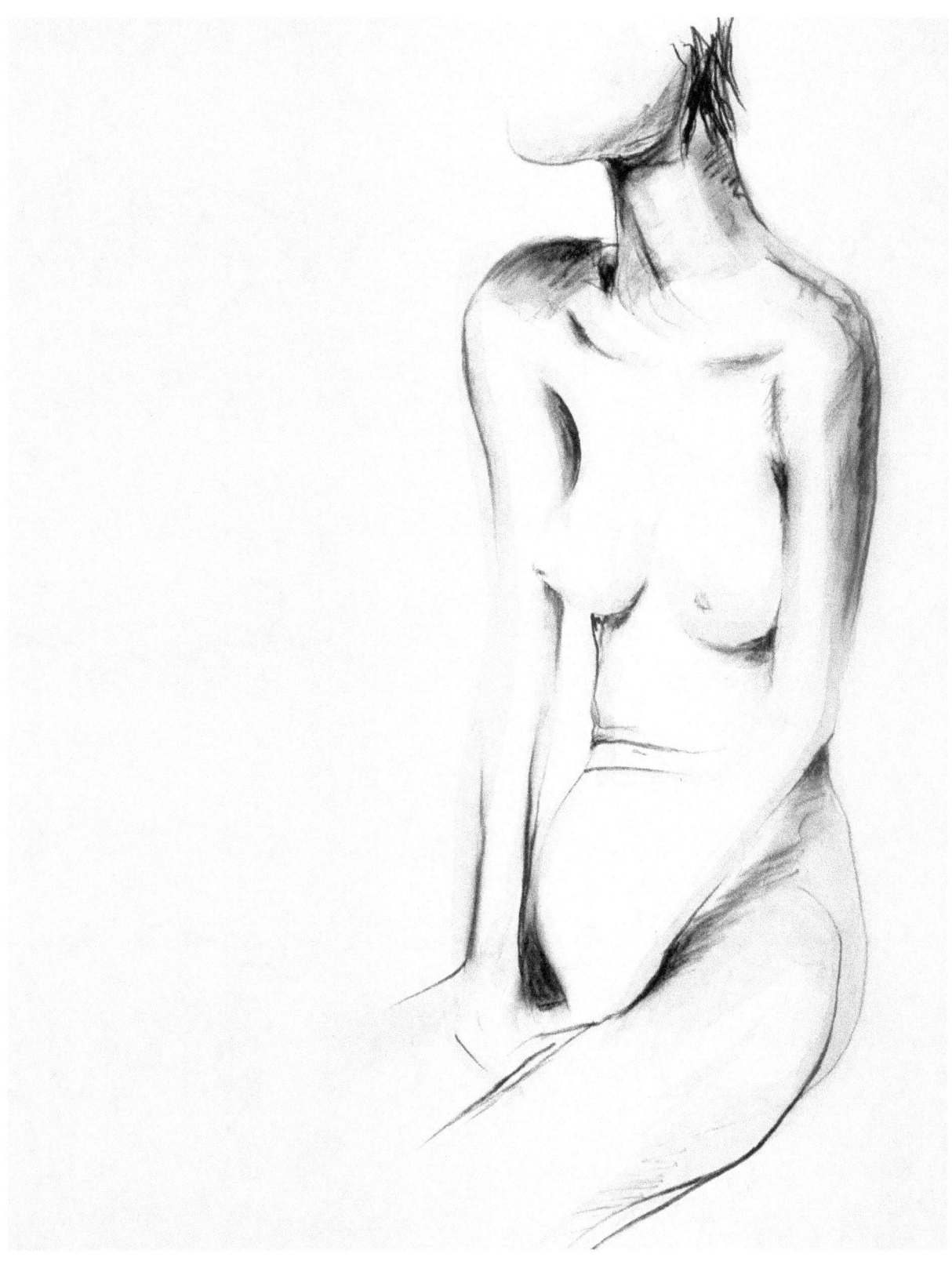

Gilles COLLETTE

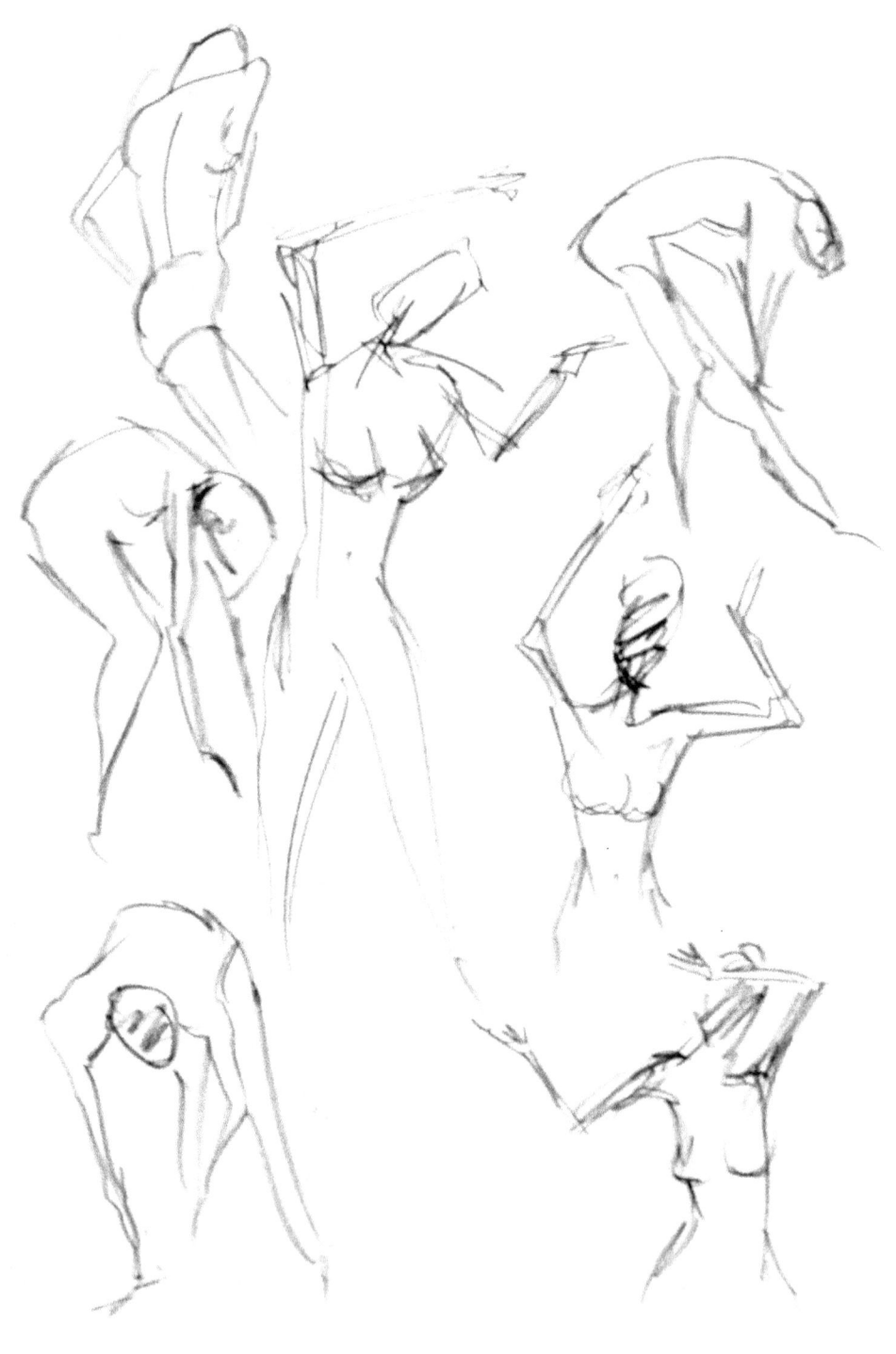

Notes and sketches

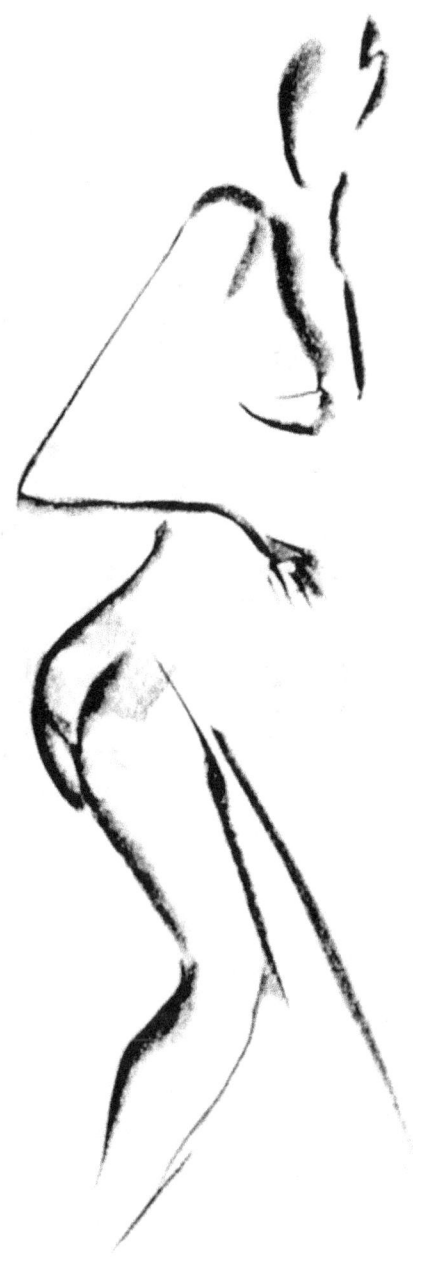

Gilles COLLETTE

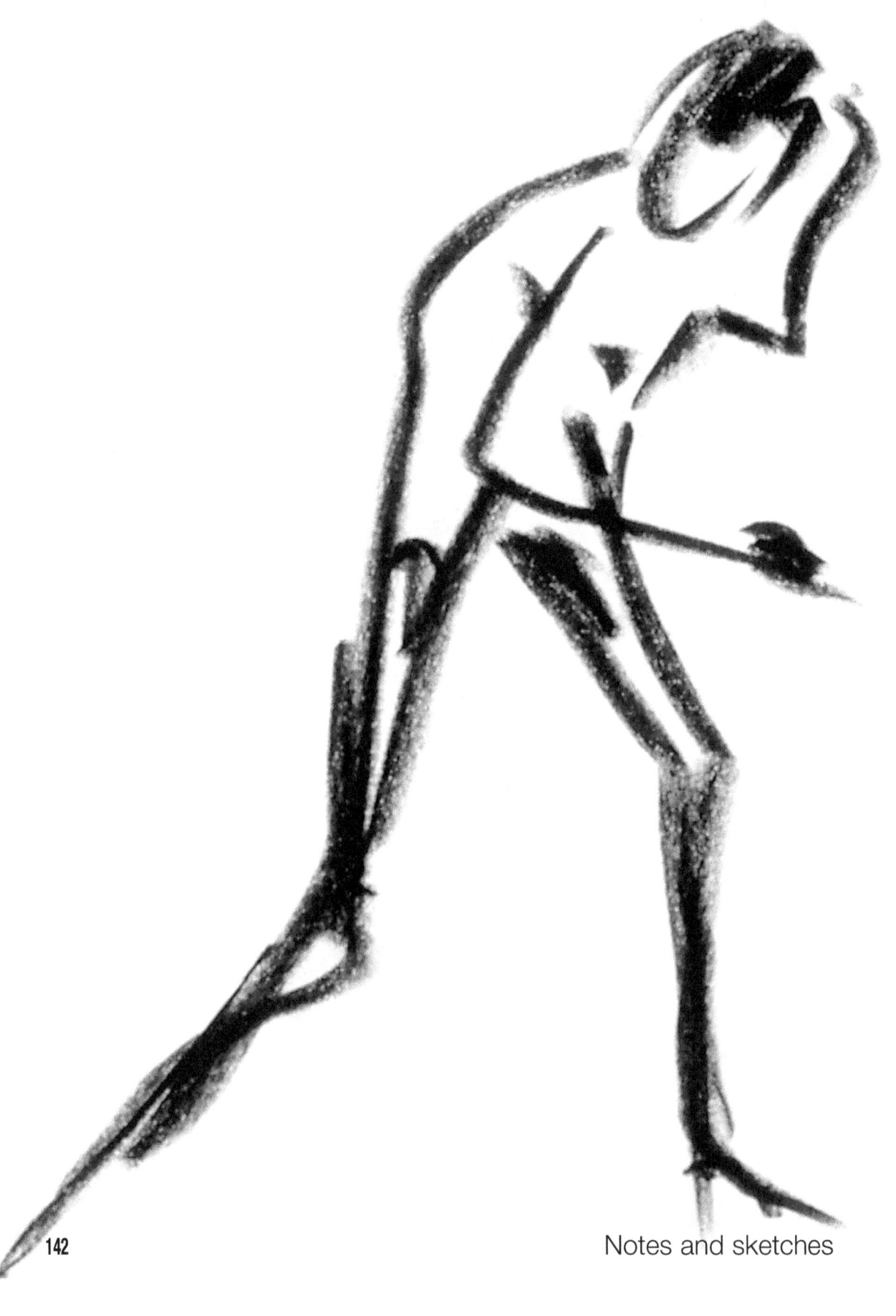

Notes and sketches

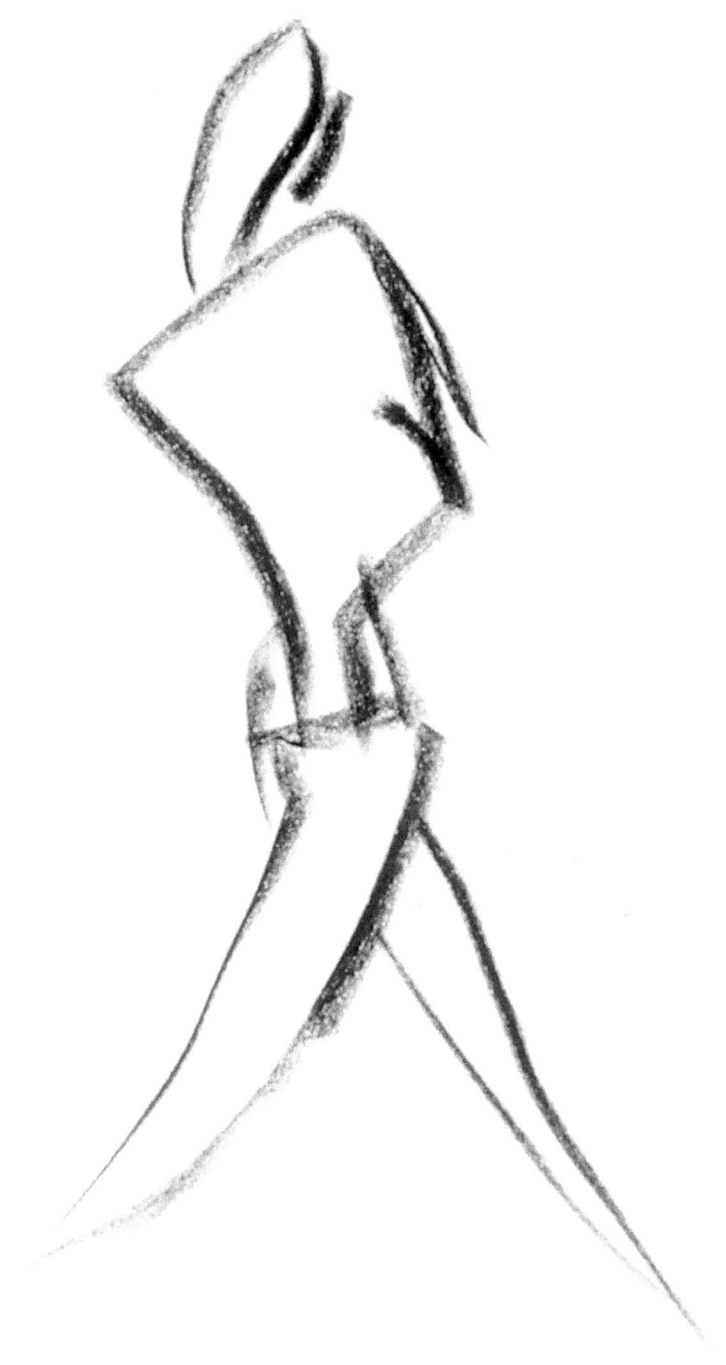

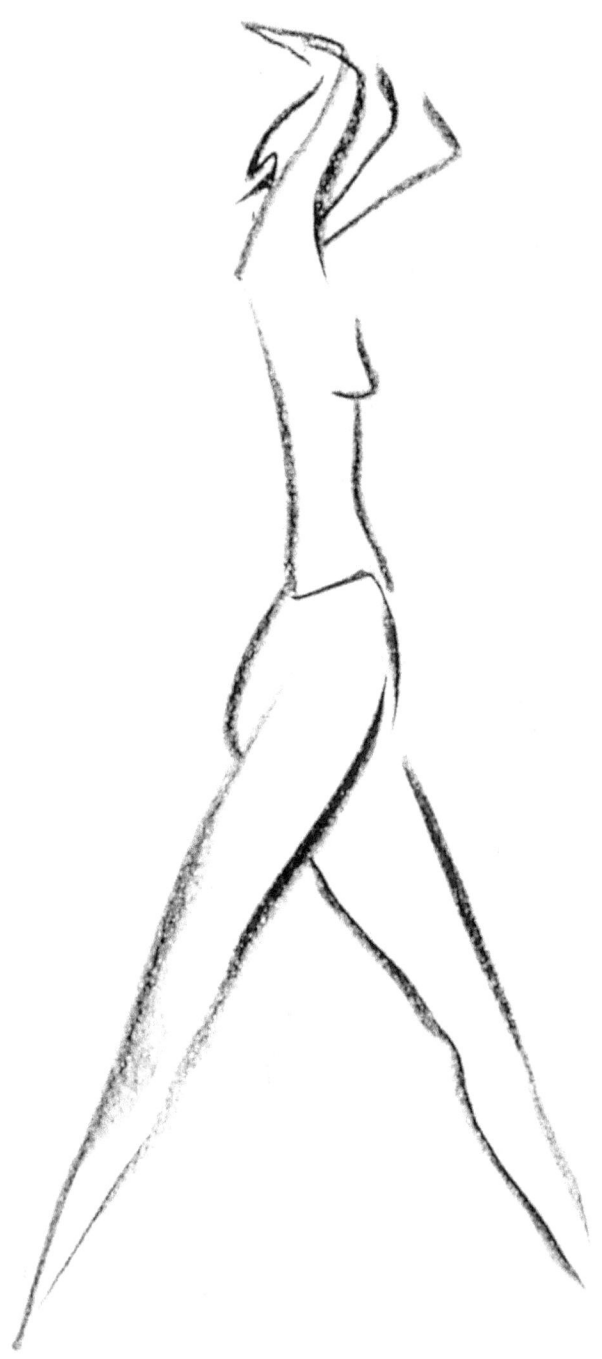

Notes and sketches

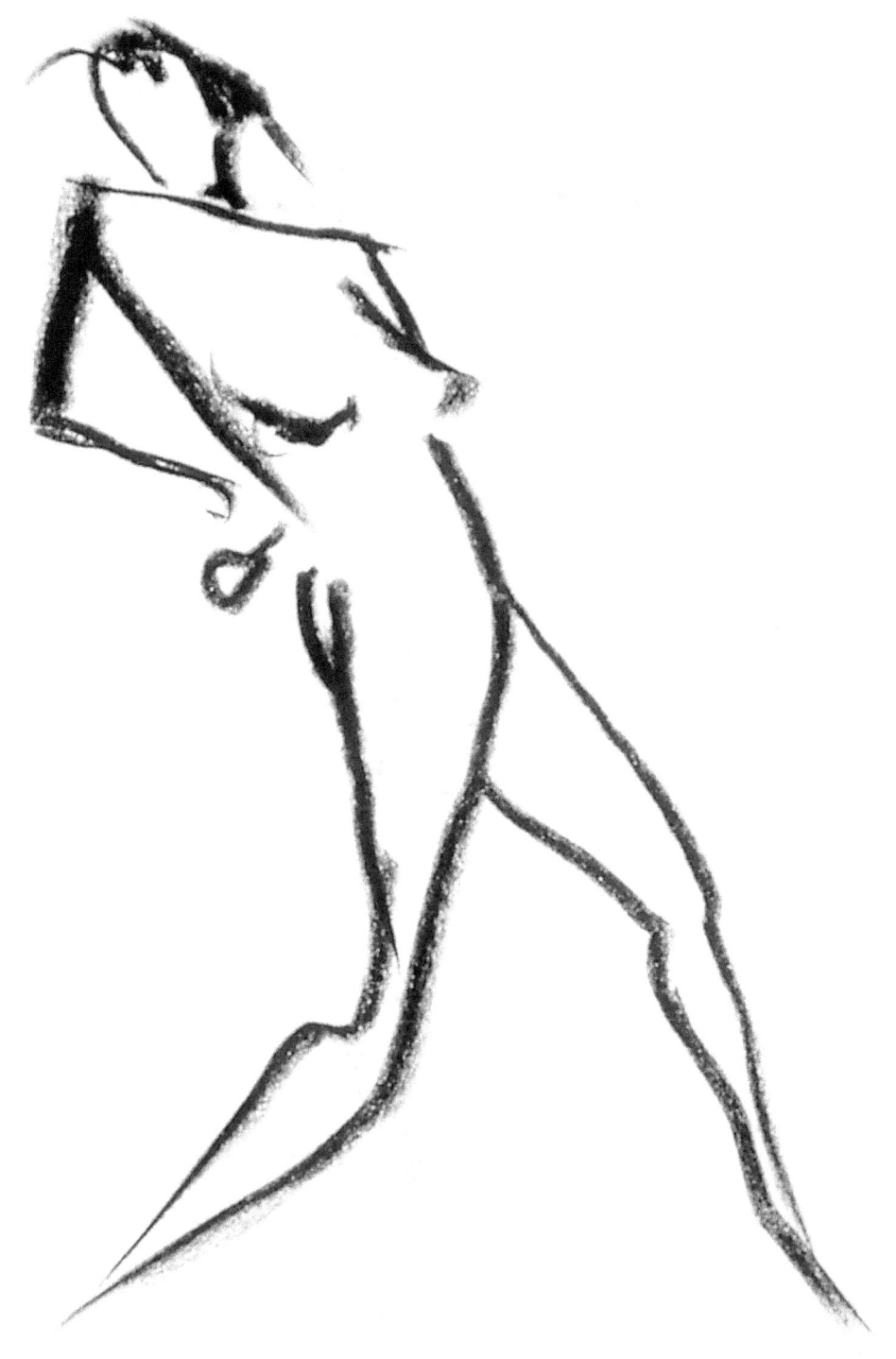

Gilles COLLETTE

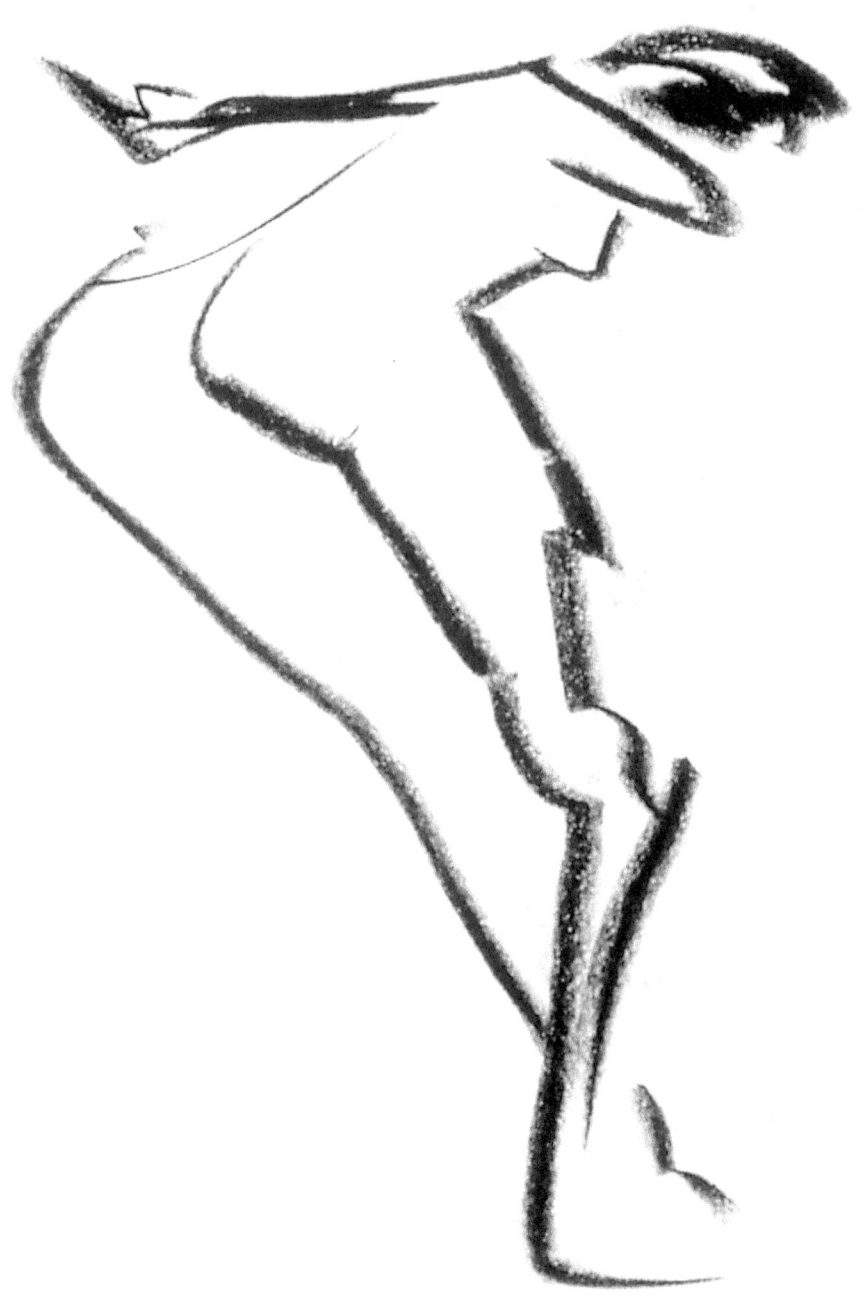

Notes and sketches

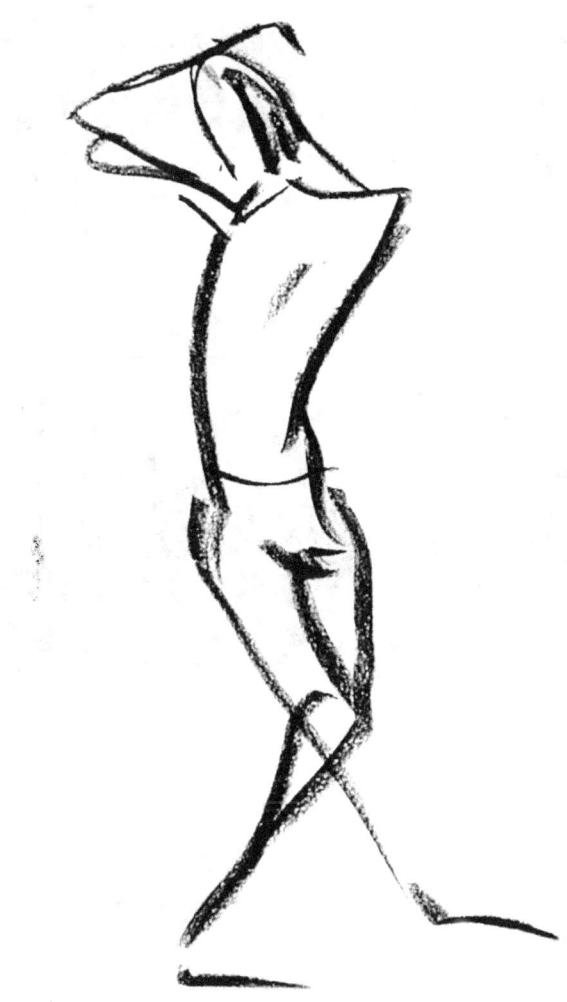

Gilles COLLETTE

147

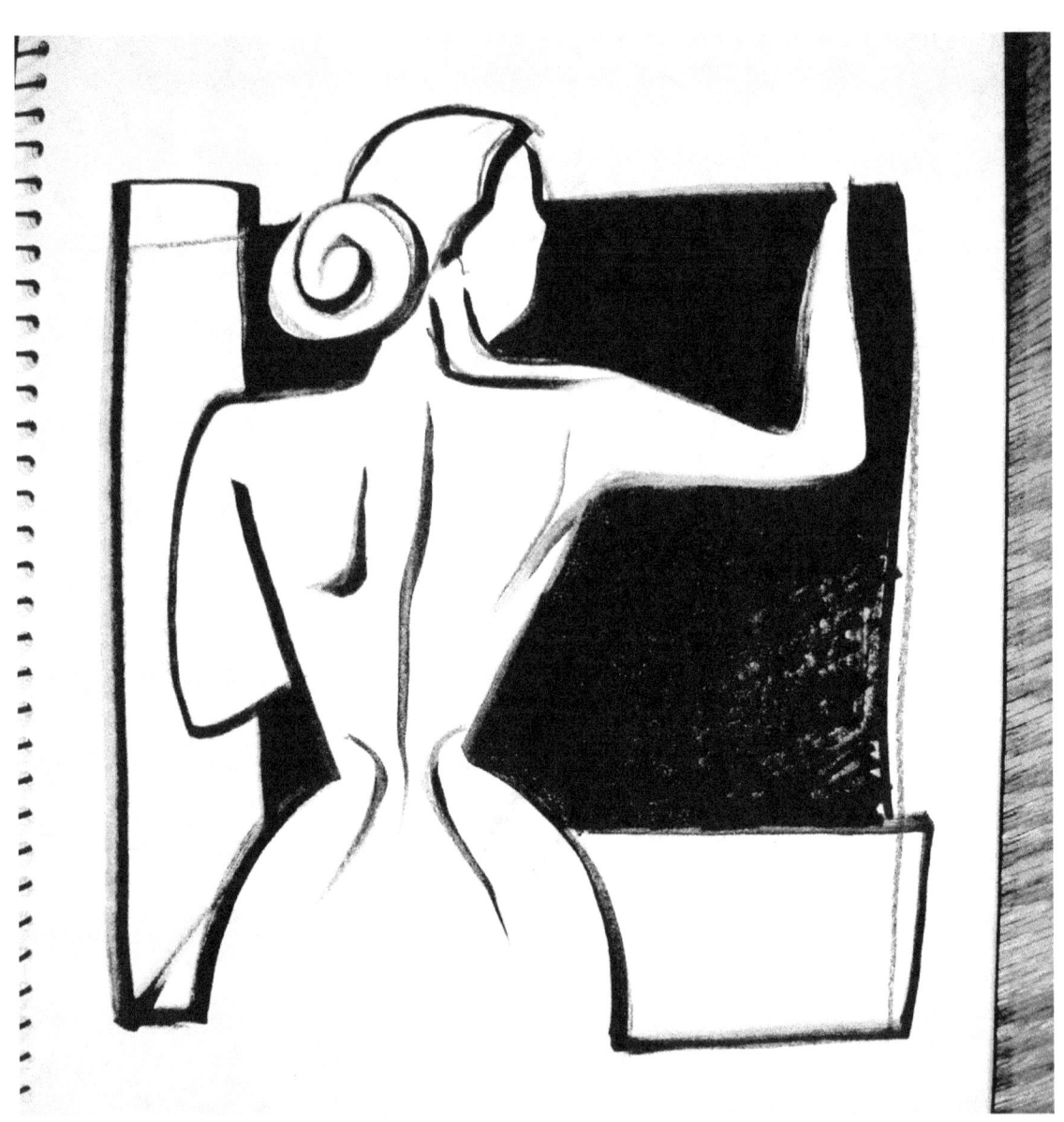

148

dolescent

rience
es.

lon
les.

hassions
calmes.

ts
es.

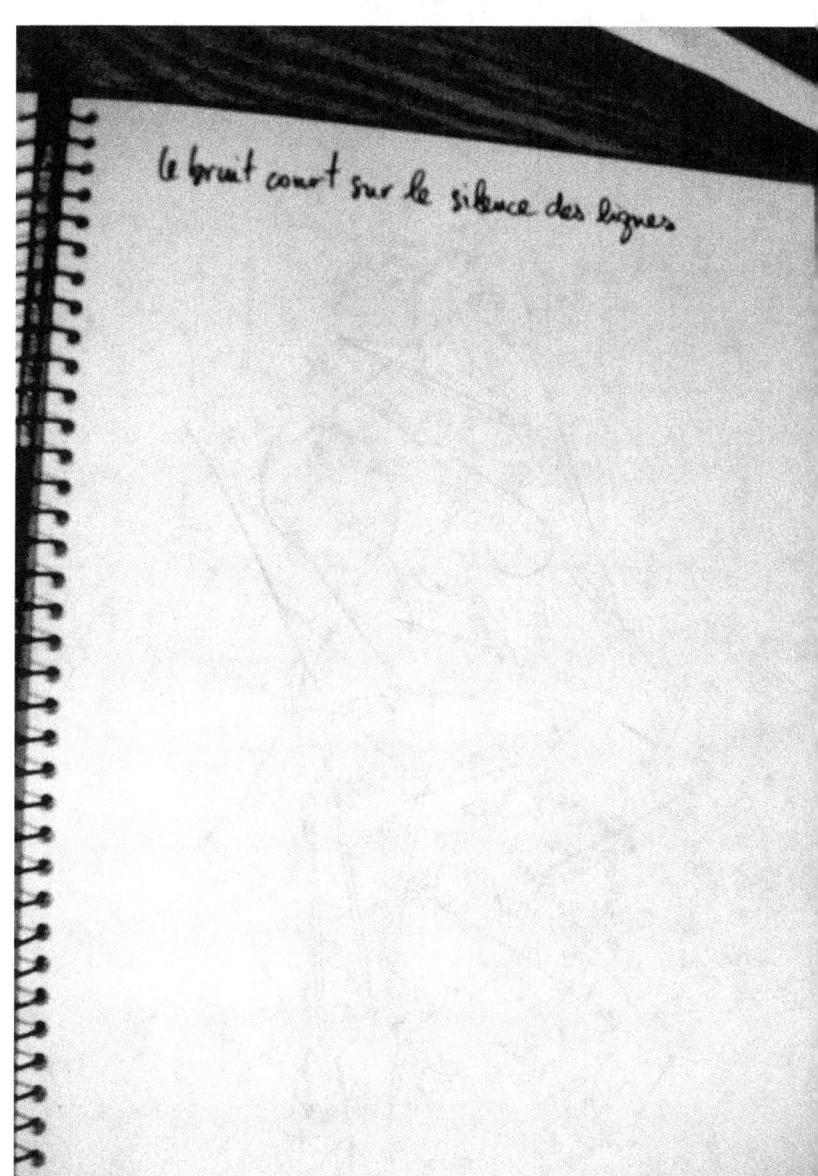

le bruit court sur le silence des lignes

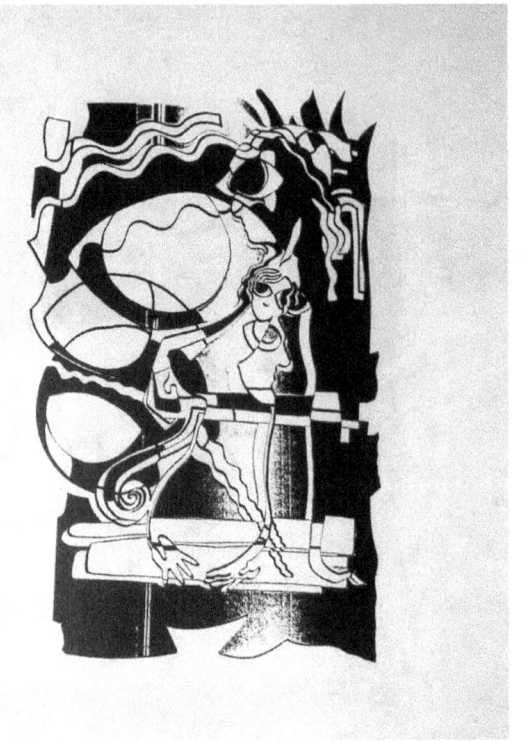

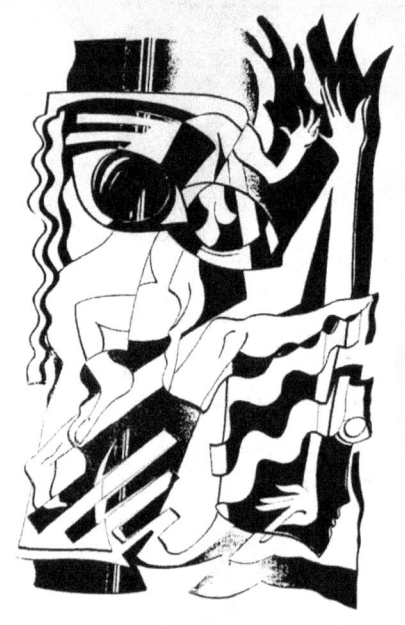

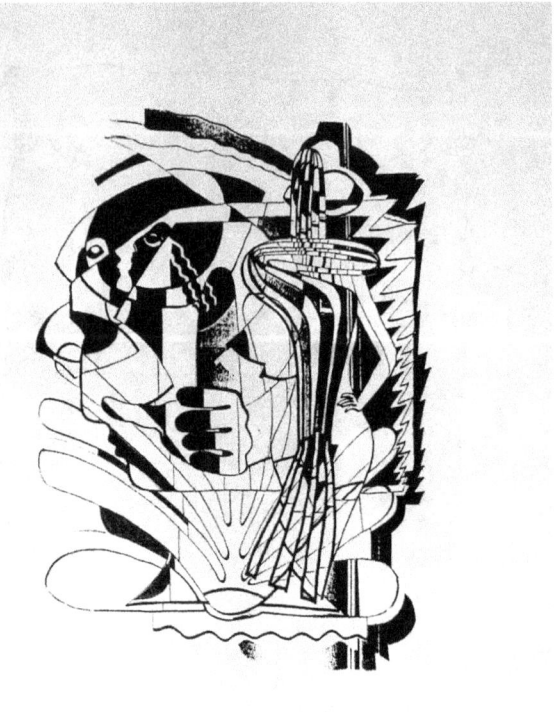

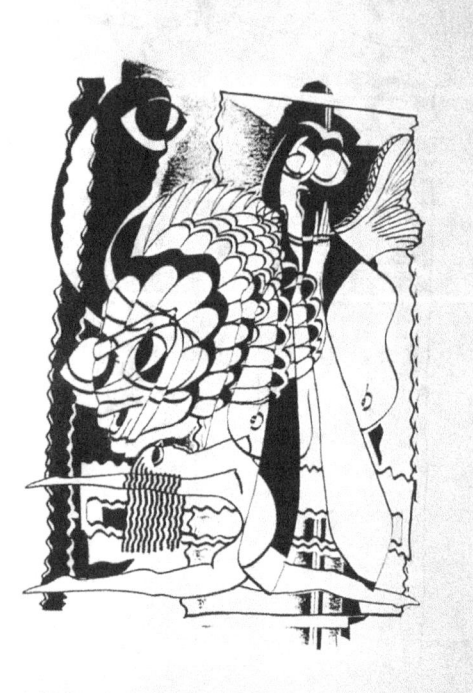

Notes and sketches

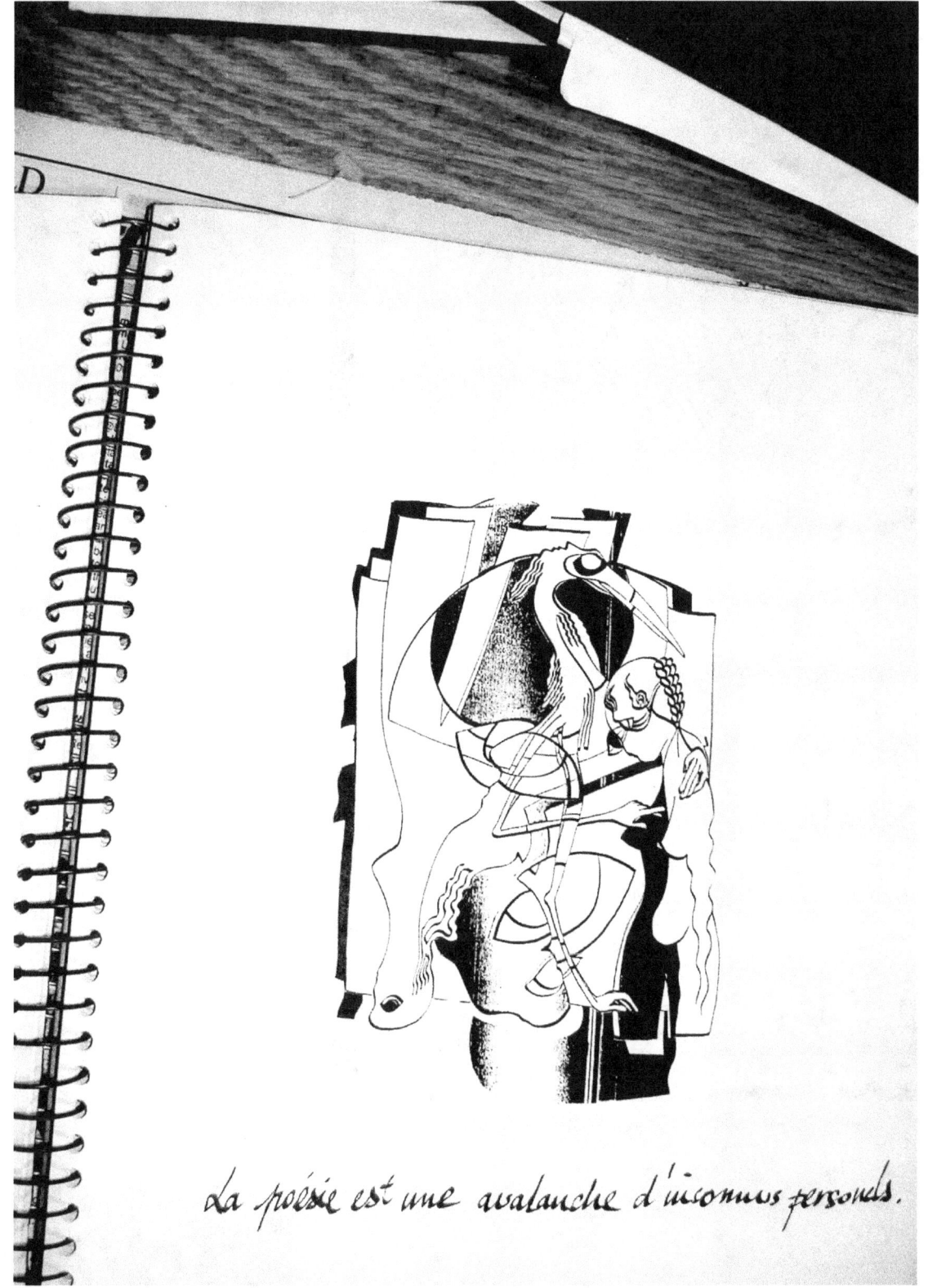

La poésie est une avalanche d'inconnus personds.

Gilles COLLETTE

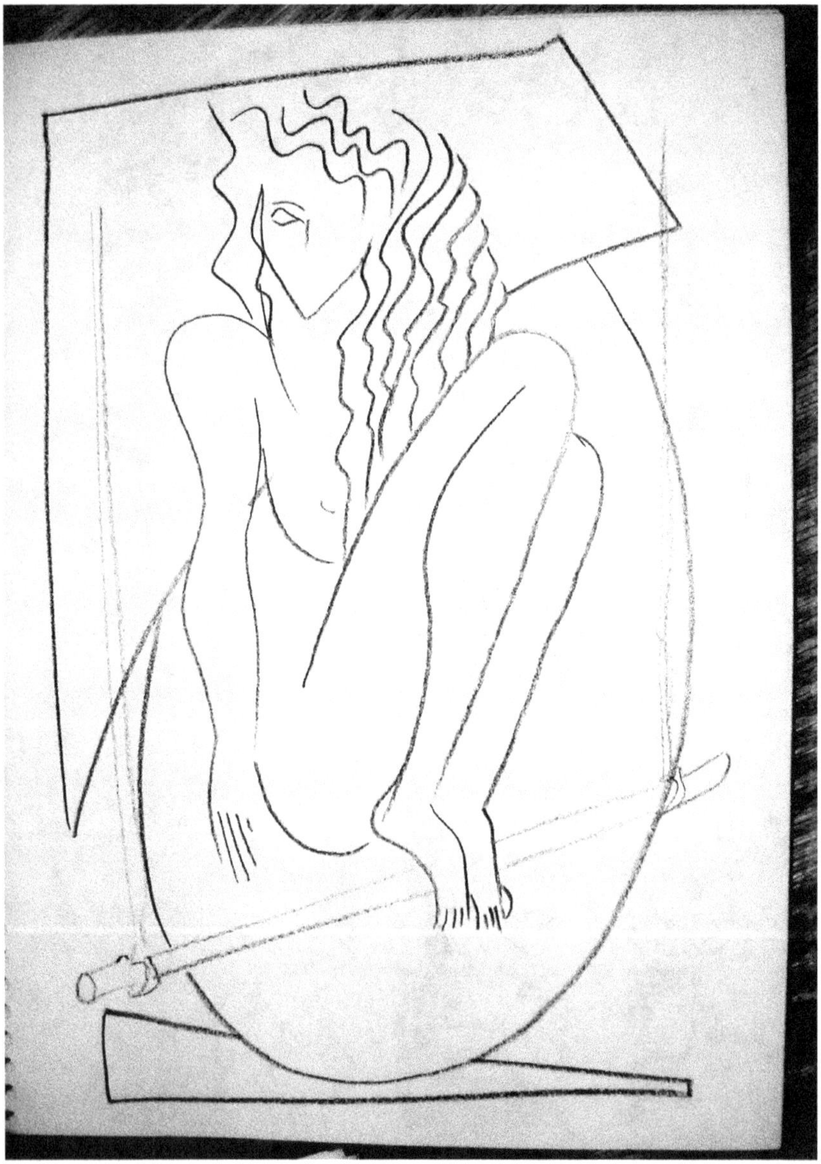

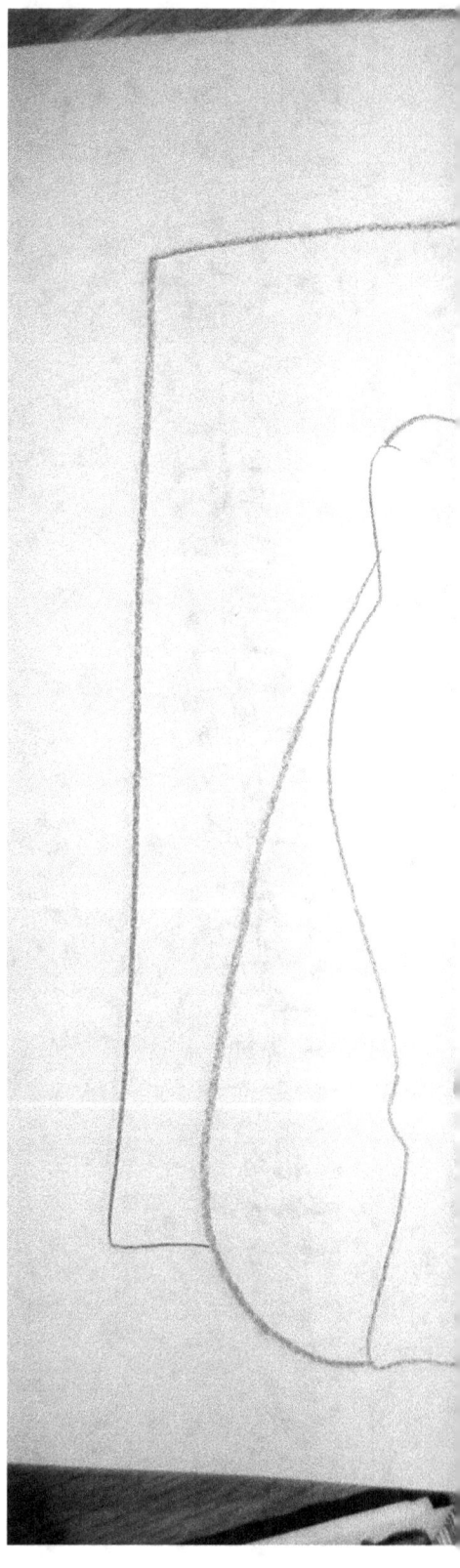

152

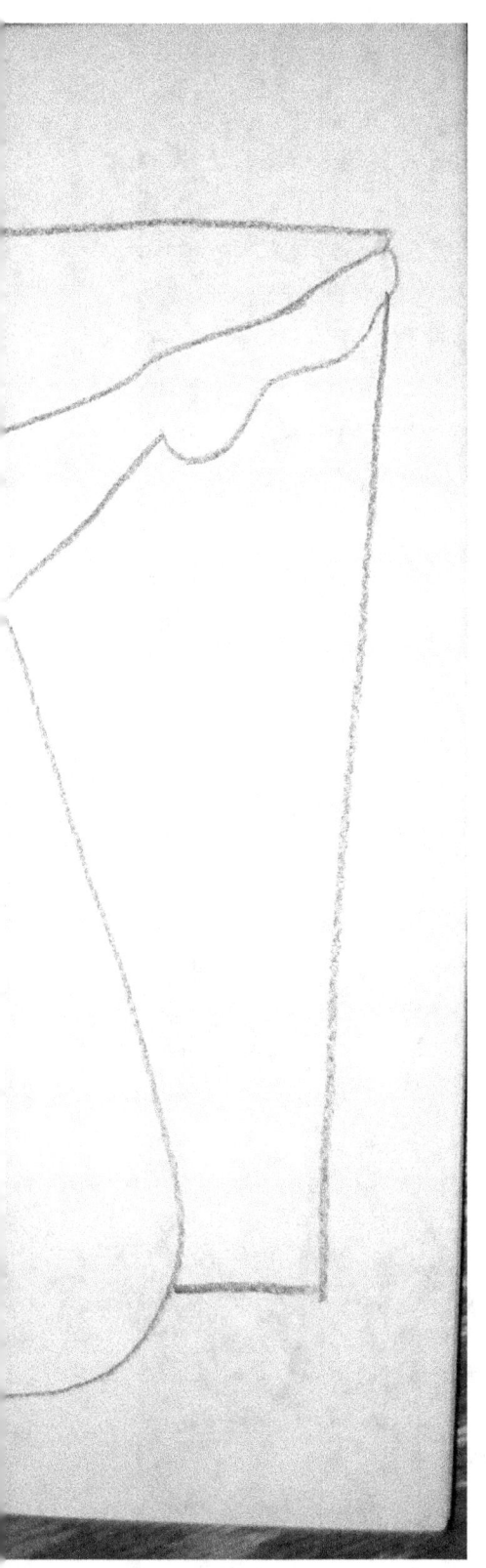

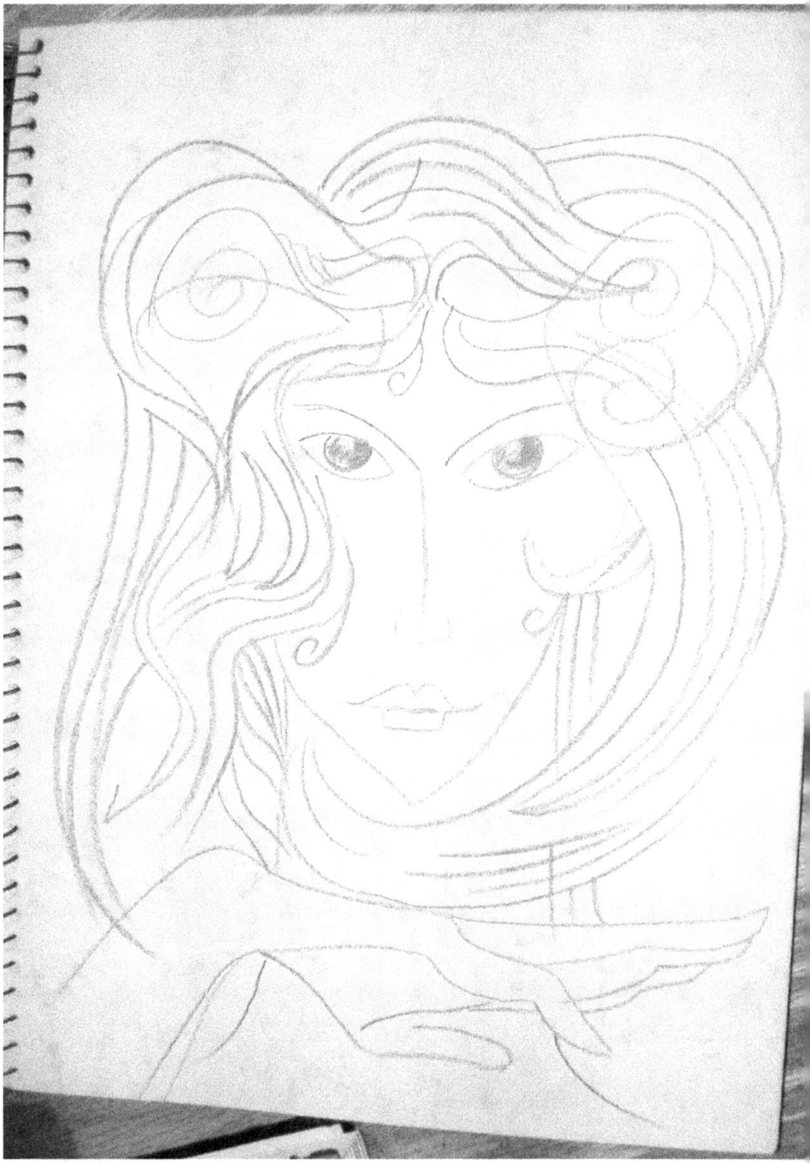

Gilles COLLETTE

153

NEWS
Stimuli of your shaking legs
you thrive on circumstances

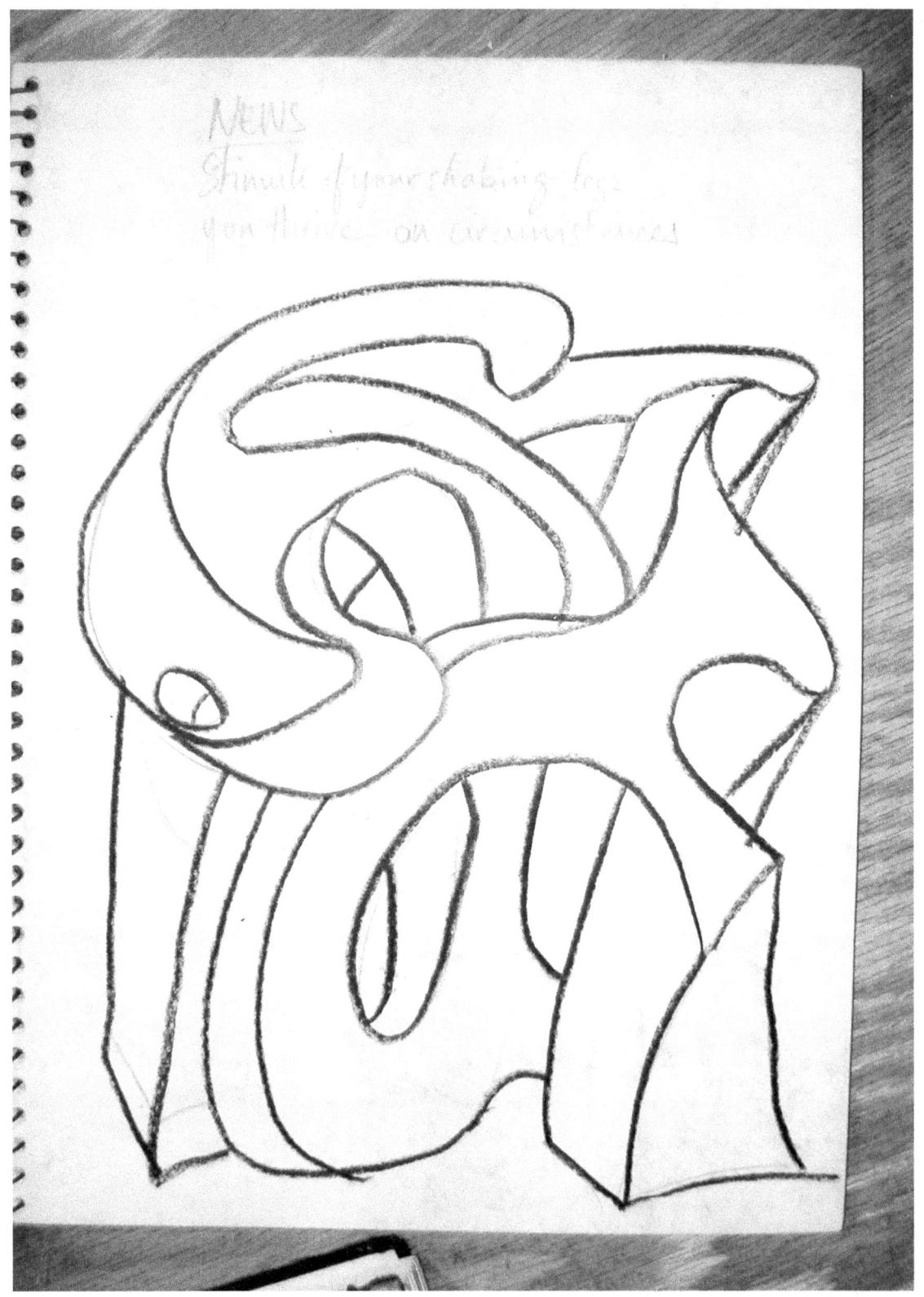

Notes and sketches

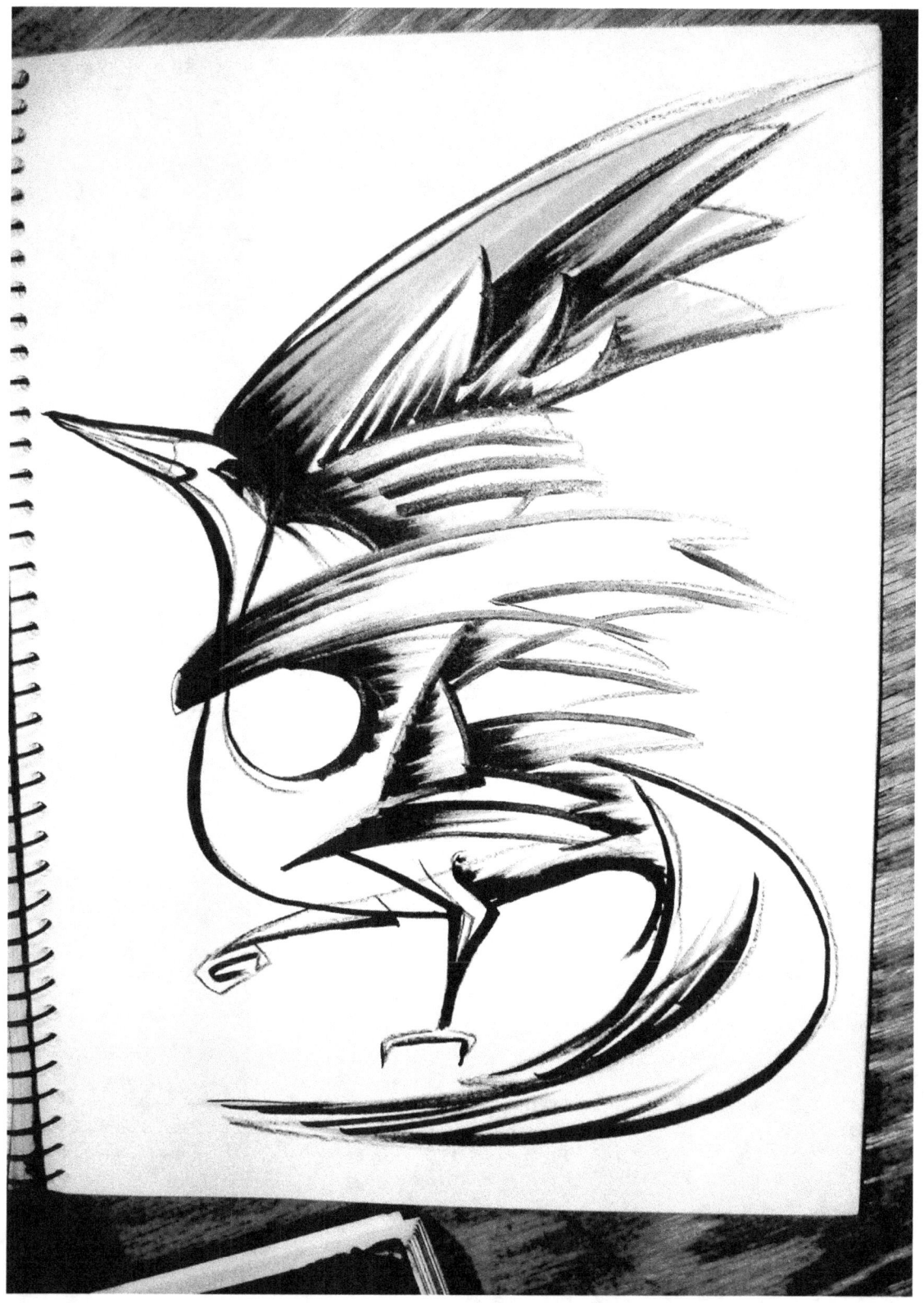

Gilles COLLETTE

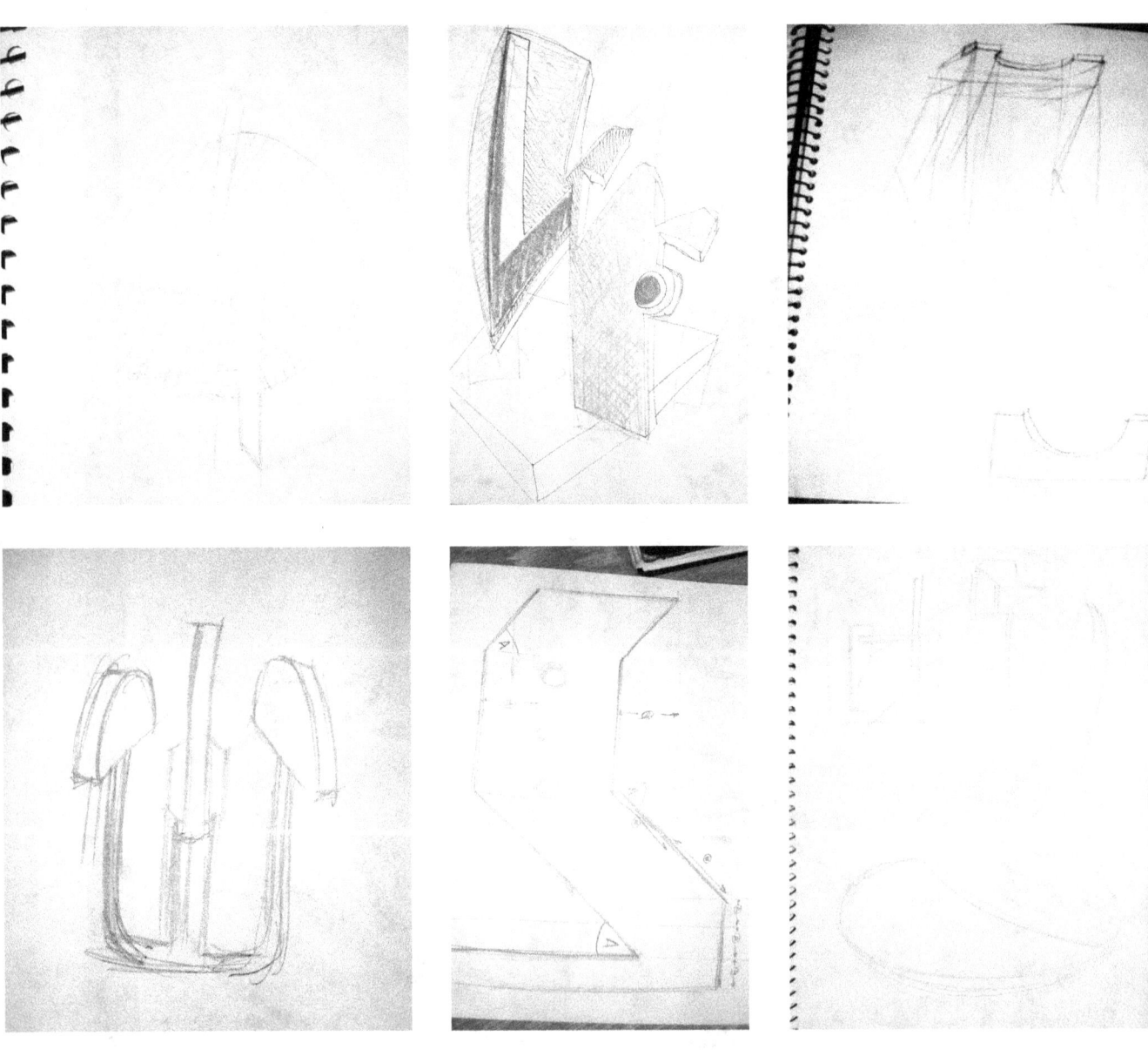

Notes and sketches

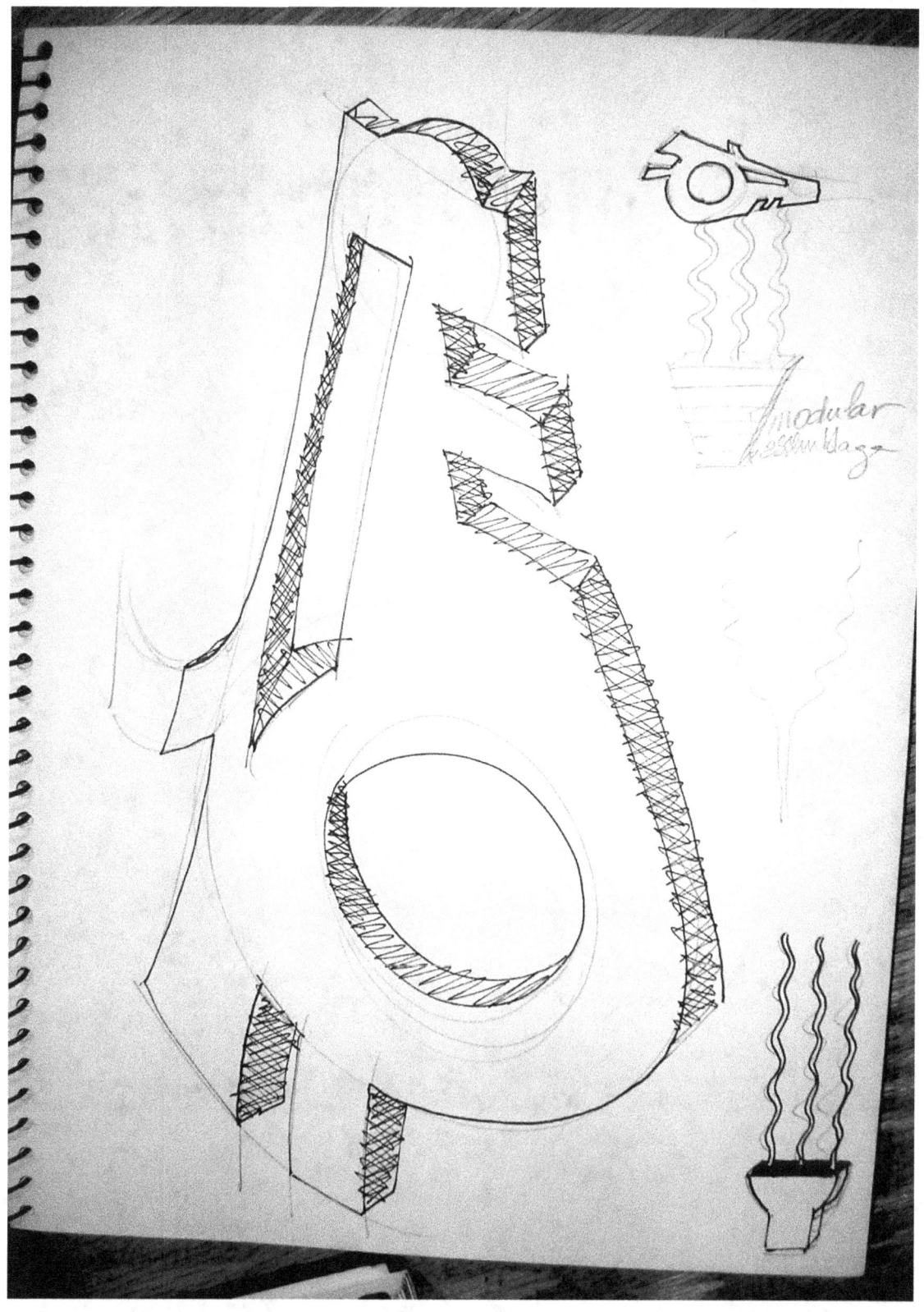

modular
assemblage

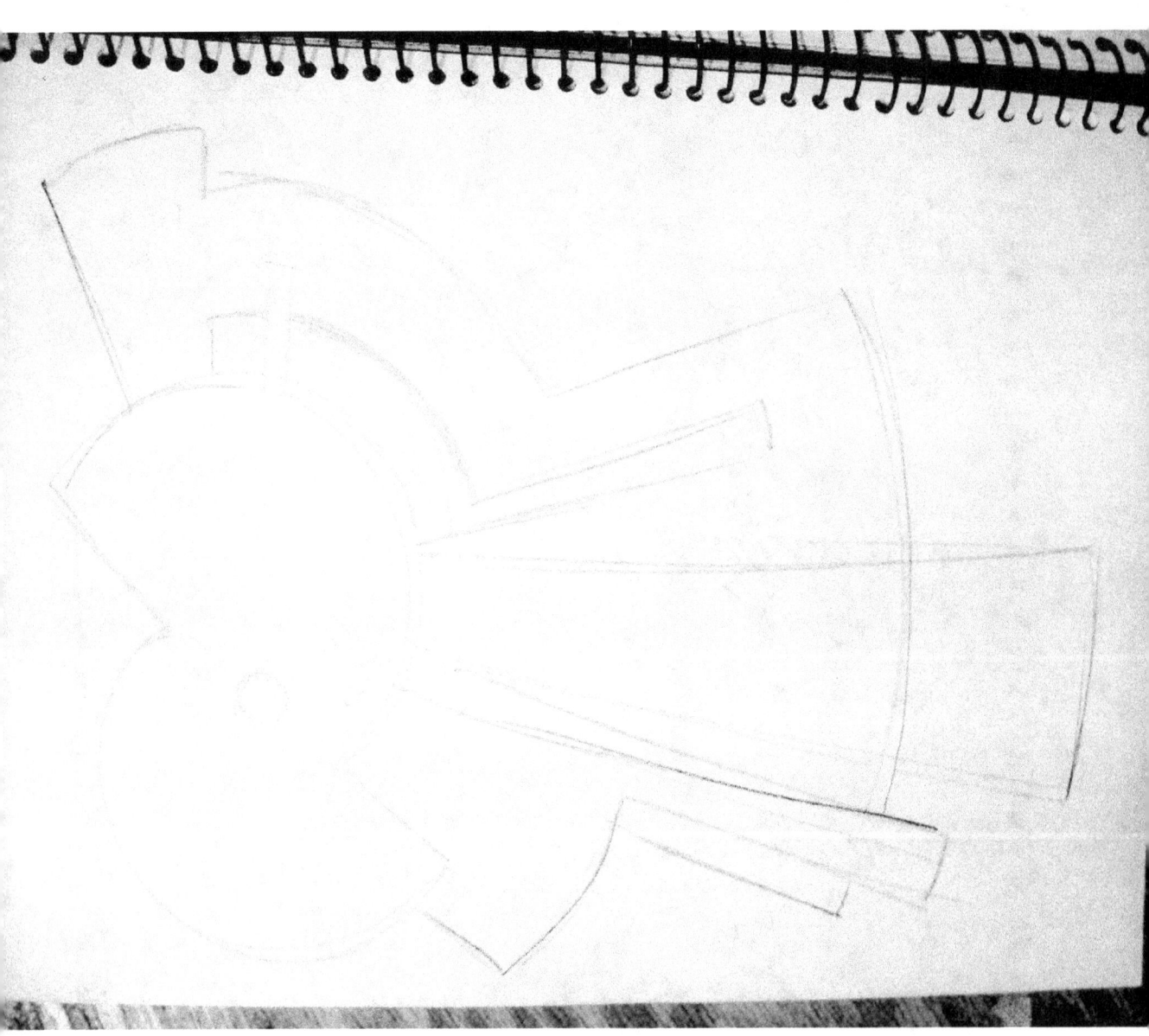

Notes and sketches

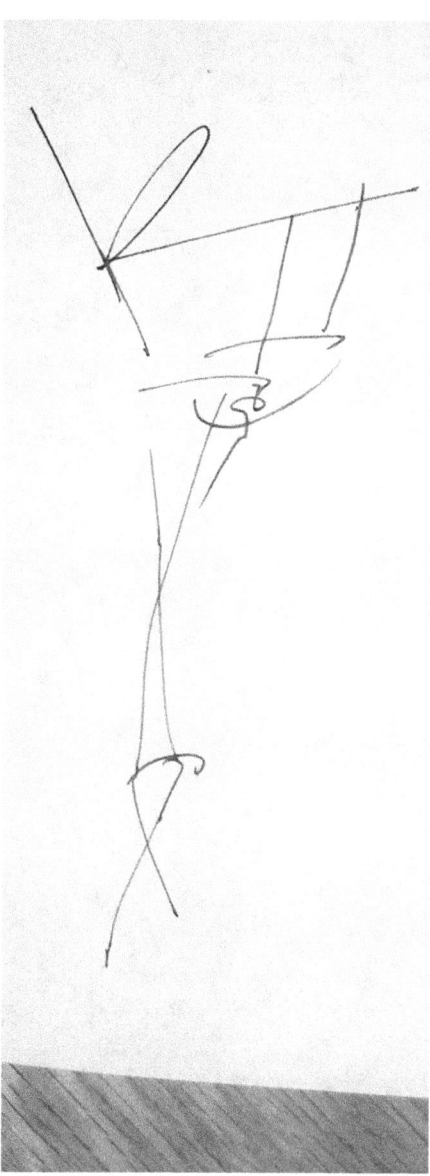
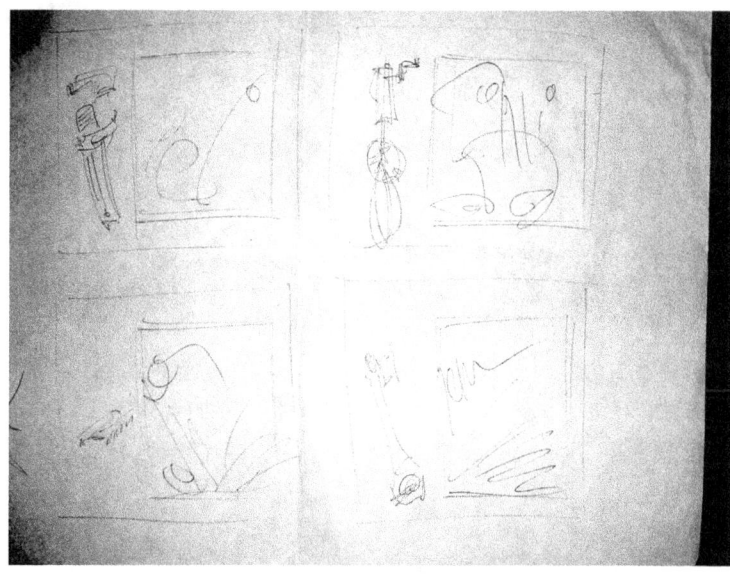

Gilles COLLETTE

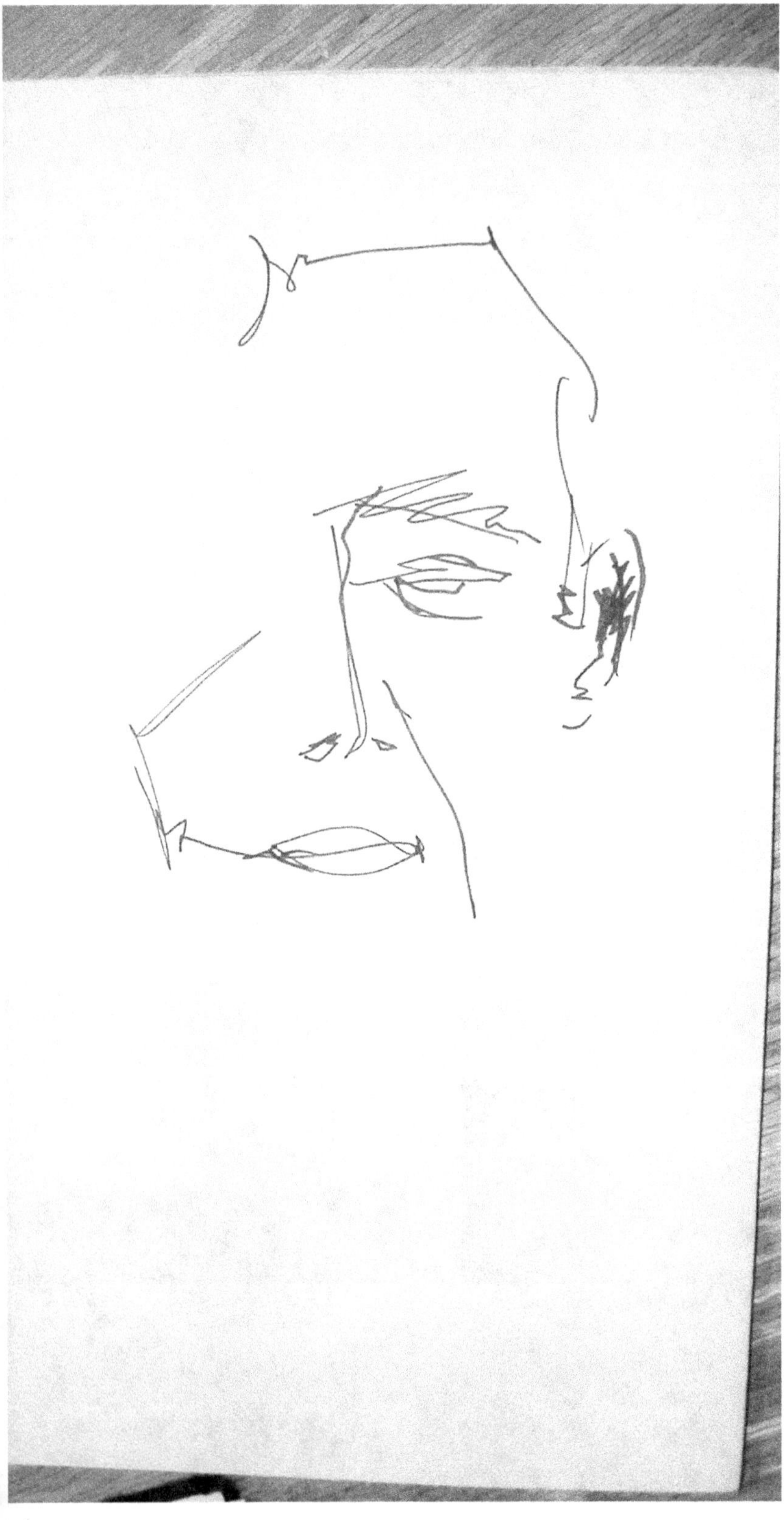

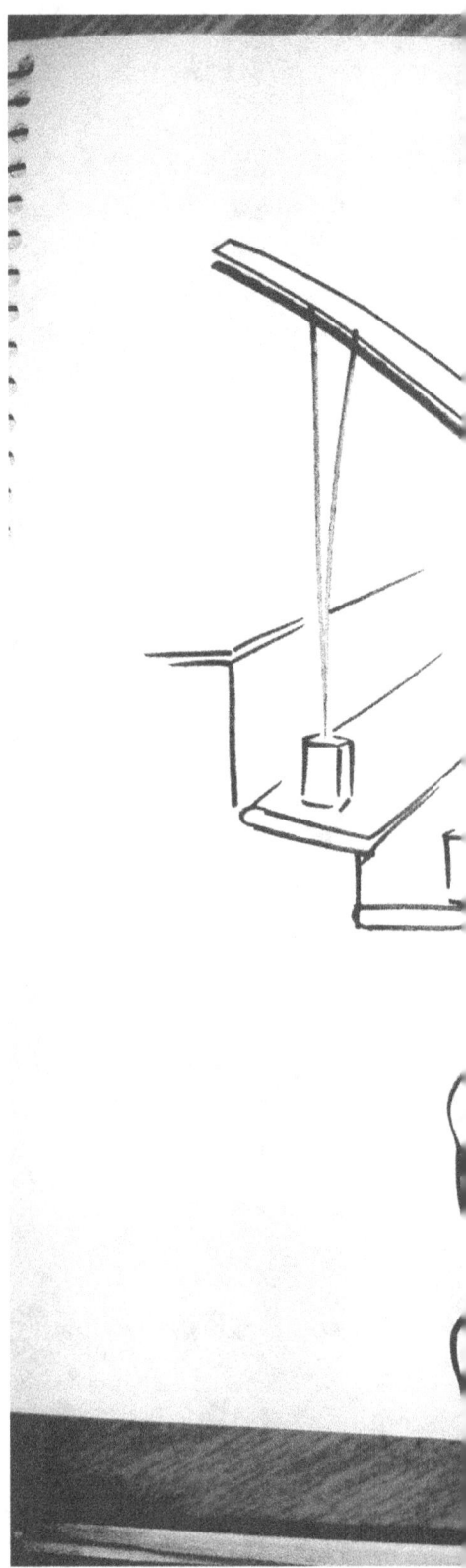

Notes and sketches

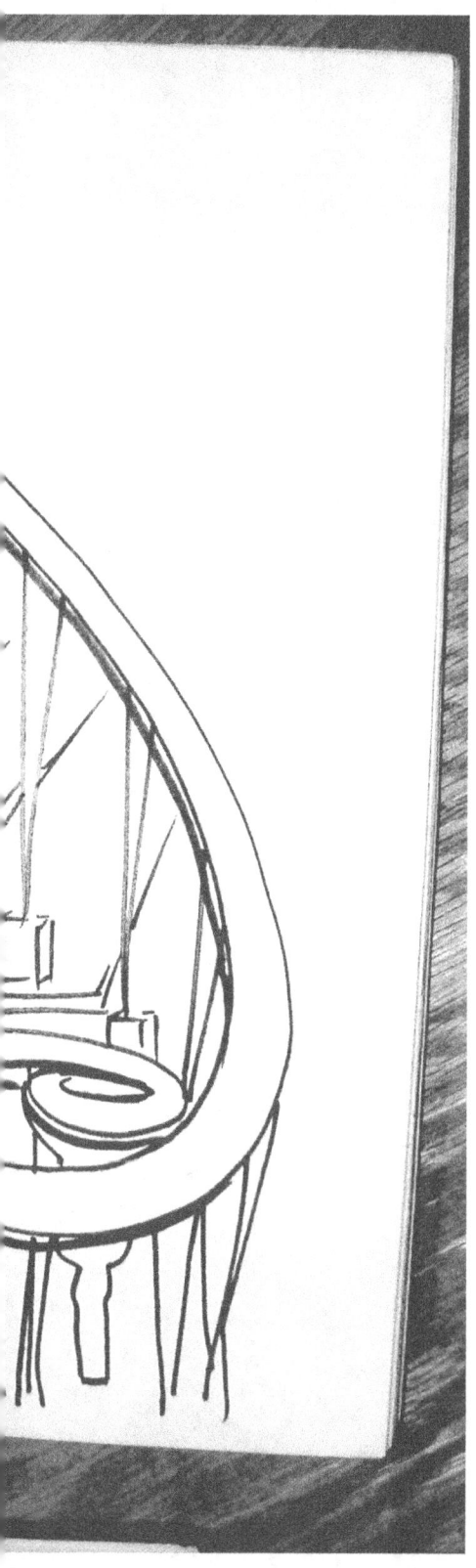

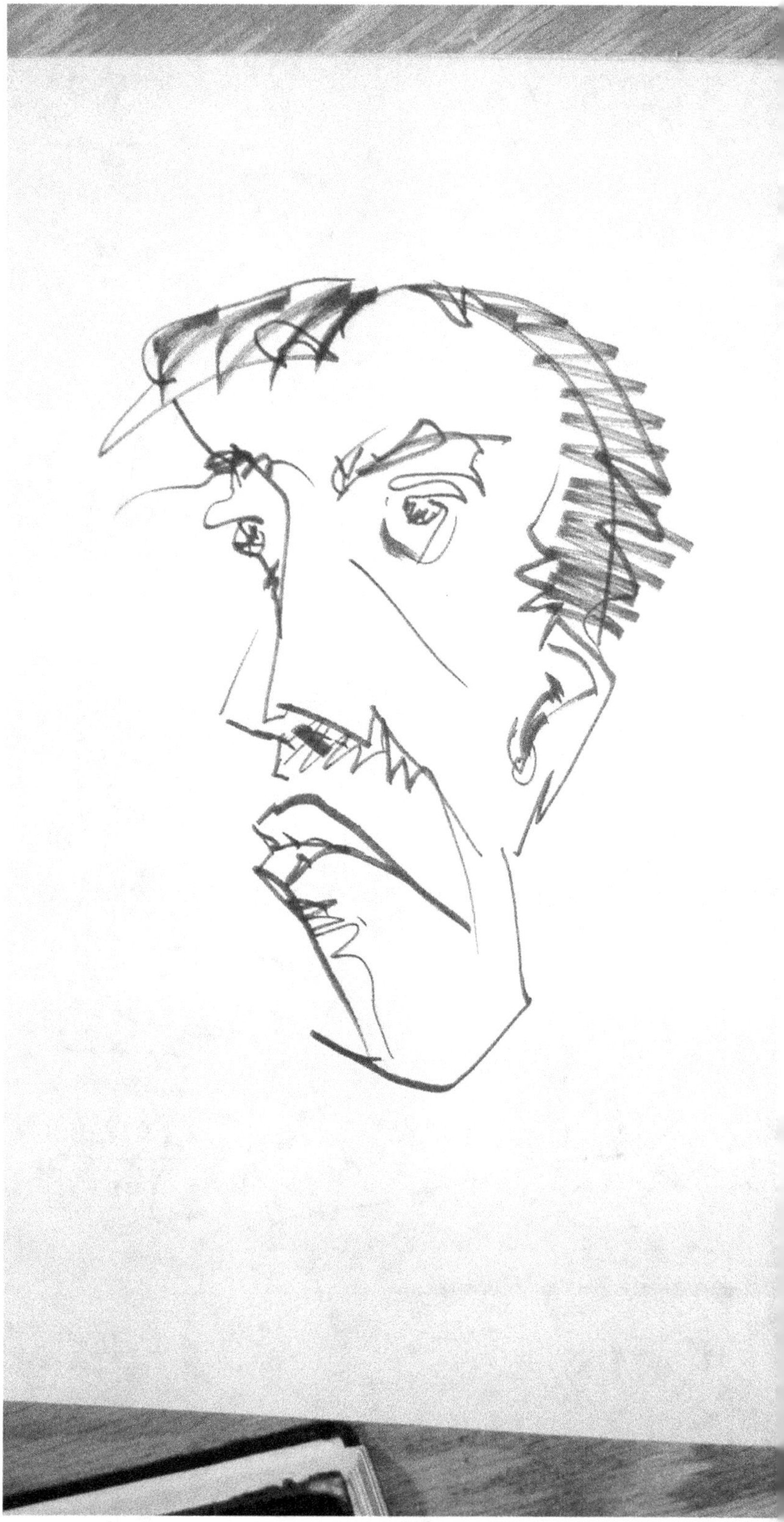

Gilles COLLETTE

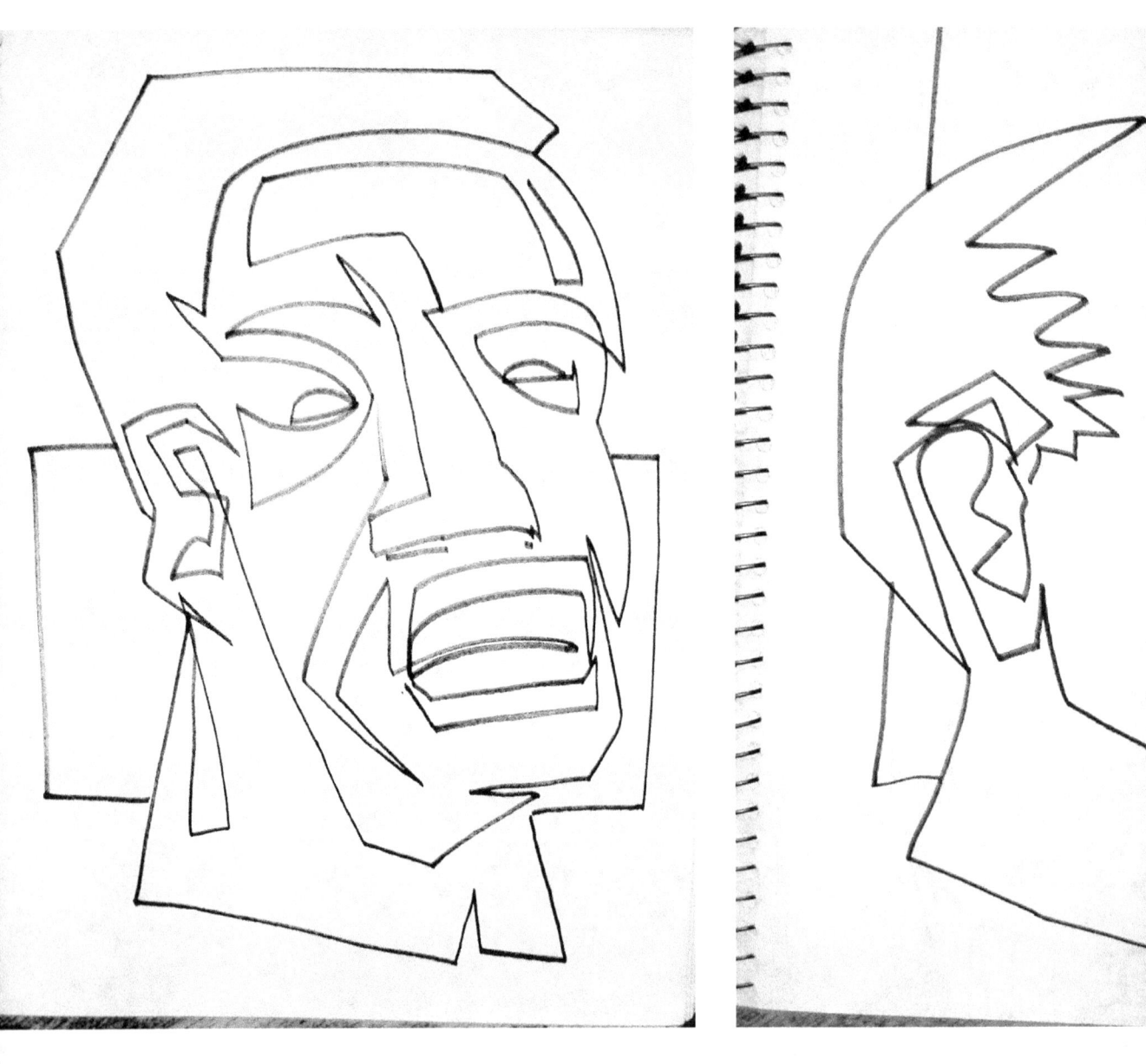

Notes and sketches

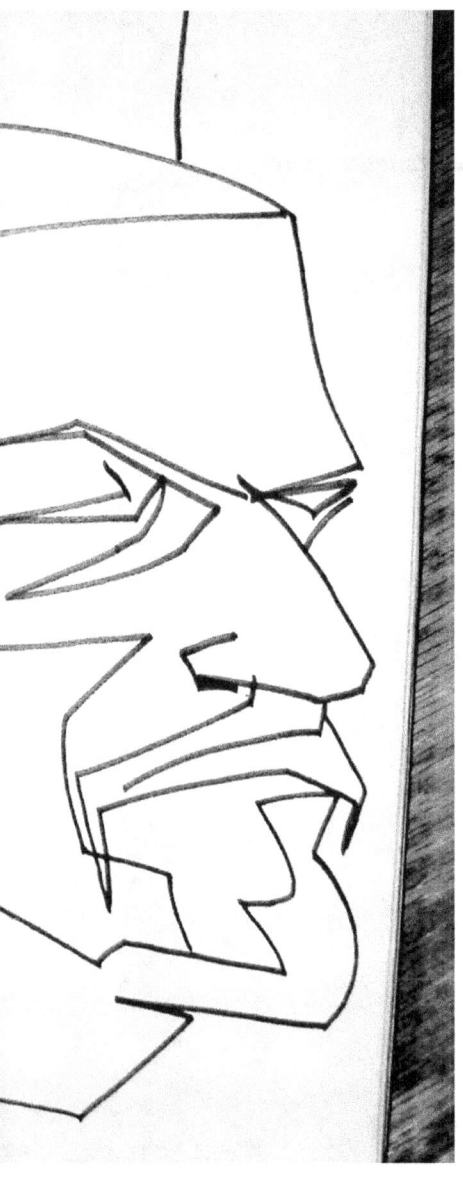

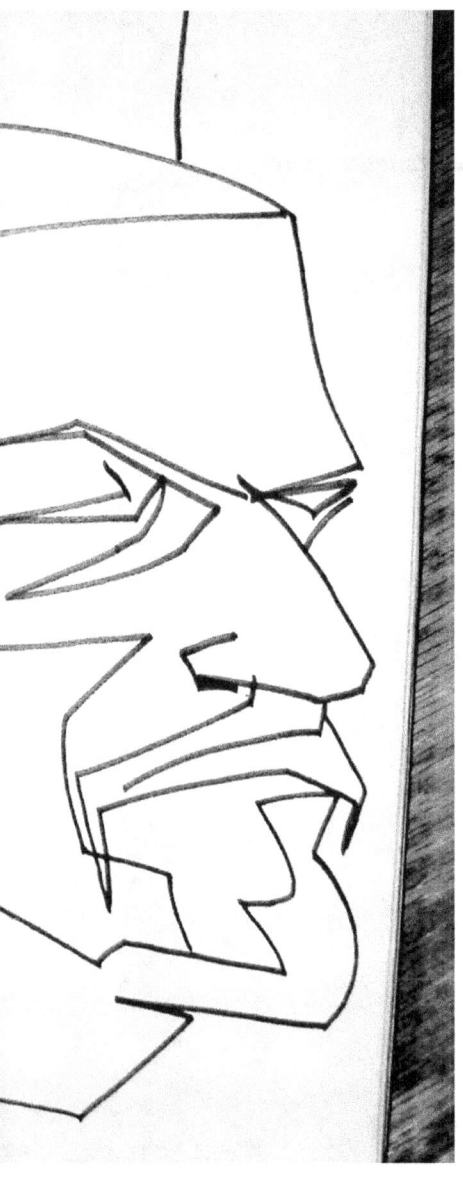

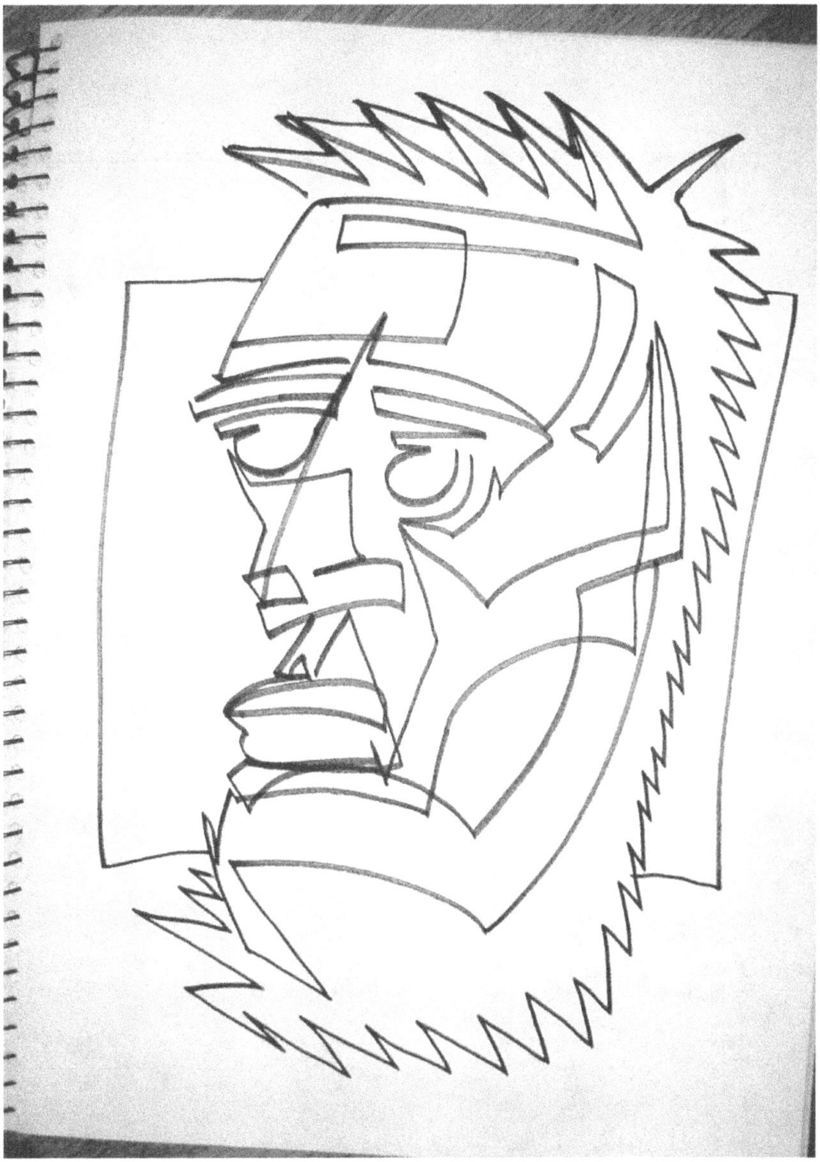

Gilles COLLETTE

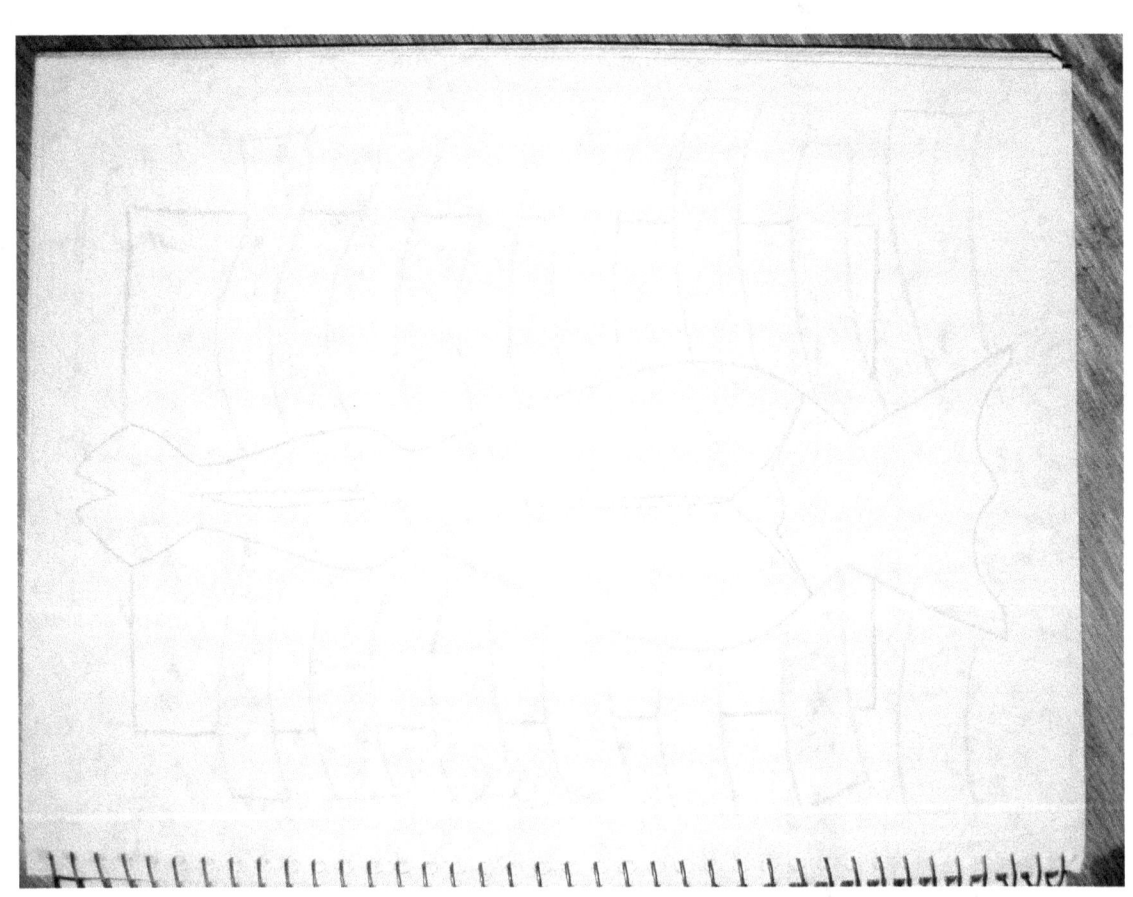

Notes and sketches

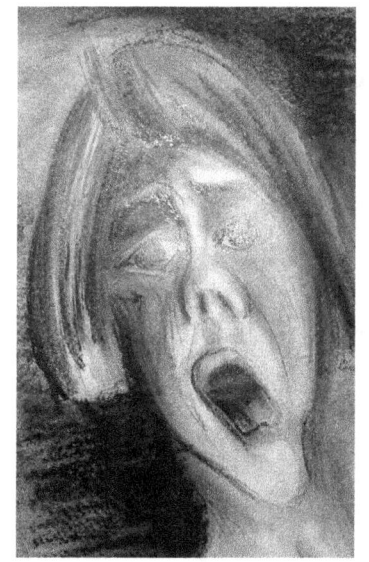

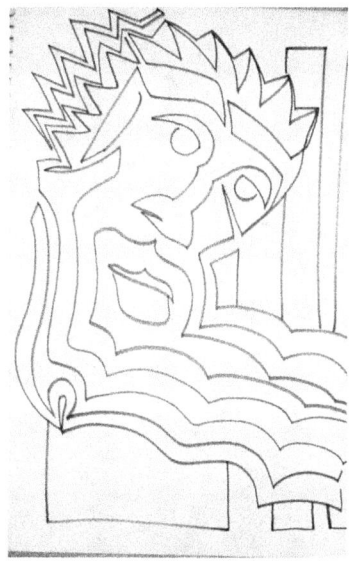

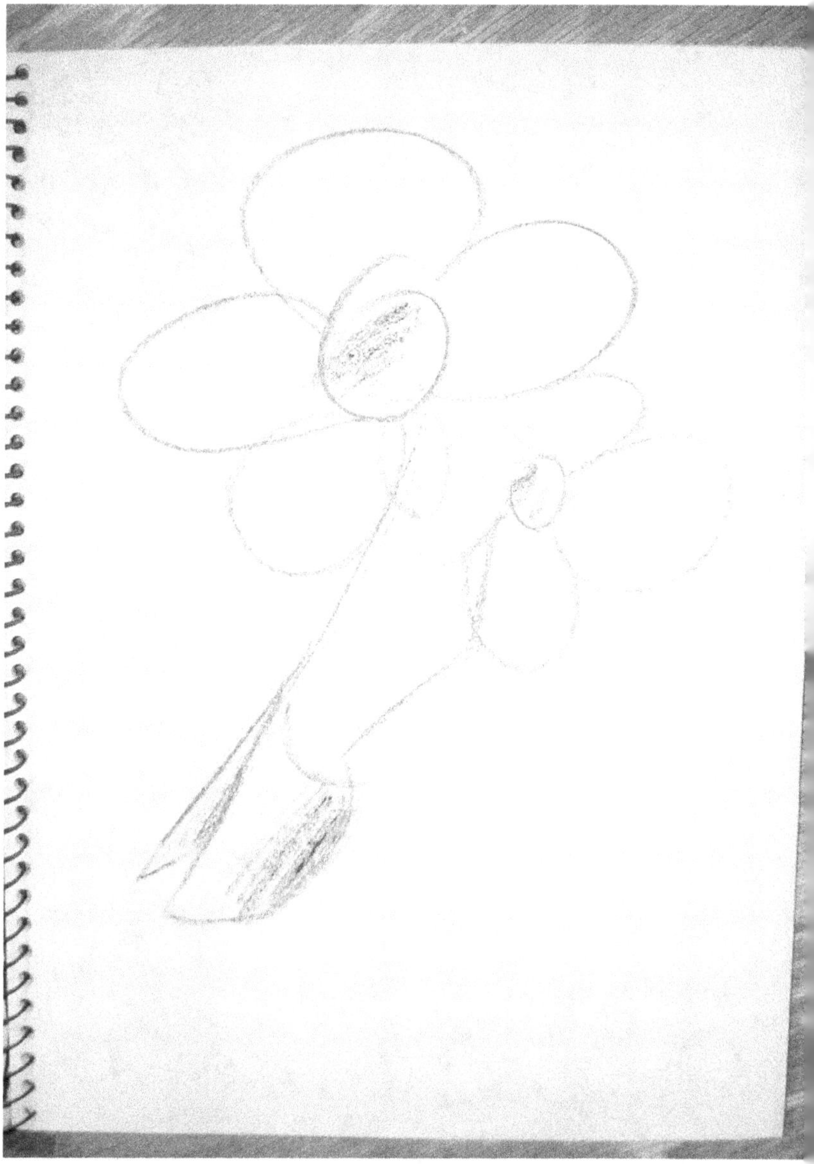

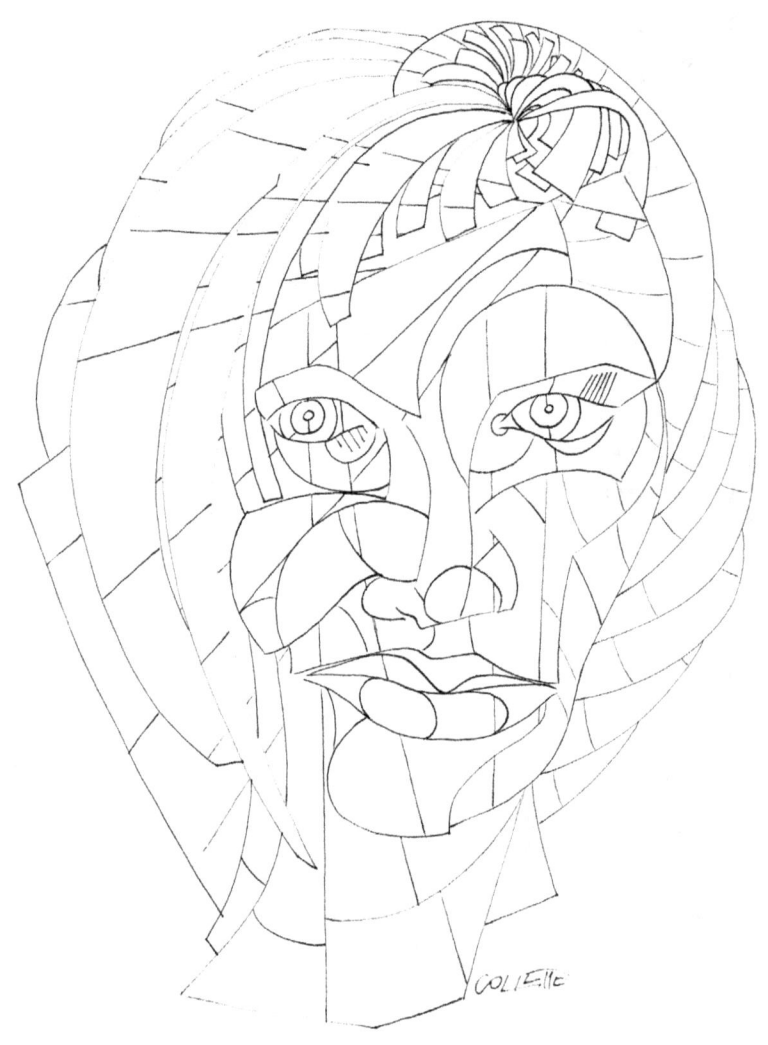

Notes and sketches

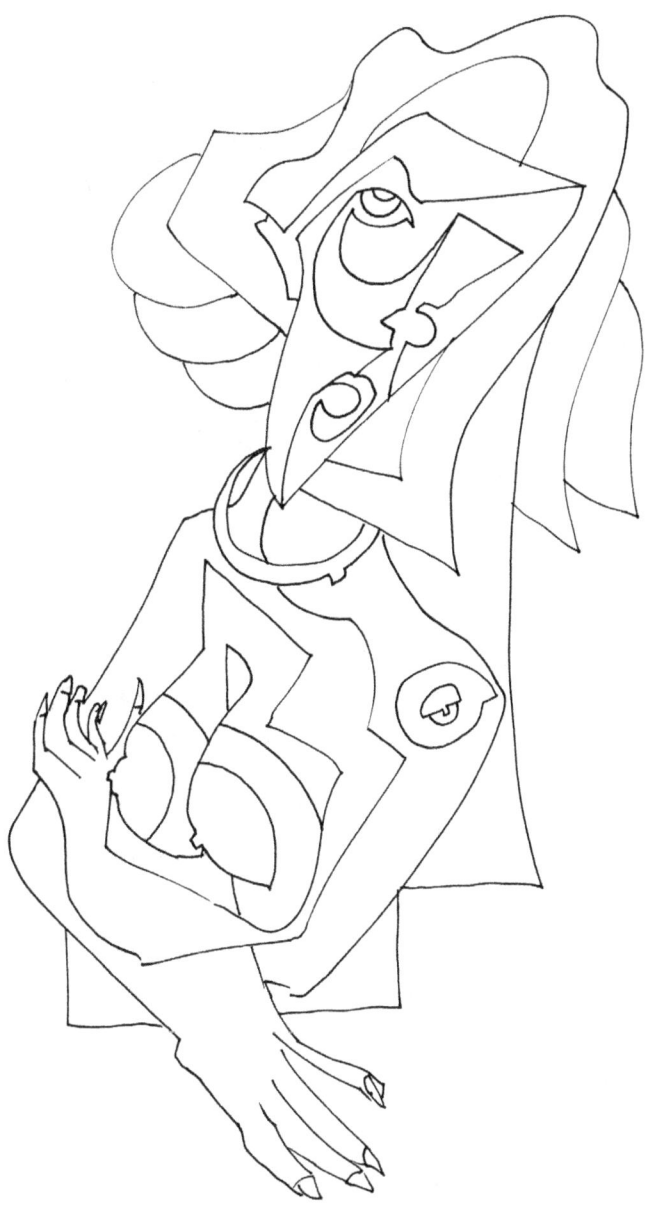

Gilles COLLETTE

167

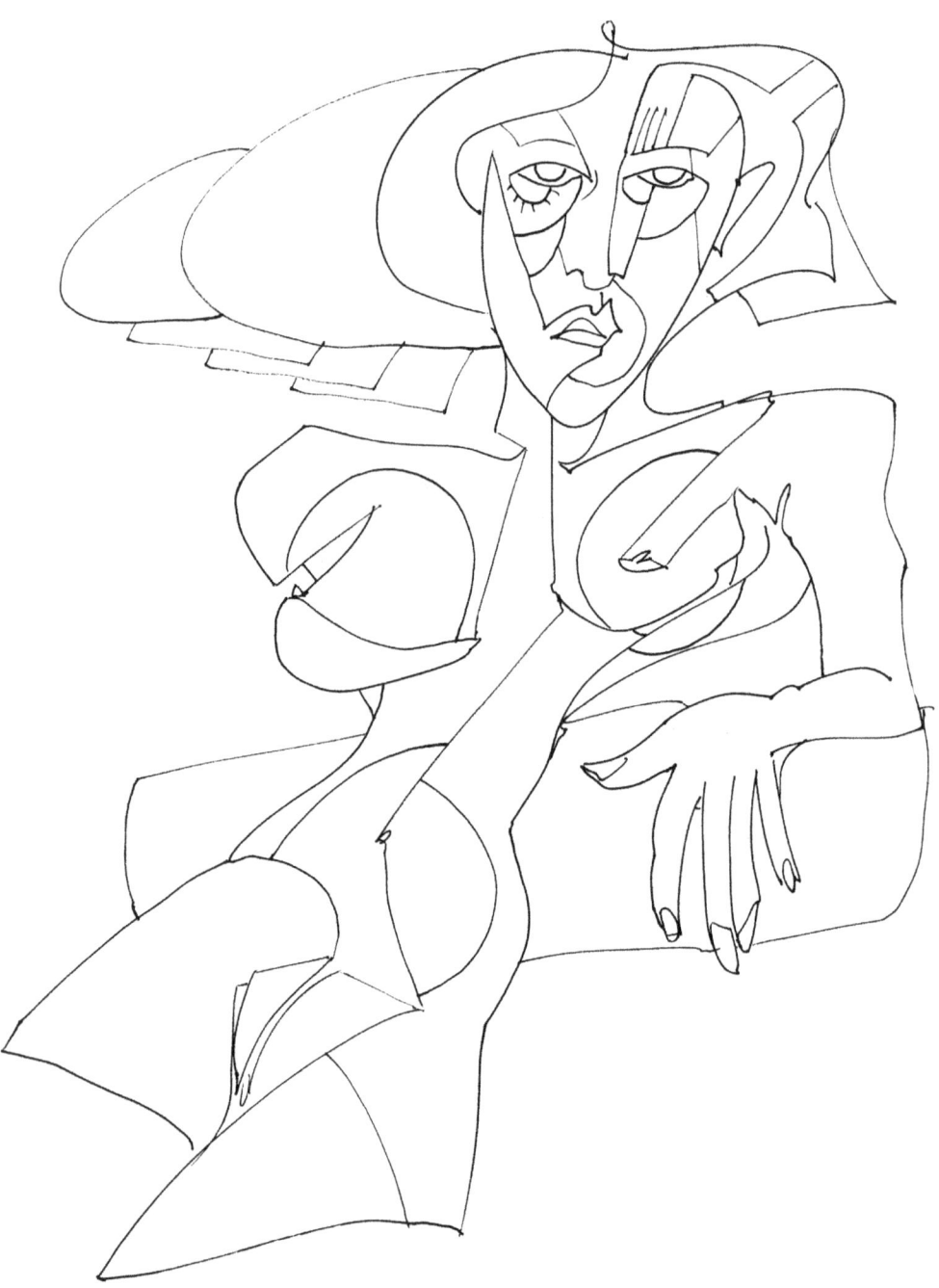

Notes and sketches

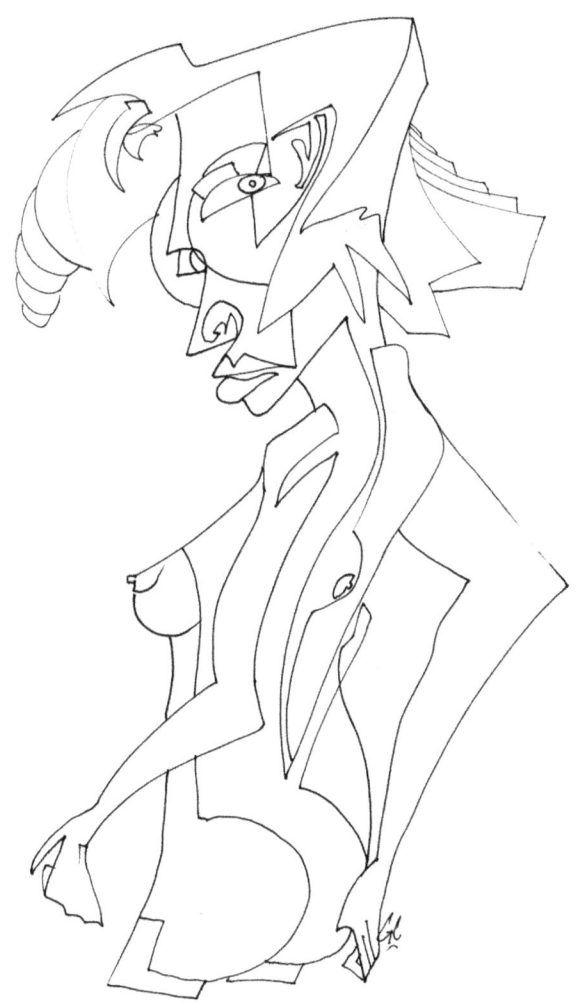

Gilles COLLETTE

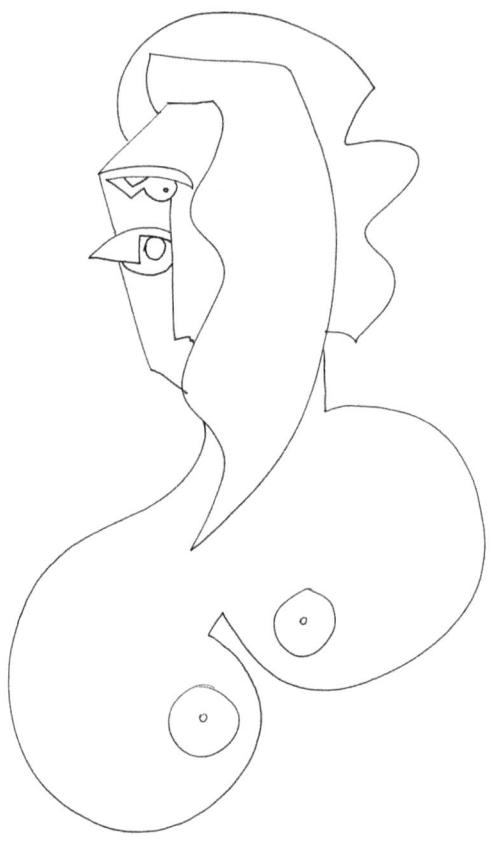

Notes and sketches

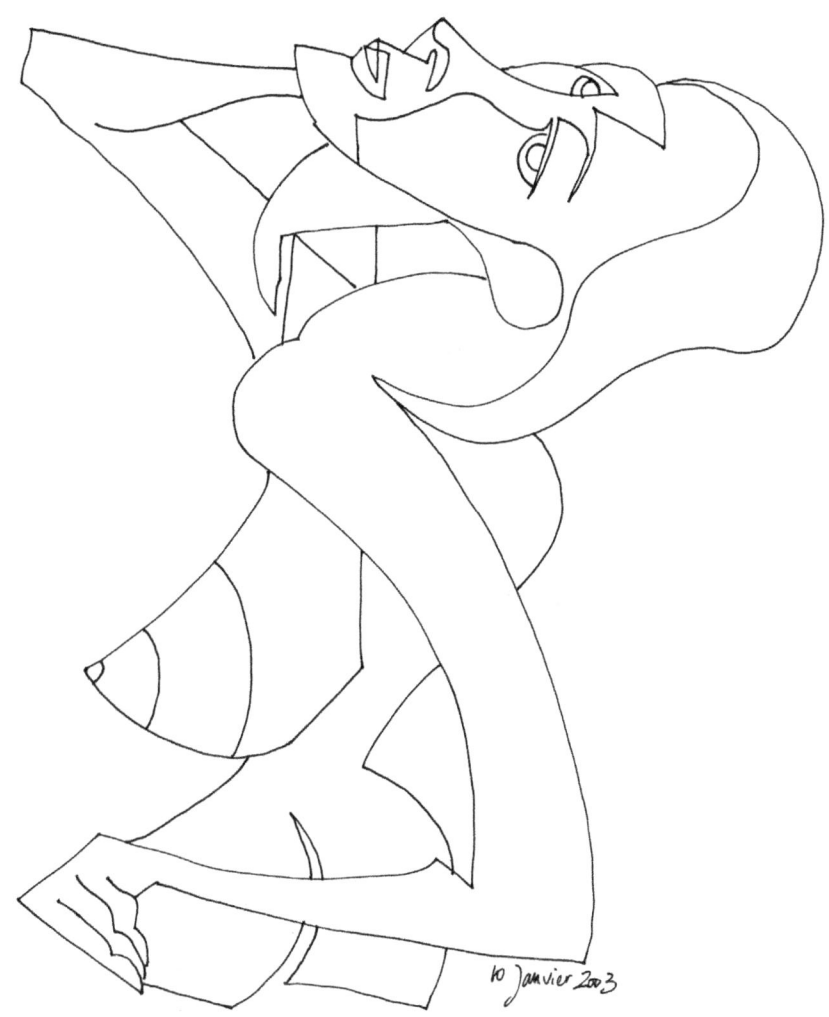

10 Janvier 2003

Gilles COLLETTE

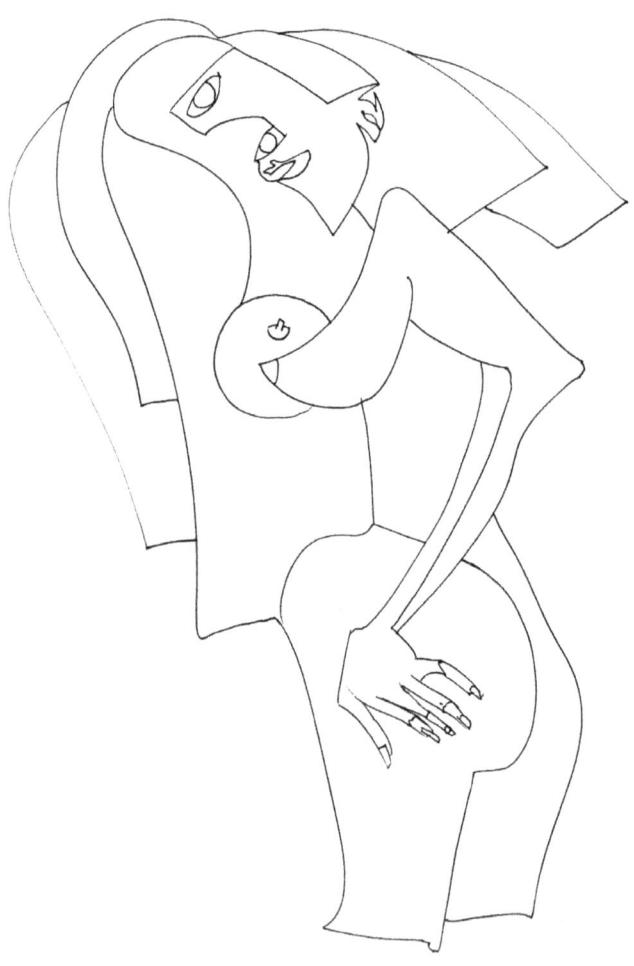

Notes and sketches

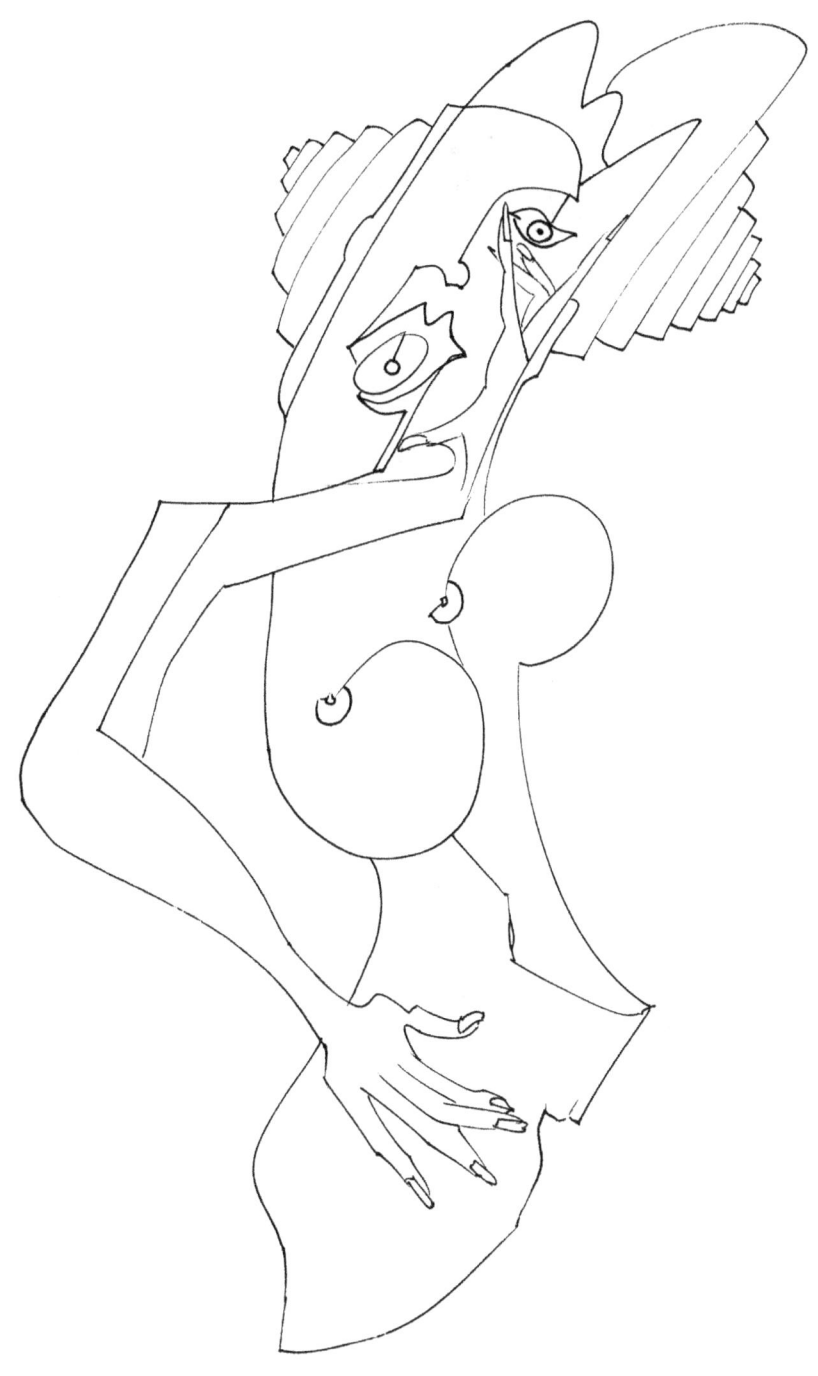

Gilles COLLETTE

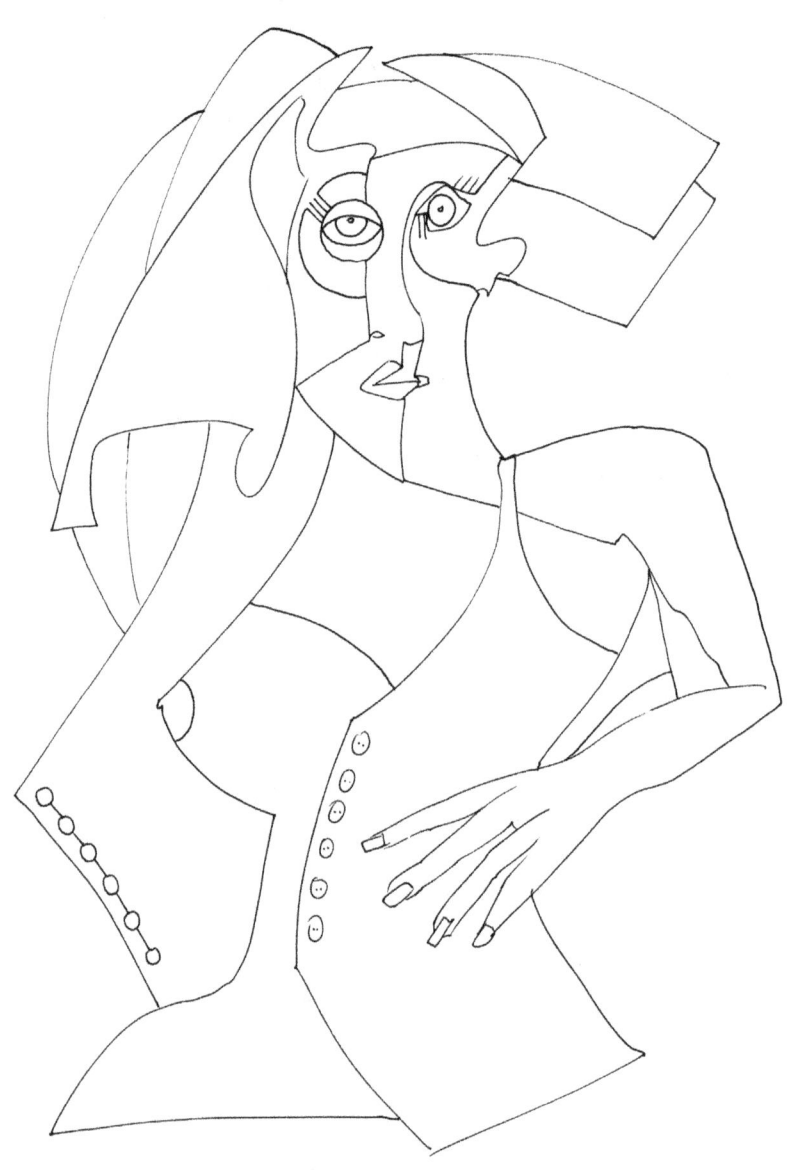

Notes and sketches

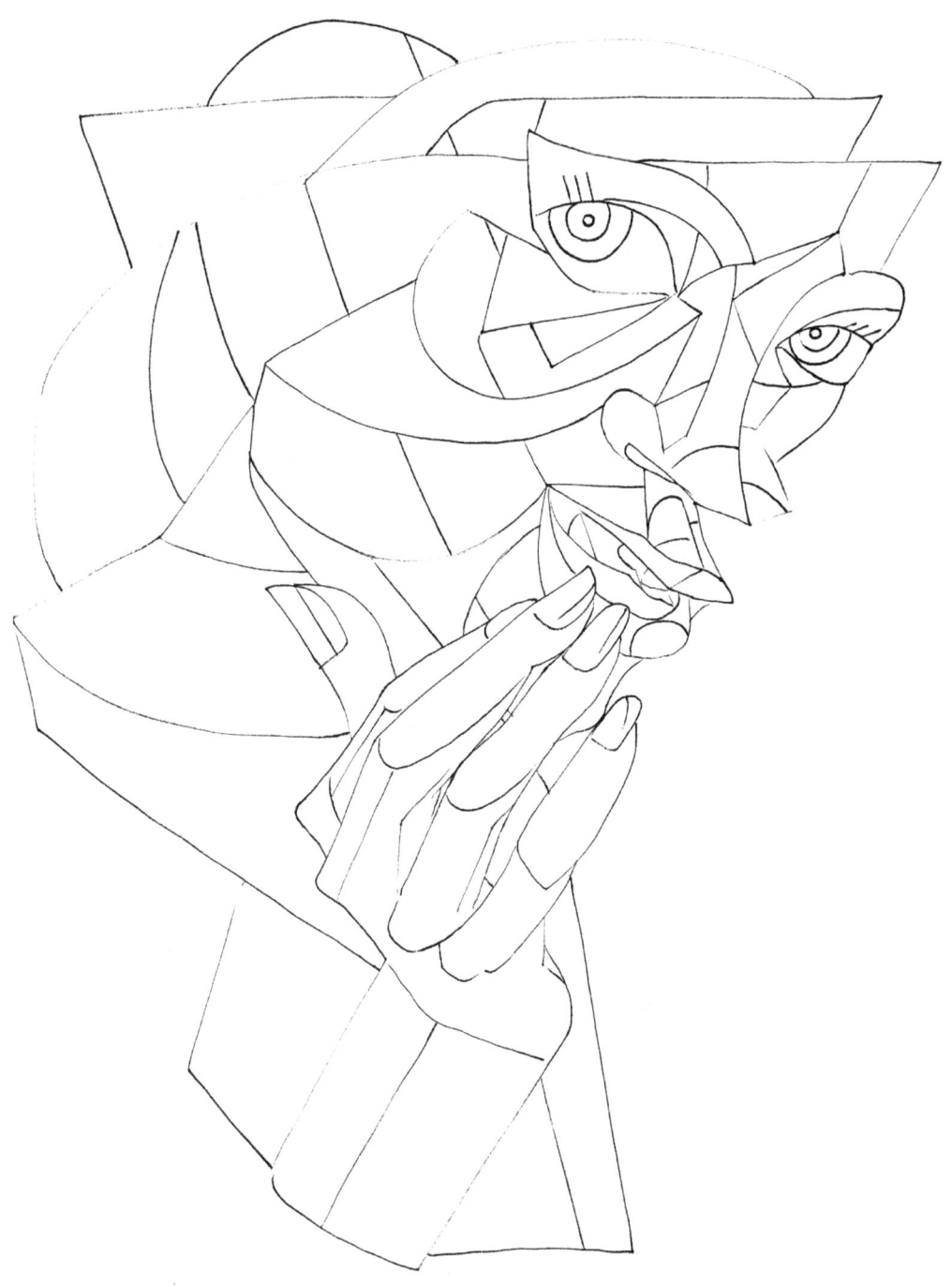

Gilles COLLETTE

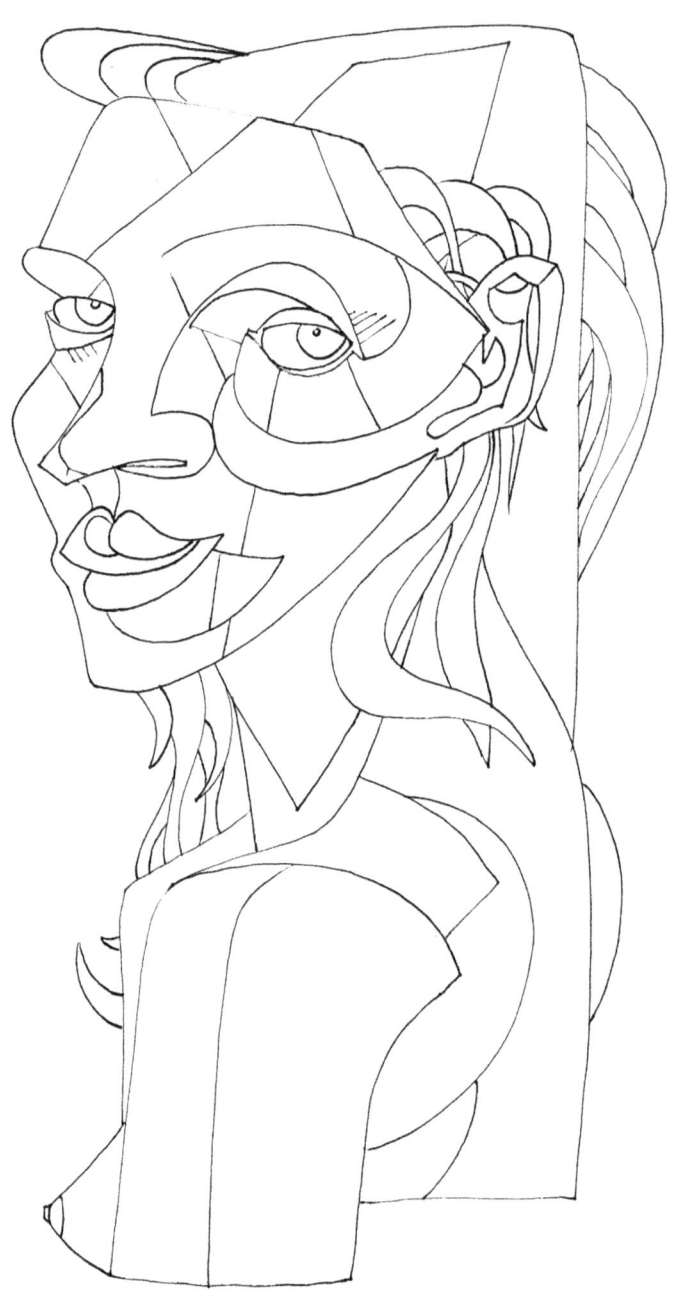

Notes and sketches

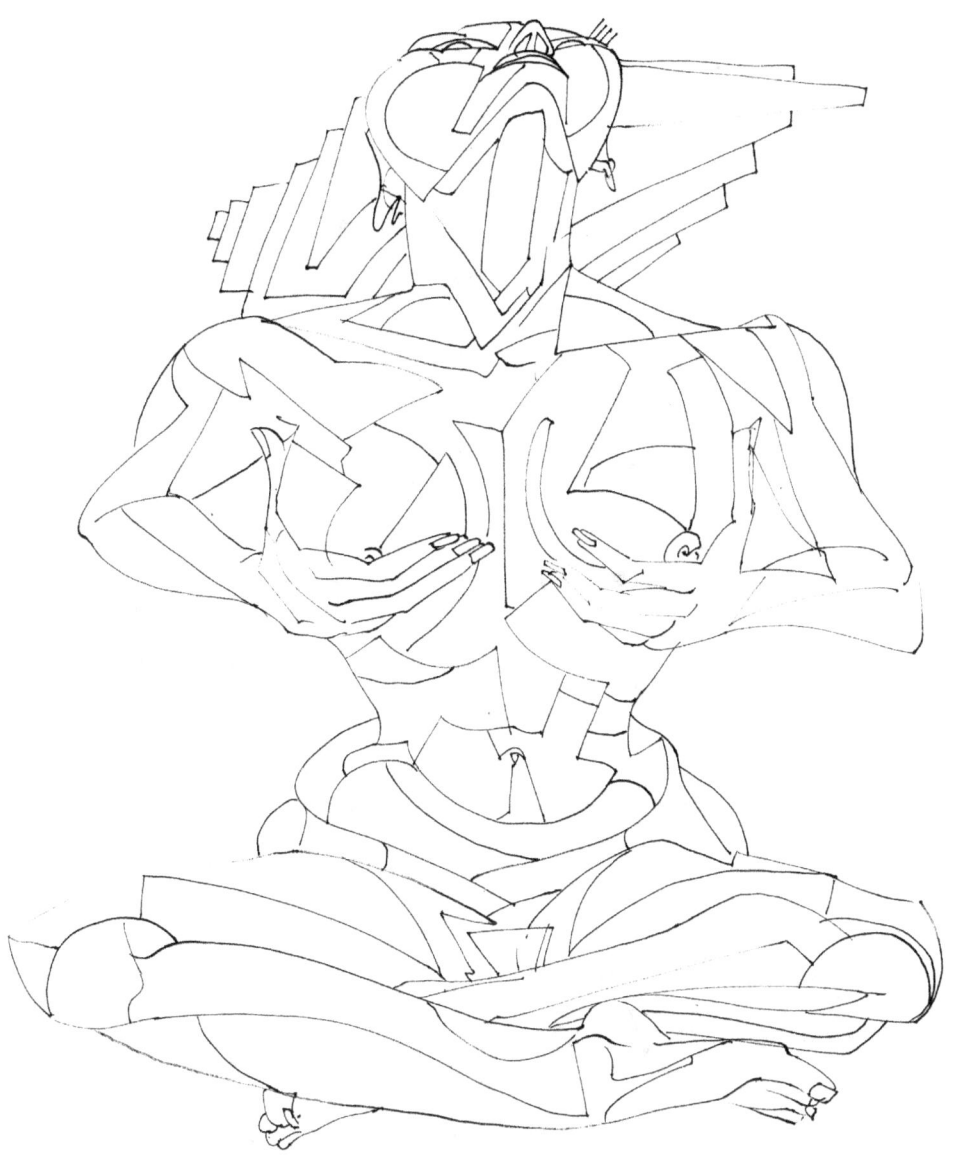

Gilles COLLETTE

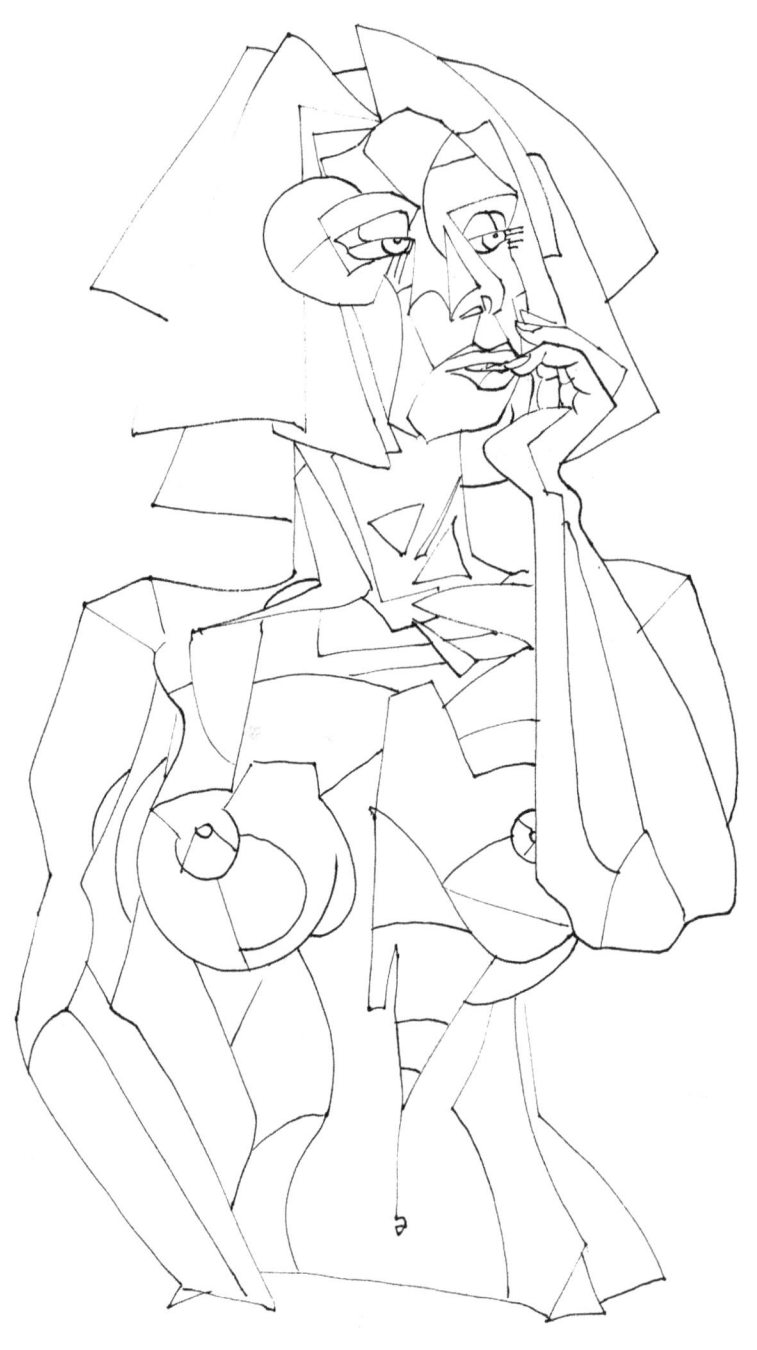

Notes and sketches

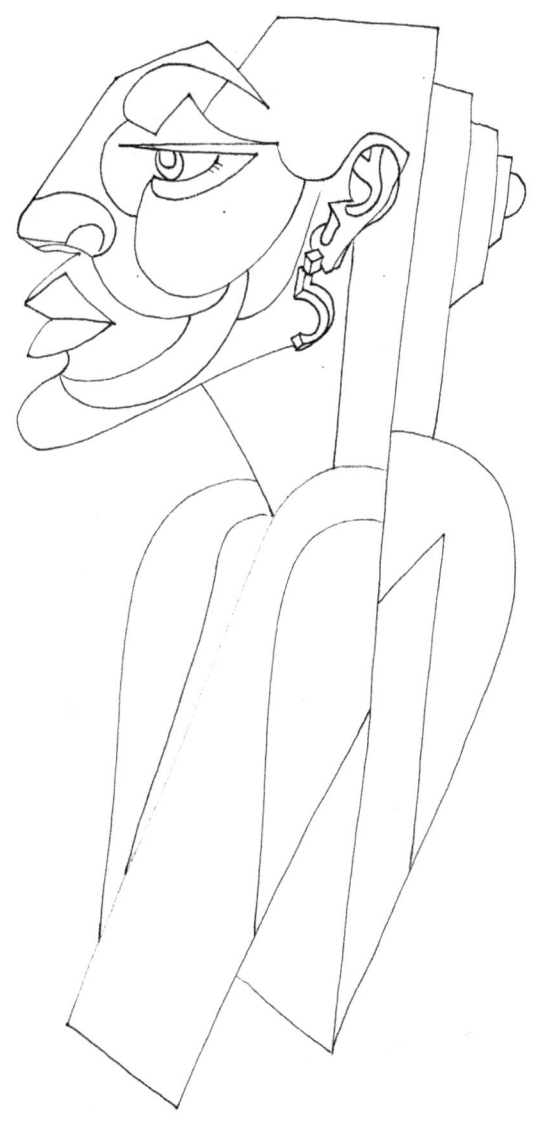

Gilles COLLETTE

179

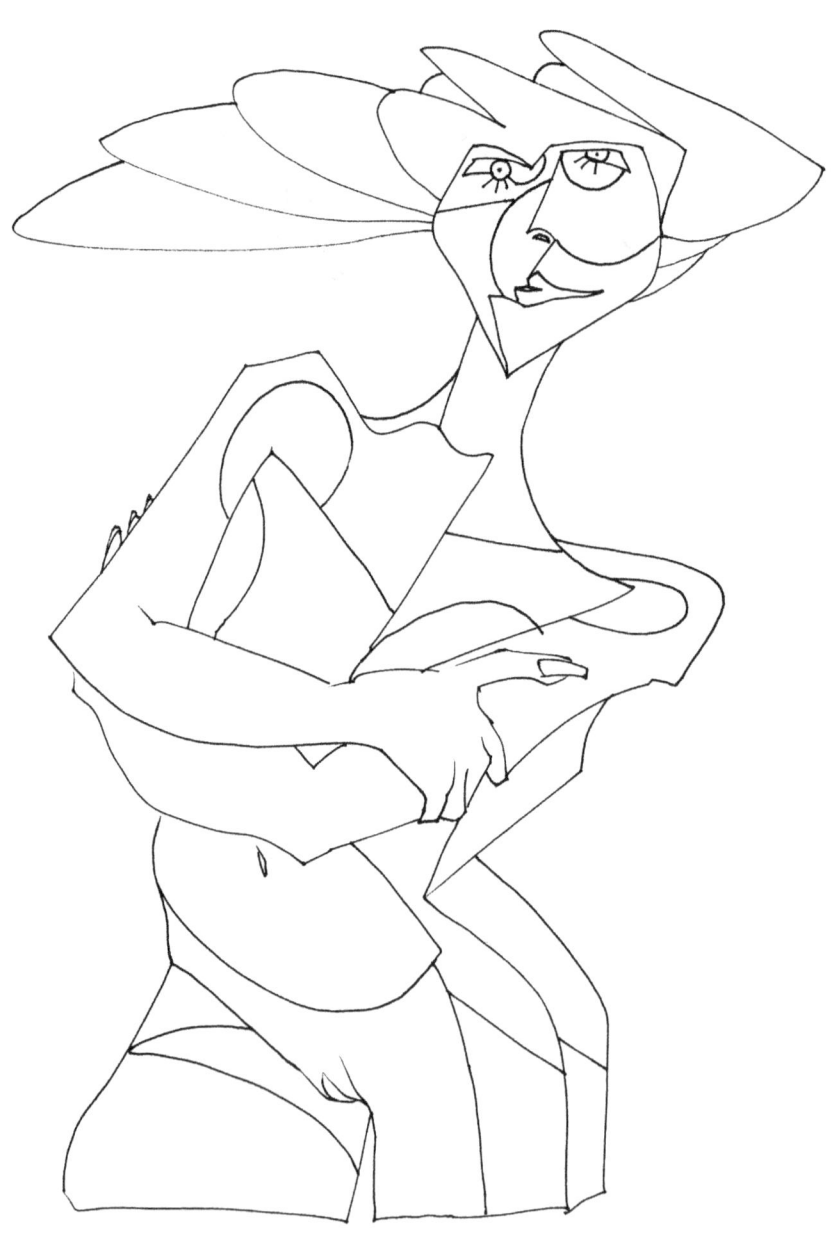

Notes and sketches

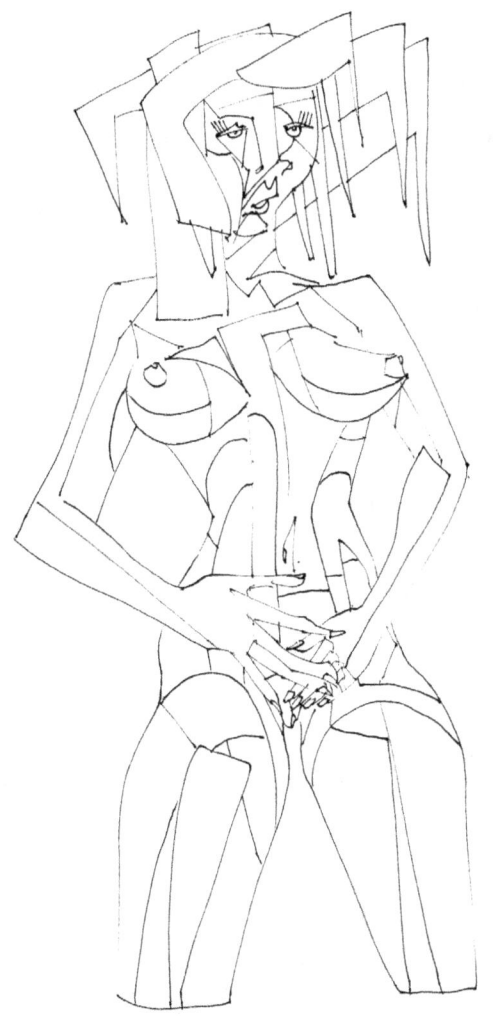
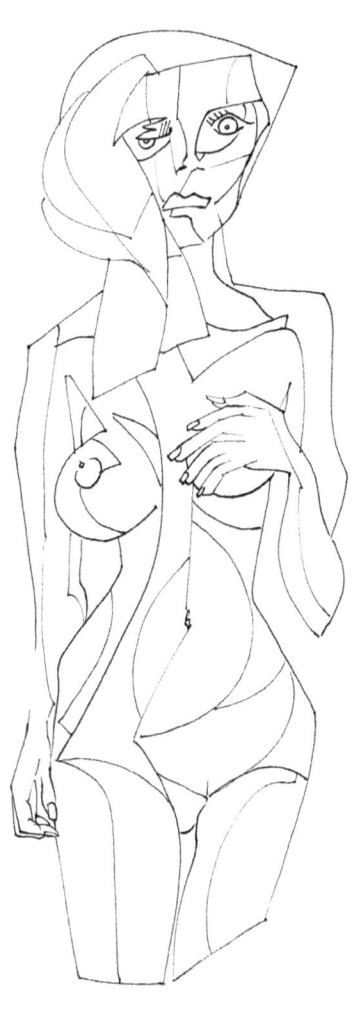

Gilles COLLETTE

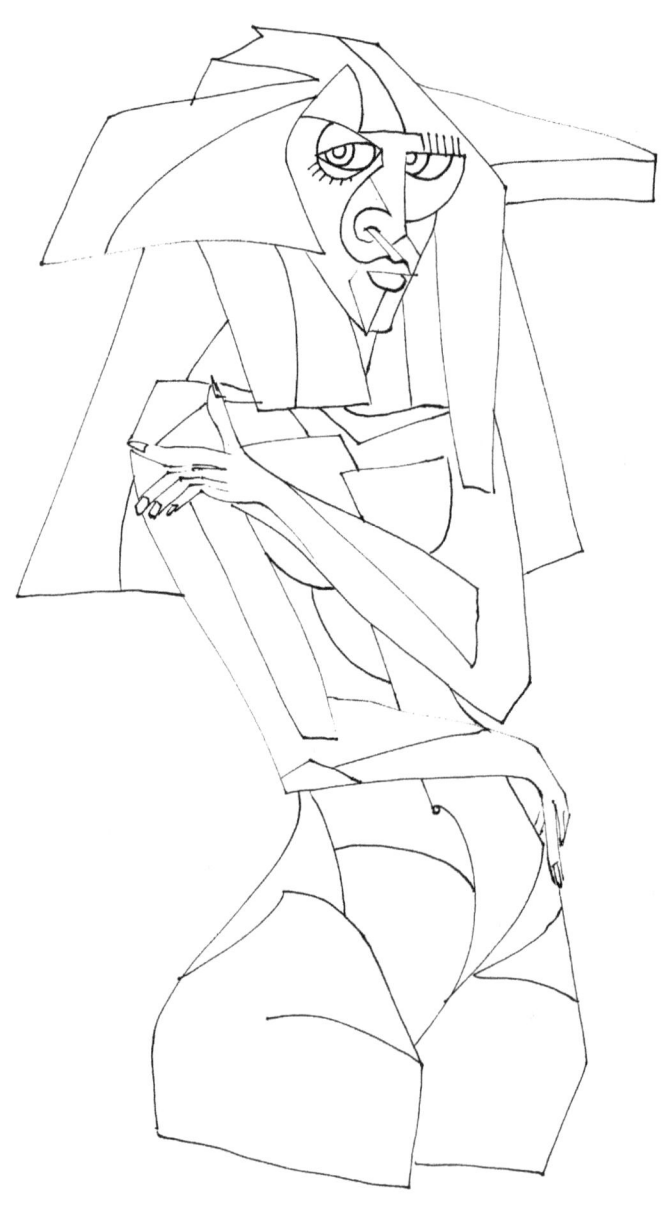

Notes and sketches

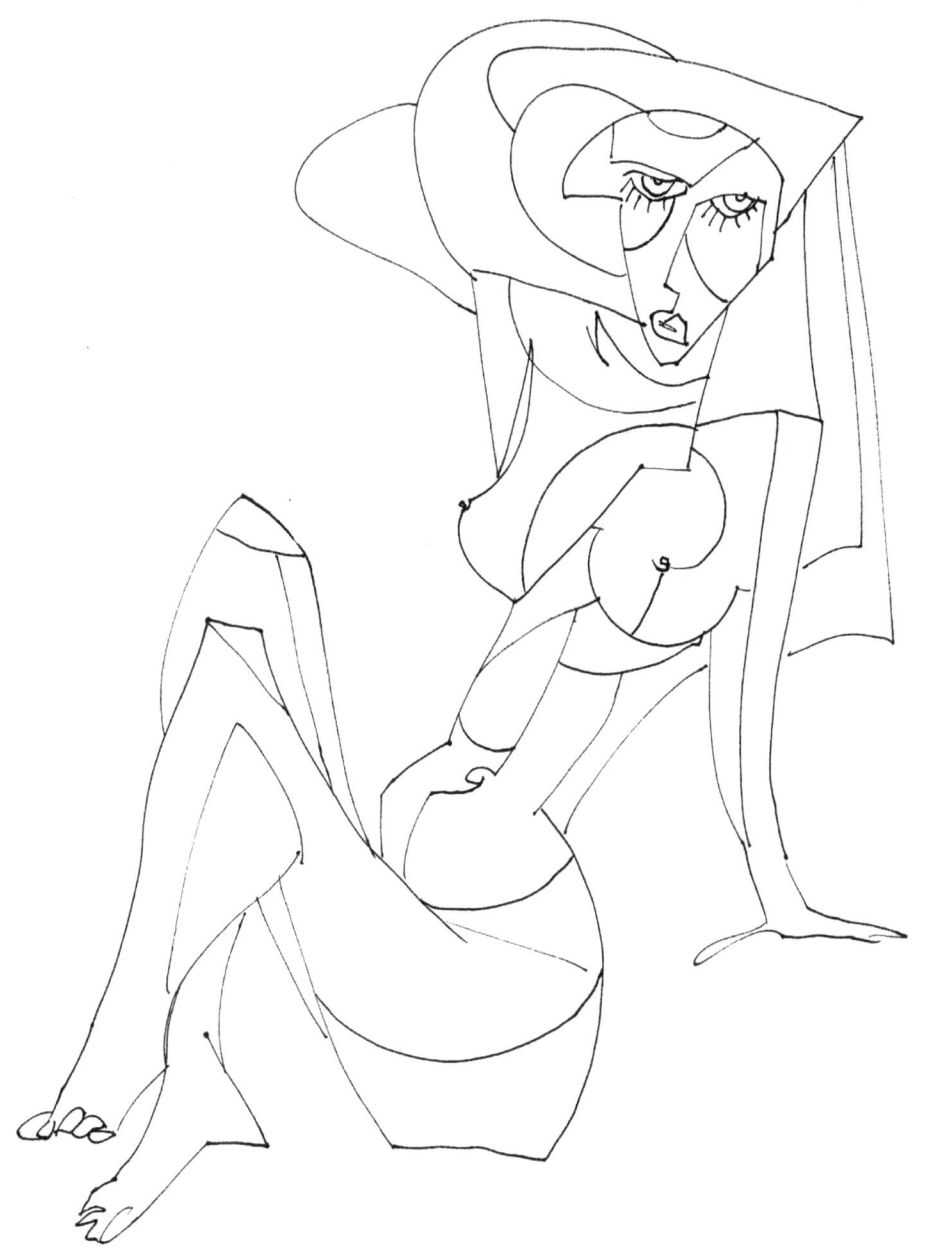

Gilles COLLETTE

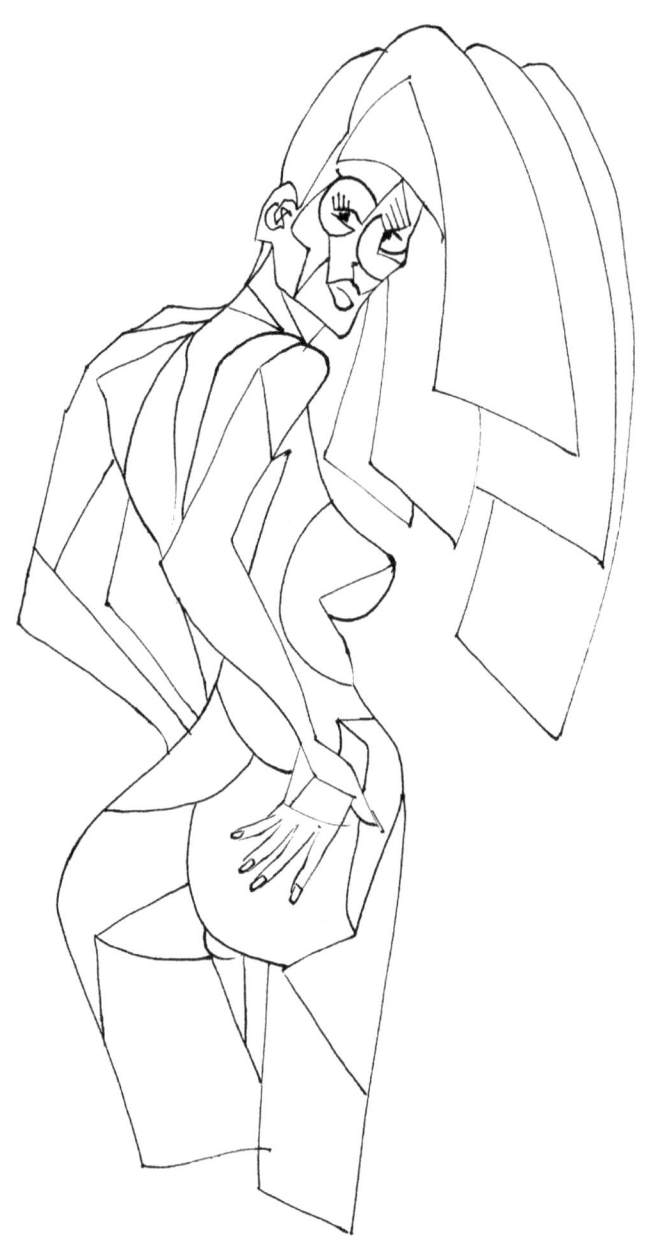

Notes and sketches

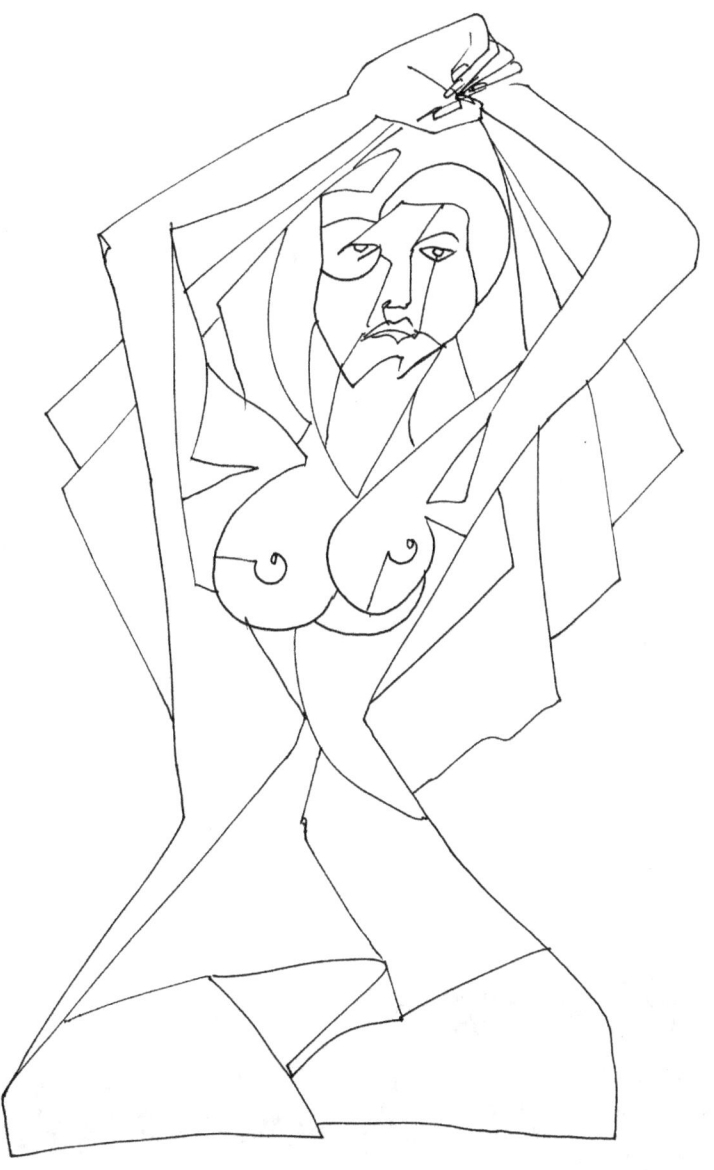

Gilles COLLETTE

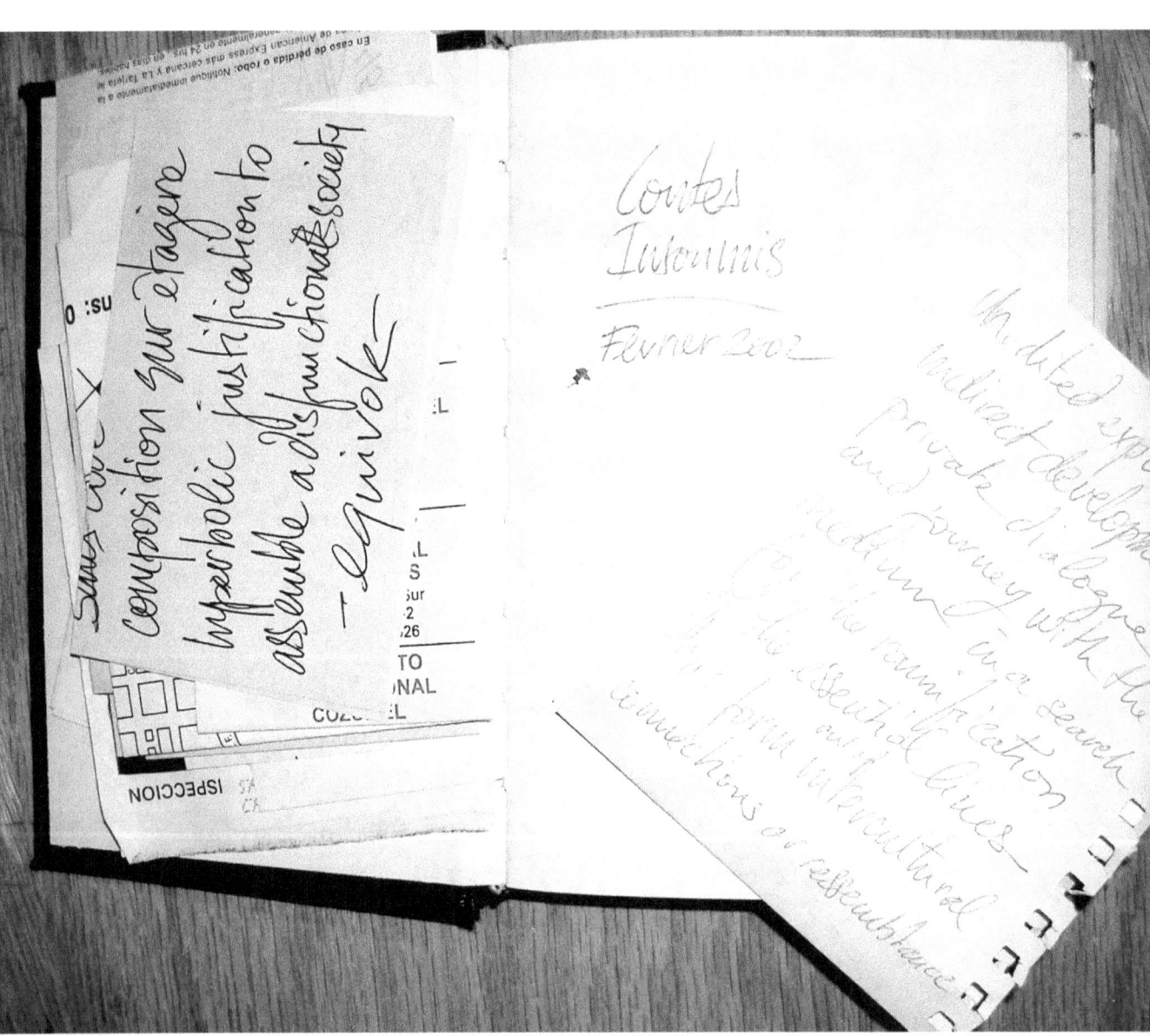

Notes and sketches

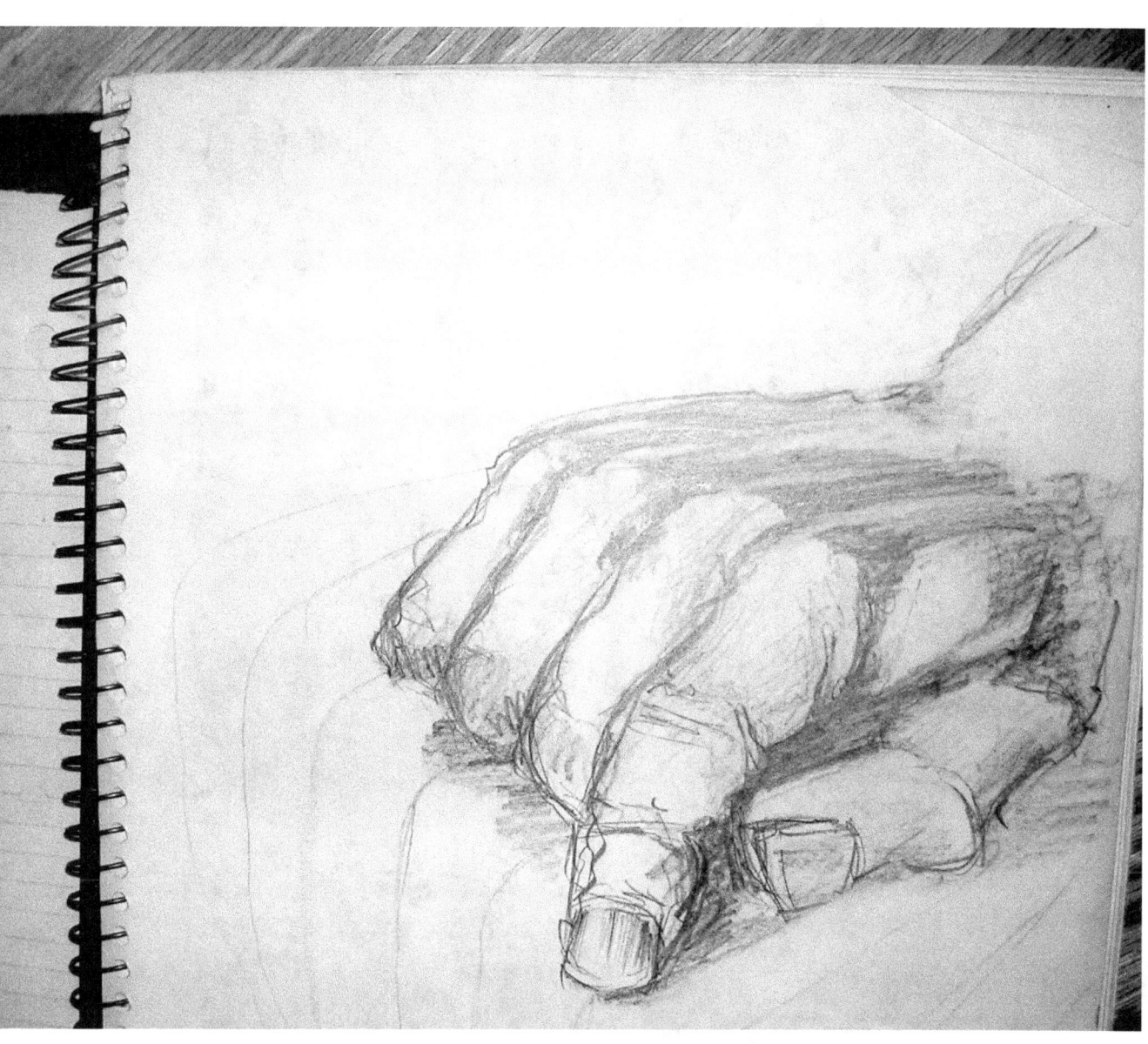

Gilles COLLETTE

187

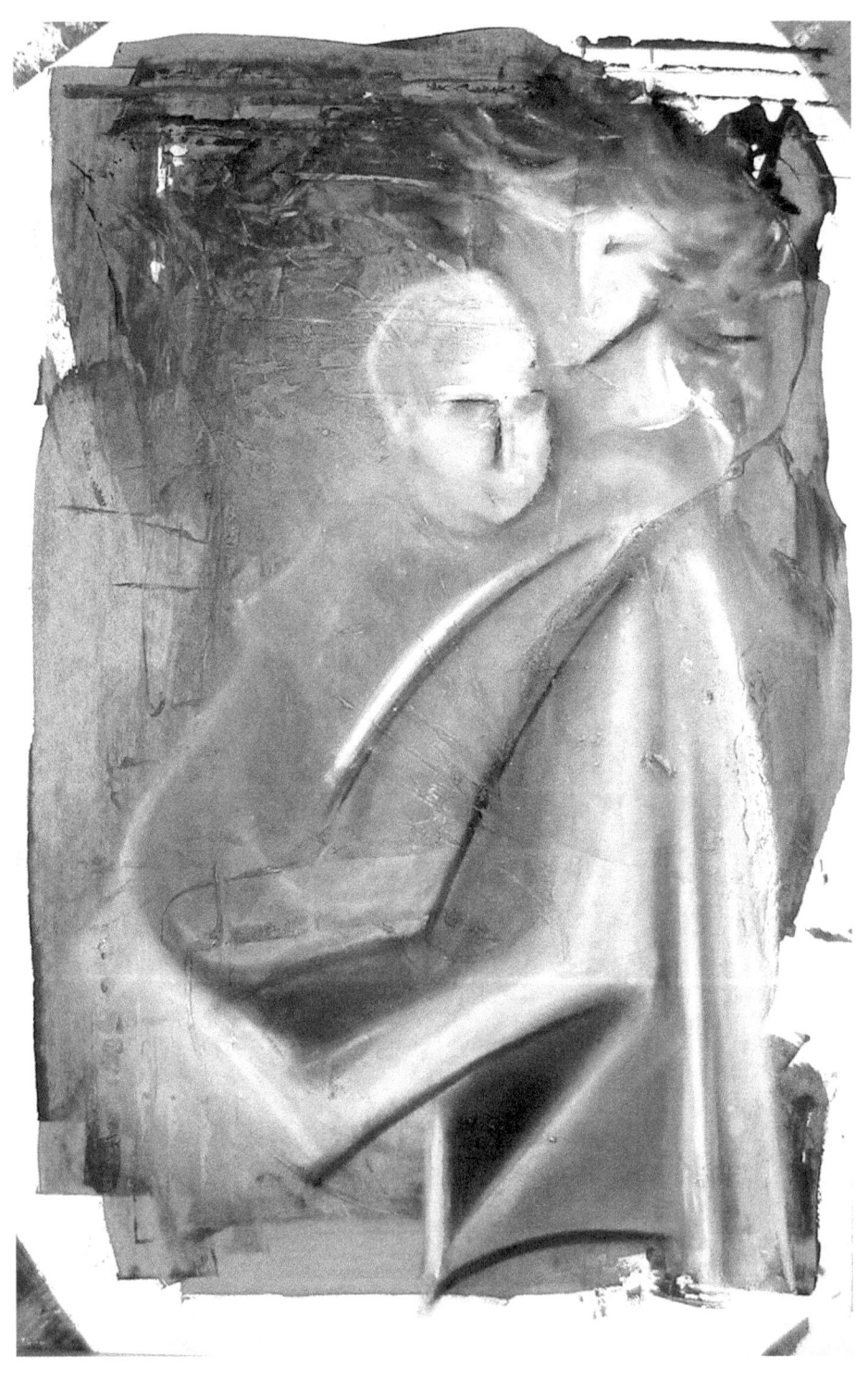

Notes and sketches

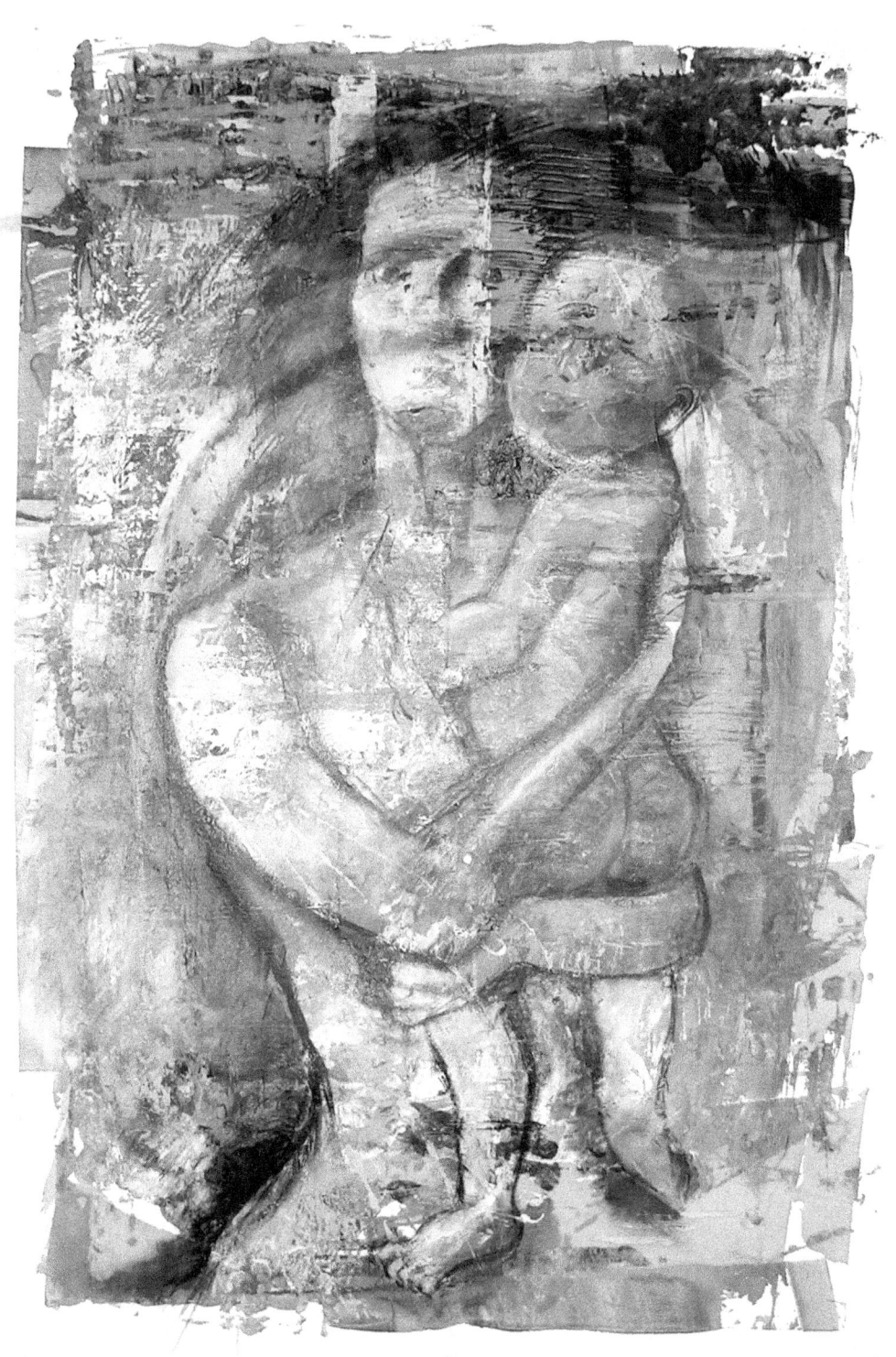

Gilles COLLETTE

189

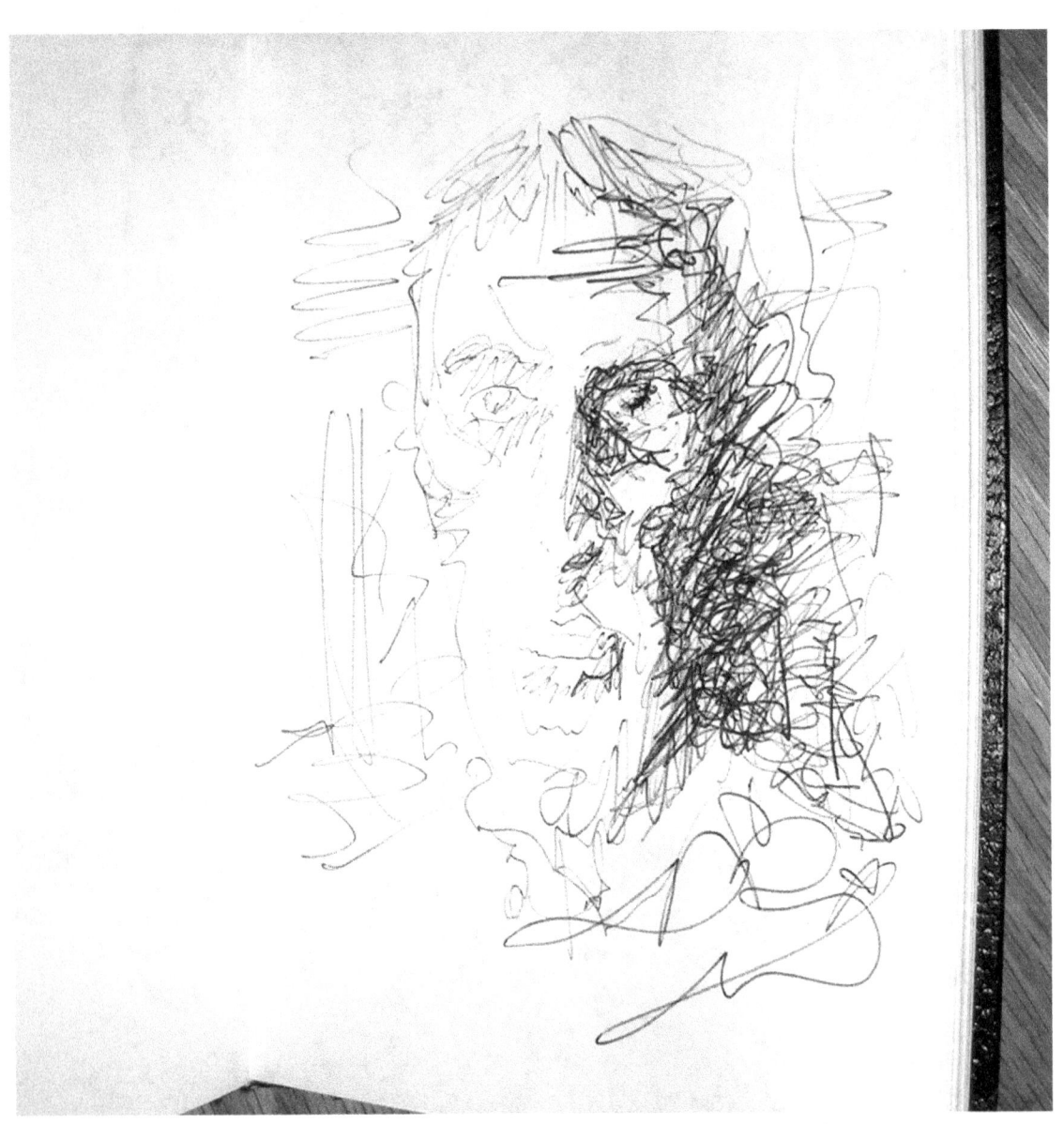

190   Notes and sketches

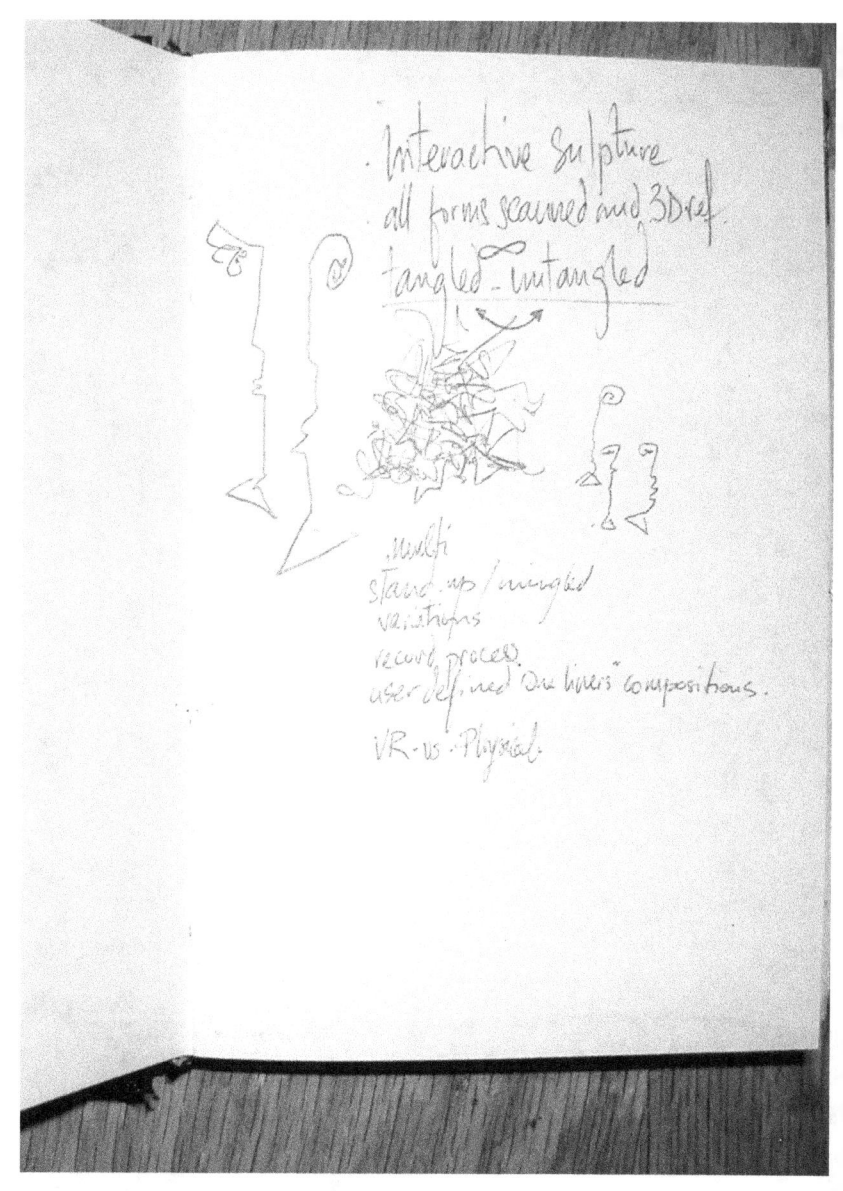

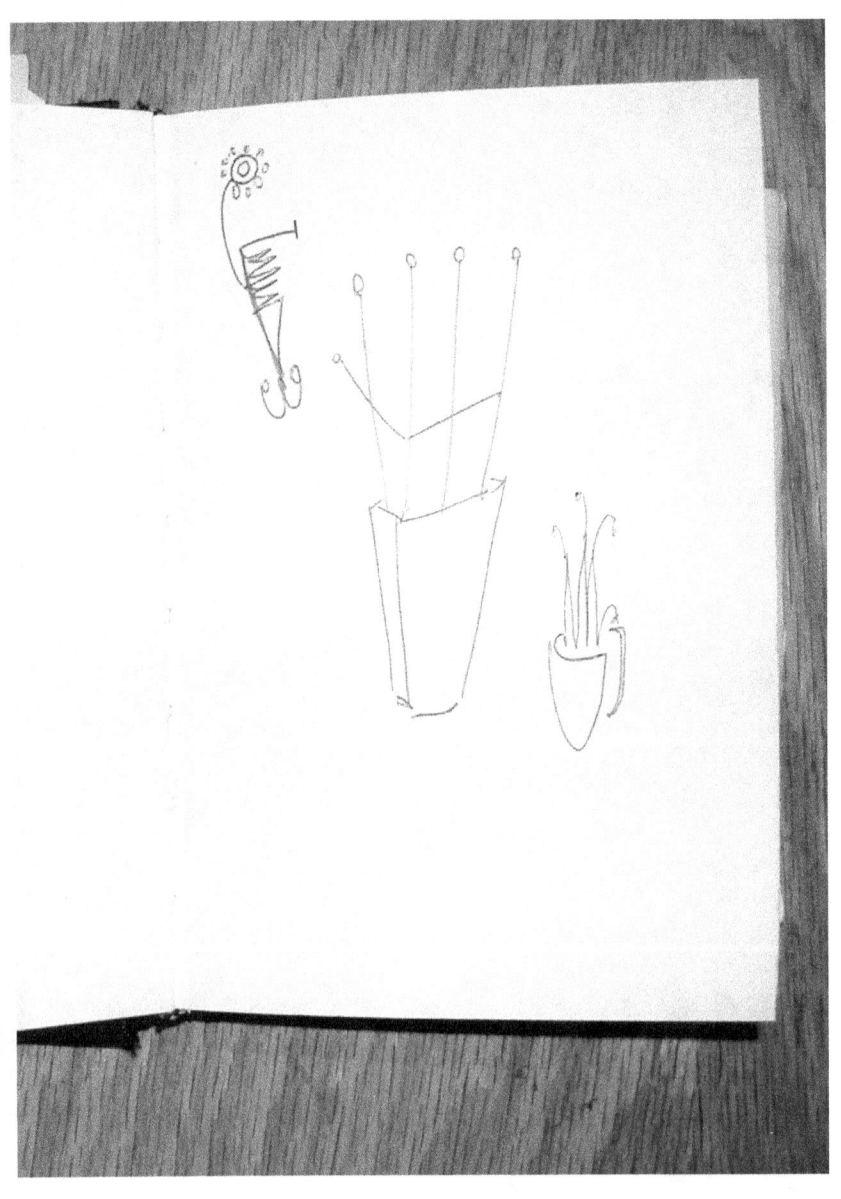

Notes and sketches

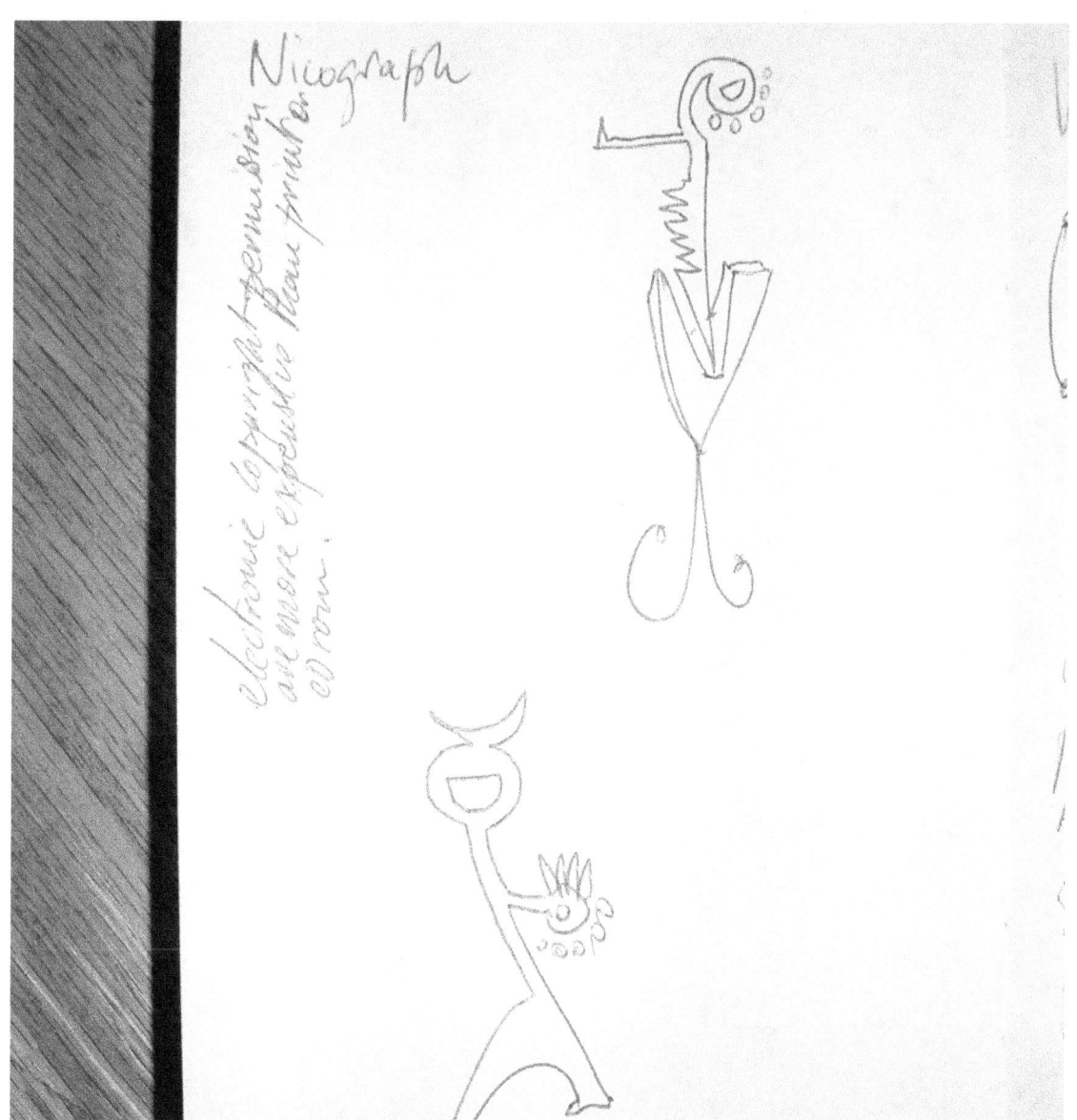

Nicograph

electronic lithograph + permission
are more expressive than printer
(Drum.

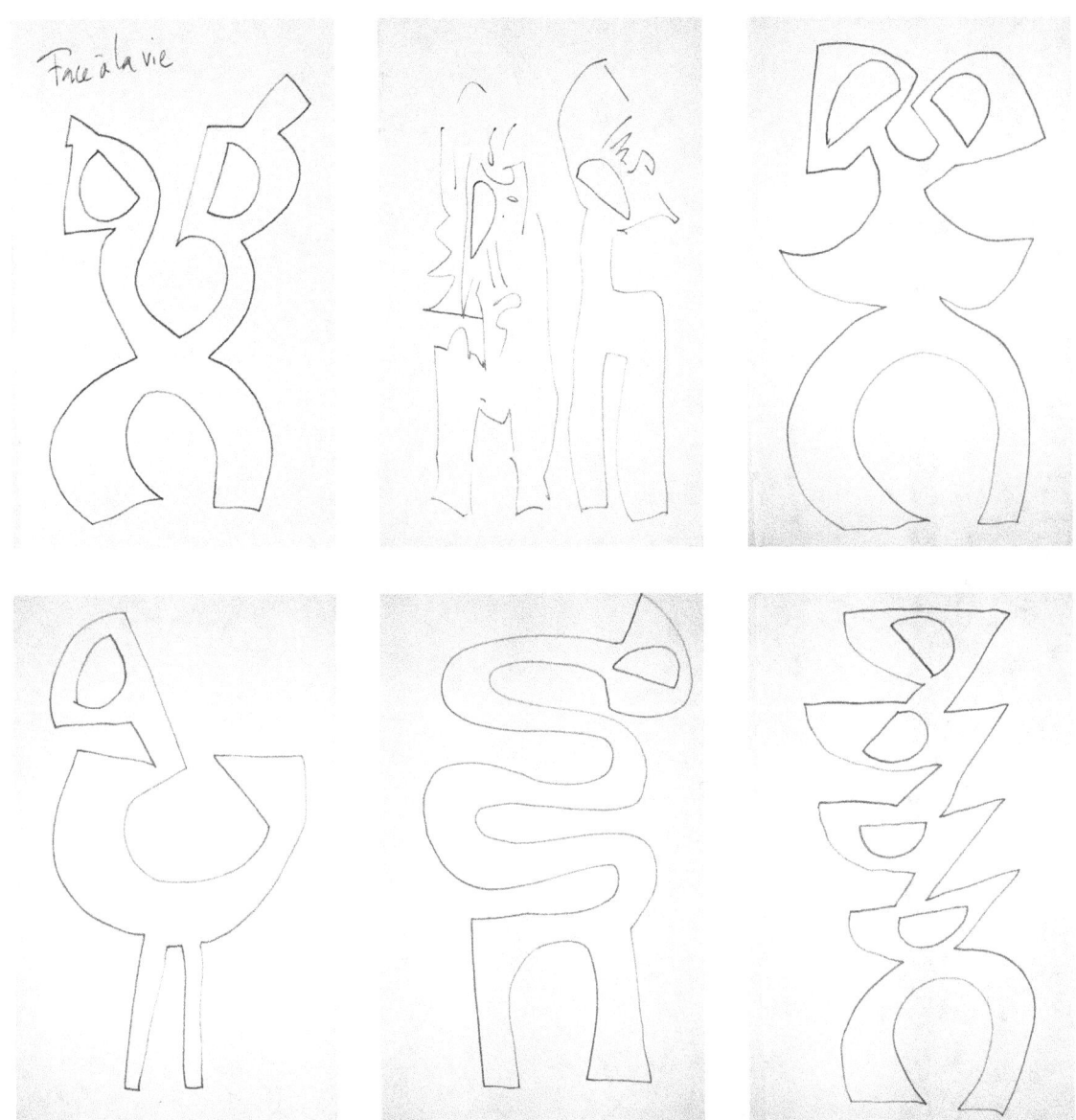

Notes and sketches

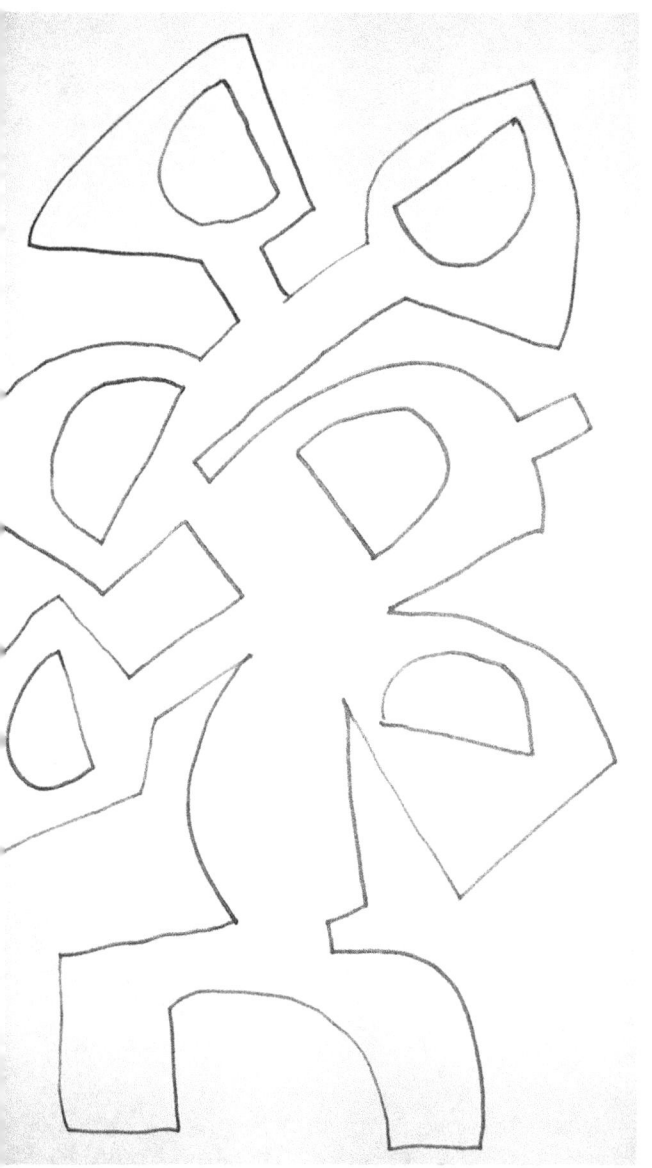 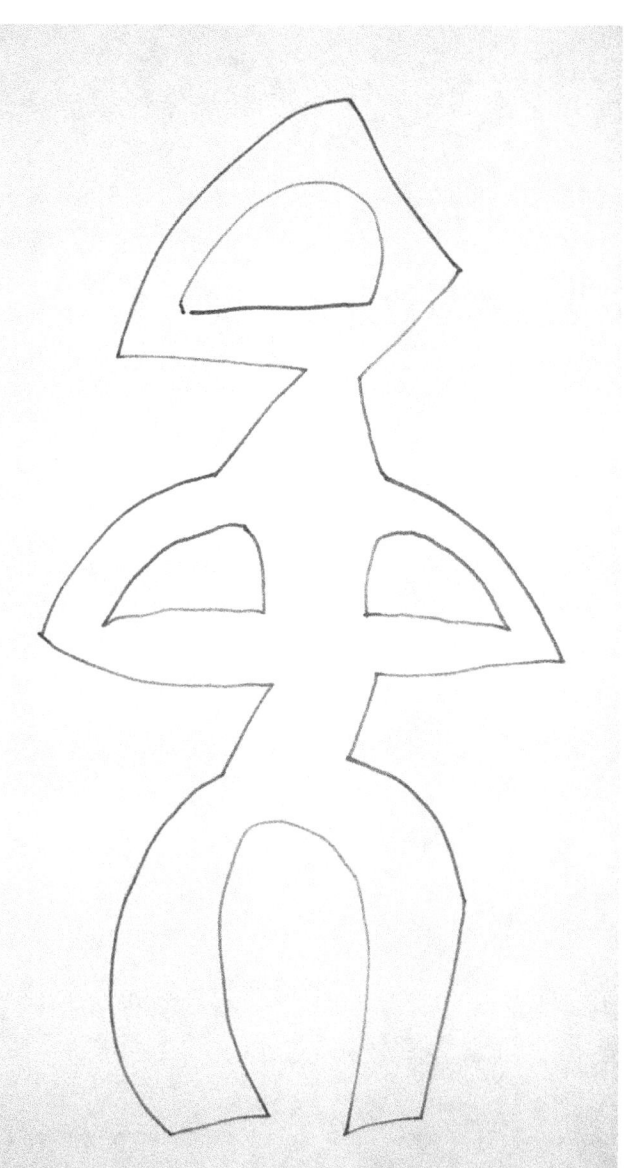

Gilles COLLETTE

195

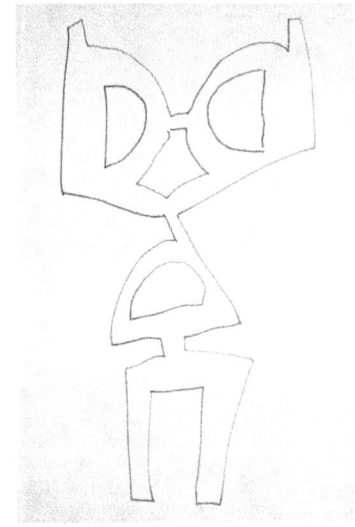 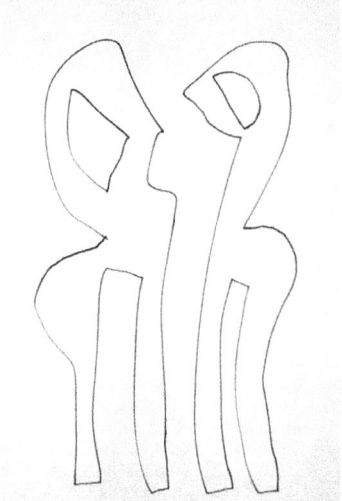 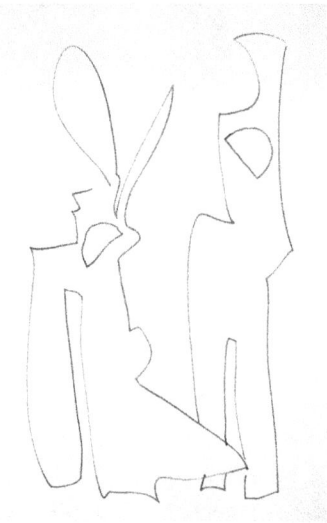

Notes and sketches

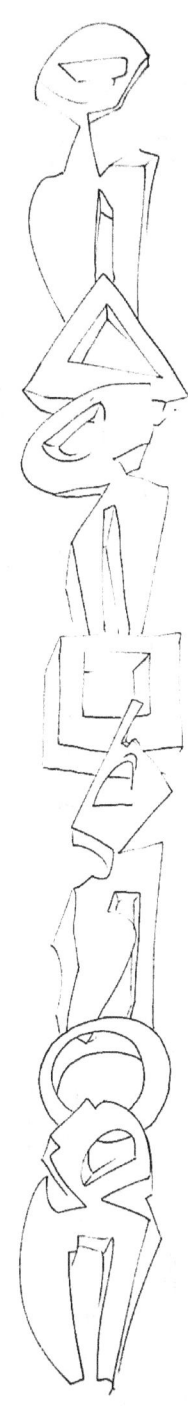

Gilles COLLETTE

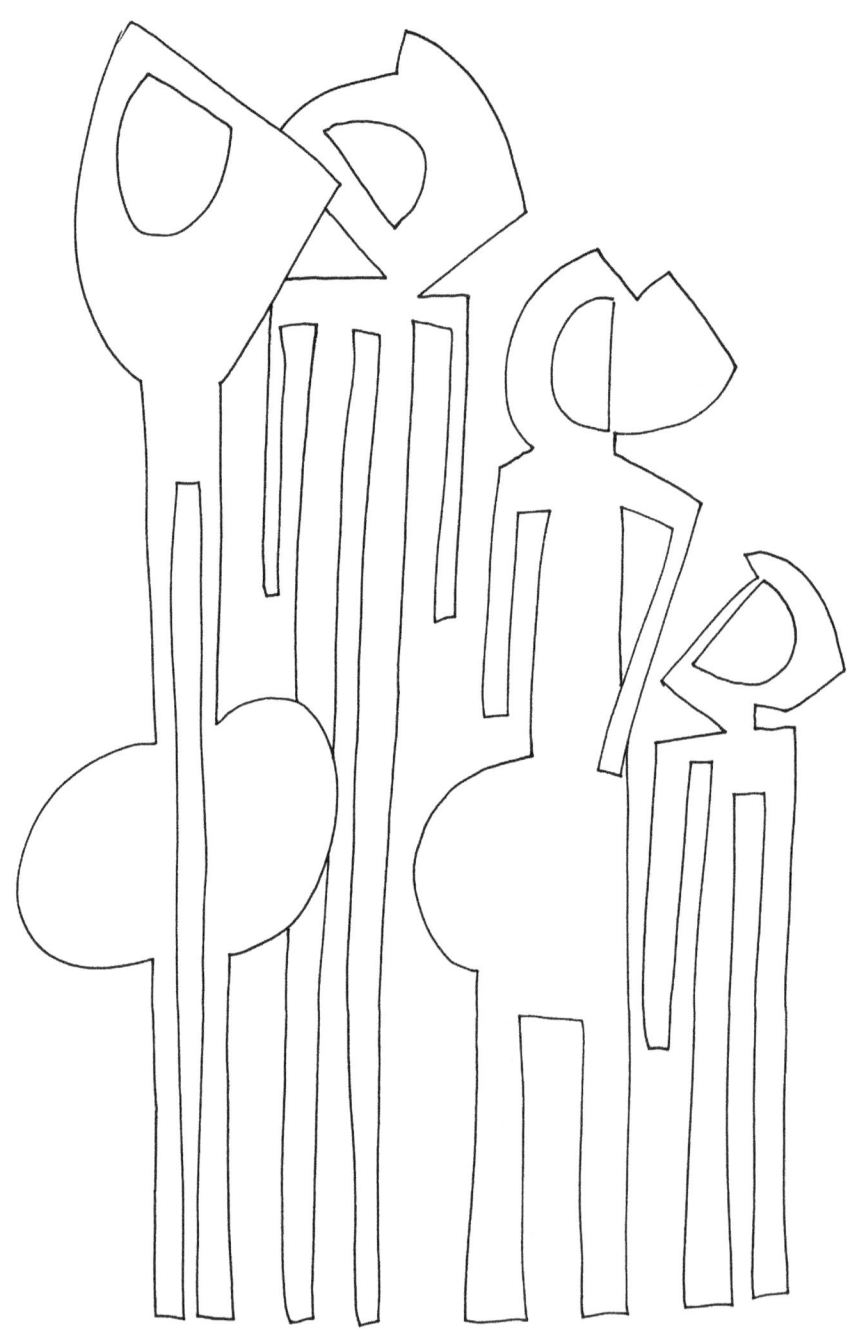

Notes and sketches

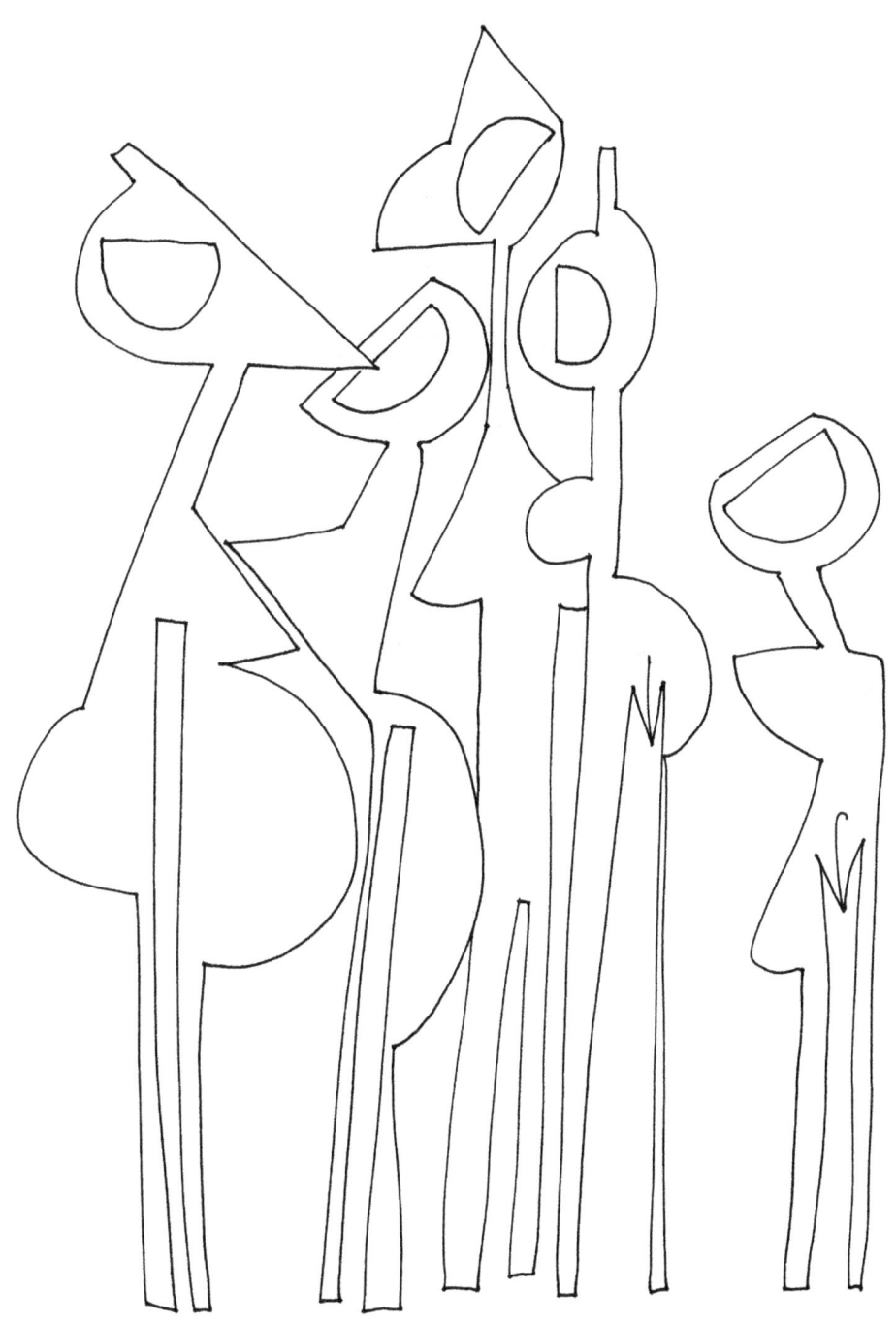

Gilles COLLETTE

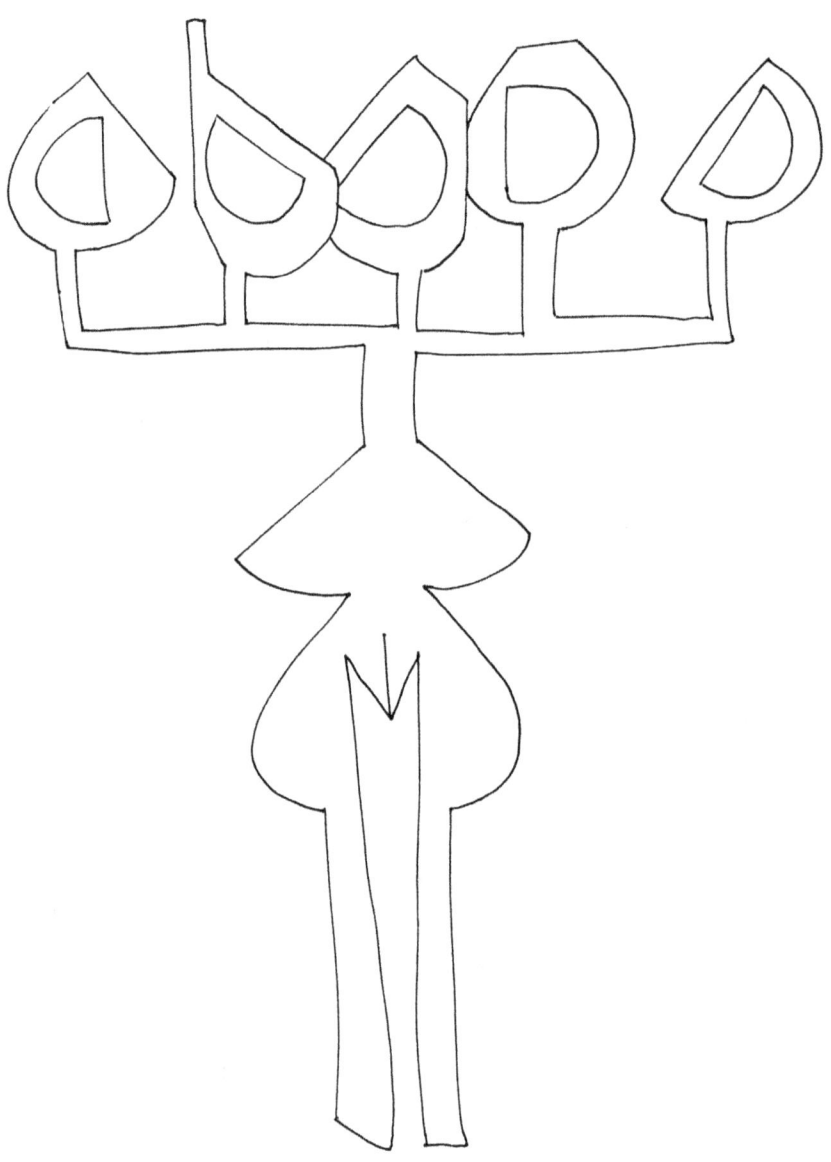

Notes and sketches

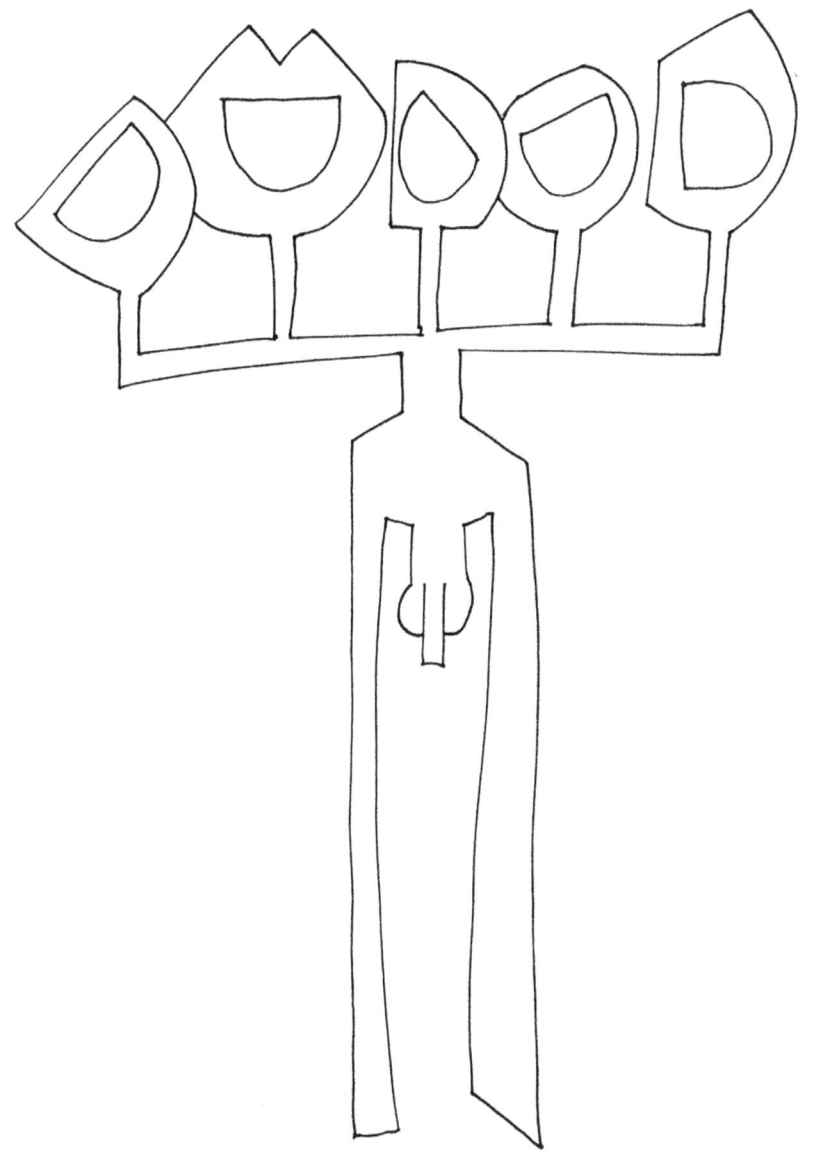

Gilles COLLETTE

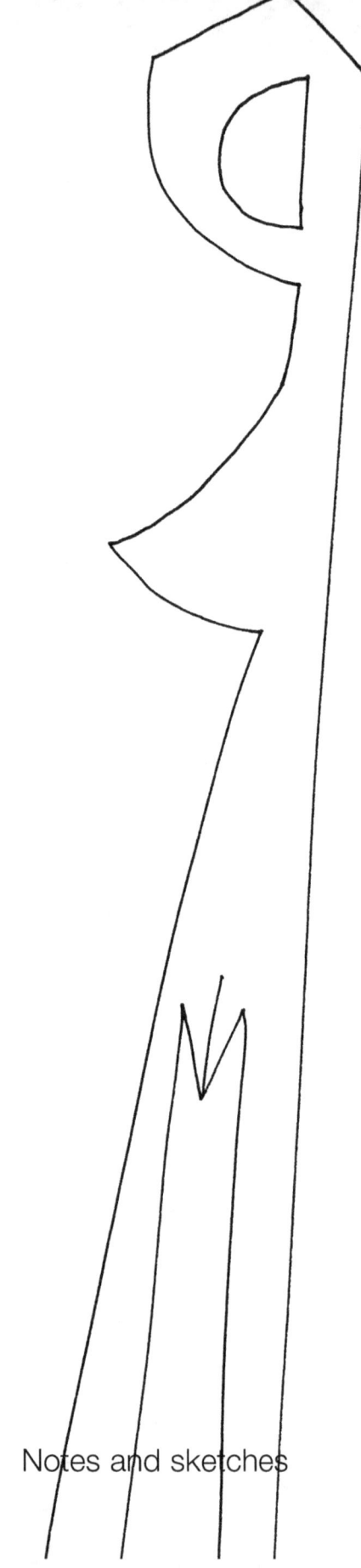

202 Notes and sketches

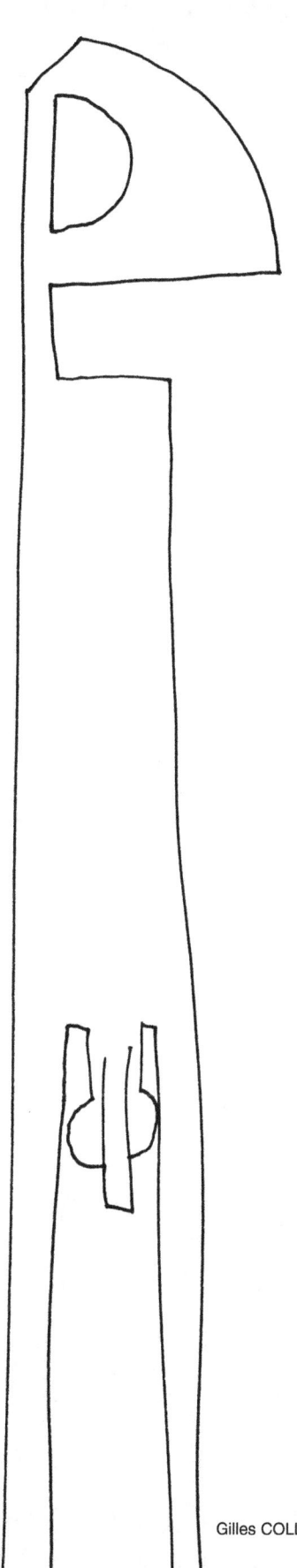

Gilles COLLETTE

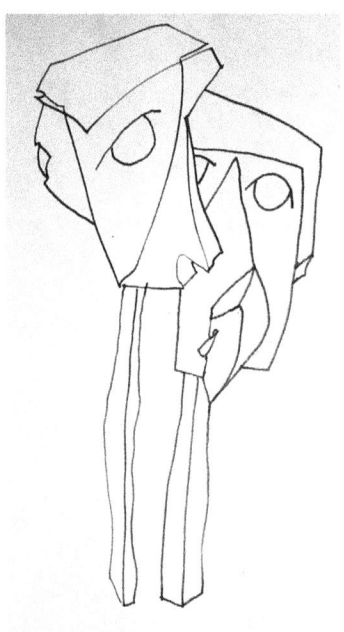

Notes and sketches

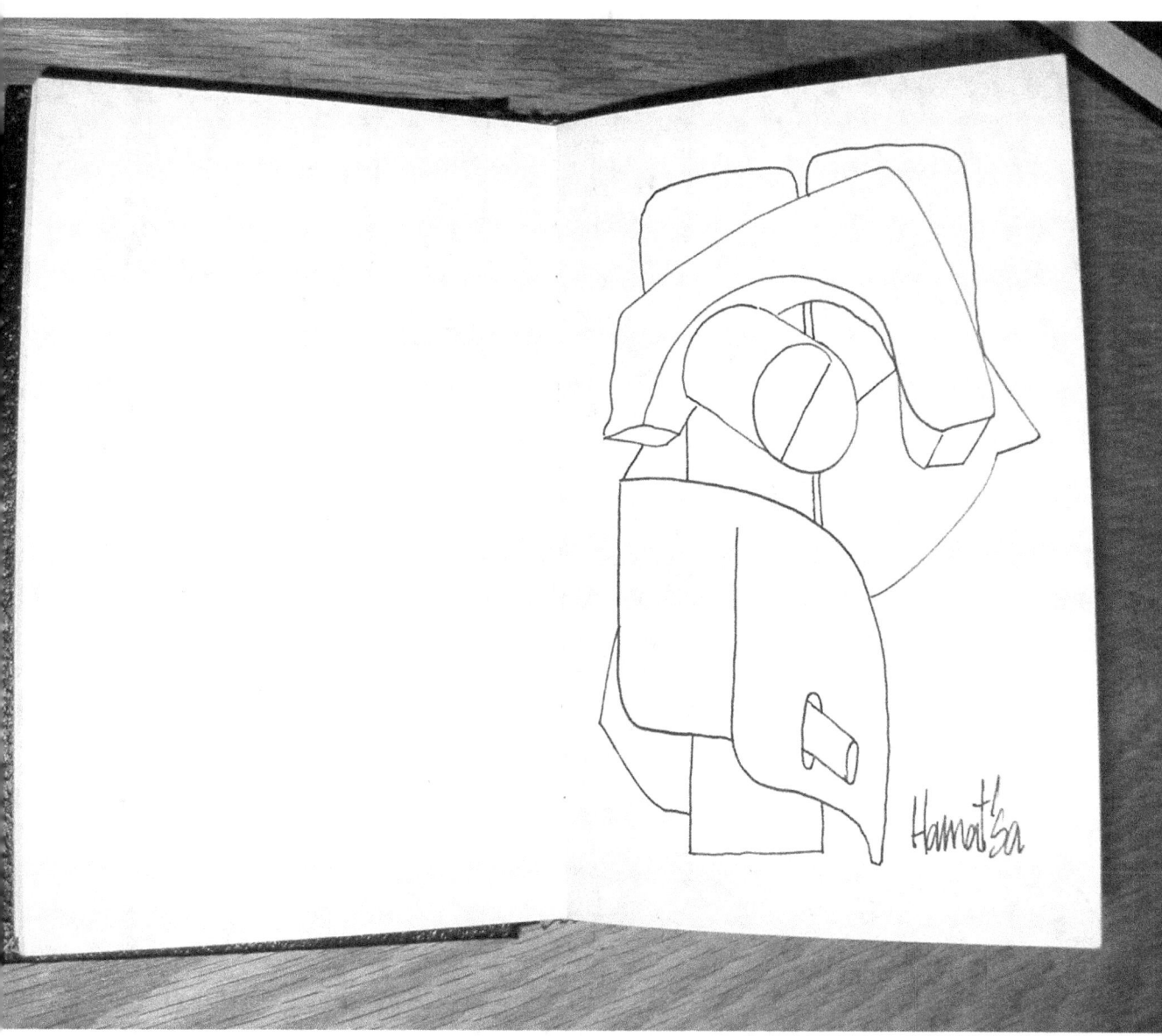

Gilles COLLETTE

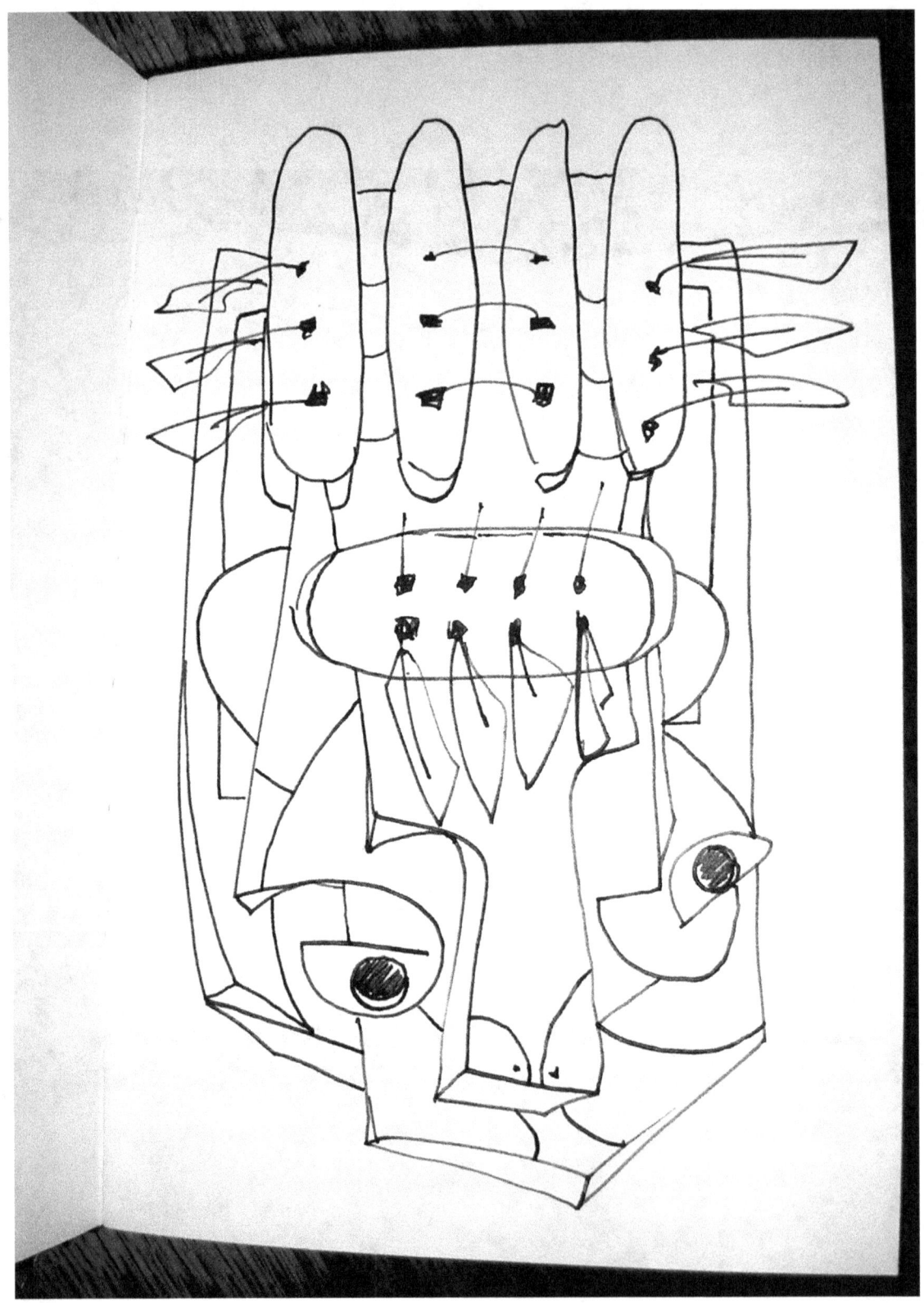

Notes and sketches

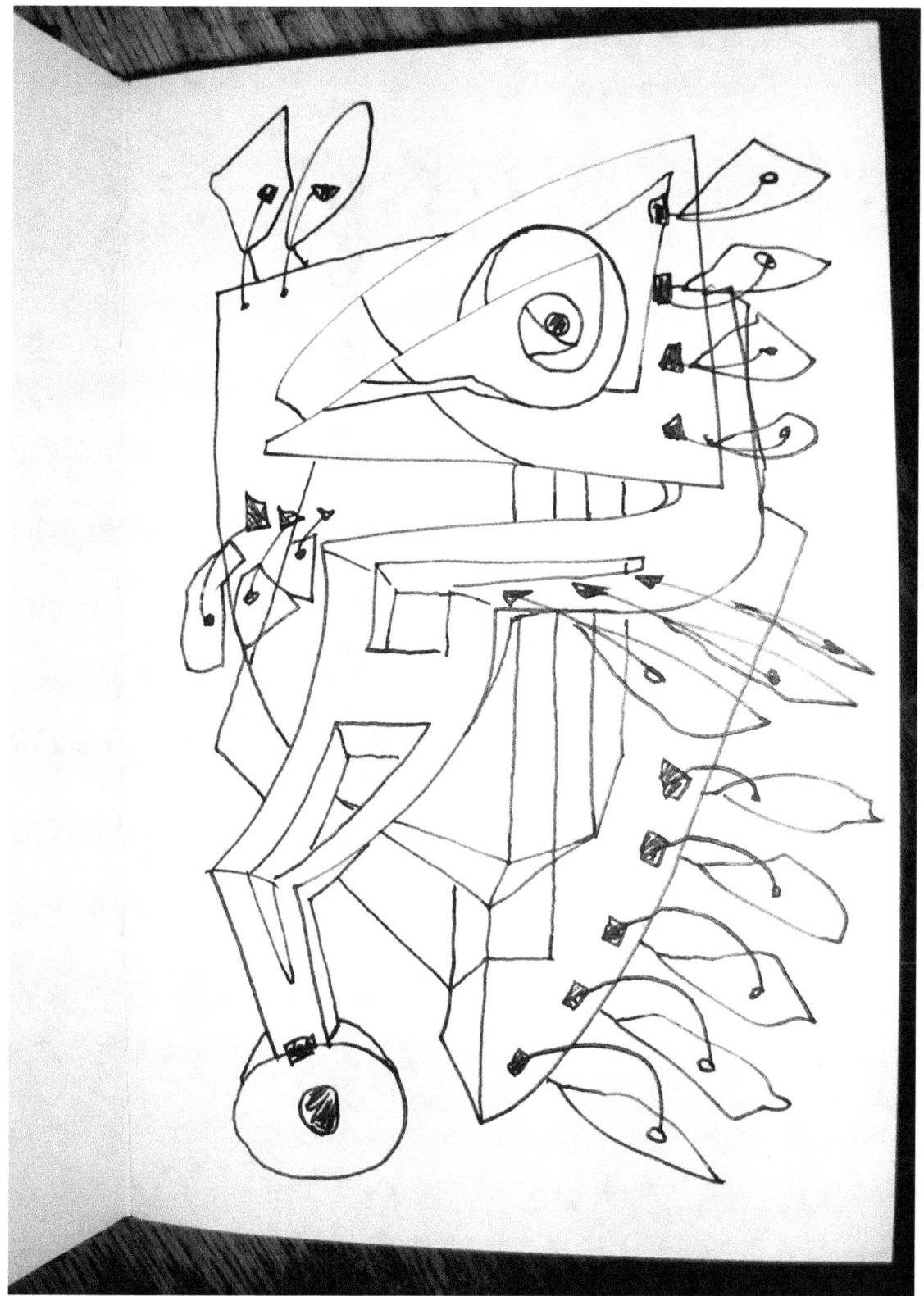

Gilles COLLETTE

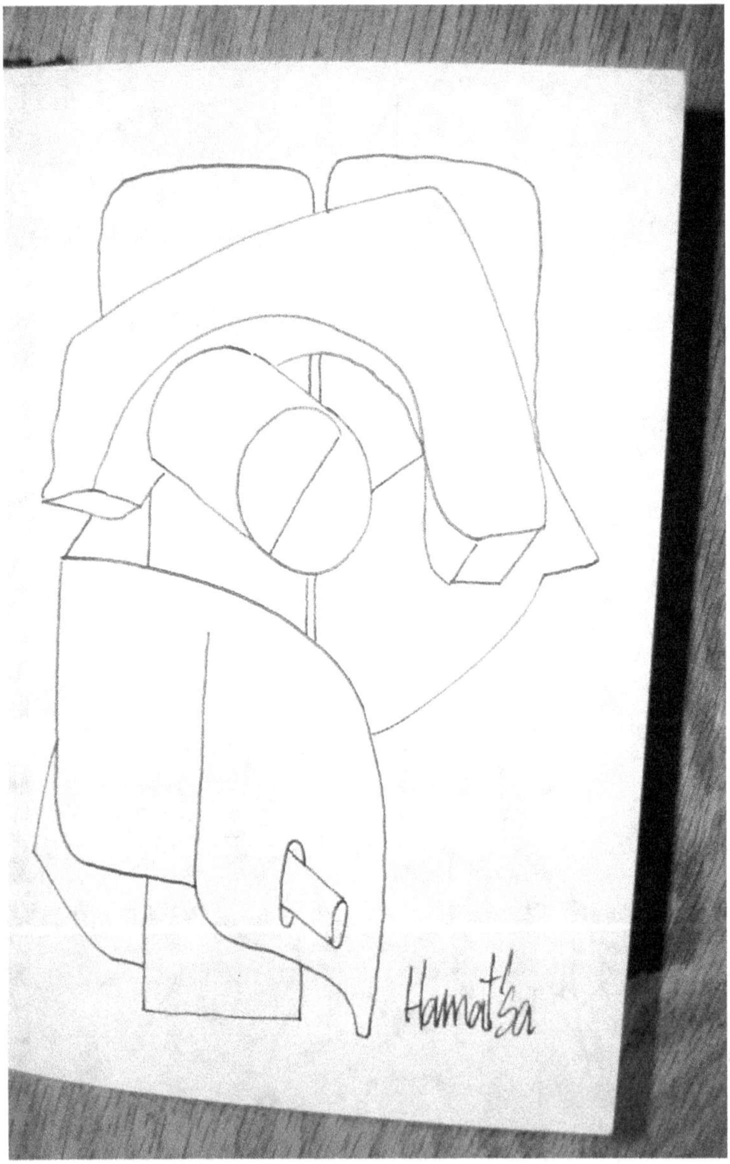

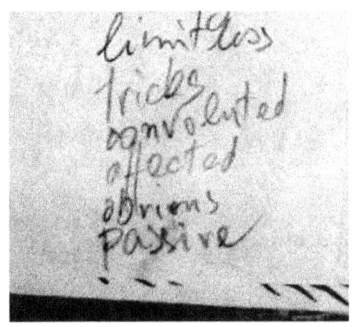

Notes and sketches

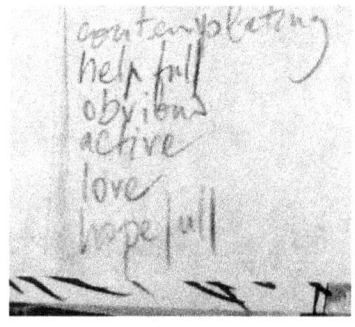

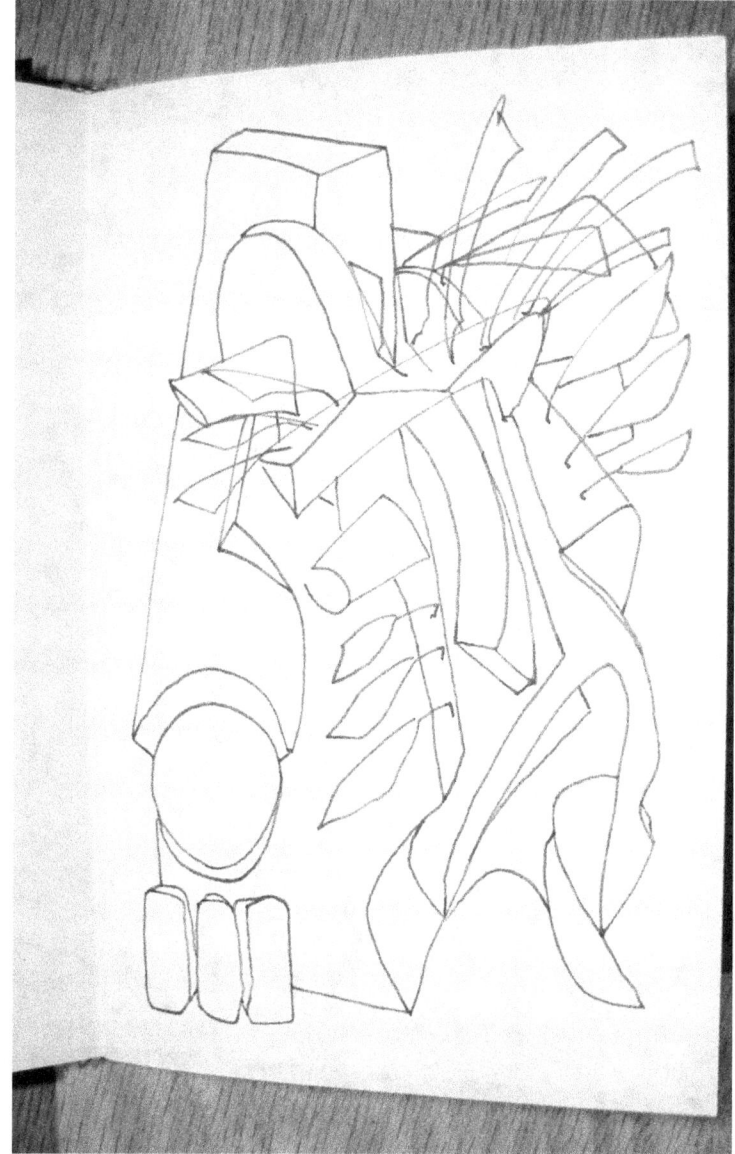

Gilles COLLETTE

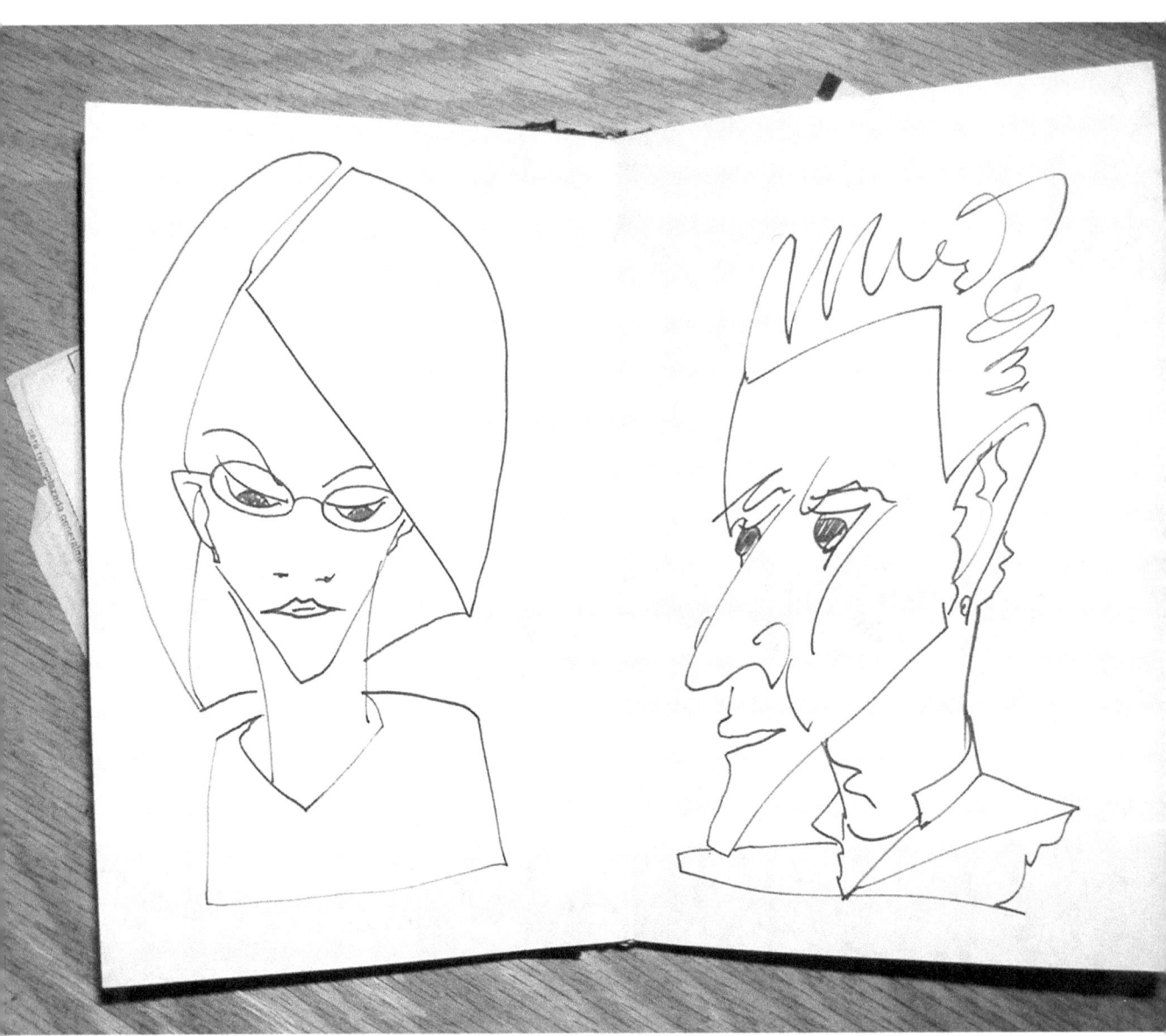

Notes and sketches

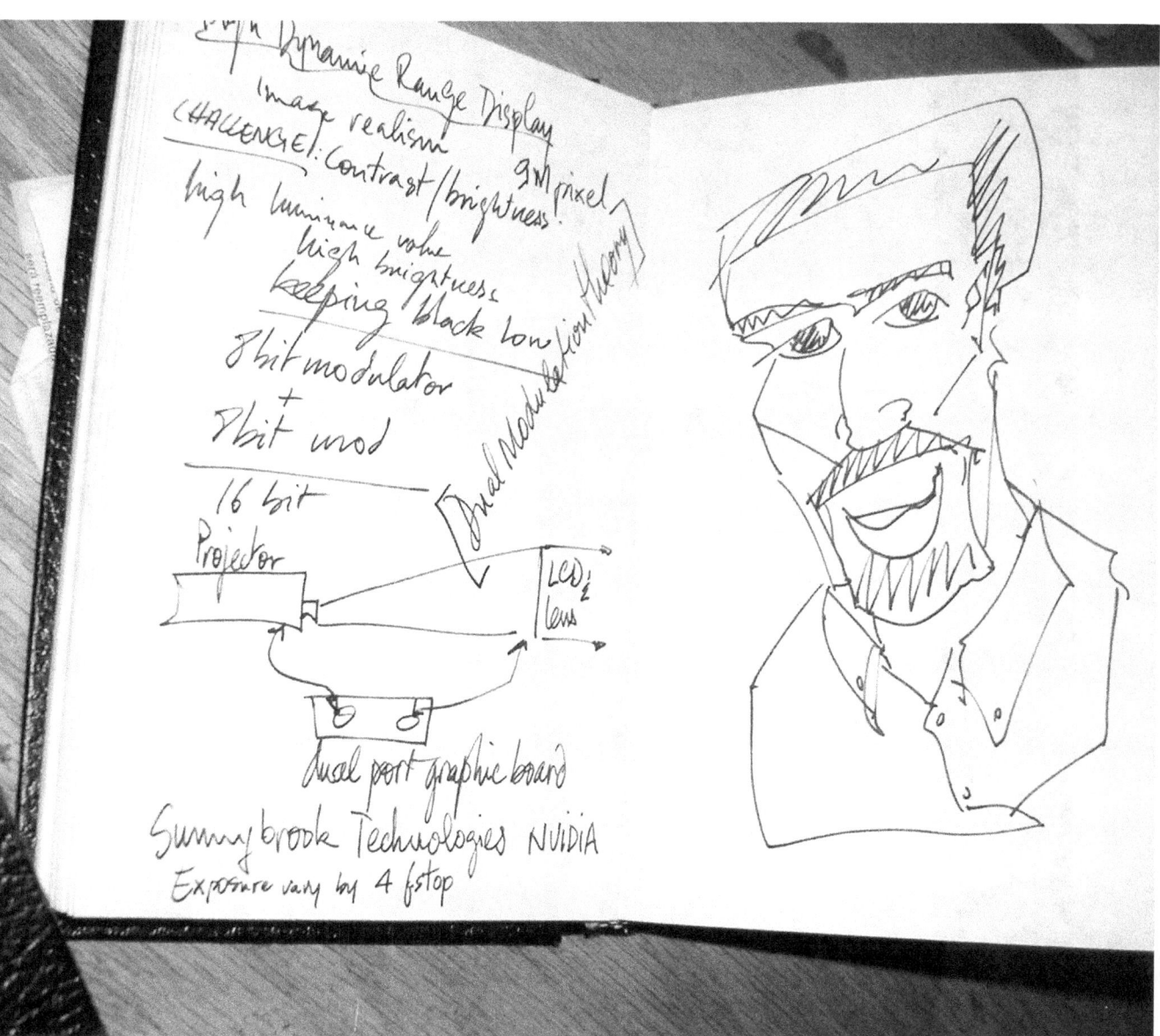

High Dynamic Range Display
Image realism
9M pixel
CHALLENGE: Contrast/brightness

high luminance value
high brightness
keeping black low

8bit modulator
+
8bit mod

Dual Modulation theory

16 bit
Projector

LCD &
Lens

dual port graphic board

Sunnybrook Technologies NVIDIA
Exposure vary by 4 f-stop

Gilles COLLETTE

211

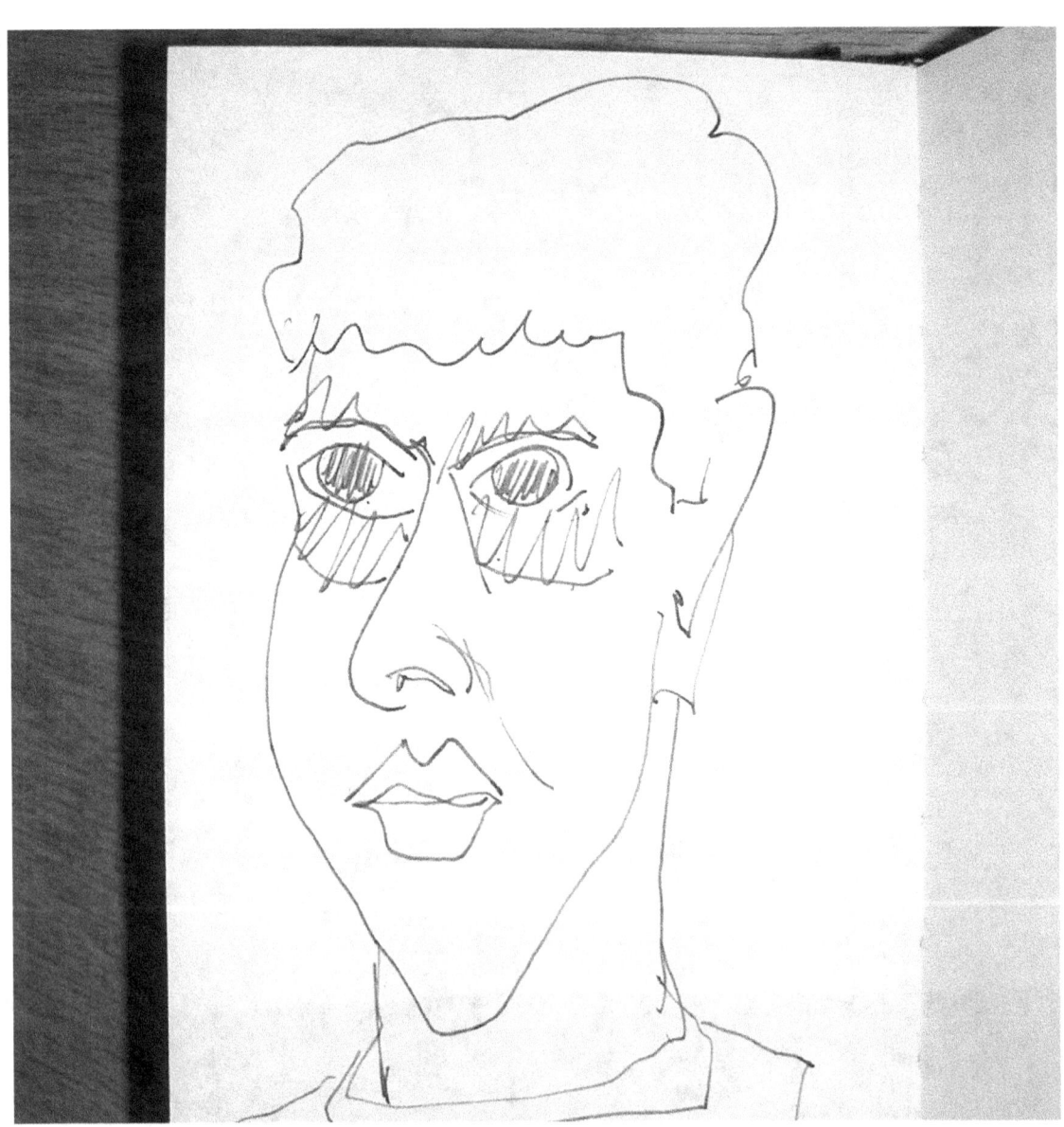

Notes and sketches

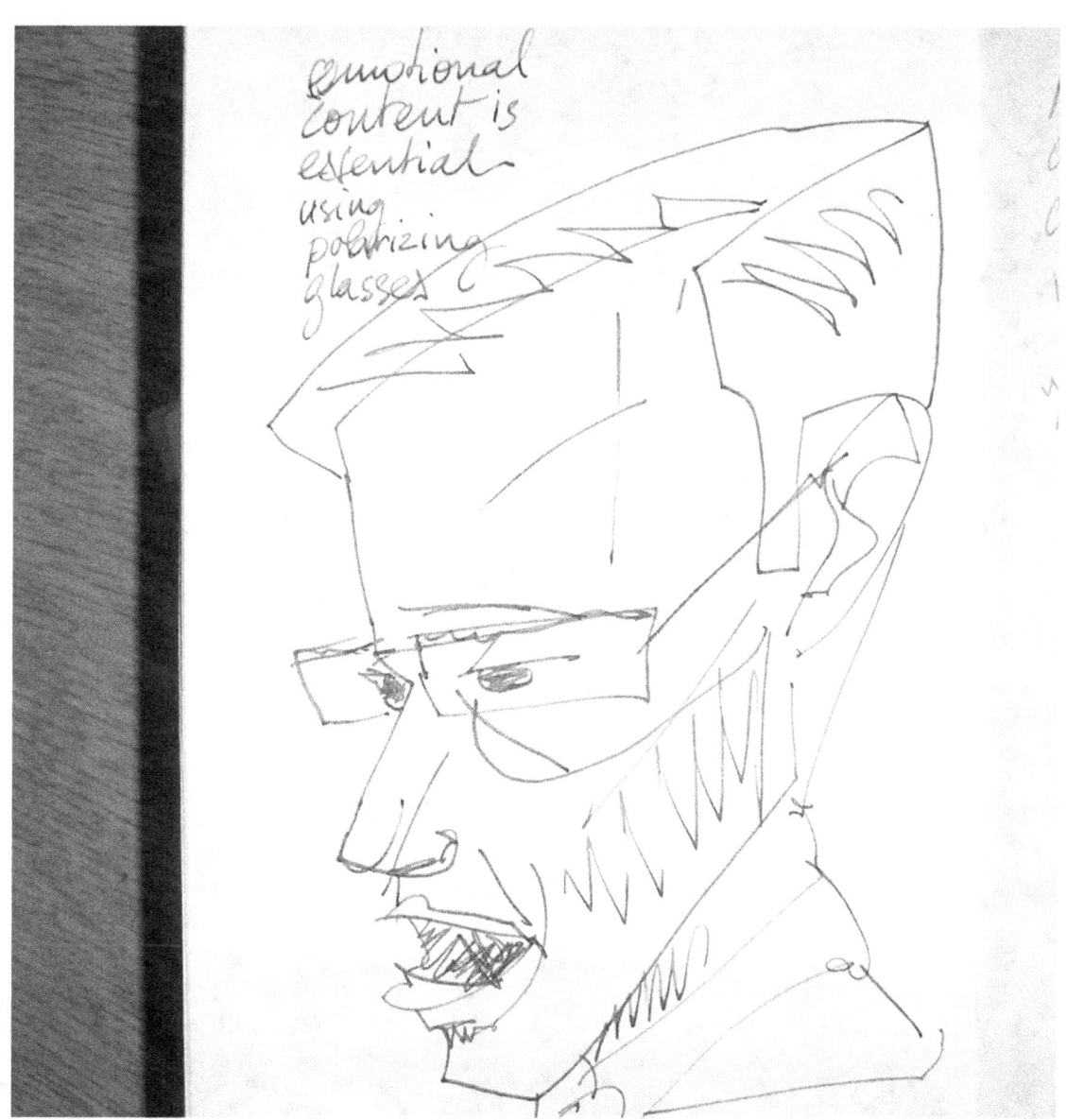

emotional
content is
essential
using
polarizing
glasses C

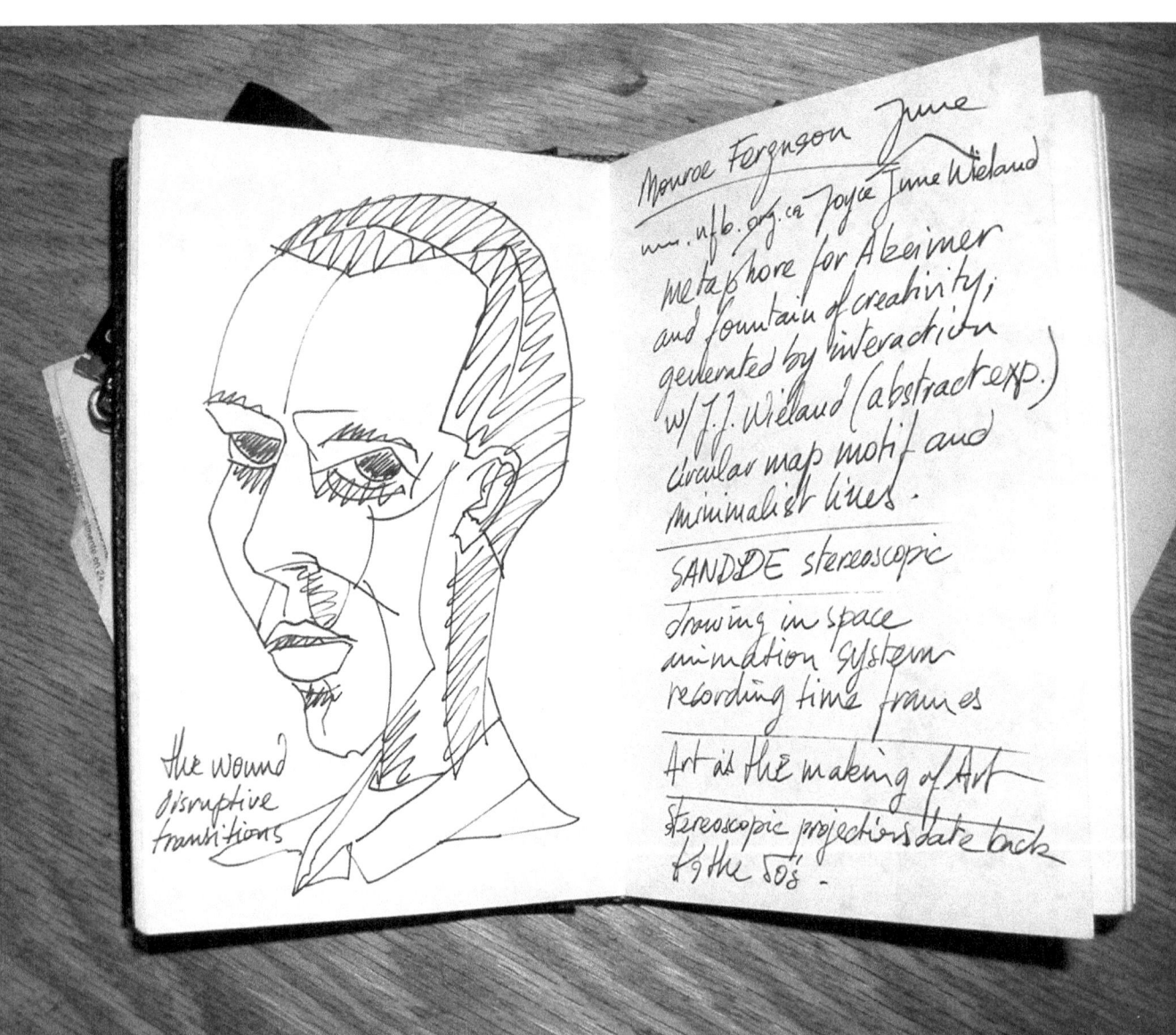

the wound
disruptive
transitions

Monroe Ferguson   June

www.nfb.org.ca Joyce June Wieland
metaphore for Alzeimer
and fountain of creativity;
generated by interaction
w/ J.J. Wieland (abstract exp.)
circular map motif and
minimalist lines.

SANDDE stereoscopic
drawing in space
animation system
recording time frames

Art as the making of Art
stereoscopic projections date back
to the 50's -

Notes and sketches

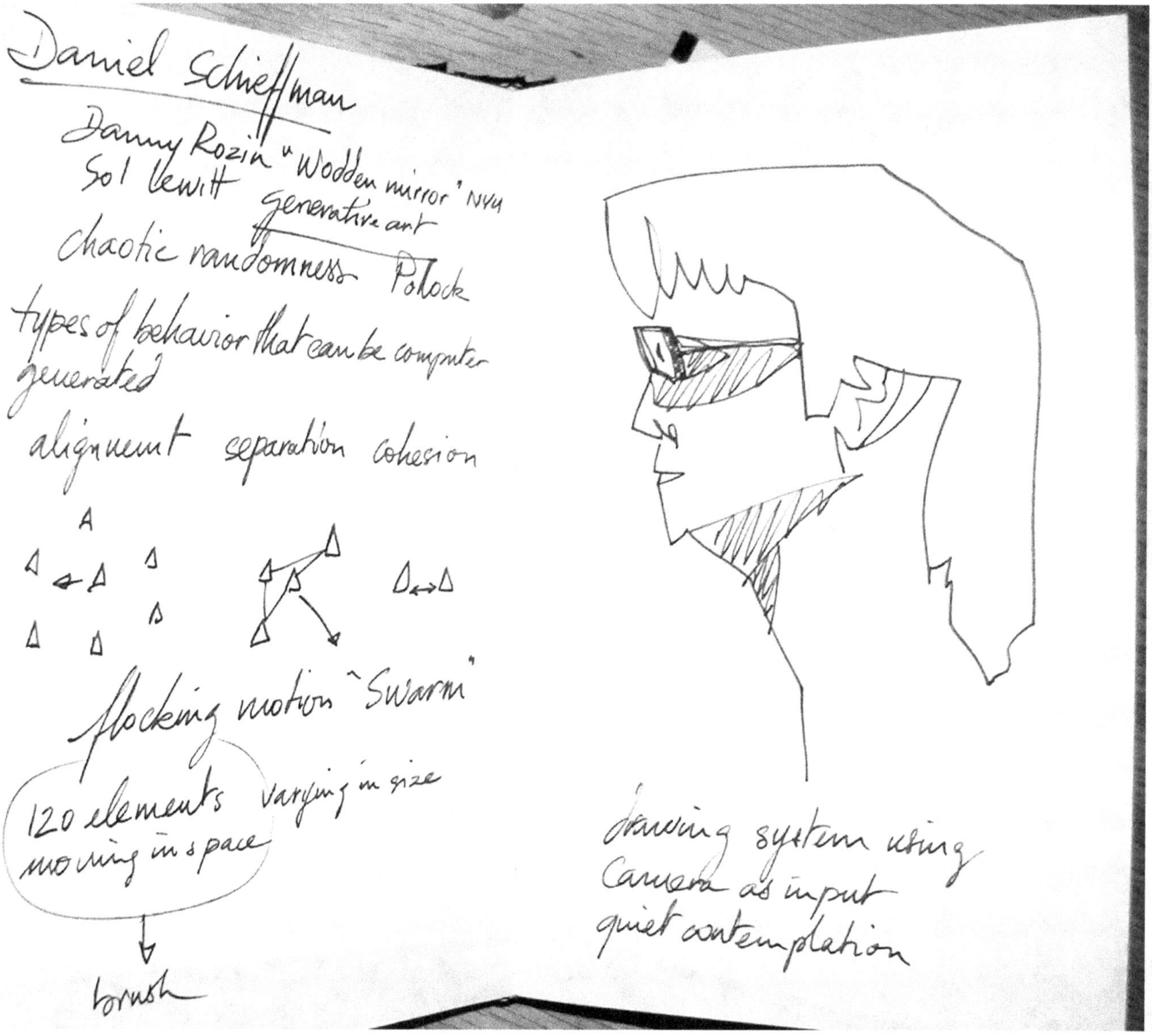

Daniel Schieffman

Danny Rozin "Wodden mirror" NYU
Sol Lewitt   generative art
chaotic randomness   Polock

types of behavior that can be computer
generated

alignment   separation   cohesion

flocking motion "Swarm"

120 elements varying in size
moving in space

brush

drawing system using
camera as input
quiet contemplation

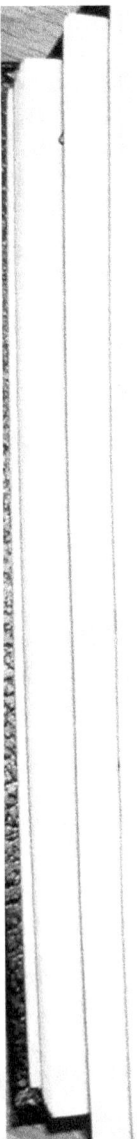

Paul Beardsley   Mitsubishi.
handheld projector w/ laser pts.
tracking cursour as a projection
project a bkg as fixed position
projective algorithm —or
fully calibrated
euclidean algorith

- to be used hand held or
  oportunistic, to be implemen
  ted in celphones or PDA as
  attached devices. (augented
  reality)-
- projected over objects to enhance
  maintenance, or physical based
  selection & do very guided processes.

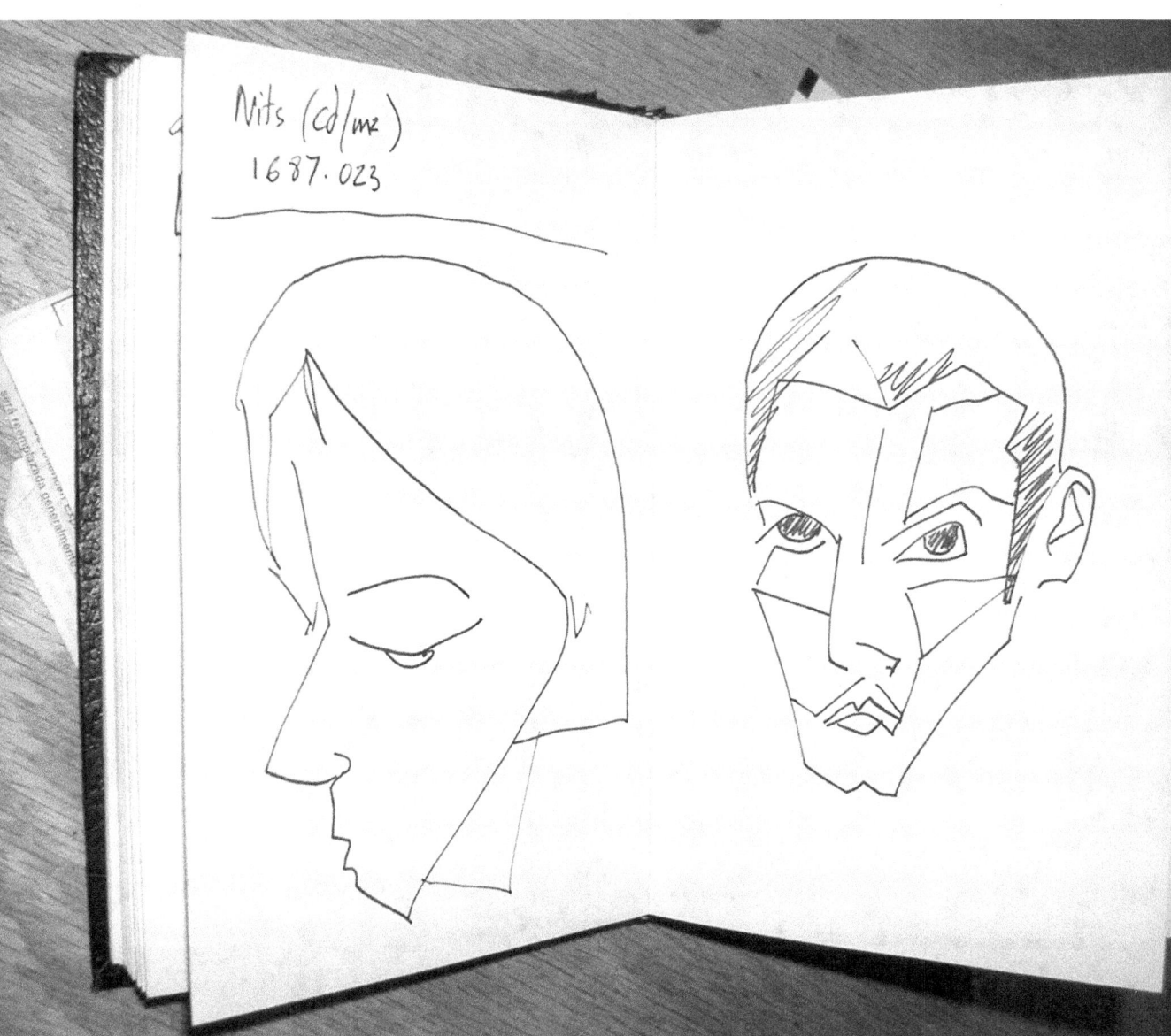

Nits (cd/m²)
1687.023

Gilles COLLETTE

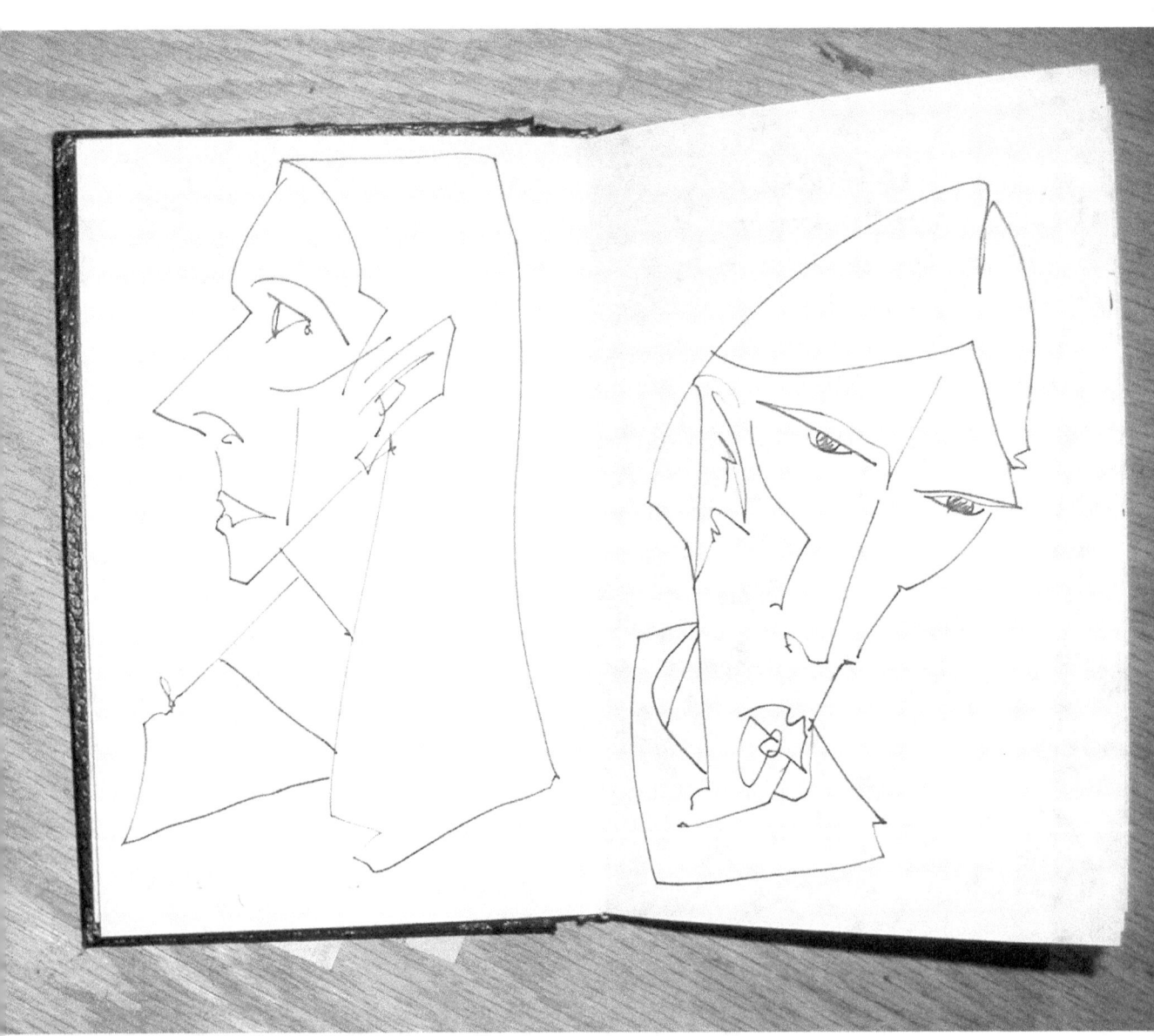

Notes and sketches

chair as closest component to the human body.

Noriyuki Fujimura

interactive public art install.
Computer controlled chair.
remote furniture | Tactile comm |

Sitting on chair. 2 people
each chair has a sensor and
tilt ↗ motor

linear
| promote communication |
echo - master / slave

Street a public space
Sp - psycho — cultural
contact
expected ≠ unexpected

Grey synthetic textile
5-red EL-wire
VU-meter like
level 1-5

Luminex fabric
fiber-optic textile
ultra bright LEDs
conductive threads for LEDs.

- Noise pollution
Car horns, fire trucks, ambulances
constructions,
- Environmental awareness

Notes and sketches

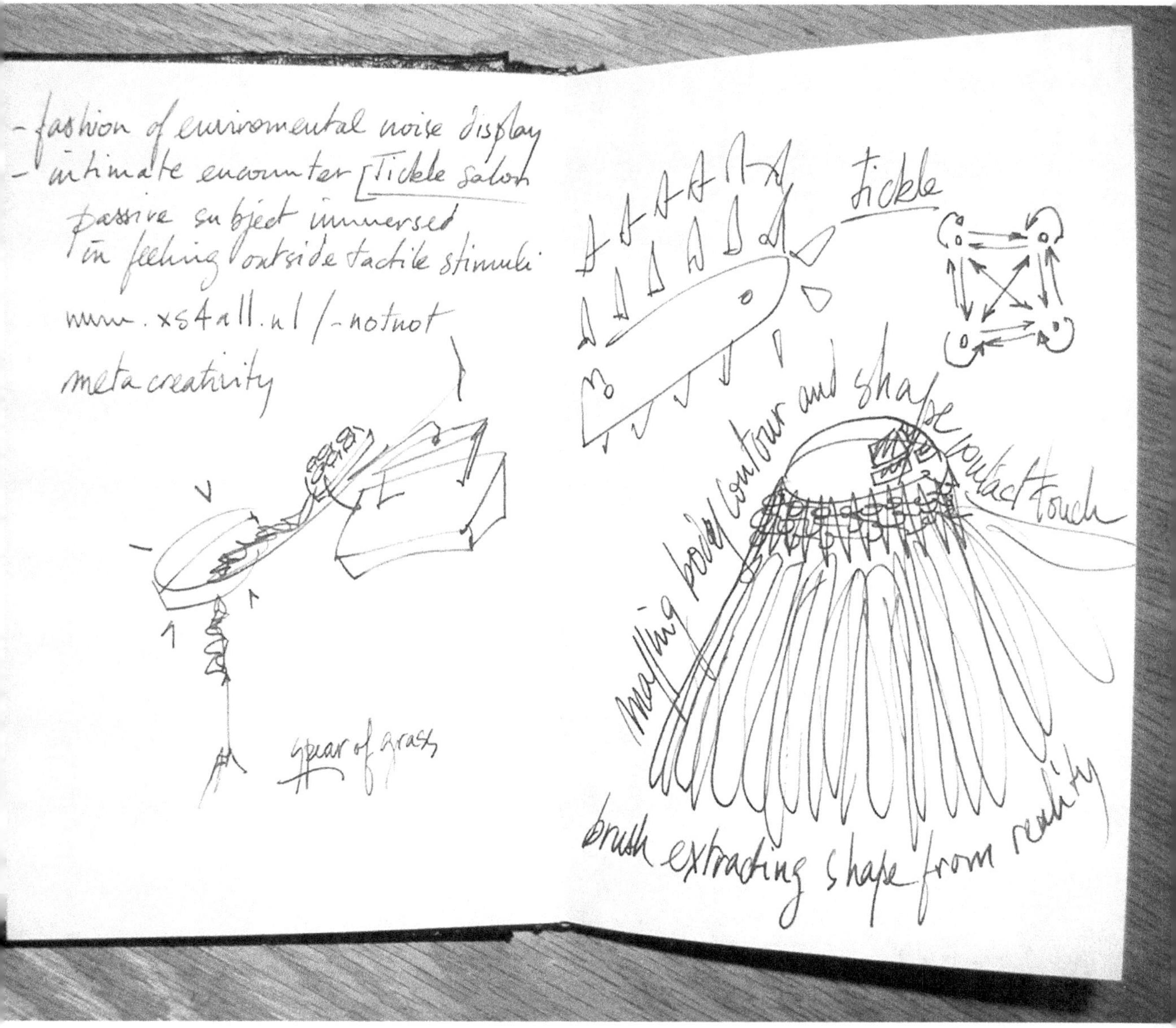

- fashion of environmental noise display
- intimate encounter [Tickle salon
  passive subject immersed
  in feeling outside tactile stimuli
  www.xs4all.nl/-notnot
  meta creativity

spear of grass

tickle

mapping body contour and shape

contact touch

brush extracting shape from reality

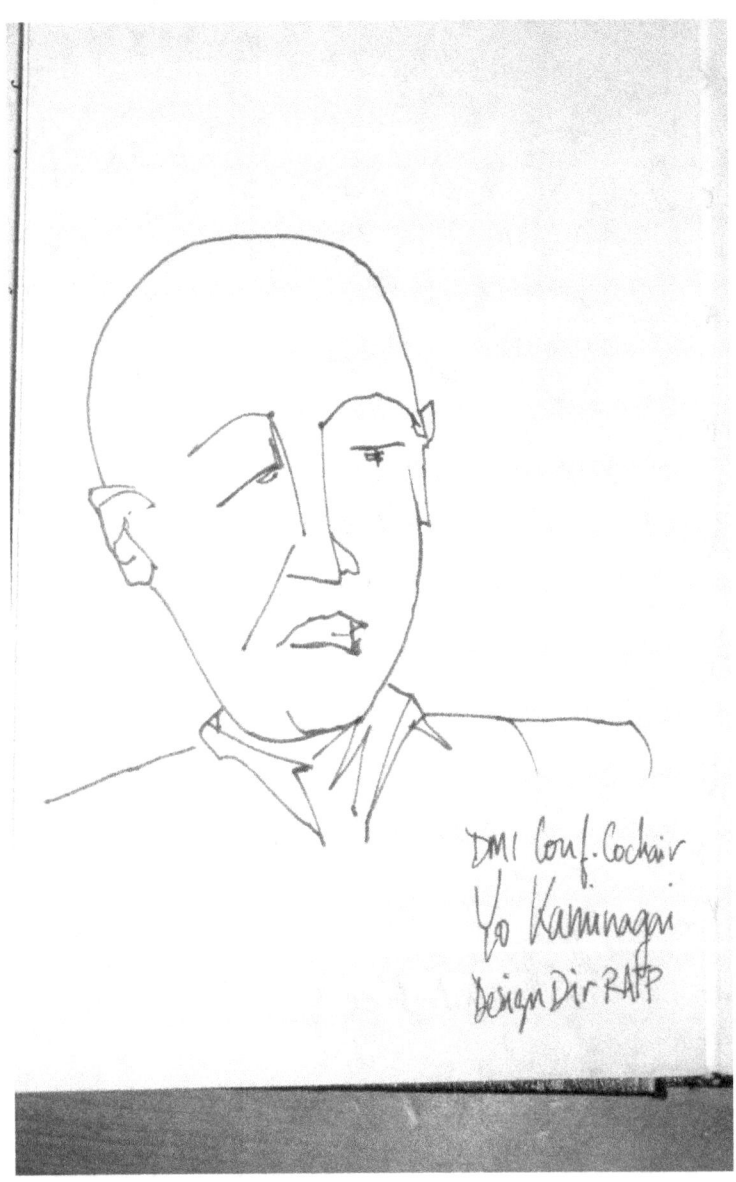

DMI Conf. Cochair
Yo Kaminagai
Design Dir RATP

Notes and sketches

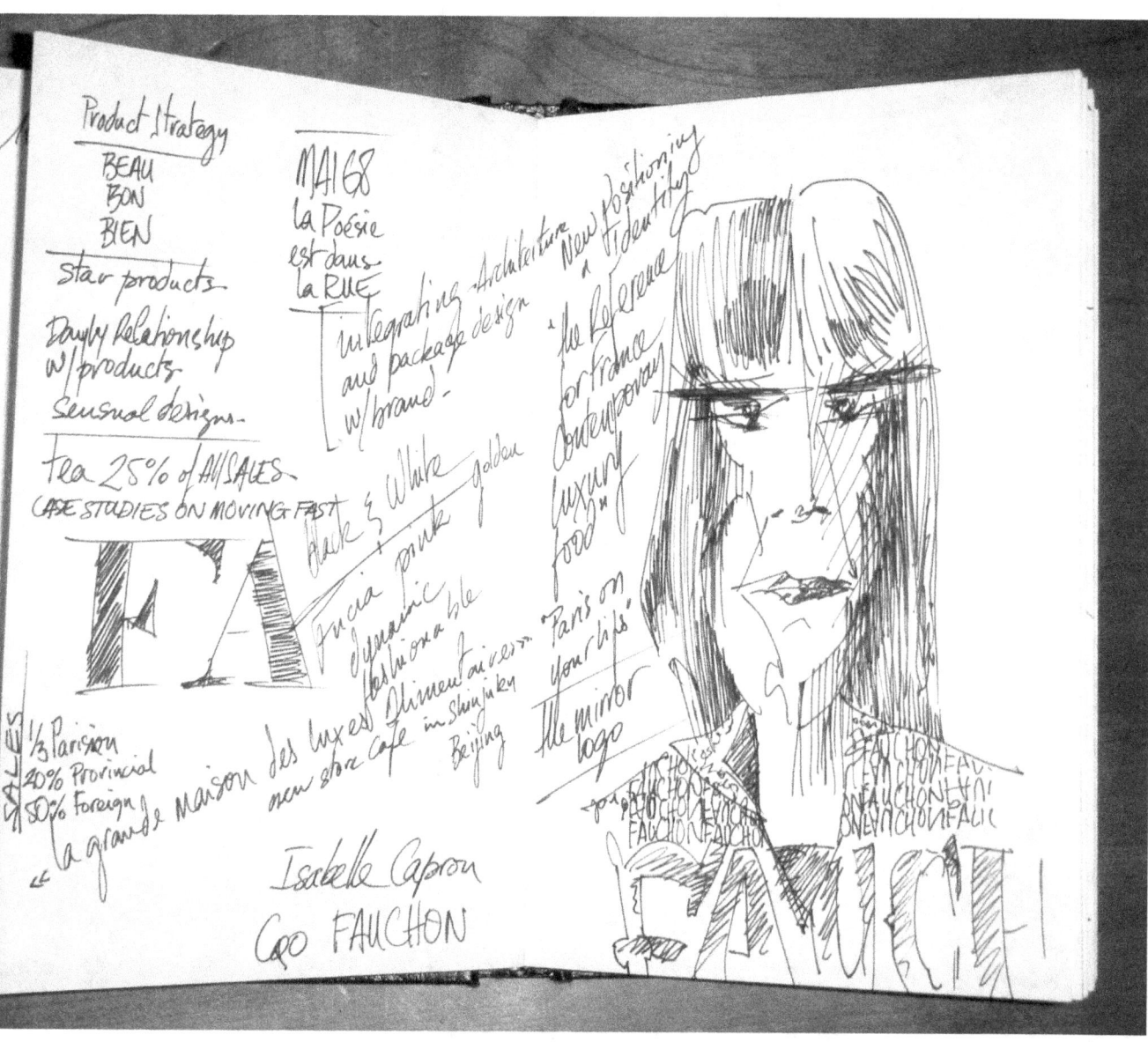

Product Strategy
  BEAU
  BON
  BIEN
Star products

Daily Relationship
w/ products

Sensual designs

Tea 25% of All SALES

CASE STUDIES ON MOVING FAST

MAI 68
La Poésie
est dans
la RUE

integrating Architecture
and package design
w/ brand

New positioning
+ identity

the Reference
for France
Contemporary
Luxury
food

black & white golden
fucia pink
dynamic
fashionable

des luxes alimentaires
new store Café in Shinjuku
Beijing

"Paris on
your lips"

the mirror
logo

SALES
⅓ Parisian
40% Provincial
50% Foreign
"la grande Maison"

Isabelle Capron
CEO FAUCHON

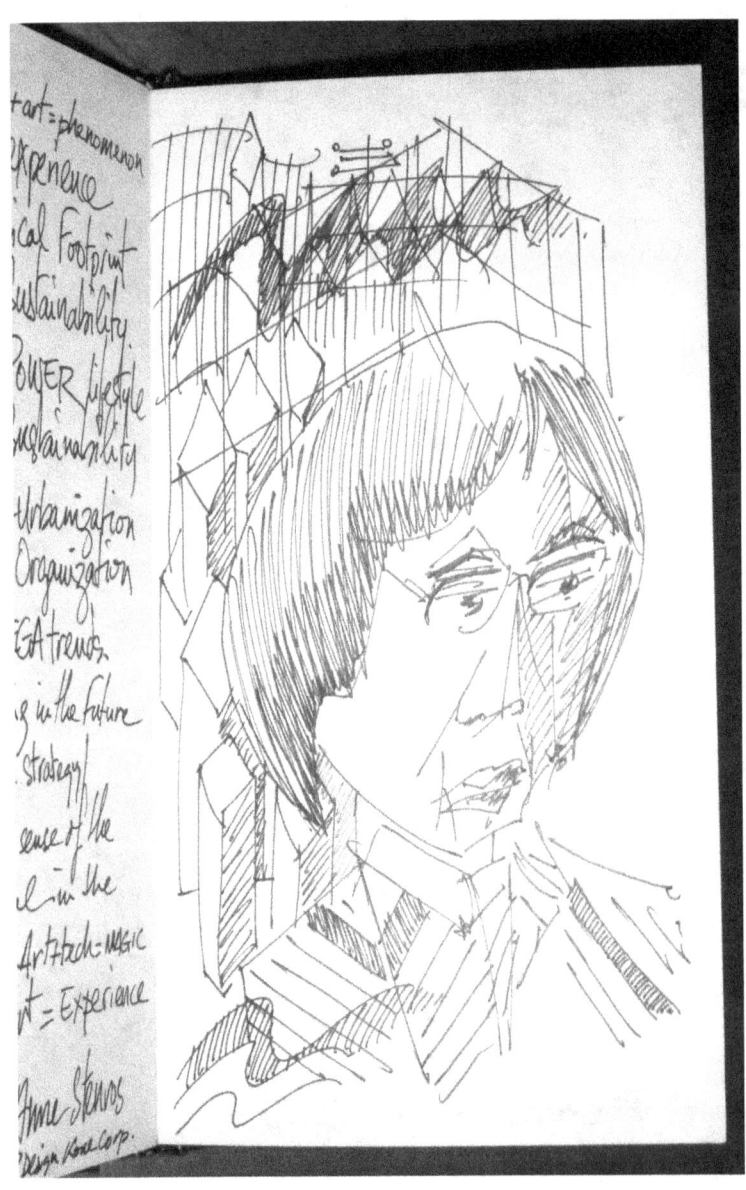

Notes and sketches

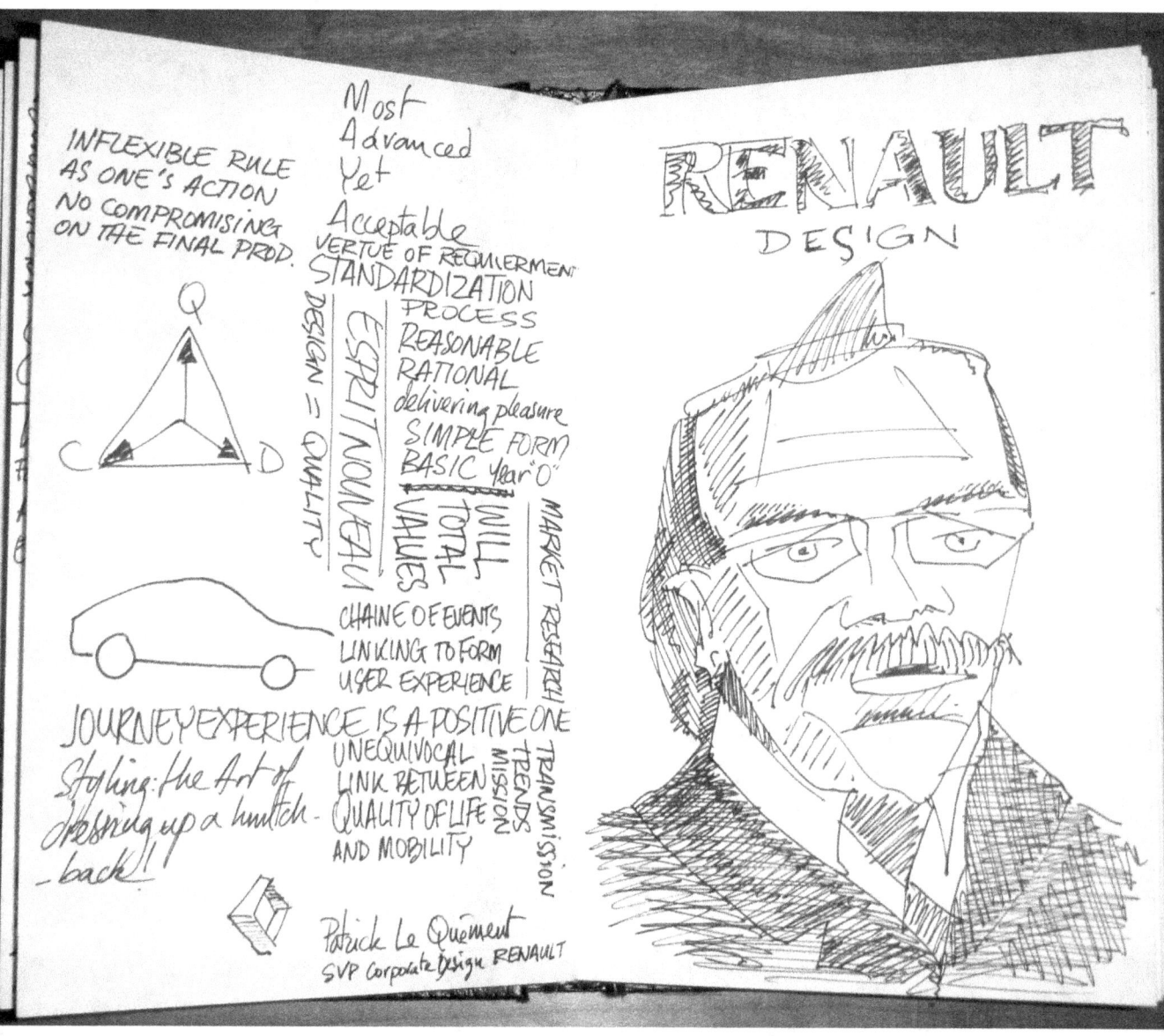

INFLEXIBLE RULE
AS ONE'S ACTION
NO COMPROMISING
ON THE FINAL PROD.

Most
Advanced
Yet
Acceptable

VERTUE OF REQUIERMENT
STANDARDIZATION
PROCESS
REASONABLE
RATIONAL
delivering pleasure
SIMPLE FORM
BASIC Year "0"

DESIGN = QUALITY

ESPRIT NOUVEAU

WILL
TOTAL
VALUES

MARKET RESEARCH

CHAINE OF EVENTS
LINKING TO FORM
USER EXPERIENCE

JOURNEY EXPERIENCE IS A POSITIVE ONE

Styling: the Art of
dressing up a hutch-
-back!

UNEQUIVOCAL
LINK BETWEEN
QUALITY OF LIFE
AND MOBILITY

TRANSMISSION
TRENDS
MISSION

RENAULT
DESIGN

Patrick Le Quément
SVP Corporate Design RENAULT

Gilles COLLETTE

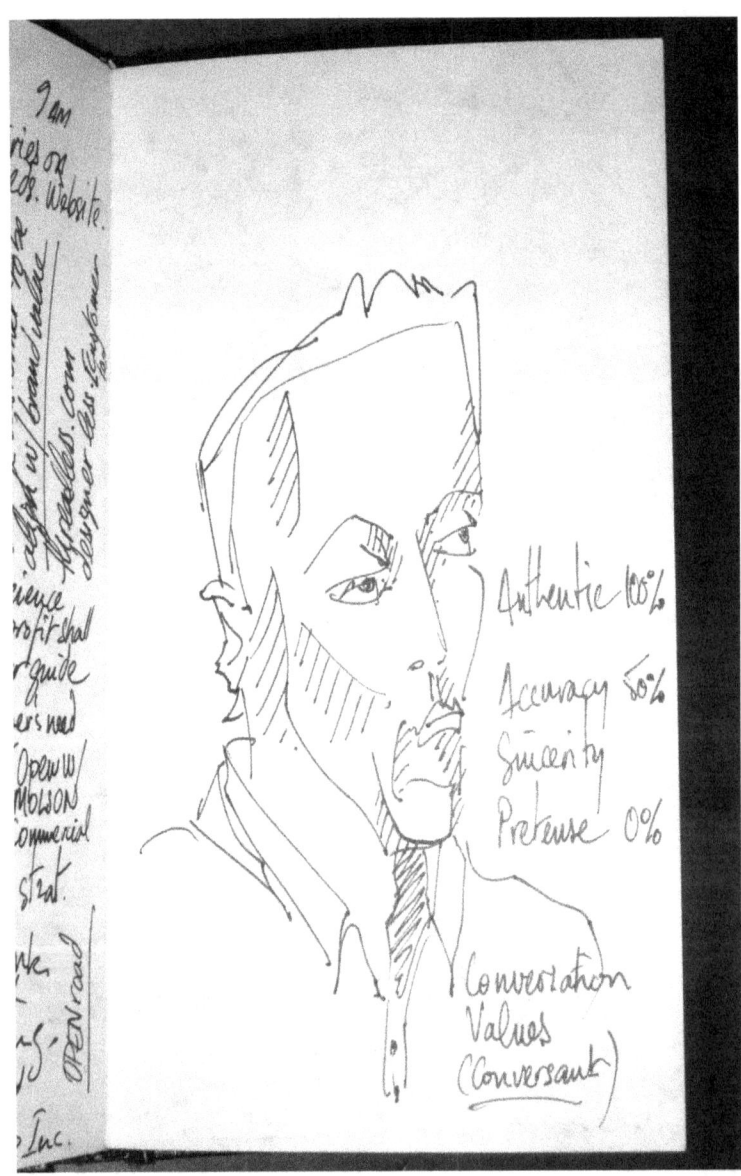

Authentic 100%

Accuracy 80%

Sincerity

Pretense 0%

Conversation
Values
(Conversant)

Notes and sketches

Red Life & human Dreams

Tech & Know.

Psycho / Socio

Techno "the Creators."

Respect sensitivity, identity culture & share in creation

SIMILAR LEVEL OF TECH diff Creative synthesis

IPSEO - Extreme
TELELANGUE - Personalisation
ESSILOR - of Prod. & Serv.
Georgio Vasari (1511-1574)
THE NET EPOQUE
HISTORICAL INNOVATION WAVES
Innovation through design
the Creative Synthesis.

INVENTIONS
INNOVATIONS
INDUSTRIALIZATION
INTERNALIZATION

World Knowledge Italy Cradle of Modern humanist vision
15th Century
Innovation & Design

Joseph Alois Schumpeter (1932 Bonn)
DISEGNO
VENTURI
CAPITALE
BREVETTO
UMANISIMO
HUMANISM
PATENT
VENTURE
CAPITAL
DESIGN

Paolo Uccello (1397-1475)

Materials energy

Marc Giget

P. & S.D. Euro. Inst. for Creat. Strat. & Innov.

the word "Design" is used for the first time by Waversbury. Eng.

Man is the measure of all things!

"All Pbs are known solutions are not!"

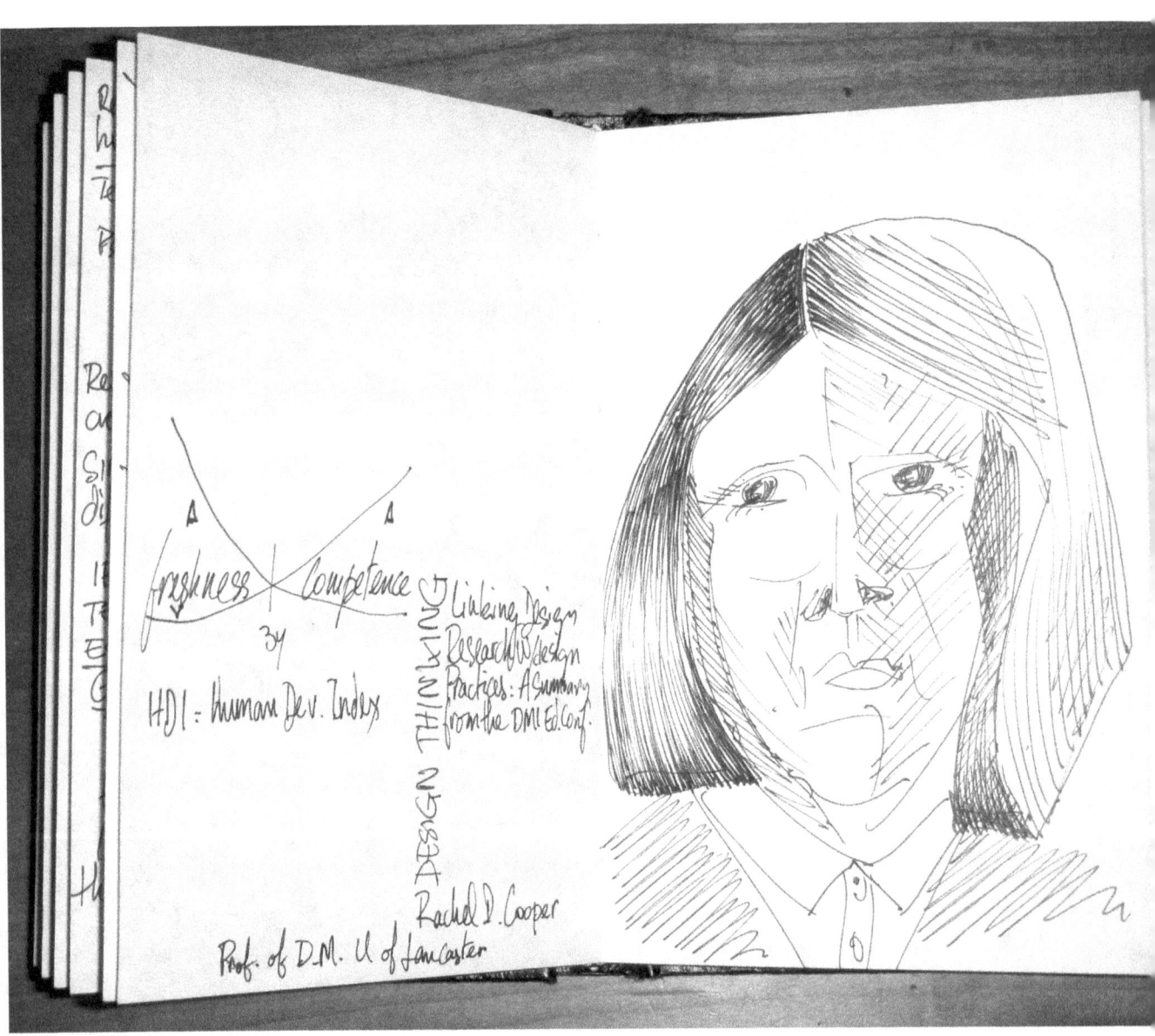

freshness × Competence

3y

HDI = Human Dev. Index

DESIGN THINKING

Linking Design Research to design Practices: A Summary from the DMI Ed. Conf.

Rachel D. Cooper

Prof. of D.M. U of Lancaster

Notes and sketches

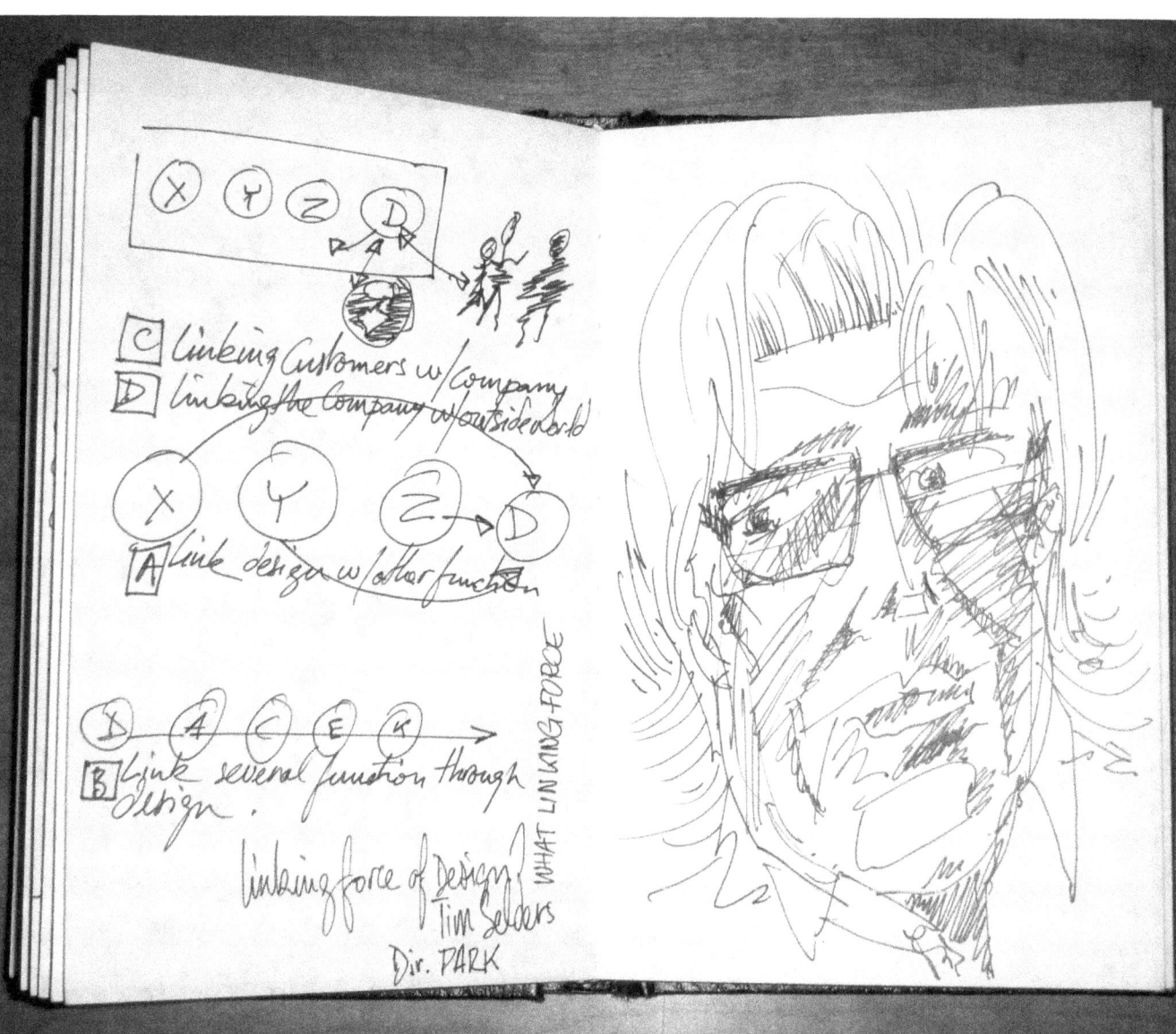

C Linking Customers w/ Company
D Linking the Company w/ outside world

A Link design w/ other function

B Link several function through design .

Linking force of Design
Tim Selders
Dir. PARK

WHAT LINKING FORCE

(TANAKA chair) inspire seat w/incorporated console

Direction KEY Innovation

Esprit LOFT (Vintage Ext. + Contempo Int.)

People pay more for products they like

NEED = DESIGN AS SOLUTION

POSITIONING = GREEN

DESIGN ISSUE = PURCHASING POWER

less esthetic sculptural to cheaper weight watchers

REDUCE EMISSION = REDUCE WEIGHT

Automotive styling 5 parts

PREMIUM ATTITUDE Andreas Wasak
                              faurecia

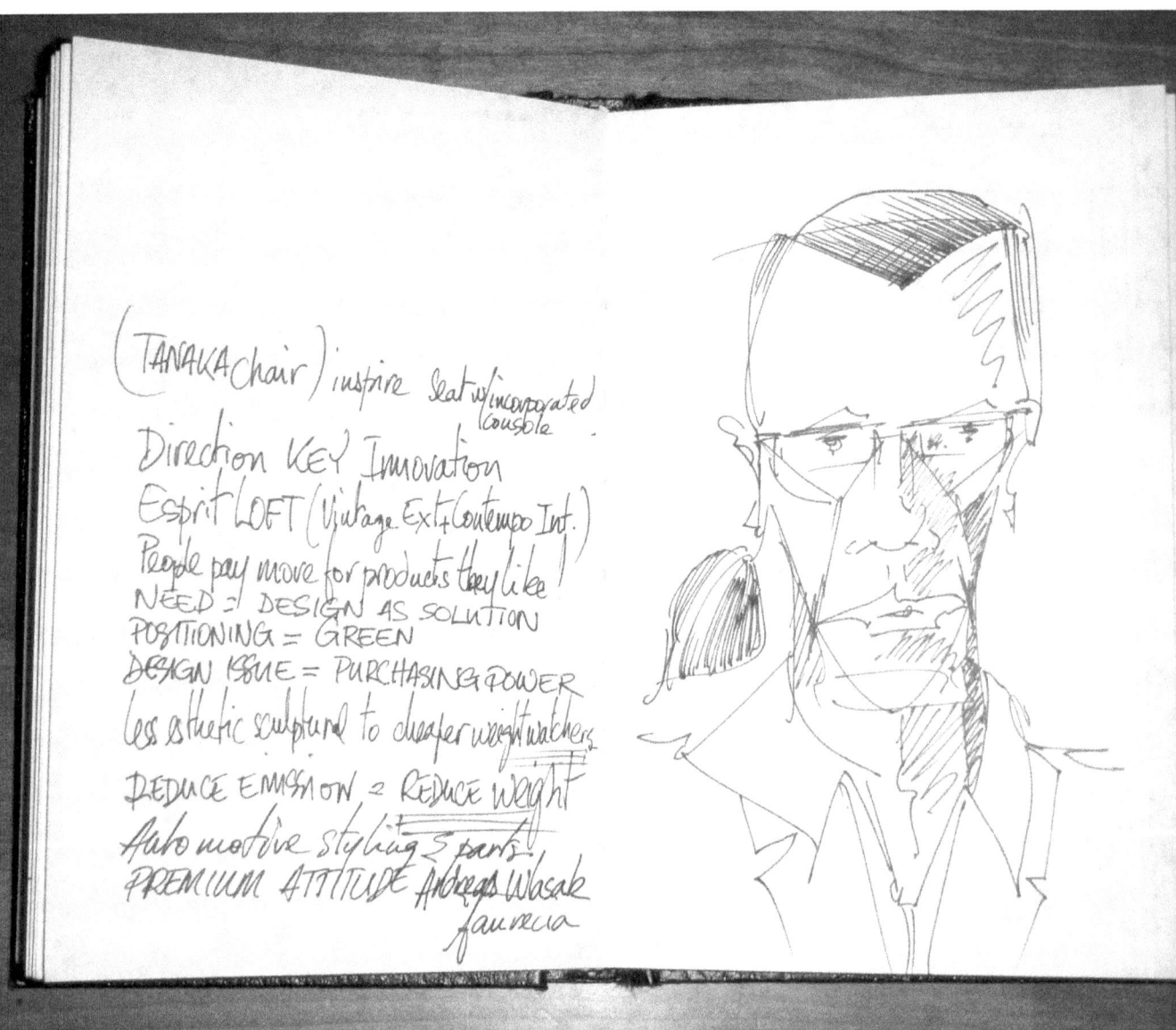

Notes and sketches

Vendredi 18 avril

Investigate ROLES
Deliver feasable concepts
LEAD TO CREATE THE FUTURE
Ethnography
TANGIBLE

Defining experiences
death from what you
are not told!

Make No Romantic

Innovation on a strategic Level

FORWARD MOMENTUM

PARADOX
FEEL/TOUCH/SEE vs
DREAM & HOPE
DESIGN DELIVERS
EXPERIENCES

MINIMIZE COST
HAVE CRITICAL MASS
DIFFERENTIATE BY
ADDING VALUE

NEED Design & Innovation on a strategic Level

VISION 2020

Miguel-Angel Munar

S. M. Dir   Roca

Envisioning
the future
through Design
Leadership

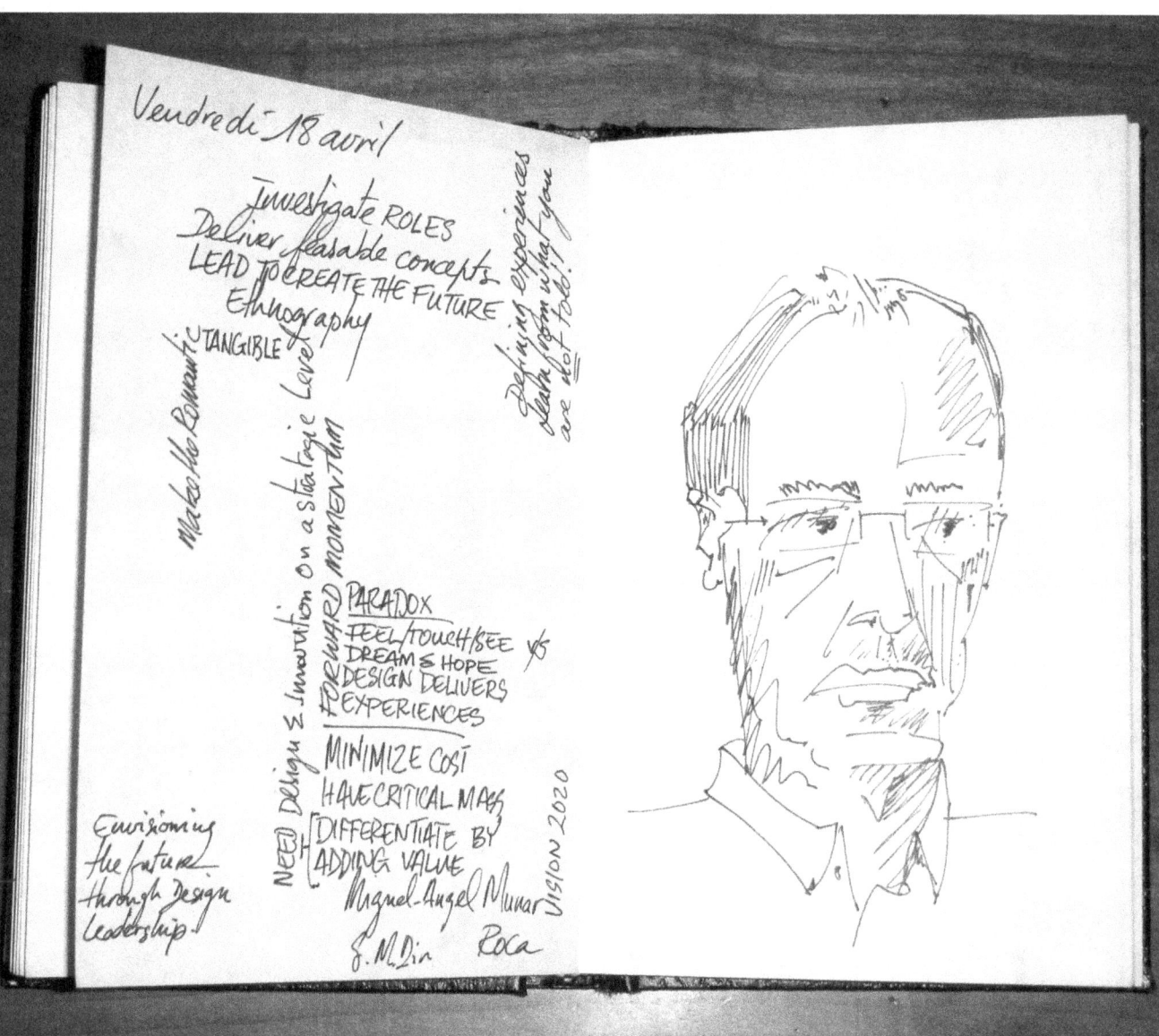

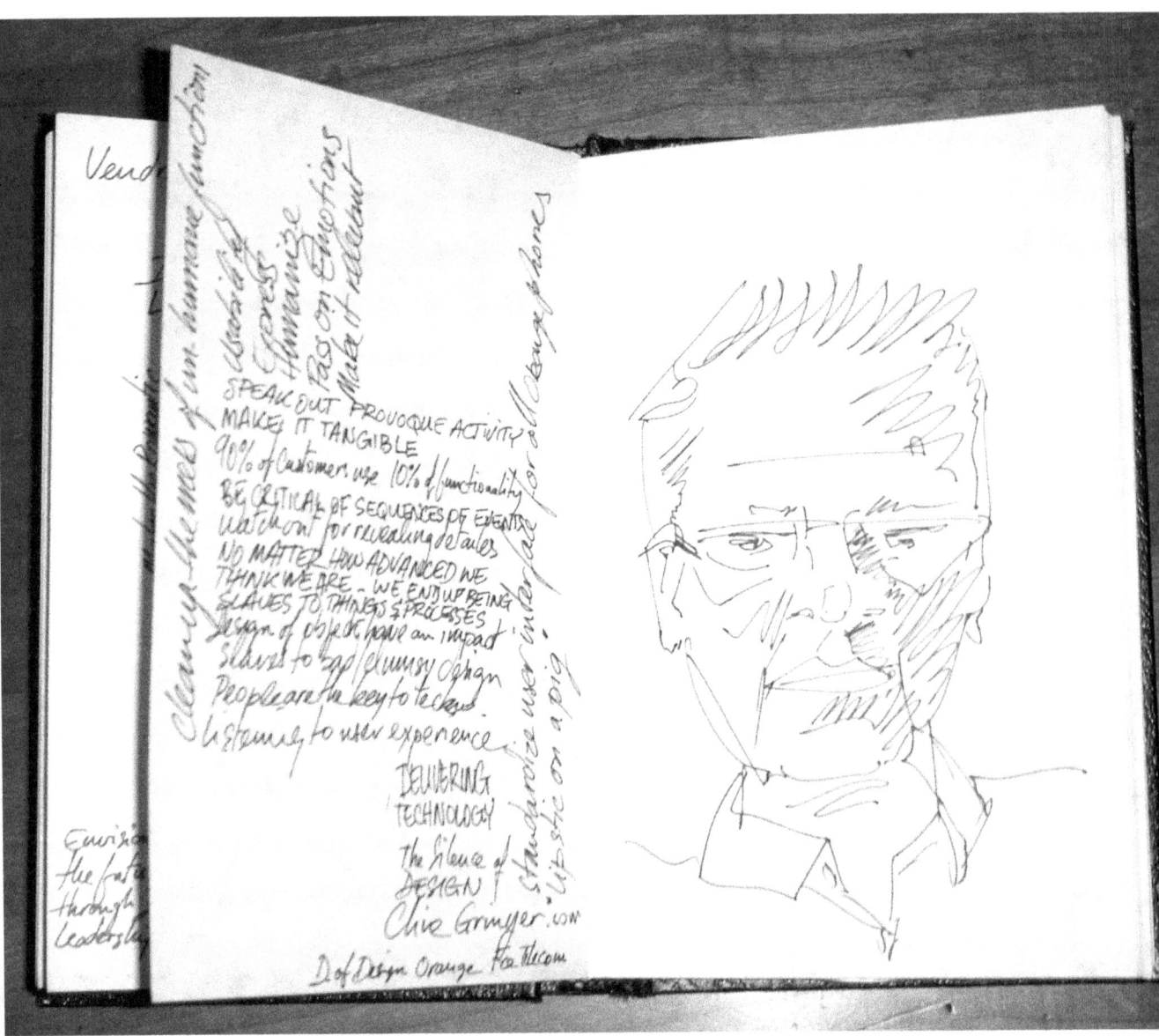

SPEAK OUT PROVOQUE ACTIVITY
MAKE IT TANGIBLE
90% of Customers use 10% of functionality
BE CRITICAL OF SEQUENCES OF EVENTS
Watch out for revealing details
NO MATTER HOW ADVANCED WE
THINK WE ARE - WE END UP BEING
SLAVES TO THINGS & PROCESSES
design of objects have an impact
Slaves to crap/clumsy design
People are the key to ideas.
Listening to user experience.

DELIVERING
TECHNOLOGY
The Silence of
DESIGN!
Clive Grinyer.com

D of Design Orange Telecom

Notes and sketches

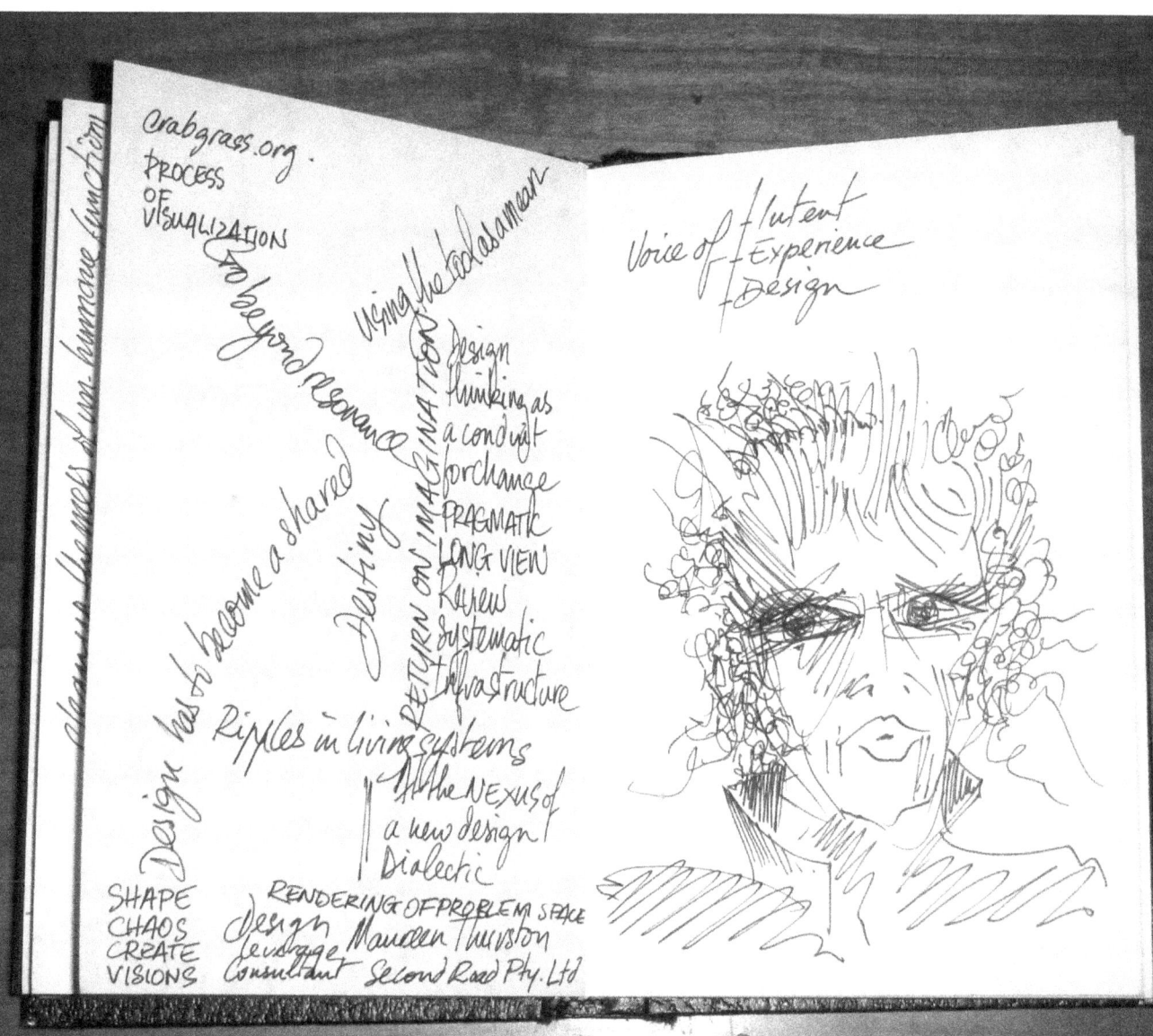

crabgrass.org.
PROCESS
OF
VISUALIZATION

to beyond resonance

using the tool as a mean

Design has to become a shared

Destiny

RETURN ON IMAGINATION

Design thinking as a conduit for change
PRAGMATIC
LONG VIEW
Review
Systematic
Infrastructure

Ripples in living systems

the NEXUS of a new design Dialectic

SHAPE
CHAOS
CREATE
VISIONS

RENDERING OF PROBLEM SPACE
Design leverage Consultant   Maureen Thurston
Second Road Pty. Ltd

Voice of Intent
Experience
Design

www.ingramcontent.com/pod-product-compliance
Lightning Source LLC
Chambersburg PA
CBHW081143180526

45170CB00006B/1913